Springer Proceedings in Business and Economics

More information about this series at http://www.springer.com/series/11960

Philip Linsley · Philip Shrives ·
Monika Wieczorek-Kosmala
Editors

Multiple Perspectives in Risk and Risk Management

ERRN 8th European Risk Conference 2018, Katowice, Poland, September 20–21

Springer

Editors
Philip Linsley
The York Management School
The University of York
York, UK

Philip Shrives
Newcastle Business School
Faculty of Business and Law
Northumbria University
Newcastle upon Tyne, UK

Monika Wieczorek-Kosmala
Faculty of Finance and Insurance
University of Economics in Katowice
Katowice, Poland

ISSN 2198-7246 ISSN 2198-7254 (electronic)
Springer Proceedings in Business and Economics
ISBN 978-3-030-16044-9 ISBN 978-3-030-16045-6 (eBook)
https://doi.org/10.1007/978-3-030-16045-6

Library of Congress Control Number: 2019934781

This Springer imprint is published by the registered company Springer Nature Switzerland AG
The registered company address is: Gewerbestrasse 11, 6330 Cham, Switzerland

Preface

A common view is that contemporary companies operate in a highly dynamic environment, accompanied by the constant development of the information technology. These circumstances impose high complexity of decision-making processes and increase the risk related to companies' performance. With the aim of stimulating cross-disciplinary research in the area of risk management, the European Risk Research Network (ERRN) was established in 2006. The network includes academics and industry experts from the disciplines of accounting, auditing, financial economics and mathematical finance. To keep the network lively and fruitful, the network regularly organizes the "European Risk Conference".

This book of proceedings is a collection of papers that were presented on the 8th European Risk Conference, held in University of Economics in Katowice, Poland, between 20 and 21 September 2018. The conference sessions embraced a wide variety of risk-related studies that reflected multiple perspectives in risk and risk management.

Part I is a collection of papers that discuss the problems related to risk disclosures and risk communication. From a corporate governance perspective, the first paper addresses the problem of appropriate risk communication, which is essential for keeping the company operating within established boundaries. The second paper responds to a call for a well-defined and comparable measure of enterprise risk management implementation, based on primary data. A deeper analysis of the practices of risk disclosures is the subject of three papers that display the variety of methodological approaches and country-specific concerns. These papers refer to the challenges of risk discourse if the public interest is threatened, the discrepancies between public and private risk disclosures and the challenge of risk disclosure from an accounting system's point of view.

Part II is a collection of papers that discuss various aspects of practical risk management implementation. Risk response is given a wider attention in the paper that discusses the application of the analysis of company's financial slack (in the buffering function) to determine its risk retention capabilities. Risk assessment is addressed in the paper that proposes a model of risk assessment process as a distributed cognitive task for a group of agents. Risk monitoring aspects are discussed in the paper that proposes the assessment of financial standing for a continuous overview of risk in SME sector. With reference to the SME sector, the problem of passive or simplistic approach risk management is addressed in one of the papers, based on the results of qualitative study. Finally, the new challenging issues of risk management are addressed by two papers considering the modelling extreme cyber losses and the benefits of robotic automation of accounting processes.

Part III collects the papers that consider risk-related issues as a social or macro-economic concern. The uncertainties related to the determination of discount rate in intergenerational investments are addressed in the first paper, with the discussion of applicability of social discount rate. The second paper in this part is related to the identification of the problem of financial inclusion and its consequences for the targets of monetary policy. Monetary policy is also addressed in the third paper, that discusses the threats for the central banks, as related to monetary policy normalization. The last two papers in this part focus on risk management in financial institutions, in the context of liquidity risk and cyber risk.

This book of proceedings is dedicated to academics and practitioners working in risk and risk management. As the collected papers display a variety of risk-related problems, as well as various methodological approaches, we believe it provides an exceptional training ground and enhances inspiration for further research ideas.

York, UK — Philip Linsley
Newcastle upon Tyne, UK — Philip Shrives
Katowice, Poland — Monika Wieczorek-Kosmala

Contents

Reviewers

René Coppe Pimentel, University of Sao Paulo, Brasil
Marijana Ćurak, University of Split, Croatia
Ewa Dziwok, University of Economics in Katowice, Poland
Tamer Elshandidy, University of Bradford, UK
Iwona Gorzeń-Mitka, Częstochowa University of Technology, Poland
Thomas Henschel, Hochschule fur Technik und Wirtschaft Berlin, Germany
Giulia Leoni, University of Verona, Italy
Artur Linke, University of Stellenbosch, South Africa
Gaia Melloni, Norwich Business School University of East Anglia, UK
Jonas Oliveira, Instituto Universitário de Lisboa, Portugal
Silvia Panfilo, Ca'Foscari University of Venice, Italy
Marco Papa, University of Bari, Italy
Francesca Rossignoli, University of Verona, Italy
Alice Francesca Sproviero, University of Verona, Italy
Simone Terzani, University of Perugia, Italy
Elżbieta Wrońska-Bukalska, Maria Curie Skłodowska University in Lublin, Poland

Part I
Risk Disclosures and Risk Communication

Directors' Duties and Risk Governance

Sergio Beretta

Abstract In recent years, growing expectations from financial markets, increasing requirements by regulators and dedicated guidelines on risk governance have raised the bar for board involvement in the management of risks. *Board risk oversight* refers to the practices used by directors to define the appropriate level of risk for their companies to communicate appetite for risk and to oversee the institution and functioning of controls aimed at keeping the company operating within established boundaries. Managerial literature offers anecdotal evidence that board risk oversight is mainly driven by the search for compliance with regulatory requirements, thus turning a value creation mechanism into an ineffective bureaucratic exercise. The inadequate risk culture of most boards is often reported as the main determinant of the gap between the expected and the actual effectiveness of board risk oversight. We provide an additional explanation based on a review of the leading guidance on corporate governance. We contend that the image of board risk oversight marketed through most of the governance literature is a simplified, unrealistic representation of a complex set of activities whose effectiveness depends on the solution of theoretical as well as practical problems. In our view, leading risk management frameworks and guidance do not address most of those critical issues but merely provide *one size fits all* solutions that are frequently derived from concepts and practices developed in highly regulated industries and later transferred to different and distant industries without adequate contextualization. We argue that this practice has led to some significant biases that make the implementation of risk oversight in different contexts less effective than the original one. We also re-examine board risk oversight in the light of directors' fiduciary duties. We contend that the well-established jurisprudential orientation of courts, inspired by the *business judgment rule*, may even encourage boards to be uninformed of aggressive risk-taking by officers and management. Nonetheless, recent jurisprudence seems to reconsider directors' responsibility (and liability) for risk oversight, apparently recognising the conflict between the weak fiduciary standards set by previous jurisprudence and the increasing requests from investors for boards to play a more active role.

S. Beretta (✉)
Accounting Department, Bocconi University, via Roentgen 1, 20136 Milan, Italy
e-mail: sergio.beretta@unibocconi.it

P. Linsley et al. (eds.), *Multiple Perspectives in Risk and Risk Management*, Springer Proceedings in Business and Economics,
https://doi.org/10.1007/978-3-030-16045-6_1

Keywords Risk governance · Board risk oversight · Risk appetite

1 Introduction

The execution of any strategy is ruled by the willingness of an organisation to accept risk in the pursuit of its goals as well as its capacity to bear that risk. When the board of directors of a corporation defines its strategy, it essentially balances opportunities and expected rewards against related risks: the governance process guides organisations in finding and pursuing their own balance between entrepreneurial opportunity-seeking for value creation and the appropriate control mechanisms for protecting shareholders' value from destruction (CIMA-IFAC 2004).

Board risk oversight indicates the practices used by directors to decide on the appropriate level of risk for their companies, to communicate the appetite for risk throughout the organisation and to external stakeholders, and to oversee the institution and functioning of controls that keep the company operating within its established boundaries (Connelly et al. 2010).

In recent years, growing expectations from financial markets and investors, new legislative provisions and requirements by regulators, and dedicated corporate governance guidelines have set challenging standards for board risk oversight (Aguilar 2015). Nonetheless, recent surveys and managerial literature offer evidence that risk governance remains a relatively low-priority topic at board meetings. A recent survey by McKinsey reveals that boards spend only 9% of their time on risk issues, even less than they declared in 2015. Governance and compliance show the same negative trend (Gius et al. 2018). Moreover, board risk oversight is mainly driven by the search for compliance with regulatory requirements (Brodeur et al. 2010), thus turning a value creation mechanism into a "somewhat sterile" exercise (Towers Watson 2013). This gap between the expected and the actual effectiveness of board risk oversight is considered a key governance weakness mostly due to the inadequate risk culture of most boards (IRM 2011; Caldwell 2012; FSB 2013a). We provide an additional explanation based on a review of the leading guidance on corporate governance. We contend that the image of board risk oversight marketed through the governance literature is a simplified, unrealistic representation of a complex set of activities whose effectiveness depends on the solution of theoretical as well as practical problems. In our view, leading risk management frameworks and guidance (COSO 2004; ISO 2009) do not give clear and univocal indications for a practical implementation of risk oversight in most industries.

Risk oversight and risk management have developed in highly regulated industries (like the financial industry) and activities (typically associated with human health and safety). Their subsequent extension to other industries and contexts has been marked by a somewhat acritical transfer of concepts and practices. We argue that this operation leads to significant biases that make the implementation of risk oversight in different contexts not very effective. In discussing this issue, we focus our analysis on two areas of weakness concerning current guidelines: the definition of the perimeter and contents of *board risk oversight* and the operationalisation of the concept of *risk appetite*.

The paper is structured in four sections. In the first section, we present a brief overview of extant corporate governance literature on board risk oversight. We examine the notion of board risk oversight emerging from corporate governance frameworks; we discuss the determinants of the increasing expectations on the role of the board in risk oversight; and we present some evidence on the practice of risk oversight in public companies.

The second section of the paper examines some critical issues implied by the operationalisation of the concept of board risk oversight from the directors' perspective, addressing their efforts in discharging their responsibilities. The most popular reference guidance on corporate governance (OECD 2014; FRC 2014a) is *principle based*. This solution allows for the flexibility required in implementing risk management in different contexts but, unfortunately, it provides little practical direction on how to guide an effective implementation of the risk oversight role by the board of directors. We contend that an effective accomplishment of risk oversight requires additional exploration of two main areas of concern that are only lightly addressed by guidance: the notion of risk and the role of risk models in risk assessment. With reference to the first issue, we demonstrate that the lack of a clear definition of the concept of *risk* that marks most governance guidelines limits their usefulness in addressing the attention and efforts of directors toward an effective risk governance. Regarding the second issue, risk assessment and risk monitoring largely depend on the use of risk models that boards frequently adopt with limited awareness of their implications on the decisions that the models will inform. We contend that *risk model management* is a foundational element of modern risk governance. Criticalities in the integration of the risk oversight activity by the board and the firm's risk management process are also highlighted.

The third section of the paper examines the notion of *risk appetite* in its connections with board risk oversight. The pivotal role of risk appetite in risk governance is recognised by the entirety of guidance published by corporate governance bodies, regulators and standard setters [among the others: (COSO 2004; SSG 2009; ISO 2009; Rittenberg and Martens 2012; FSB 2013a; OECD 2014; NYSE 2014)]. The concept of risk appetite has found wide popularity and diffusion in regulated industries (like the financial industry and those industries associated with human health and safety), where it has been recognised by regulators as the starting point in the design of a company's sound risk management system and a key object for their supervisory activity. We contend that the concept of risk appetite has suffered a simplistic representation in its transfer to different businesses: critical issues in its definition and in the operationalisation of its measurement have not been adequately faced yet. Simplification has been an effective strategy for increasing the diffusion of the concept but does not effectively support directors in discharging their oversight responsibilities.

The fourth section re-examines risk oversight in light of directors' fiduciary duties. Jurisprudence testifies that courts refrain from holding boards of directors responsible for harmful outcomes that are derived from risk mismanagement unless fraud, misappropriation of corporate funds or other illegal acts are involved. Thus, established jurisprudential orientation may even encourage boards to be uninformed of aggressive risk-taking by officers and management. Nonetheless, recent jurisprudence seems to reconsider the responsibility (and liability) of directors for inadequate risk oversight, apparently recognising the existence of a conflict between weak fiduciary standards set by previous jurisprudence and the increasing requests coming from investors for the board to play a more active role in the management of risks.

2 Board Risk Oversight: An Overview

2.1 Risk Oversight and Directors' Duties

The execution of any strategy is ruled by the willingness of an organisation to accept risk in the pursuit of value creation, as well as by its capacity to bear that risk. Thus, in defining a company's strategy, the board of directors essentially balances opportunities and expected rewards against related risks. Sound risk management does not imply that all risks should be avoided at any cost; that would exclude any single opportunity to create value for shareholders. Instead, it does imply that it will make informed and coherent choices regarding the risks that the company agrees to take in pursuit of its objectives and the measures it has adopted to manage and mitigate those risks. Thus, addressing the balance of entrepreneurial opportunity that seeks to create value with the appropriate control mechanisms for protecting value is one of the key elements of corporate governance.

A fundamental part of directors' duties concerns making decisions on how a company should approach the principal risks it faces (FRC 2014b). The board of directors is responsible for determining the nature and extent of the principal risks it faces and for selecting those risks that the organisation is willing to take to achieve its strategic objectives (FRC 2014a).

Board risk oversight indicates the practices used by directors to decide on the appropriate level of risk for their companies, to communicate appetite for risk throughout the organisation and to external stakeholders, and to oversee the institution and functioning of controls that keep the company operating within these established boundaries (Connelly et al. 2010). In contrast, *risk management* represents management's role in planning, coordinating, executing and handling the activities of the organisation in order to minimise the impact of unwanted risk on desired outcomes (Ittner and Keusch 2015).

Generally recognised corporate governance standards define in detail the board's responsibility for an organisation's overall approach to risk management and internal control (FRC 2014a) by taking the following measures:

- ensuring the design and implementation of appropriate risk management and internal control systems that identify the risks facing the company and enable the board to make a robust assessment of the principal risks;

- determining the nature and extent of the principal risks faced and those risks that the organisation is willing to take to achieve its strategic objectives (determining its risk appetite);
- ensuring that appropriate culture and reward systems have been embedded throughout the organisation;
- agreeing on how principal risks should be managed or mitigated to reduce the likelihood of their incidence or their impact.

Balancing the search for performance with conformance to laws, codes and standards is not a "once in a lifetime" decision (CIMA-IFAC 2004). Thus, the board of directors must periodically reconsider this balance in light of the risk profile that it periodically negotiates with shareholders and major stakeholders, also taking into account the evolution of the environment. For these reasons, monitoring and reviewing the risk management system and the internal control system is a key responsibility of directors. In order to discharge their duties, directors should ensure that systems are properly aligned with strategic objectives, that they are functioning effectively, and that corrective action is being taken where necessary (FRC 2014a).

2.2 Drivers that Elevate Expectations on Board Risk Oversight

In the last few decades, boards' expectations for effective risk oversight have continuously increased. On one hand, boards are expected to oversight compliance risks, i.e. to assure adequate conformance to the law and alignment with corporate governance standards. On the other hand, boards are expected to provide stable, and possibly increasing, financial and business results to investors and financial markets. Regarding conformance requirements, security regulators, intergovernmental economic organisations, international regulatory bodies and professional bodies are among the key players of the risk governance game.

Security regulators ask boards and directors for a strong commitment to risk oversight and for an effective disclosure to markets concerning how they discharge their oversight responsibilities. In the UK, the Financial Reporting Council requires that boards of directors "provide entrepreneurial leadership of the company within a framework of prudent and effective controls which enables risk to be assessed and managed" (FRC 2014a). A robust assessment of the principal risks implied by the company's business model and of the effectiveness of control systems aimed at managing and mitigating them is requested. In the US, in adoption of the Securities and Exchange Commission [SEC] Rule 10A-3, which required audit committees to comply with the Sarbanes-Oxley Act of 2004, the NYSE revised its listing standards.[1] The revision introduced additional guidelines for Audit Committees concerning their

[1]The Sarbanes-Oxley Act of 2002 in Section 205 states that the Audit Committee was "established by and amongst the board of directors of an issuer for the purpose of overseeing the accounting and financial reporting processes of the issuer and the audits of the financial statements of the issuer".

role in discussing companies' major financial risk exposures and the steps that management must take in order to monitor and control such exposures (NYSE 2014: Section 303A.07(c)(iii)(D)). Additionally, the SEC requires companies to disclose specific details in their annual proxy statements about how their boards discharge their risk oversight responsibilities [SEC].[2] In Canada, the Securities Regulatory Authority requires that listed companies disclose that their boards are formally responsible for risk oversight and detail in their Annual Information Form (AIF) how their boards meet risk oversight expectations (OSC: Section 1.1(1), Principle 7). In Singapore, the Corporate Governance Council, established by the Monetary Authority of Singapore, published a "Risk Governance Guidance for Listed Boards" (CGC 2012) which defines clear roles and responsibilities. Boards of listed companies are "responsible for the governance of risks" (Section 5.1) and "have ultimate responsibility for approving the strategy of the company in a manner which addresses stakeholders' expectations and does not expose the company to an unacceptable level of risk" (Section 5.2). Oversight of risk management and internal control systems is a qualified element of risk governance by the board (Section 5.4).

Intergovernmental economic organisations and international regulatory bodies emphasise the centrality of board risk oversight in pursuing an effective governance (OECD 2014) and even require that supervisory agencies verify the effective role played by boards in executing their oversight role in order to avoid 'rubber stamping' behaviours (FSB 2013b).

Professional bodies contend that boards must take an active and direct role in risk governance, well beyond the bureaucratic "getting informed once a year" (Caldwell 2012). On the side of performance assurance, credit rating agencies and institutional investors play a decisive role in promoting boards' active involvement in risk oversight and are increasingly exerting extensive monitoring about how boards discharge this duty.

Credit rating agencies started scoring boards' risk oversight at the beginning of the 2000s. A review of risk governance is currently part of the process of credit rating, thus influencing the cost of raising capital (Standard & Poor's 2005; Moody's Investor Services 2006; Standard & Poor's 2013).

Institutional investors' organisations recommend that their members include an evaluation of corporate governance and board risk oversight in their due diligence process when making investment decisions (ICGN 2015). The Canadian Coalition for Good Governance explicitly declares: "Effective oversight of all relevant types of risk is a core function of the board and a process in which every director should be actively involved. [...] Directors are responsible for risk oversight, including overseeing management's systems and processes for identifying, evaluating, prioritising, mitigating and monitoring risks" (CCGG 2013). According to The Vanguard Group, Inc., one of the world's largest investment management companies: "Directors are

---

[2]SEC Regulation S-K, Item 407(h) and Schedule 14A: Item 7—require a company to disclose the extent of its board of directors' role in the risk oversight of the company, such as how the board administers its oversight function and the effect this has on the board's leadership structure [see: SEC: Item 407(h) of Regulation S-K [17 CFR 229.407(h); 17 CFR 240.14a-101—Schedule 14A] and (SEC 2009)].

shareholders' eyes and ears on risk". When evaluating corporate governance practices, risk oversight is one of the four pillars upon which the evaluation of corporate governance practices stands along with the characteristics of the board, the governance structure and the management compensation system (The Vanguard Group 2017a, b).

2.3 *Risk Oversight and Directors' Duties*

The financial crisis of 2008 unveiled extremely deficient risk oversight and management practices even in large public companies. In a significant number of cases, boards were ignorant of the risks facing their companies, and risk was not adjusted to corporate strategy; neither was it managed on an enterprise-wide basis (OECD 2010). From then onwards, the monitoring of boards by external agents has significantly increased, and board composition and functioning have been revised in a quite large number of companies. Nonetheless, board risk oversight is still a critical issue, as formal accomplishment tends to prevail over substantial fulfillment of directors' duties. According to a survey conducted in 2016 regarding a significant sample of large companies, in 93% of cases, boards of directors review and approve the overall risk management policy or ERM framework, showing a substantial increase from 81% in 2012 (Hida 2016). Meanwhile, a parallel survey reveals that in only 30% of cases, the boards of directors extensively discuss top-risk exposures within the definition of a company's strategic plan. According to the same source, in more than one-third of cases, the board when evaluating new strategic initiatives makes no formal assessments of emerging strategic, market, or industry risks (Beasley et al. 2016). Furthermore, a survey conducted in 2017 shows that reports on the implementation of enterprise-wide risk management systems (ERMs) are reviewed at the board level in less than half of cases and that in only 6 cases out of 10, ERM programs are used to inform and influence corporate strategy (RIMS 2017). It is not surprising that risk professionals express a diffuse dissatisfaction with the state (or lack thereof) of performance management as it is tied to handling risk issues.

In 2014, the world of business was astonished when the California Public Employees' Retirement System (CalPERS) and the New York City Pension Funds, which were among the major shareholders in Duke Energy, urged fellow shareholders to oppose the re-election of four members of Duke's board of directors, accusing them of lax risk oversight in a toxic waste spill (Ormazabal 2016).

In April 2017, influential proxy adviser Institutional Shareholder Services (ISS) recommended that investors vote to replace the majority of directors at Wells Fargo & Company on the basis that they failed "to provide a timely and sufficient risk oversight process" (Reuters).

Recent cases of enforcement action by the Federal Reserve against banks' boards of directors confirm this issue. On February 2, 2018, the Federal Reserve issued an enforcement action against the board of directors of Wells Fargo & Company, imposing a careful evaluation of the firm's risk management capacity and a near oversight of the implementation of adequate risk management systems (Board of Governors of the Federal Reserve System 2018).

Notwithstanding the meaningful pressures that both conformance and performance arguments put on boards, there are contrasting evidences of a convinced and committed alignment of the boards of public companies with best practices in risk oversight.

Inadequate risk culture of most boards is frequently called into question (IRM 2011; Caldwell 2012; FSB 2013a). We contend that the image of board risk oversight marketed through the governance literature is a simplified, unrealistic representation of a complex set of activities whose effectiveness depends on the solution of theoretical as well as practical problems. We concentrate our attention on two major areas of weakness of most corporate governance guidance: (1) an unclear definition of the perimeter and contents of board risk oversight; and (2) the inadequate operationalisation of the concept of risk appetite. We also argue that the mechanistic transfer of concepts and practices originally developed in highly regulated industries to different industries and contexts has injected significant biases that compromise the effectiveness of risk oversight.

3 Defining the Perimeter and Contents of Board Risk Oversight

3.1 The Foundations of Board Risk Oversight: The Notions of Risk and Uncertainty

The increasingly high expectations for an effective board risk oversight have not always been seconded in corporate governance guidance by a clear definition of what should be intended for "risk". For example, the authoritative OECD Guidance defines *risk management,* but *risk* is not defined (OECD 1997). Similarly, the FRC Guidance on risk management does not contain any definition of risk (FRC 2014a).[3]

The issue is critical, as the current use of the term *risk* has different meanings in association with different contexts. For example, it may refer to the volatility of the stock market for an investor; the possibility of insolvency of an insurer for a regulator; the manifestation of a natural event (like a hailstorm) for a farmer; or the success of integrating an acquired business to the management of a buying company. As it emerges from previous examples, the notion of risk spans from volatility to insolvency and from exposure to natural disasters to consequences of management decisions. A common element among the different notions of risk is *uncertainty of outcomes*: what differentiates risk in the proposed examples are the contexts and

[3] An occasional recognition of the variety of circumstances subtended by the concept of risk appears in Section 1: "33. Risks will differ between companies but may include financial, operational, reputational, behavioural, organisational, third party, or external risks, such as market or regulatory risk, over which the board may have little or no direct control" (FRC 2014a).

the contents of that uncertainty, which shape the management of each type of risk (Towers Watson 2013).

Thus, a practical and effective definition of *board risk oversight* requires a sound qualification of the notion of risk. Frank Knight provided the arguably most famous definition of risk: "To preserve the distinction … between the measurable uncertainty and an unmeasurable one, we may use the term 'risk' to designate the former and the term 'uncertainty' for the latter" (Knight 1921: 233).[4] According to Knight, in assessing risks, decision-makers may rely upon a priori and statistical probabilities (as in the case of a credit loss distribution), when and where information is available; or on estimates in case of a lack of or poor information from which to draw reliable inferences. From his perspective, business decisions are a typical decision context for uncertainty. While Knight's distinction addresses only the dimension of probability (Holton 2004; Brooke 2010), the notion of risk in its common use entails both *likelihood* (the possibility of something happening) and *impact* (the exposure to the possible consequences).

A well-known classification of *risk* is based on the joint consideration of the level of knowledge that a decision-maker has about the *occurrence* of a risky event (likelihood, stated at the extreme as *known or unknown*) as well as about its *impact* (either *known or unknown*). Four basic possible states emerge from the combination of the two dimensions (Willows and Connell 2003; Cleden 2009), as depicted in Fig. 1.

Fig. 1 Possible states of uncertainty (adapted from Willows and Connell 2003; Cleden 2009)

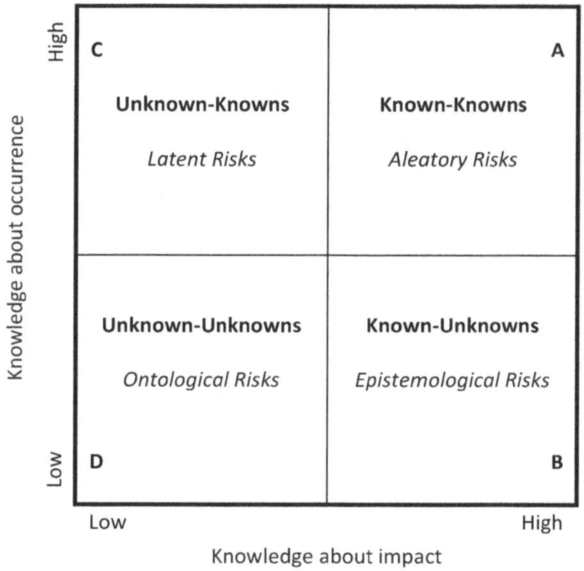

[4]The relationships and distinctions between risk and uncertainty have been discussed extensively in literature. For a review (Aven 2012).

Quadrant A depicts a context of knowledge where substantial information exists about likelihood as well as about the impact of potential events (*aleatory risks*). This is the typical case of "rolling dices": the context is clearly set (number of dices, number of rolls); knowledge of the context is high (number of faces and points associated to each face for each dice); and there are reliable historical data about the outcomes of previous rolls. In sum, a probability theory is available and can guide decision-making. An exemplification of this decision context can be found in the management of risk of machinery breakage, where statistics on breakage of mechanical equipment drive most decisions about the amount and timing of maintenance and even about the opportunity to provide related insurance coverage.

Quadrant B depicts a context of partial knowledge where potential events are reasonably identifiable and their impact can be estimated reasonably well, but information (in terms of both experience and knowledge) about the possibility of occurrence is quite limited. It is a decision context where knowledge gaps can be reduced through data gathering, research and model building, and knowledge can be increased through the analysis of emerging issues (*epistemological risks*). This is the typical case of pricing new products: no algorithm is available from the beginning, but market tests can provide additional information that helps reduce the ambiguity of expected outcomes.

Quadrant C depicts a context where potential events are reasonably identifiable (known), but solid data and evidences that could be used in decision-making (especially in estimating the expected impact of a foreseeable event) are difficult to draw from previous experience. Risks like the entrance of a new competitor in the arena or the launch of a new product by an existing competitor belong to this category. Companies may have already experienced events like those in the past, and previous experiences may have generated unconscious knowledge among managers of what can happen but this kind of knowledge is hidden within the organisation and needs to be brought to consciousness in order to be used (*latent risks*).

Quadrant D depicts a context of complete lack of knowledge both about the existence of potential risks as well as about their measurement (*ontological risks*). These are contexts in which individual as well as social biases in learning and decision-making (Kahneman 2013) may induce an inadequate awareness of some risks, thus exposing the company to potentially catastrophic events in the absence of mitigation activities. This is the real realm of the "unexpected" (Taleb 2007).

The proposed classification may be helpful in mapping the territory of risk management with the aim of defining a conscious approach to the management of uncertainty *latu* sensu. Meanwhile, the differentiation drawn among the various contexts does not represent an unmodifiable state of nature: through knowledge building, organisations increase their capability to manage uncertainty, thus changing the *status quo*. Assuming that the context depicted in quadrant A is optimal from a risk management perspective, risk management in quadrant B should be aimed at refining available knowledge about uncertainty through data gathering, model building and testing in order to move decision contexts towards quadrant A. In quadrant C, risk management should be directed towards unleashing hidden knowledge, i.e., unshared information and skills available within the organisation in order to subsequently model and measure it, as in quadrant B. In quadrant D, efforts should be addressed to educate managers to identify low probability—high-impact, risky events in order to limit investments and operations in business contexts characterised by complex decisions with a fat-tail distribution of results (Taleb 2009; Taleb and Goldstein 2012).

As the notion of *oversight* implies "responsibility for a job or activity and for making sure it is being done correctly" (The English Cambridge Dictionary 2018), the above-referenced classification of different states of uncertainty and associated risks has relevant implications in defining both the perimeter and the content of board risk oversight in identifying, prioritising, managing and monitoring critical risks (Ittner and Keusch 2015).

As the board of directors must "provide entrepreneurial leadership of the company within a framework of prudent and effective controls which enables risk to be assessed and managed" (FRC 2014c), the board is responsible for determining the nature and the extent of the principal risks it is willing to take in achieving its strategic objectives and for maintaining sound risk management and internal control systems (FRC 2014c: Section C2). More specifically, the same guidance qualifies the board's responsibilities as, among others, "ensuring the design and implementation of appropriate risk management and internal control systems that identify the risks facing the company and enable the board to make a robust assessment of the principal risks" (FRC 2014a: Section C2, Item 24). "Robust" in current use stands for *solidly built* (versus *weak, fragile)*, *realistic* and *pragmatic* (as opposed to *impractical*). Robust statistics are statistics that yield good performance when data is drawn from a wide range of probability distributions that are largely unaffected by outliers or small departures from model assumptions in a given dataset. According to both the current use and the statistical meaning, a "robust assessment of the principal risks" implies a high level of knowledge about both the probability of occurrence and the expected impact of risky events. Thus, the decision context depicted in quadrant A stands as "the" typical area of concern for the board of directors in discharging their responsibilities for risk oversight.

Nonetheless, "ensuring the design and implementation of appropriate risk management and internal control systems that identify the risks facing the company" is explicitly mentioned. Thus, boards should take care of the implementation of effective risk assessment processes that also promote knowledge building with the aim of identifying principal risks.

In case of limited knowledge of the probability of occurrence of relevant risks, as in quadrant B, the board should verify that adequate processes are in place and aimed at improving the forecasting capabilities through data gathering, model building and testing.

Taking into consideration the left side of the risk classification matrix, the oversight activity of the board must largely surrender to the *hidden knowledge* of unidentified risks (quadrant C) and to the complete lack of insight about possible risky events (quadrant D). Nonetheless, the board can certainly play a key role in challenging management's tendency to focus only on well-known contexts (Taleb et al. 2009).

In sum, an unclear definition of *risk* may induce the board to focus on easily identifiable and quantifiable risks. Unfortunately, other risks that remains un-monitored, as they are difficult to identify and quantify, can put the sustainability and the execution of a firm's strategy in jeopardy (Taleb 2007).

3.2 Board Risk Oversight and the Use of Risk Models

Over the last few decades, companies have developed models intended to address and support risk management through the identification and quantification of risks and their subsequent aggregation and management across geographies and business areas. Pressed by regulation, banks have led the process of innovation and diffusion of quantitative models for managing market and credit risks. Nonetheless, also manufacturing and service companies are making increasing use of quantitative risk models (Arboleda et al. 2016; Deloitte 2017).

Risk models largely influence management estimation of future potential adverse consequences of decisions or events. As models are simplified representations of real-world relationships among observed characteristics, values, and events, their use presents *model risk*; that is, the potential for adverse consequences from decisions based on incorrect or misused model outputs and reports. Model risk occurs primarily for two reasons (Board of Governors of the Federal Reserve System 2011):

- Models may embody errors and/or may produce inaccurate outputs when viewed against the design objective and intended business uses—Errors can occur at any point from design through implementation: selection of theories underlying the model, choice of sample design and numerical routines, selection of inputs and estimation, and implementation in information systems may be less than optimal when not totally wrong. Moreover, the quality of model outputs depends on the quality of input data and assumptions.
- Models may be used incorrectly or inappropriately—By their nature, models are simplifications of reality, and real-world events may prove those simplifications inappropriate, especially if a model is used outside the context for which it was designed.

In sum, a model's capabilities and limitations must be appreciated in the light of the simplifications and assumptions underlying the model. A model's users must also understand its intrinsic limitations in order to avoid misuses.

Rigorous model validation and monitoring is thus required for effective use (Board of Governors of the Federal Reserve System 2011; ECB 2018). Models must be challenged through critical analysis by objective and competent subjects in order to make their underlying assumptions explicit and to signal their limitations. If management does not possess adequate technical preparation or management's objectivity is at stake due to the incentive system, external parties should be involved in the challenge of risk models.

It is somewhat surprising that this issue is not discussed in reference guidance on risk governance. This lack may lead the guidance's recipients to believe that *model risk management* is a purely technical issue that belongs to the sphere of risk management, not to the sphere of risk governance. This belief is wrong for many reasons. First, model design implies making choices among different theoretical approaches that may subtend different views on the management of risks. Second, a relevant amount of subjective judgment is implied in the implementation, use and even in the validation of the models adopted. These activities are only apparently *technical*: they are qualifying elements of risk governance. Third, risk models act like cognitive filters, heavily influencing management risk perception (Stulz 2008). Moreover, as decision contexts change, management must regularly monitor the adequacy of risk models and the appropriateness of their use. Thus, model risk management implies a political dimension that must address the technical issues in coherence with the firm's strategic vision.

For these reasons, model risk management emerges as a relevant component of board risk oversight, raising the issue of the availability of technical competences within the board of directors.

3.3 Risk Oversight and Risk Management: Integration and Substitution

As said previously, *risk oversight* refers to the practices used by the board to determine that the firm has a robust process in place for identifying, prioritising, managing, and monitoring its critical risks. In contrast, *risk management* is concerned with management's role in planning, coordinating, executing, and handling the activities of the organisation in order to minimise the impact of unwanted risk on desired outcomes (Ittner and Keusch 2015).

For an effective governance of risks, risk oversight and risk management need to complement each other, which implies a close cooperation of directors and management. According to the Financial Reporting Council: "The board retains ultimate responsibility for the risk management and internal control systems and should reach its own conclusions regarding the recommendations it receives" (FRC 2014a: Section 2, Item 27). Moreover, when receiving assurance from management: "The board should satisfy itself that these sources of assurance have sufficient authority, independence and expertise to enable them to provide objective advice and information to the board" (FRC 2014a: Section 2, Item 27).

Effective cooperation does not exclude a challenging role for the board: the board is not a passive recipient of information that senior managers pass on to it. It is management's duty to bring the board's attention to the company's material risks and to assist the board in evaluating them, in understanding how they interrelate and in appreciating how they are managed. Meanwhile, it is the board of directors' duty to contribute to the definition of their information needs, to monitor the adequacy and the quality of information flows, and to provide useful feedback to management.

Moreover, there are circumstances in which the challenging role of the board is of utmost importance. This occurs when decisions that can expose the company to highly negative impacts cannot be adequately mitigated, and when management bias can compromise the smooth functioning of the usual information channels.

Examples of circumstances of the first type are financial transactions that expose the company to an extremely high (and risky) leverage that could compromise its liquidity and/or solidity; business decisions that expose the company to compliance infringement or to possible hard retaliations by powerful competitors; changes in business models that could heavily impact customer retention; and decisions to enter totally new businesses. In circumstances like these, the board is expected to take very active role in the process of understanding, quantifying, prioritising, mitigating and monitoring such risks.

A second area of criticality materialises when senior managers are directly involved in the review of risks associated with strategic decisions that they themselves have taken and implemented in the past. It seems unreasonable to expect unbiased self-evaluations of previous strategic decisions or objective self-assessments of their abilities to execute these decisions. In these circumstances, an effective risk oversight must consider a quite active and direct role for the board to challenge assumptions and assessments presented by senior management (Caldwell 2012).

4 Operationalising the Concept of Risk Appetite

4.1 A Simplistic View of a Complex Concept

In defining a company's strategy, the board of directors essentially balances opportunities and expected rewards against related risks. The willingness of a company to accept risks in pursuit of its goals is commonly defined as *risk appetite*. The definition of risk appetite is at the heart of a firm's strategy (Stulz 2008). Thus, it is widely recognised as a typical competence of the board and a key element in the execution of boards' duties (OECD 2010).

The concept of risk appetite is key within the oversight role of the board for two reasons. First, different strategies expose a firm to different risks or different amounts of similar risks. The governing body of the firm must manage its strategy and business objectives in coherence with the types and amount of risks it is willing to accept in its pursuit of value. Risk appetite provides guidance on the practices that an organisation is encouraged to pursue or not pursue (COSO 2017: 48). Second, in order to provide effective guidance to decision-making at any level of the firm, risk appetite must be cascaded within the organisation. This can be done by defining the amount of risk associated with management objectives at any relevant organisational

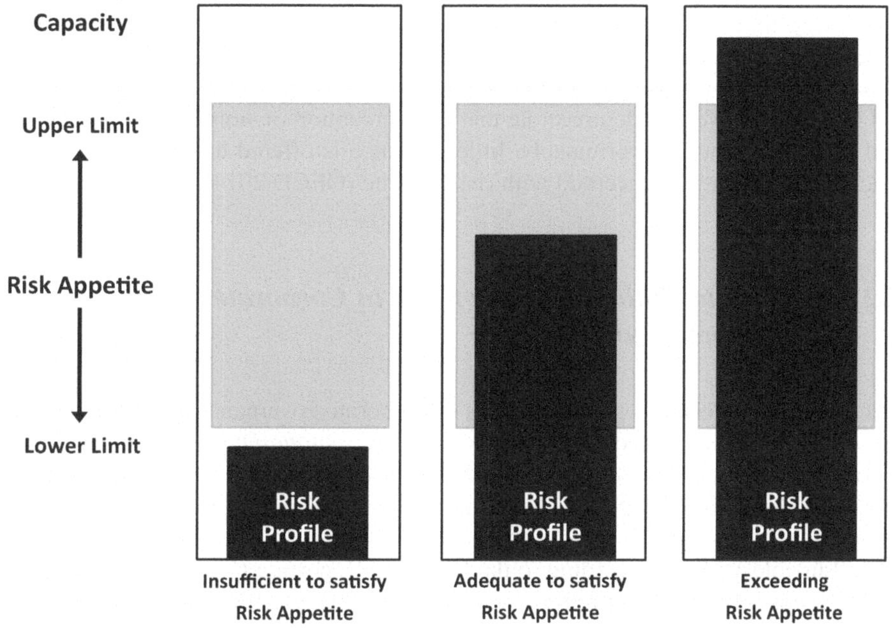

Fig. 2 Interactions of risk profile and risk appetite (adapted from Deloitte 2014a, b)

level (*risk tolerance*).[5] Operating within risk tolerances helps ensure that the entity remains within its risk appetite and, in turn, that the entity is able to achieve its objectives (COSO 2004: 20). The process of cascading risk appetite is of utmost importance for the effectiveness of risk management and should be guided by the governing body of an organisation.

In recent times, the concept of *risk appetite* has acquired wide popularity and diffusion among consultants, professional associations and even regulators as a metaphor for communicating the desired *risk-reward balance* (COSO 2004, 2017; SSG 2010; ISO 2009; Rittenberg and Martens 2012; RIMS 2012; FSB 2013b; KPMG 2013; Towers Watson 2013; IIA 2017).

An evocative capacity and an apparent simplicity are among the main ingredients of its popularity and growing diffusion. Consider the following representation of the interactions of the concepts of *risk profile* and *risk appetite* (see Fig. 2).

The concept of risk appetite is intuitive: it captures the attitude of the board and senior management for risk acceptance that is implied in the firm strategy as well as the urgency to re-establish the desired alignment of risk profile with risk appetite when trigger thresholds are exceeded. Recent guidance recommends the definition of both upper and lower risk appetite limits in order to provide a range of desired

[5]"*Risk tolerance* is the acceptable level of variation relative to achievement of a specific objective, and often is best measured in the same units as those used to measure the related objective" (COSO 2004: 20).

risk-taking that expands the application of risk appetite from a pure risk control concept to one that also incorporates strategic risk-taking (COSO 2017: 100).

Unfortunately, realising a similar representation of risk appetite in real life is not that simple. We will demonstrate that this perception of simplicity is unrealistic and even dangerous. Unfortunately, little guidance is offered to boards on how to discharge their duties concerned with risk appetite (OECD 2014).

4.2 The Pivotal Role of Risk Appetite in Corporate Governance Guidance

According to widely accepted principles of corporate governance, risk appetite is a key element of the risk governance function. The *Annotations to the Principles of Corporate Governance* issued by OECD state that boards have an essential responsibility in setting the risk policy, including the specification of "the types and degree of risk that a company is willing to accept in pursuit of its goals" (OECD 2014: 11—Principle VI.D.). According to the Financial Reporting Council, the board has the "responsibility for determining the nature and extent of the principal risks faced and those risks which the organisation is willing to take in achieving its strategic objectives (determining its *risk appetite*)". The same guidance requires that the board, in its annual review of the effectiveness of the risk management system, consider the company's "willingness to take on risk (its *risk appetite*)"(FRC 2014a: Section 5, Item 43).

In the financial industry, regulators consider the definition and monitoring of risk appetite as one of the key elements for the effectiveness of the risk management system. The Senior Supervisors Group (SSG) identifies the "failure of some boards of directors and senior managers to establish, measure, and adhere to a level of risk acceptable to the firm" as one of the areas of weakness that generated the financial crisis of 2008 (SSG 2009). The European Central Bank considers a well-developed risk appetite statement "a cornerstone of a sound governance framework" (ECB 2016).

The concept of risk appetite is pivotal also for the Committee of Sponsoring Organizations of the Treadway Commission (COSO), one of the most authoritative standard setters in the field of risk management practices, within its Enterprise Risk Management (ERM) Frameworks.[6]

---

[6]"Align risk appetite and strategy—Risk appetite is the degree of risk a company or other entity is willing to accept in pursuit of its goals. Management considers the entity's risk appetite in evaluating strategic alternatives, setting related objectives and developing mechanisms to manage related risks" (COSO 2004: 3). The concept of risk appetite is pivotal also in the recent ERM Framework, where the term *risk appetite* appears more than 200 times: "An organization must manage risk to strategy and business objectives in relation to its risk appetite—that is, the types and amount of risk, on a broad level, it is willing to accept in its pursuit of value. The first expression of risk appetite is an entity's mission and vision. Different strategies will expose an entity to different risks or different amounts of similar risks" (COSO 2017: 48).

4.3 *The Notion of Risk Appetite in the Financial Industry*

The concept of risk appetite has been extensively explored in regulated industries. Regulators have found the concept of *risk appetite* conceptually aligned with their need to set limits to aggressive risk-taking by industry operators. By modeling risk appetite, regulators impose on regulated actors to identify material risks to their objectives, to design controls and mitigations that produce a residual risk consistent with a target risk appetite, and to monitor the entire process, making feedback adjustments as necessary (Power 2009). Thus, the definition of risk appetite is the cornerstone of the risk management approach in regulated industries.

In particular, the financial industry is a standard setter among regulated industries in the definition of risk appetite. Regulators in the financial industry aim to avoid firms' failures (that could enact chain reactions at a systemic level) and to assure full compliance with laws and regulations (in order to promote a well-ordered functioning of the economic system) (FSB 2013b). Consequently, they have addressed their efforts to the definition of standardised quantitative measures of risk capacity and of associated measures of risk appetite, defined as "The aggregate level and types of risk a financial institution is willing to assume, within its risk capacity, to achieve its strategic objectives and business plan" (FSB 2013b).

A practical implementation of the concept of risk appetite in the financial service industry requires a sequence of methodological steps that include the definition of synthetic measures of risk at the firm level; the allocation of risk appetite to organisational units and groups within the firm; the systematic monitoring with respect to the limits set; and the regular re-evaluation of the risk appetite (Deloitte 2014b).

The nature of the financial business and the focus of regulators on risk limitation address the definition of risk appetite at the firm level towards risks whose quantification is supported by observable financial exposure data (mainly: credit risks, market risks, liquidity risks). Accordingly, practice has developed a wide range of commonly accepted metrics (capital-at-risk amounts; liquidity ratios; VaR limits; risk sensitivity limits; expected loss ratios; credit spreads; and others) along with measurement methodologies defined or accepted by regulators.

Once it has been quantified at the firm level, risk appetite can be allocated to organisational units and entities within the firm (typically business lines and divisions within the financial industry). Generally accepted concepts like *risk capacity* (i.e., the maximum level of risk that a financial institution can assume given its current level of resources before breaching regulatory constraints) and *risk limits* (i.e., the amounts of acceptable risk related to specific types of risks or to a specific level or unit of the organisation) drive the allocation process (FSB 2013b).

The following step is the implementation of ongoing monitoring mechanisms: limits and thresholds aligned with risk appetite must be integrated into the reporting system. In case of breaches of risk limits and thresholds, the reporting line should guarantee the timely information of senior management and, eventually, it should activate an escalation to the board of directors.

Finally, risk appetite should be reviewed and updated periodically in order to assure its alignment with changes in market conditions, regulation, strategy, risk capacity, or other relevant factors that may affect it.

The dominance of measurable aspects that characterise key industry business factors and the strong guidance offered by regulators in approaching measurement issues, have shaped the implementation of the concept of risk appetite within the financial industry. Observed from the outside, the process appears quite *mechanistic* and strongly anchored to hard measures, thus inducing a perception of simplicity and objectivity. It is an incorrect perception indeed, as non-financial risks (operational, reputational, strategic risks) still represent a quite uncertain context for risk measurement within the financial industry. In those risk areas (where hard data on risk exposure and probability are not available), risk estimates are heavily based upon subjective measurement practices (as risk self-assessment scoring methods). In those areas, risk quantification largely relies on the adoption of proxy measures whose reliability and precision is quite limited (Deloitte 2014a). Aside from pure financial risks, the perception of simplicity and objectivity disappears, unveiling an implementation process of risk appetite that is as complex and subjective as it is in non-financial businesses.

In sum, no quick troubleshooting of most of the critical issues associated with the practical implementation of risk appetite for non-financial risks is offered by best practices developed within the financial industry.

4.4 Criticalities in the Implementation of Risk Appetite

Empirical evidences testify to a limited diffusion of best practices concerning the implementation of risk appetite outside the financial industry. A survey recently conducted on a population of large non-financial companies reveals that nearly half of respondents have not developed risk appetite statements at any firm or business level (RIMS 2017). The limited implementation of the concept of risk appetite within management systems clearly contrasts with its large popularity. We contend that this is not only the consequence of the poor risk culture of some directors, but also a symptom of the theoretical and practical challenges associated with the definition and implementation of risk appetite in non-financial contexts.

Issues in the definition of Risk Appetite To begin, the definition of risk appetite proposed by different guidance is not univocal (Purdy 2011; RIMS 2012). Let us consider the definitions proposed by the two leading standard setters in the risk management practice: the Committee of Sponsoring Organizations of the Treadway Commission (COSO) and the International Organization for Standardization (ISO). COSO, in its Enterprise Risk Management Framework, defines risk appetite as "the amount of risk an entity is *willing* to accept in pursuit of value" (COSO 2004: 11). ISO, in its guide on risk management, defines risk appetite (3.3.6.2) as the "amount and type of risk an organization is *prepared* to pursue or take" (ISO 2008). One guidance associates risk appetite with the *willingness* of management to accept risks, while the other assumes the *preparedness* of the firm in taking risks. *Willingness* does not necessarily imply *preparedness*.

Definitions offered by popular guidance are not only different, but also quite vague and ambiguous. For example, the Basel Committee on Banking Supervision defines risk appetite as "a high level determination of how much risk a firm is willing to accept taking into account the risk/return attributes; it is often taken as a forward looking view of risk acceptance" (Basel Committee on Banking Supervision 2011). No further explanation is provided about the key concepts of "high level determination" and "forward looking view of risk acceptance".

In light of the examples provided, the guidance offered by leading standard setters in defining *risk appetite* in practical terms is quite poor and far from unambiguous. In addition to that, methodological issues are associated both with the quantification of risk appetite and with its timely reporting to senior management and to the board of directors.

Issues in the quantification of Risk Appetite Boards of directors can express different appetites for different risks. COSO classifies risks in four categories: strategic risks, operational risks, reporting risks and compliance risks (COSO 2004). Different types of risks show different attitudes toward quantification and present different dilemmas in measurement.

Operational risks affect the effectiveness and efficiency of the entity's operations, including performance and profitability goals and the safeguarding of resources' value against loss (COSO 2004: 36). Most operational risks in non-financial firms can be modeled by linking operational indicators to financial measures. This kind of expertise is widely diffused in planning and control functions as demonstrated by the progressive integration of risks within typical performance measurement and control systems (Cheng et al. 2014). Thus, for most operational risks, risk appetite is based on available measurements.

Reporting risks pertain to the reliability of internal and external reporting and may involve financial and non-financial information (COSO 2004: 36). Listed companies have a long established tradition of managing these types of risks as they are required to adopt and apply accounting and reporting standards and are subject to systematic control by external auditors. The financial accounting and reporting activity is on average quite structured and regulated by internal procedures designed in order to match external reporting requirements. Internal auditors (IAs) and Chief Financial Officers (CFOs) regularly assess financial reporting risk by systematically reviewing the processes by which accounting data is obtained and reported and the systems through which data are collected, treated and presented (Deloitte 2010). The market impact of financial restatements can also be fairly estimated (Stunda 2017). Thus, a reliable quantification of current financial reporting risk is a sound point of reference for the definition of risk appetite.

Strategic risks and compliance risks definitely raise the bar for risk quantification. *Strategic risks* affect the attainment of strategic objectives aligned with and supporting the entity's mission (COSO 2004: 21). Myriad external and internal factors drive events that can affect the achievement of strategic objectives. Among the outside factors one can consider are economic factors, political factors, social factors, technological factors and natural environment factors (COSO 2004: 42). Inside factors associated with the management of human resources, infrastructure, and business process and technology can also affect the attainment of strategic objectives. For most of the listed factors, an exhaustive identification of associated risky events is almost impossible, thus making any definition of risk appetite conceptually weak. Moreover, many of the so-called strategic risks are difficult to quantify. For example, companies struggle to quantify reputational risk. Events that inflict reputational damage to a firm will ultimately result in losses far greater than the direct cost of the particular event and can potentially have a devastating impact. This could also be the case for breaks in product quality and safety, fraud, disasters attributed to a firm's responsibility and so on. Conceptually, reputation risk can be estimated by measuring the market capitalization loss associated to the risky event that affects the firm's reputation. Assessment models have been proposed in recent years (Mahon 2002; Roberts and Dowling 2002; Chalmers and Godfrey 2004; Perry and Fontnouvelle 2005), but their diffusion is still quite limited. Difficulties in defining the risk, complex and largely subjective models for risk assessment, and insufficient data availability are factors that limit the practical quantifications of the risk appetite associated with these types of risks (Wartick 2002; Walker 2010; Scandizzo 2011).

Compliance risks are associated with the adherence to a firm's behaviour regarding relevant laws and regulations (COSO 2004: 36). Organisations can act only through agents and, under federal criminal law, generally are vicariously liable for offenses committed by their agents. The United States Sentencing Commission lists in its guidelines two factors that mitigate the ultimate punishment of an organisation in case of criminal conduct of individual agents of the organization (USSC 2016: §3E1.1) (i) the existence of an effective compliance and ethics program; and (ii) self-reporting, cooperation, or acceptance of responsibility (USSC 2016: 525—Chap. 8). In order to reduce the risk of punishment, firms must implement an effective compliance and ethics program, exercise due diligence to prevent and detect criminal conduct and promote an organisational culture that encourages ethical conduct and a commitment to compliance with the law.[7] In implementing those requirements, the organisation shall periodically assess the risk of criminal conduct.[8] The board of directors plays a pivotal role in assuring compliance, as the failure to meet compliance standards is

[7]USCC (2016) Ch. 8 "Sentencing of Organizations"—§8C2.5 (Culpability Score) and §8D1.4 (Recommended Conditions of Probation—Organizations).

[8]USSC (2016) Ch. 8 "Sentencing of Organizations"—The Application Notes to the rule state: "7. Application of Subsection (c). To meet the requirements of subsection (c), an organization shall: (a) Assess periodically the risk that criminal conduct will occur, including assessing the following: (i) the nature and seriousness of such criminal conduct; (ii) the likelihood that certain criminal conduct may occur because of the nature of the organization's business. [...]; (iii) the prior history of the organization. The prior history of an organization may indicate types of criminal conduct that it shall take actions to prevent and detect; (b) Prioritize periodically, as appropriate, the actions taken pursuant to any requirement set forth in subsection (b), in order to focus on preventing and detecting the criminal conduct identified under subparagraph (A) of this note as most serious, and most likely, to occur. [...]".

likely to breach the board members' fiduciary obligations (Roach 2007). According to established practices in risk assessment, the quantification of compliance risks requires both the estimate of the impact of the sanctions imposed over the organisation because of the violation of the law, and the measurement of the probability that the event happens. Concerning the first issue, direct and indirect effects of sanctions must be considered. While the estimation of direct effects (fines, compensation to victims and other remedies to the harm caused by the offense, community service) is relatively easy, the estimation of indirect effects of sanctions (i.e., the impact of temporary interdiction and disqualification from the business and the reputation damage) is much more difficult. With regard to the second issue, the implementation of procedures and internal controls aim to reduce the possibility that individual conducts may infringe upon the law and its regulations. Nonetheless, the evaluation of the effectiveness of preventive controls represents a quite tough challenge. Thus, the intensity of compliance risk is frequently expressed in qualitative terms, making use of *traffic lights*, *heat maps*, and *risk barometers*. While effective for intuitive communication, this symbology is of little help in the quantification of the risk appetite that must be subsequently cascaded within the organisation.

Implications for Board Risk Oversight In sum, the quantification of risk appetite is more problematic than a merely intuitive interpretation may suggest. The risks that an organisation faces may have many different kinds of consequences, not all of which can be measured on a common scale (incommensurability of measures). Financial measures attract the attention of management, quite often excluding from their view other, less tangible but not less important outcomes such as staff morale, brand value and reputation, which legitimise the social license to operate (unidimensionality of measures). Different types of risks deserve different measurement methodologies that are not always easy to match across a portfolio of risks (inhomogeneity of measures) (Purdy 2011).

Incommensurability, unidimensionality, and inhomogeneity of measures dramatically limit the process of cascading risk tolerances along the management pyramid. Difficulties in the definition of specific limits and triggers whose breach requires appropriate escalation to the next level of oversight compromise the capability of senior management and governing bodies to monitor actual risk profiles against defined risk appetites. Vagueness and ambiguity in defining risk appetite are not the best attributes for a sound and effective oversight role.

The role of the board in managing Risk Appetite The board of directors plays a central role both in the definition of the firm's risk appetite and in its management. The ideal process depicted by most popular standards of corporate governance and risk management frameworks includes the following steps: the board of directors, with input from senior management, sets overarching expectations for the risk profile and communicates the approved risk appetite; senior management translates those expectations into objectives, constraints and incentives for line managers; the board holds the business accountable for performance related to expectations; and the board asks for and receives the adequate type and amount of information in order to monitor adherence to risk appetite (SSG 2010).

Recent studies offer a quite different picture of the actual risk oversight process in public companies. On one side, communication from the board and senior management concerning the expected alignment of strategy execution with risk appetite is quite poor: in more than one-third of cases, there is no explicit reference to the firm's risk attitude, and only in a very limited fraction of the population examined (14%) does communication from the board include explicit references to defined risk appetite and tolerances (Ittner and Keusch 2015). Conversely, most boards do not contribute actively in shaping the risk reporting that is directed to them: they are often passive recipients of predefined sets of information about the risk environment (FSB 2013b).

Guidelines on risk oversight offer quite different and somewhat contrasting pictures of the role that the board of directors is expected to play in managing risk appetite. Two basic approaches emerge from our review: a *principal role* versus a *supporting role* for the board.

The board plays a *principal role* when it takes the lead of the process aimed at defining the risk appetite at the firm level; it guides the risk allocation process and the associated cascading process of risk tolerances; it monitors that risk limits and thresholds are respected; and it aligns incentive systems with risk appetite (FSB 2013b).

The board plays a *supporting role* when the burden of risk management remains mainly on management. The board is a rather passive recipient of risk reports that has not contributed to design. Challenging the assurances offered by management is rare, and support given to the definition and management of risk appetite is more formal than substantial, mainly induced by a bureaucratic adhesion to standards of corporate governance.

In previous paragraphs, we have contended that different competitive and regulatory contexts justify, or at least contribute to the explanation of, different approaches to boards' risk oversights. Internal factors also contribute in shaping the role that boards play. It is well documented that boards are exposed to the risk of information asymmetry when overseeing management's risk appetite and tolerance. Due to their roles, senior-level executives, who naturally have deeper knowledge about the firm's operations (and associated risks) than the board, select and filter the information presented to the board. Information asymmetry is frequently associated with the reluctance of senior management to share their real risk appetite/tolerance with their boards, as this may conflict with compensation systems and career advancement goals (Gupta and Leech 2015). As directors rely upon those filtered data, the definition of risk appetite by a less-than-active board is unavoidably biased (NACD 2013; Brennan et al. 2016). A challenging role of the board is thus required in order to limit the gap between the *declared* risk appetite and *real* risk appetite of senior management. Unresolved issues in the quantification of risk appetite make this gap utterly difficult to detect.

5 Directors' Duties and Risk Governance

A board's risk oversight responsibilities arise primarily from legal fiduciary duties that directors owe to the company and its shareholders. From a common law perspective, fundamental duties can be re-conducted to (Black 2001):

- duty of *loyalty*—the duty to act in the interests of the company;
- duty of *disclosure*—the duty to provide reasonably complete disclosure to shareholders;
- duty of *care*—the duty to pay attention and to try to make good decisions. Directors must display the care, skill and competence that is reasonable for someone carrying out the functions of the office.

In substantial terms, the duty of care implies a *duty to monitor* in order to prevent harm to the corporation: directors as individuals and the board may breach this duty if harm occurs due to their inattention or inaction (Pan 2010).

This duty assumes special relevance within the issue of board risk oversight as it applies to two of its fundamental components: the monitoring that risk acceptance lies within the risk appetite limits set by the board and the monitoring of the effectiveness of control systems set for the protection of shareholders and stakeholders. Jurisprudence has established that directors breach their duty to monitor when they "fail [ ] to implement any reporting or information systems or controls" or if "having implemented such systems or controls, consciously fail [ ] to monitor or oversee its operations, thus disabling themselves from being informed of risks or problems requiring their attention" (Stone vs. Ritter 2006).

As most popular catastrophic losses suffered by shareholders and stakeholders of large public companies are largely associated with severe weaknesses in board risk oversight, there is an interest in verifying how strongly this duty is enforced in practice. Two popular case studies concerning litigations involving large public companies operating in naturally high-risk industries can be helpful in fixing some points. The first concerns Merck & Co., Inc., a primary actor of the pharmaceutical industry; the second refers to Citigroup Inc., one of the giants of the banking sector.

Merck & Co., Inc. On 15 January 2016 (WSJ 2016), The Wall Street Journal published an article titled "Merck to Pay \$830 Million to Settle Vioxx Shareholder Suit". The news referred to a shareholders' action linked to the withdrawal from the market of Vioxx, a champion painkiller drug and one of the most relevant products within Merck's portfolio. As a consequence of the withdrawal of Vioxx at the beginning of October 2004, Merck's market capitalisation plunged more than \$37 billion (roughly about −30%) in the following month. Shareholders alleged they paid inflated prices for Merck shares because of the company's conduct. A quick review of the story behind the withdrawal of Vioxx (Presley 2008) can be helpful in depicting the role of board risk oversight in this case.

In November 1998, Merck asked the Food and Drug Administration (FDA) for approval of Vioxx after testing the drug. Shortly before the FDA approved Vioxx,

Merck launched a study aimed at proving that Vioxx was superior to older painkillers because it caused fewer gastrointestinal problems. Instead, the study would eventually provide evidence that Vioxx could cause cardiovascular problems, heart attacks and strokes. In January 1999, Merck launched the Vioxx Gastrointestinal Outcomes Research study (VIGOR), a clinical trial designed to demonstrate that Vioxx was safer for the digestive system than older painkillers based on *Naproxen*. In May 1999, after the approval of the FDA, Vioxx was put on the market in the United States.

In November 1999, at a meeting of the VIGOR safety panel, it was reported that 79 patients out of 4000 who took Vioxx had had serious heart problems or even died, compared with 41 patients who took *Naproxen*. The panel voted to continue the study and to meet again in a month. At a December 1999 meeting, it was confirmed that the risk of serious heart problems and death among Vioxx patients was twice as high as in the *Naproxen* group. It was decided to continue the study. DSMB (Data and Safety Monitoring Board) Chairman Michael Weinblatt and Merck statistician Deborah Shapiro sent a letter to Merck's Alise Reicin, V.P. of Merck's clinical research committee and a steering committee member, reporting the collected evidence.

In September 2001, the FDA issued a warning to Merck for misrepresenting the safety of Vioxx by downplaying the cardiovascular risks associated with the drug's use. The following year, new safety information was added to Vioxx's labeling.

Between 2002 and 2004, several epidemiological studies pointed to Vioxx's increased risk of cardiovascular problems. In May 2004, a Canadian study revealed that patients in the study using Vioxx had an 80% increased risk of heart diseases compared to those taking the competing drug Celebrex. In August 2004, an FDA-sponsored study reported that patients taking the recommended dose of Vioxx had three times the risk of heart attacks and sudden cardiac death than did those patients taking Celebrex.

On 30 September 2004, Merck made a public announcement that it planned to withdraw Vioxx from the market. Research published in the medical journal Lancet estimates that 88,000 Americans had heart attacks from taking Vioxx, and 38,000 of them died.

The reported "January 2016 agreement" brought Merck's total payouts to settle Vioxx-safety-related litigation to an estimated amount of \$6 billion, excluding Merck's own legal-defense costs and Vioxx-related litigations still pending.

Merck's Vioxx story depicts a clear case of inadequate risk oversight by the board. Clinical risk is one of the most critical issues for pharmaceutical companies: it seems reasonable to expect that the monitoring of this risk falls within the board's duty to monitor. Merck's board of directors included qualified specialists in health care and expert managers of the pharmaceutical industry: no competence gap can justify the board's "inattention" to the safety issues raised about Vioxx since its launch. Information channels to and from the board were apparently working well: no information block can justify the "inaction" of the board in front of the many red flags raised and communicated to one of the members of its executive committee.

Notwithstanding the previous arguments, Merck said that the settlement of the shareholders' lawsuit did not constitute an admission of liability or wrongdoing by the company or individual executives named as defendants in the case.

Citigroup Inc. By the end of 2002, under the guidance of Charles O. Prince III (CEO) and Robert Rubin (Chairman of the Executive Committee), Citigroup pursued high-risk strategies aimed at increasing the bank's earnings. Three major areas were involved in this strategy between 2003 and 2007: originating and securitising subprime loans; creating and marketing collateralised debt obligations (CDOs); and originating and securitising leveraged corporate loans (Wilmarth 2013). The booming housing market injected additional opportunities in the CDO market: from 2003 to 2005, Citigroup more than tripled the issuance of CDOs to more than $20 billion (NYT 2008).

In June 2007, when the first shockwaves of the subprime mortgage crisis hit Bear Stearns and examiners from the SEC began scrutinising subprime mortgage holdings, Citigroup's executives communicated that the probability of those mortgages defaulting was so limited that they excluded them from their risk analysis.

In late summer 2007, when the subprime crisis became evident and the value of CDOs began to fall, the senior management of Citigroup more directly involved in security trading met to review Citigroup's exposure. They concluded that, based on the judgement expressed by rating agencies, the company's probability of default was extremely low (NYT 2008).

In September 2007, when the subprime mortgage market was already in turmoil, Citigroup decided to expand its subprime securitisation business by purchasing a company operating in the wholesale lending and servicing business (Terris 2007).

On October 2007, the CEO warned the market of a potential write-off of more than $1 billion in subprime mortgage-related assets. In November 2007, Citigroup communicated estimated write-downs between $8 billion and $11 billion.

In late 2008, the firm submitted two government rescue packages. Under the plan, Citigroup and the government identified a pool of about $306 billion in troubled assets. Its shareholders bore heavy losses: share prices lost about 90% of their market value in 2008 (WSJ 2008).

Post-mortem evaluations of Citigroup's near-collapse revealed that the bank's senior executives did not recognise the systemic risks embedded in the bank's high-risk strategy in conjunction with its broad spectrum of operations.

Post-crisis analyses revealed two major shortcomings of Citigroup's risk governance that led to its crash. On one side, a hyper-focus on revenue growth, supported by compensation policies that encouraged excessive risk-taking, induced directors and senior managers to ignore the risks associated with the company's aggressive expansion into speculative activities. On the other side, a weak, if not absent, risk oversight characterised the board's guidance of the implementation of the selected strategy. Complementary elements of Citigroup's risk governance support this judgement (Wilmarth 2013). The first element was the inadequacy and ineffectiveness of the risk management system: due to insufficient independence of its risk management team from a fixed-income business manager, the control of risk managers over the compliance of the trading floor with policies and regulation was weak and biased. The second element concerned the insufficient monitoring activity of senior managers and directors: they systematically disregarded the monitoring and review of mortgage loans even when red flags were raised, as in the case of investment decisions taken in contrast with Citigroup's stated criteria for buying subprime loans. The third element was concerned with risk assessment. Notwithstanding the high risk implied by the aggressive strategy pursued, risk assessments ignored "tail risks" and did not perform firm-wide consolidated stress tests in order to evaluate the impact of extreme outcomes on the entire bank. Moreover, the decentralised nature of Citigroup created silos that resulted in poor communication across businesses.

In addition to internal signals of inadequacy of internal control and risk management systems, red flags were raised from outside regulators. In 2005, the Federal Reserve Board (FRB) and the Office of the Comptroller of the Currency (OCC) issued a moratorium on further acquisitions by Citigroup until the company had provided substantial improvements in corporate compliance and risk management procedures (Wilmarth 2013).

A derivative litigation began against the Citigroup board of directors in the attempt to hold the board liable for the firm's losses and consequent damage to shareholders (In re Citigroup Inc. 2009). Shareholders claimed that the directors breached their fiduciary duties by not properly monitoring and managing the risks associated with problems in the subprime market, not disclosing Citigroup's exposure to subprime assets, and ignoring "red flags" in the real estate and credit markets in favour of short-term profits, to the detriment of long-term viability of the company.

The Delaware Court of Chancery dismissed this attempt, finding that the board did not breach any of its fiduciary obligations. Chancellor Chandler rejected the plaintiffs' claims on two grounds (Pan 2010). First, a board should not be held liable for failure to monitor business risk. Delaware's duty to monitor risk required only that a board implemented oversight programs to monitor corporate activities for fraud or illegal conduct. Second, a board cannot be held liable for making business decisions that later prove to have been unwise. Expanding the duty to monitor to hold boards responsible for bad business outcomes would place the court in the inappropriate position of second-guessing the business judgment of the board.

Legal enforcement of the duty to monitor The two cases examined do not represent exceptions in the enforcement of the duty of care by directors and boards. In application of the *business judgement rule*, U.S. courts do not hold directors liable for business decisions made without a conflict of interest unless those decisions are completely irrational, clearly disloyal or illegal. The scope of the duty of the board to monitor depends on two elements that must be considered: the care that the board must take to detect possible harm, and the types of harm that require board intervention (Pan 2010). Any evaluation of both elements is largely subjective and hard to frame in terms of optimal choices.

Moreover, in administering their judgments, courts must consider the potential impact of their sentences upon boards' decision-making. A mechanical recognition of liability of directors for damages caused to the company by their business decisions may negatively affect shareholders in two ways. First, due to the risk aversion induced in directors and boards, shareholders could lose risky but rewarding opportunities. Second, in the attempt to self-protect from litigations, directors may charge shareholders with extra costs of monitoring, both in terms of additional resources devoted to controls, and in terms of less reactivity of decision-making processes induced by formal authorization procedures. The recognition of this conflict between direct and indirect damages to shareholders and the difficulty to quantify the net balance of managerial decisions systematically leads courts to refer to the *business judgment rule* in their ruling.[9] The principle underlying the rule is diffused in most common law countries, including the United States, Canada, England and Wales and Australia (Gurrea-Martínez 2018).

In sum, the current standard for breach of the duty to monitor exposes directors to possible liability only if they are inattentive and/or inactive in the face of red flags associated with legal violations (Pan 2010).

6 Concluding Remarks

In this paper, we have contended that the increasing expectations about the oversight role of boards in risk management remain largely unsatisfied due to the vagueness of most popular corporate governance guidance in providing practical directions on how to implement an effective board risk oversight. The absence of a clear definition of the notion of *risk*, the simplistic delimitation of the perimeter of *board risk oversight*, and the inadequate operationalisation of the concept of *risk appetite* offered by corporate governance guidance and risk management frameworks severely limit their practical usefulness for those boards of directors willing to align risk governance to best practices.

Moreover, the law seems to provide little help in promoting the fulfillment of a board's risk oversight responsibilities. Under the doctrine of the *business judgment rule*, current US courts' standards pose three challenges for litigations associated with the breach of the duty of care (and of the duty to monitor):

- plaintiffs must show scienter, i.e., that the board acted with actual or constructive knowledge that its inaction would harm the corporation;
- the board is responsible only for preventing wrongful or illegal acts, i.e., the board has no responsibility to prevent acts that are legal, but that lead to harmful business results;

[9]Given the uncertainty associated with most managerial decisions and the expected competence of decision-makers, the business judgment rule specifies that the court will not review the business decisions of directors who performed their duties (1) in good faith; (2) with the care that an ordinarily prudent person in a like position would exercise under similar circumstances; and (3) in a manner the directors reasonably believe to be in the best interests of the corporation. See: Aronson vs. Lewis (1984), Kaplan vs. Centex Corp. (1971), Robinson vs. Pittsburgh Oil Refinery Corp. (1926).

- boards cannot be held responsible for monitoring the outcomes of previous board decisions.

A consequence of the strong presumption of the *rule* in favor of the board of directors of a corporation is a meaningful reduction of the exposure of directors to possible liability for behaviours that result in damages to the corporation.

As jurisprudential orientation of courts may even encourage boards to be uninformed of aggressive risk-taking by officers and management (Pan 2010), recent jurisprudence seems to have reconsidered responsibility (and liability) of directors for ineffective risk oversight, apparently recognising the conflict between the weak fiduciary standards set by previous *Delaware-based* jurisprudence and the increasing request for a more active role of the board in risk management coming from the same investors that the rule intended to protect.

A recent case involving Wells Fargo & Co. has challenged the limits of the *Delaware doctrine*. In 2017, a California court denied the defendants' motion to dismiss because the plaintiffs pointed to numerous *red flags* of which the company's directors allegedly were or should have been aware and took no substantial remedial actions (Shaev vs. Baker et al. 2017). The plaintiffs asserted that Wells Fargo's directors knew or consciously disregarded that Wells Fargo employees were creating millions of deposit and credit card accounts for customers without the customers' knowledge or consent. The court rejected defense efforts to explain away the alleged *red flags* as "insignificant when viewed in their larger context". Rather than look at the *red flags* in isolation, as the defendants urged, the court viewed them collectively, finding that "Defendants ignore the bigger picture by addressing each of these *red flags* in piecemeal fashion". The court concluded that while the *red flags* might "appear relatively insignificant to a large company like Wells Fargo when viewed in isolation, when viewed collectively they support an inference that a majority of the Director Defendants consciously disregarded their fiduciary duties despite knowledge regarding widespread illegal account-creation activities, and … that there is a substantial likelihood of directors' oversight liability" (Lipton et al. 2018).

Thus, while there is no evidence of a structural change in the administration of the business judgment rule by US courts, this case reaffirms the relevance of risk oversight within the fiduciary role of the board. In order to enforce directors' duties for risk oversight, courts need best practices to refer. Unfortunately, current guidelines are not supportive in clarifying what directors are expected to do in discharging their risk oversight duties.

Acknowledgements The Author acknowledges the financial support of the Accounting Department of Bocconi University. The Author thanks Marco Ventoruzzo (Department of Legal Studies, Bocconi University) for sharing his views on the topic and for providing useful comments.

References

Aguilar, L.A.: The important work of boards of directors. In: 12th Annual Boardroom Summit and Peer Exchange, New York, 15 October, 2015. https://www.sec.gov/news/speech/important-work-of-boards-of-directors.html. Last accessed 25 July 2018

Arboleda, P., Bagheri, S., Khakzad, F.: Model risk. In the context of the regulatory climate change. Working Paper (2016), https://www.risknet.de/.../eb8f4afc5add139265982d0a46f459be. Last accessed 26 July 2018

Aronson vs. Lewis, 473 A.2d 805, 812 (1984)

Aven, T.: The risk concept. Historical and recent development trends. Reliab. Eng. Syst. Saf. **99**, 33–44 (2012)

Basel Committee on Banking Supervision: Principles for the Sound Management of Operational Risk, pp. 1–27. Bank for International Settlements, Geneva, June 2011

Beasley, M., Branson, B., Hancock, B.: An Overview of Enterprise Risk Management Practices, 7th edn., pp. 1–31. American Institute of Certified Public Accountants—AICPA, North Carolina State University—Poole College of Management, April 2016

Black, B.S.: The Principal Fiduciary Duties of Boards of Directors. Presentation at Third Asian Roundtable on Corporate Governance Singapore, 4 April 2001

Board of Governors of the Federal Reserve System: Supervisory Guidance on Model Risk Management, April 4, 2011. https://www.federalreserve.gov/supervisionreg/srletters/sr1107a1.pdf. Last accessed 25 July 2018

Board of Governors of the Federal Reserve System: Re: Performance of the Wells Fargo & Company Directors, February 2, 2018. https://www.federalreserve.gov/newsevents/pressreleases/files/enf20180202a2.pdf. Last accessed 25 July 2018

Brennan, N.M., Kirwan, C.E., Redmond, J.: Accountability processes in boardrooms: a conceptual model of manager-non-executive director information asymmetry. Acc. Auditing Accountability J. **29**(1), 135–164 (2016)

Brodeur, A., Buehler, K., Patsalos-Fox, M., Pergler, M.: A board perspective on enterprise management. McKinsey Working Papers on Risk, Number 18, pp. 1–22. McKinsey & Company (2010). https://www.mckinsey.com/~/media/mckinsey/dotcom/client_service/risk/working%20papers/18_a_board_perspective_on_enterprise_risk_management.ashx. Last accessed 25 July 2018

Brooke, G.T.F.: Uncertainty, profit and entrepreneurial action: Frank Knight's contribution reconsidered. J. Hist. Econ. Thought **32**(2), 221–235 (2010)

Caldwell, J.E.: A Framework for Board Oversight of Enterprise Risk, pp. 1–90. The Chartered Professional Accountants of Canada (2012)

CCGG (Canadian Coalition for Good Governance): Building High Performance Boards, CCGG, pp. 1–22 (2013). https://www.ccgg.ca/site/ccgg/assets/pdf/building_high_performance_boards_august_2013_v12_formatted__sept._19,_2013_last_update_.pdf. Last accessed 25 July 2018

CGC (Corporate Governance Council): Risk Governance Guidance for Listed Boards, pp. 1–45. Monetary Authority of Singapore (2012). http://www.mas.gov.sg/~/media/resource/fin_development/corporate_governance/RiskGovernanceGuidanceforListedBoards.pdf. Last accessed 27 July 2018

Chalmers, K., Godfrey, J.M.: Reputation costs: the impetus for voluntary derivative financial instrument reporting. Acc. Organ. Soc. **29**(2), 95–125 (2004)

Cheng, M.M., Humphreys, K.A., Zhang Y.: Does integrating strategic risk information in the balanced scorecard affect managers' strategy evaluations and recommendations? WP (2014). https://www.business.uq.edu.au/sites/default/files/events/files/chz_may9_14_uq.pdf. Last accessed 27 July 2018

CIMA-IFAC (Chartered Institute of Management Accountants, International Federation of Accountants): Enterprise Governance. Getting the Balance Right, pp. 1–61 (2004). http://www.cimaglobal.com/Documents/ImportedDocuments/tech_execrep_enterprise_governance_getting_the_balance_right_feb_2004.pdf. Last accessed 27 July 2018

Cleden, D.: Managing Project Uncertainty. Gower Publishing Ltd, Aldershot (2009)

Connelly, K.M., Eadie, C.C., Harper, V.R.: The Growing Role of the Board in Risk Oversight. Point of View, pp. 1–6. Spencer Stuart (2010)
COSO (The Committee of Sponsoring Organizations of the Treadway Commission): Enterprise Risk Management. Conceptual Framework, pp. 1–121 (2004)
COSO (The Committee of Sponsoring Organizations of the Treadway Commission): Enterprise Risk Management. Integrating with Strategy and Performance, pp. 1–227 (2017)
Deloitte: Reducing Financial Reporting Risk, pp. 1–12. Deloitte Development LLC (2010). https://www.iasplus.com/en/binary/dttpubs/1002reducingrisk.pdf. Last accessed 25 July 2018
Deloitte: Risk Appetite and Assurance, pp. 1–12. Deloitte Development LLC (2014a). https://www2.deloitte.com/.../Deloitte/.../risk/lu-risk-appetite-ass. Last accessed 25 May 2018
Deloitte: Risk Appetite in the Financial Services Industry. A Requisite for Risk Management Today, pp. 1–19. Deloitte Development LLC (2014b). https://www2.deloitte.com/content/dam/Deloitte/ie/Documents/FinancialServices/investmentmanagement/us_aers_grrs_riskappetite_03102014.pdf. Last accessed 25 July 2018
Deloitte: Model Risk Management. Driving the value in modellin, Risk Advisory. Deloitte Network, April 2017. https://www2.deloitte.com/content/dam/Deloitte/fr/Documents/risk/deloitte_model-risk-management_plaquette.pdf. Last accessed 27 July 2018
ECB (European Central Bank): SSM Supervisory Statement on Governance and Risk Appetite, pp. 1–21, June 2016. https://www.bankingsupervision.europa.eu/ecb/pub/pdf/ssm_supervisory_statement_on_governance_and_risk_appetite_201606.en.pdf. Last accessed 25 July 2018
ECB (European Central Bank): ECB guide to internal models, European Central Bank, pp. 1–55, March 2018. https://www.bankingsupervision.europa.eu/legalframework/publiccons/pdf/internal_models/ssm.guidegeneraltopics.en.pdf?450d12852b90a730172529b462c7d6e3. Last accessed 5 Oct 2018
FRC (Financial Reporting Council): Guidance on Risk Management, Internal Control and Related Financial and Business Reporting, pp. 1–30. The Financial Reporting Council Limited (2014a)
FRC (Financial Reporting Council): Guidance on the Strategic Report, pp. 1–60. The Financial Reporting Council Limited (2014b)
FRC (Financial Reporting Council): The UK Corporate Governance Code, pp. 1–636. The Financial Reporting Council Limited (2014c)
FSB (Financial Stability Boar): Increasing the Intensity of Effectiveness of Supervision. Guidance on Supervisory Interaction with Financial Institutions on Risk Culture. Consultative Document, pp. 1–13 (2013a)
FSB (Financial Stability Board): Principles for an Effective Risk Appetite Framework. Consultation Draft, pp. 1–15 (2013b)
Gius, D., Mieszala, J., Panayiotou, E., Poppensieker, T.: Value and resilience through better risk management. McKinsey & Co., October 2018. https://www.mckinsey.com/business-functions/risk/our-insights/value-and-resilience-through-better-risk-management. Last accessed 5 Oct 2018
Gupta, P.P., Leech, T.: The Next Frontier for Boards: Oversight of Risk Culture, Director Notes, pp. 1–12. The Conference Board (2015). https://corpgov.law.harvard.edu/2015/07/13/the-next-frontier-for-boards-oversight-of-risk-culture/. Last accessed 25 July 2018
Gurrea-Martínez, A.: Re-examining the law and economics of the business judgment rule: notes for its implementation in Non-US jurisdictions. J. Corp. Law Stud. **18**(2), 417–438 (2018)
Hida, E.: Global Risk Management Survey, Inside Magazine, pp. 1–6. Deloitte (2016)
Holton, G.A.: Defining risk. Financ. Anal. J. **60**(6), 19–25 (2004)
ICGN (International Corporate Governance Network): Guidance on Corporate Risk Oversight, pp. 1–24 (2015). https://www.icgn.org/sites/default/files/ICGN%20Corp%20Risk%20Oversightweb_0.pdf. Last accessed 25 July 2018
IIA (Chartered Institute of Internal Auditors): Risk Appetite and Internal Audit, pp. 1–15 (2017). https://www.iia.org.uk/resources/risk-management/risk-appetite/. Last accessed 27 July 2018
In re Citigroup Inc. Shareholder Derivative Litigation, No. 3338-CC, 2009 WL 481906 (Del. Ch. Feb. 24 (2009). https://courts.delaware.gov/opinions/download.aspx?ID=118110. Last accessed 27 July 2018

IRM (The Institute of Risk Management): Risk Appetite and Risk Tolerance. Guidance paper, pp. 1–42 (2011)
ISO (The International Organization for Standardization): ISO/IEC CD 2 Guide 73:2008 Risk Management—Vocabulary (2008)
ISO (The International Organization for Standardization): ISO 31000:2009(en). Risk management—Principles and guidelines (2009). https://www.iso.org/obp/ui/#iso:std:iso:31000:ed-1:v1:en. Last accessed 25 July 2018
Ittner, C.D., Keusch, T.: The Influence of Board of Directors' Risk Oversight on Risk Management Maturity and Firm Risk-Taking, pp. 1–70. Working Paper, March 12, 2015
Kahneman, D.: Thinking, Fast and Slow. FSG, New York (2013)
Kaplan vs. Centex Corp., Del. Ch., 284 A.2d 119, 124 (1971)
Knight, F.H.: Risk, Uncertainty and Profit. Hart, Schaffner, and Marx, New York (1921). https://www.econlib.org/library/Knight/knRUP.html?chapter_num=13#book-reader. Last accessed 25 July 2018
KPMG: Developing a Strong Risk Appetite Program. Challenges and Solutions, pp. 1–20. KPMG International (2013). https://assets.kpmg.com/content/dam/kpmg/pdf/2013/11/risk-appetite-v2.pdf. Last accessed 25 July 2018
Lipton, M., Niles, S.W., Miller, M.L.: Risk Management and the Board of Directors, Harvard Law School Forum on Corporate Governance and Financial Regulation, March 20, 2018. https://corpgov.law.harvard.edu/2018/03/20/risk-management-and-the-board-of-directors-5/. Last accessed 25 July 2018
Mahon, J.F.: Corporate reputation: research agenda using strategy and stakeholder literature. Bus. Soc. **41**, 415–445 (2002)
Moody's Investor Services: Best Practices for a Board's Role in Risk Oversight, pp. 1–8. Moody's Investors Service, Inc., August 2006. https://www.moodys.com/sites/products/AboutMoodysRatingsAttachments/2005700000435561.pdf. Last accessed 25 July 2018
NACD (National Association of Corporate Directors): Mitigating Board Information Risk, pp. 1–15. White Paper, Washington DC, (2013). https://rsmus.com/pdf/wp_mitigating_board_information_risk.pdf. Last accessed 25 July 2018
NYSE (New York Stock Exchange): Corporate Governance Guide, pp. 1–358 (2014). https://www.nyse.com/publicdocs/nyse/listing/NYSE_Corporate_Governance_Guide.pdf. Last accessed 25 July 2018
NYSE (New York Stock Exchange): Listed Company Manual. http://wallstreet.cch.com/LCM/. Last accessed 25 July 2018
NYT (The New York Times): Citigroup Saw No Red Flags Even as It Made Bolder Bets. The New York Times, 22 Nov 2008. https://www.nytimes.com/2008/11/23/business/23citi.html. Last accessed 15 Oct 2018
OECD (Organization for Economic Co-operation and Development): Glossary of Environment Statistics, Studies in Methods, Series F, No. 67, United Nations. New York (1997)
OECD (Organization for Economic Co-operation and Development): Corporate Governance and the Financial Crisis—Conclusions and Emerging Good Practices to Enhance Implementation of the Principles, pp. 1–34. OECD Publishing (2010). http://www.oecd.org/daf/ca/corporategovernanceprinciples/44679170.pdf. Last accessed 25 July 2018
OECD (Organization for Economic Co-operation and Development): Risk Management and Corporate Governance, Corporate Governance, pp. 1–96. OECD Publishing (2014). http://dx.doi.org/10.1787/9789264208636-en. Last accessed 25 July 2018
Ormazabal, G.: Are Risky Boards Getting Riskier? Risk Oversight: What Every Director Should Know, IESE Insight, Issue 28 (2016)
OSC (Ontario Securities Commission): Securities Law & Instruments—National Instrument. http://www.osc.gov.on.ca/en/SecuritiesLaw_51-102.htm. Last accessed 25 July 2018
Pan, E.J.: A board's duty to monitor. New York Law School Law Review **54**, 717–740 (2010)
Perry, J., De Fontnouvelle, P.: Measuring reputational risk: the market reaction to operational loss announcements. Federal Reserve Bank of Boston (2005). https://www.semanticscholar.

org/paper/Measuring-Reputational-Risk-%3A-The-Market-Reaction-%E2%88%97-Perry-Fontnouvelle/919660bdf95542207ee1278b79ccb2b24cae7fa6?tab=references. Last accessed 27 July 2018
Power, M.: The risk management of nothing. Acc. Organ. Soc. **34**, 849–855 (2009)
Presley, H.: Vioxx and the Merck team effort. The Kenan Institute for Ethics (2008). https://web.duke.edu/kenanethics/CaseStudies/Vioxx.pdf. Last accessed 5 Oct 2018
Purdy, G.: Risk appetite: is using the concept worth the risk? Broadleaf Risk Post, Sept 2011. http://broadleaf.com.au/resource-material/risk-appetite-is-using-this-concept-worth-the-risk/. Last accessed 20 May 2018
Reuters: https://www.reuters.com/article/us-wells-fargo-directors-idUSKBN1792H4. Last accessed 25 July 2018
RIMS: Exploring Risk Appetite and Risk Tolerance, pp. 1–14 (2012). https://www.rims.org/resources/ERM/Documents/RIMS_Exploring_Risk_Appetite_Risk_Tolerance_0412.pdf. Last accessed 25 July 2018
RIMS: Enterprise Risk Management Benchmark Survey, pp. 1–19 (2017). https://www.rims.org/RiskKnowledge/RISKKnowledgeDocs/2017_ERM_survey_1162017_84825.pdf. Last accessed 25 July 2018
Rittenberg, L., Martens, F.: Understanding and Communicating Risk Appetite, pp. 1–32. COSO (2012)
Roach, D.R.: The board of directors' role in compliance and ethics. J. Health Care Compliance 53–56 (2007) (Nov–Dec)
Roberts, P.W., Dowling, G.R.: Corporate reputation and sustained superior financial performance. Strateg. Manag. J. **23**(12), 1077–1093 (2002)
Robinson vs. Pittsburgh Oil Refinery Corp., Del. Ch., 14 Del. Ch. 193, 126 A. 46 (1926)
Scandizzo, S.: A framework for the analysis of reputational risk. J. Oper. Risk **6**(3), 41–63 (2011)
SEC (United States Securities and Exchange Commission): Final Rules. https://www.sec.gov/rules/final.shtml. Last accessed 25 July 2018
SEC (United States Securities and Exchange Commission): Final Rules: Proxy Disclosure Enhancements, Release No. 33-9089 (Dec 16, 2009) [74 FR 68334 (Dec. 23, 2009)] (2009). http://www.sec.gov/rules/final/2009/33-9089.pdf. Last accessed 25 July 2018
Shaev vs. Baker et al. Case No.16-cv-05541-JST, United States District Court—Northern District of California (2017). https://casetext.com/case/shaev-v-baker. Last accessed 25 July 2018
SSG (Senior Supervisors Group): Risk Management Lessons from the Banking Crisis of 2008, 21 Oct 2009. http://www.fsb.org/2009/10/r_0910a/. Last accessed 25 July 2018
SSG (Senior Supervisors Group): Observations on Developments in Risk Appetite Frameworks and IT Infrastructure, pp. 1–17 (2010). https://www.newyorkfed.org/medialibrary/media/newsevents/news/banking/2010/an101223.pdf. Last accessed 25 July 2018
Standard & Poor's Ratings Services: Standard & Poor's Ratings Direct, Evaluating The Enterprise Risk Management Practices of Insurance Companies, pp. 1–17. Standard & Poors, 17 Oct 2005
Standard & Poor's Ratings Services: Standard & Poor's RatingsDirect, Enterprise Risk Management, pp. 1–29. Standard & Poors, 7 May 2013
Stone vs. Ritter, 911 A.2d 362, Supreme Court of Delaware (2006). https://www.courtlistener.com/opinion/2334726/stone-v-ritter/. Last accessed 25 July 2018
Stulz, R.: Risk management failures: what are they and when do they happen? J. Appl. Corp. Finan. **20**(4), 39–48 (2008)
Stunda, R.: Financial restatements by industry and their market impact. Int. J. Acad. Bus. World **11**(1), 49–56 (2017)
Taleb, N.N.: The Black Swan. The Impact of the Highly Improbable. Random House, New York (2007)
Taleb, N.N.: Errors, robustness and the fourth quadrant. Int. J. Forecast. **25**(4), 744–759 (2009)
Taleb, N.N., Goldstein, D.G.: The problem is beyond psychology: the real world is more random than regression analyses. Int. J. Forecast. **28**(3), 715–716 (2012)

Taleb, N.N., Goldstein, D.G., Spitznagel, M.W.: The six mistakes executives make in risk management. Harvard Bus. Rev. **87**, 78–81 (2009)
Terris, H.: Citi-ACC: A Bet Vertical Integration Still Has Legs, American Banker (Sept 13, 2007)
The English Cambridge Dictionary: https://dictionary.cambridge.org/dictionary/english/oversight. Last accessed 24 Apr 2018
The Vanguard Group Inc.: An open letter to directors of public companies worldwide (2017a) (31 Aug). https://www.vanguardinvestments.com.au/au/portal/homepage.jsp. Last accessed 25 July 2018
The Vanguard Group Inc.: Investment Stewardship 2017 Annual Report, pp. 1–36. The Vanguard Group Inc. (2017b). https://about.vanguard.com/investment-stewardship/annual-report.pdf. Last accessed 25 July 2018
Towers Watson: Another Bite at the Apple. Risk Appetite Revised, pp. 1–20. Towers Watson (2013)
USSC (United States Sentencing Commission): Guidelines Manual, Nov 2016. https://www.ussc.gov/sites/default/files/pdf/guidelines-manual/2016/GLMFull.pdf. Last accessed 25 July 2018
Walker, K.: A systematic review of the corporate reputation literature: definition, measurement, and theory. Corp. Reputation Rev. **12**, 357–387 (2010)
Wartick, S.L.: Measuring corporate reputation: definition and data. Bus. Soc. **41**(4), 371–393 (2002)
Willows, R., Connell, R.: Climate adaptation: Risk, uncertainty and decision-making, UKCIP Technical Report, pp. 1–166, May 2003. https://ukcip.ouce.ox.ac.uk/wp-content/PDFs/UKCIP-Risk-framework.pdf. Last accessed 25 July 2018
Wilmarth, A.E.: Citigroup: a case study in managerial and regulatory failures. Indiana Law Rev. **47**, 69–137 (2013)
WSJ (The Wall Street Journal): U.S. Agrees to Rescue Struggling Citigroup. Wall Street J. (Nov 24, 2008). https://www.wsj.com/articles/SB122747680752551447. Last accessed 15 Oct 2018
WSJ (The Wall Street Journal): Merck to Pay $830 Million to Settle Vioxx Shareholder Suit. The Wall Street J. (Jan 15, 2016). https://www.wsj.com/articles/merck-to-pay-830-million-to-settle-vioxx-shareholder-suit-1452866882. Last accessed 15 Oct 2018

Enterprise Risk Management Measurement: Insights from an Interdisciplinary Literature Review

Arthur Linke and Cristina Florio

Abstract Enterprise Risk Management (ERM) represents a paradigm envisioned to provide an organization both resilience and opportunity in the face of uncertainty. The debate around ERM's value contribution to the organization has led to key ERM research questions arising, highlighting the need for further investigation of empirical measurement of ERM and its implementation. Calls from several scholars specifically request extending the academic body of knowledge on ERM measurement. Motivated by the above calls, this study presents the findings of a systematic review of the ERM literature. The review examines the academic discipline of journals existing ERM studies are published in, these journals' H-indices, the location of the studies, and the methodology of how ERM is measured in the studies. The review establishes that the ERM literature cuts across several academic research disciplines such as accounting, finance and strategy. Moreover, the extant literature underscores that it is very difficult to quantify and measure ERM in practice within organizations. Consequential to this, most empirical studies of ERM have emphasized either a qualitative approach focusing in depth on specific organizations, or a quantitative approach relying on accessible, basic secondary data available in company reports. A gap in knowledge is presented around extending ERM measurement, in particular in terms of methodologies based on primary data collection and analysis. This paper concludes that further development of empirical measurement scales based on primary data, whereby direct, first-hand input from members of organizations implementing ERM is collected, will augment the ERM body of knowledge. Such scales will allow for important aspects of ERM as it is implemented in the organization to be empirically measured.

Keywords Enterprise risk management · Empirical measurement · Literature review · Qualitative research · Quantitative research · Primary data

A. Linke
University of Stellenbosch Business School, Bellville 7535, South Africa

C. Florio (✉)
University of Verona, Via Cantarane, 24, 37129 Verona, Italy
e-mail: cristina.florio@univr.it

P. Linsley et al. (eds.), *Multiple Perspectives in Risk and Risk Management*, Springer Proceedings in Business and Economics,
https://doi.org/10.1007/978-3-030-16045-6_2

1 Introduction

Enterprise risk management (ERM) has been called the fundamental new paradigm for managing the portfolio of risks confronting organizations according to Gordon et al. (2009: 302), who provided a preliminary review of the ERM literature and stated that by "adopting a systematic and consistent approach (or process) to managing all of the risks confronting an organization, ERM is presumed to lower a firm's overall risk of failure and thus increase the performance, and in turn, the value of the organization." ERM is thus envisioned to provide a holistic framework for the risk management process, thereby providing both resilience and opportunity to the organization, enabling it to meet its objectives in the face of uncertainty. Hoyt and Liebenberg (2011: 795) summarized the comprehensive nature of ERM, stating that unlike "traditional risk management where individual risk categories are separately managed in risk 'silos,' ERM enables firms to manage a wide array of risks in an integrated, enterprise-wide fashion. More broadly, ERM is said to promote increased risk awareness that facilitates better operational and strategic decision-making."

Beyond the academic context of ERM which is examined in detail in this paper, the importance of ERM in management practice and the current business environment is well testified by the number of frameworks and guidelines on the subject. There are two predominant international frameworks that organizations may utilize to implement ERM, which are also considered the two main practitioner standards applied globally for ERM, namely COSO (2017) and ISO 31000 (2018). These standards or frameworks provide the 'critical success factors' or 'best practices' for ERM in terms of its implementation within the organization. Fraser and Simkins (2010) concluded that COSO and ISO are quite simply the two most widely applied constructs for practical management applications of ERM. These frameworks are structured to help resolve the many inconsistencies and ambiguities that have existed between various approaches and definitions within the realms of ERM practice. Both standards were updated since their first issuances in 2004 (COSO 2004) and 2009 (ISO 31000 2009) respectively, with the most recent releases being in 2017 (COSO) and 2018 (ISO 31000). Both standards are referenced in the canon of the academic ERM literature and thus form a contribution to ERM theoretical conceptualization. Additionally, there are global and local guidelines incorporating risk management that continue to be issued in different countries, by regulators, stock exchanges and corporate governance codes such as the UK Corporate Governance Code (2018) and South Africa's King IV Report (2017).

The ERM literature and its discourse are still growing in maturity, especially given that the first mention of the exact term 'enterprise risk management' in an academic journal was only at the beginning of this century (Dickinson 2001). The discussion of ERM is multifaceted, for example, whilst some empirical evidence confirmed a value contribution of ERM (Hoyt and Liebenberg 2011; Florio and Leoni 2017), some articles criticized ERM's value contribution (Power 2009; Arena et al. 2011), even more so in the aftermath of the last global financial crisis. Such debate has led to the following core ERM research questions arising for further investigation: Is the actual ERM implementation in organizations currently being empirically measured? If so, in which disciplines is ERM discussed and measured? What is the relevance and impact of articles facing the issue of ERM measurement in the literature? Where are studies on ERM measurement located geographically? And perhaps most critically, which methodologies do extant studies adopt to measure ERM? These questions highlight the need to further investigate the empirical measurement of ERM and its implementation, and suggest extending the academic body of knowledge on ERM in this regard.

Authors such as Kaplan (2011), McShane et al. (2011) and Bromiley et al. (2015) have in fact all made very specific calls in the literature for empirical measurement of ERM to feature prominently on the risk management research agenda. These papers argue that there is a significant gap in the literature with regards to the empirical measurement of ERM. Paape and Speklé (2012) explicitly lamented that a main roadblock to academic risk management research is the difficulty in developing a valid and reliable measure for a risk management construct, i.e. a proxy that can act as a variable within empirical studies examining measurement of ERM. The lack of empirically validated ERM measurement scales, which incorporate constructs that comprise the broad spectrum of ERM implementation components (i.e. the theoretical ERM domain construct), limits the prospects to assess ERM's effectiveness as a management instrument.

Motivated by the above calls, this paper analyses how ERM is measured within the existing body of literature. To such purpose, the study systematically reviews the literature emerging from a Google Scholar search of academic resources and their classification by relevance to ERM measurement. As a preliminary analysis, the study provides an overview of the academic subject areas of the journals the existing studies are published in; it includes journals that are represented in the Scimago database, as well as the journal's H-indices according to Scimago. Scimago is one of the leading resources to determine the impact and quality of peer-reviewed journals.

The study also shows a classification according to the location of the study, which is important to consider because different environmental contexts and regulatory frameworks may be in place from region to region and affect ERM 'measurement'. To answer the research question of how ERM is measured within the existing literature, the study relies on a well-established classification of research by methodology and distinguishes between qualitative and quantitative studies of ERM. Within the latter methodology it is demarcated whether the papers rely on secondary or primary data sources or both. Certain literature review articles dealing specifically with the topic of ERM measurement are also included in the review.

The findings underline that the ERM literature is multi-disciplinary and references a variety of research streams and methodologies, many of which are not necessarily interconnected. This is paradoxically unlike ERM itself, which as it is defined should adopt a holistic and integrated approach. The study examines examples of papers featuring qualitative and quantitative methodologies, and specifically highlights limitations and a paucity of studies that measure ERM based on primary data—i.e. by receiving and investigating direct, first-hand input from members of organizations.

With its findings, the study contributes to the literature on ERM by providing the first holistic review of the ERM literature across all the research disciplines it is represented in. It addresses the call by scholars to measure ERM by providing a systematic review of measurement in the ERM literature, building the foundation of identifying the various streams of ERM measurement both qualitative and quantitative. Finally, the study proposes a research direction to further develop the empirical measurement of ERM.

The remainder of the paper is structured as follows: Sect. 2 describes the research design adopted for reviewing the literature; Sect. 3 presents and discusses the main findings in terms of discipline, citations and geography; Sect. 4 presents and discusses the main findings on the methodologies adopted for empirically investigating ERM; finally, Sect. 5 provides concluding remarks, limitations and suggestions for future research, especially with reference to the development of ERM primary data measurement.

2 Research Design

2.1 Article Search

The study is centered on a systematic and comprehensive review of the cross-disciplinary ERM literature in order to select peer-reviewed articles related to the research questions of determining how ERM is defined and measured. A keyword search on the terms ('Enterprise Risk Management' Measure), with Enterprise Risk Management in quotes as one term, was performed in Google Scholar. The search results were updated and finalized on 12.08.2018. The search went to the first 15 pages of 20 'hits' per page for the indicated search terms, in other words, the top 300 articles returned based on relevance and also listing the number of citations. In order of relevance, the citations of the articles dwindled into the low single digits. To ensure recent articles were not excluded, a similar search was also conducted on Google Scholar for articles specifically published since 2017, thus identifying recent articles based on relevance, and any not appearing in the first, undated search were included in the literature review (Massaro et al. 2016).

The first criterion in selecting and reviewing the articles was thus specifically Google Scholar relevance to the search terms.

2.2 Journal Classification and Citations

The articles were then reviewed and assessed for whether the journals they were published in are included in the Scimago (SJR) journal ranking, as well as the journal's H Index, which measures the journal's number of articles (h) that have received at least (h) citations. The H Index quantifies both journal scientific productivity and scientific impact. This criterion thus ensured peer-reviewed articles from leading journals were included in the assessment. The journals were classified based on the Scimago subject area and category, and the number of citations each article received according to Google Scholar was also noted. The findings of the review with regards to specific aspects of the articles from the literature are discussed in Sect. 3 of this paper.

2.3 Content Analysis

A focal point of the literature review, which is incorporated in the methodological design of this study, was to determine whether in the broad body of ERM academic literature there are empirical measures for ERM and if so, what these are. To address the research questions, beyond understanding how the articles define the ERM construct, there is an emphasis on understanding the various methodologies utilized to measure ERM, for example, qualitative and quantitative studies, and within quantitative studies those based on secondary data as contrasted with those based on primary data. The articles that progressed through the first level of analysis outlined in the previous section, namely that were included in the Scimago journal index and registering an H Index, were then reviewed for content as the next step in the methodological design. The first criterion examined was to determine whether these articles did examine the topic of ERM measurement as part of a literature review or if they purported to provide their own measure of ERM. If they did so, the type of empirical study—qualitative or quantitative—was noted with further differentiation of quantitative studies in terms of their reliance on primary or secondary data. It was also noted, to determine the complexity of the ERM variable, whether the quantitative studies employed a monistic or holistic measure of ERM.

The methodological design of the study also incorporated examining the geographical location of the studies in the literature review as this information could provide context to the circumstances of the ERM measurement within the article, for example differences in regulatory regimes towards corporate governance and reporting requirements. Finally, the methodology called for an assessment of whether the article referred to either the COSO or ISO ERM frameworks or both. As outlined in the introduction, these are the two predominant ERM frameworks found in both industry and the ERM literature. The emphasis on one or both of these frameworks could relate to the article's ERM measurement methodology, for example, for a quantitative primary data study, the choice of ERM framework would affect the ERM construct definition.

The methodological design of the study called for determining whether ERM measures were found in the literature, and examining those studies and ERM measures found, to explicate why and how they were developed. These studies were then classified as outlined above, thus providing a contribution to the body of ERM and measurement literature. The outcomes of the measurement classifications, as well as the discussion of the findings, are presented in Sect. 4.

2.4 Seminal Articles from the ERM Literature

The body of academic ERM literature was reviewed and classified according to the methodology outlined in the previous sections. Table 1, following, provides a summary of the top 10 seminal ERM measurement articles based on descending number of citations and depicts the aspects of the articles reviewed as discussed in the previous sections i.e. the methodological design (classification) of the study. In total 51 articles were selected for the literature review based on the Scimago rating and ERM measurement criteria as summarized in Table 1.

3 ERM Articles by Discipline, Citations and Geography

As outlined in Sect. 2, the methodological design considered several key aspects of the articles, including the academic disciplines of the journals they were published in, the Scimago H Index of the journals and the relevance in terms of article citations, as well as the geography of the studies.

3.1 ERM in Various Academic Disciplines Literature

Figure 1 illustrates the academic disciplines of the journals as provided in the Scimago Subject Area 1. The journals predominantly feature Scimago Subject Area 1 as Business, Management and Accounting. Some journals, within which the ERM measurement articles were found, demonstrate up to four Scimago Subject Areas. Some more eclectic Subject Areas of the journals within which the ERM measurement articles were found include Social Sciences and Mathematics.

Figure 2 illustrates the academic disciplines of the journals as provided in Scimago's Category 1—in this case these reflect the first category within Subject Area 1 as indicated above. Scimago generally rates journals based on the Category Areas and which quartile the journal is in within each Category Area (from quartile 1 to 4). There was a broad variety of Category Areas demarcated within the up to four Subject Areas per journal that the ERM measurement articles were found in. These included Applied Psychology, Artificial Intelligence, Computer Science, Control and Systems Engineering, Decision Sciences, Electrical and Electronic Engineering, Finance, Geography, Planning and Development, Industrial and Manufacturing Engineering, Information Systems and Management, Management Science and Operations Research, Marketing, Mathematics, Organizational Behavior and

Human Resource Management, Psychology, Safety, Risk, Reliability and Quality, Social Sciences, Sociology and Political Science, Software, Strategy and Management, and Theoretical Computer Science.

The review of the literature referring to ERM measurement indicated that there are multiple academic disciplines, as outlined in the section above, in which ERM is considered part of, some of which are quite far removed from each other with regards to theoretical underpinnings, e.g. accounting and strategy. There are different definitions of ERM within these academic disciplines and contexts, sometimes even in contradicting terms. To investigate this aspect systematically, each of the 51 articles that were included in the study as per the methodology detailed above was analyzed in terms of the discipline of the journal it was published in. Whilst the broad list of

Table 1 Top 10 relevant articles emanating from the ERM measurement literature review

Author/date/citations	Article title/journal/discipline/H Index	Methodology/region
MS Beasley, R Clune, DR Hermanson/2005/606	Enterprise risk management: An empirical analysis of factors associated with the extent of implementation/Journal of Accounting and Public Policy/Business, Management and Accounting/58	Quantitative; Secondary Data/USA
RE Hoyt, AP Liebenberg/2011/586	The value of enterprise risk management/Journal of risk and insurance/Business, Management and Accounting/53	Quantitative; Secondary Data/USA
AP Liebenberg, RE Hoyt/2003/556	The determinants of enterprise risk management: Evidence from the appointment of chief risk officers/Risk Management and Insurance Review/Business, Management and Accounting/12	Quantitative; Secondary Data/USA
V Aebi, G Sabato, M Schmid/2012/520	Risk management, corporate governance, and bank performance in the financial crisis/Journal of Banking & Finance/Economics, Econometrics and Finance/126	Quantitative; Secondary Data/North America

(continued)

Table 1 (continued)

Author/date/citations	Article title/journal/discipline/H Index	Methodology/region
M Power/2004/509	The risk management of everything/The Journal of Risk Finance/Business, Management and Accounting/24	Literature review incorporating ERM measurement
M Power/2009/434	The risk management of nothing/Accounting, organizations and society/Business, Management and Accounting/110	Literature review incorporating ERM measurement
LA Gordon, MP Loeb, CY Tseng/2009/430	Enterprise risk management and firm performance: A contingency perspective/Journal of Accounting and Public Policy/Business, Management and Accounting/58	Quantitative; Secondary Data/USA
AE Kleffner, RB Lee/2003/359	The effect of corporate governance on the use of enterprise risk management: Evidence from Canada/Risk Management and Insurance Review/Business, Management and Accounting/12	Qualitative/Canada
A Mikes/2009/354	Risk management and calculative cultures/Management Accounting Research/Business, Management and Accounting/72	Qualitative/Europe
G Purdy/2010/304	ISO 31000: 2009—setting a new standard for risk management/Risk Analysis: An International Journal/Engineering/105	Literature review incorporating ERM measurement

subject areas and categories demonstrates the diversity of disciplines within which ERM is considered, on closer review for content, the majority of the articles could in fact be classified within their respective journals Subject Area 1 as detailed in Fig. 1, namely predominantly Business, Management and Accounting.

With regards to the Category 1 classification of the journals within which the ERM measurement articles were found, Accounting represented the most frequently selected category, with Strategy and Management the second most selected category and a number of other categories represented relatively consistently with a few articles found in each.

3.2 Journal H Index and Article Citations

The journals were assessed as per the Scimago H Index as described in the methodology. The journals of the 51 articles ranged from an H Index of 141 to 10. It can be considered fairly authoritative, for example, for the article on ERM maturity models (Oliva 2016) published in the *International Journal of Production Economics*, to score an H-Index of 141, meaning the journal has had more than 141 citations in more than 141 journals each. According to Scimago, this specific journal is consistently ranked in the first quartile of Business, Management and Accounting Subject Area and Category.

The 51 articles were also assed in terms of citations. According to Google Scholar, the ERM measurement articles selected ranged from 17 to 606 citations at the time of the review. The most cited article was an empirical analysis of factors associated with the extent of ERM implementation by Beasley et al. (2005) as presented in Table 1.

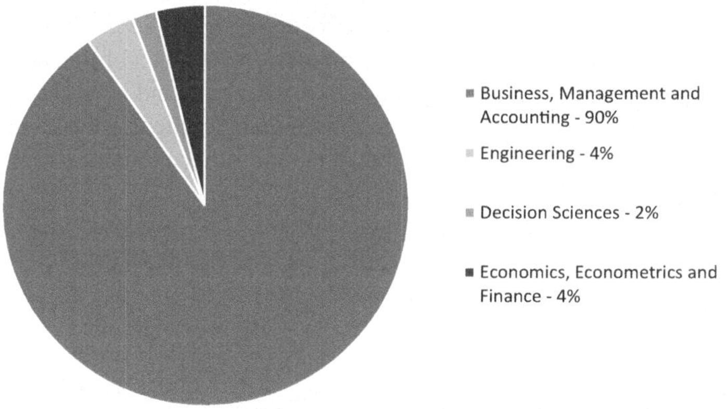

Fig. 1 Scimago Subject Area 1 of the journals the ERM measurement articles are published in

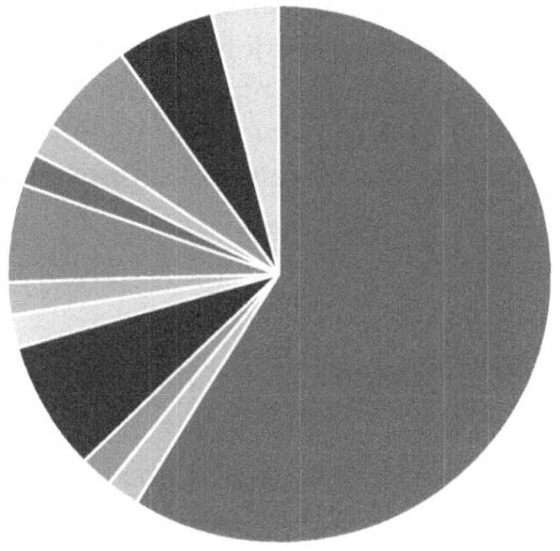

Fig. 2 Scimago Category 1 (within Subject Area 1) of the journals the reviewed ERM measurement articles are published in

3.3 Location of the Studies and Reference to Frameworks

For each of the 51 articles, the geographical location of the study empirically measuring ERM was noted. As was outlined in the methodology section, the environment of the study can provide context to the study and its methodology, for example with regulatory frameworks or reporting requirements being implemented in a specific region. The findings indicated that whilst initially, there was a clustering of studies within the US, and also specifically studies in the banking and insurance industries, over time the studies expanded their geographies, and included countries and regions such as Brazil, Italy, Denmark, India and Asia, and other industries such as Oil & Gas and Energy.

With regard to reference to ERM frameworks, COSO was predominantly mentioned in the earlier articles; more recent articles mention both COSO and ISO 31000, confirming the predominance of these frameworks globally.

4 Measurement of ERM and ERM Practices

In a review of ERM measurement instruments, Kimbrough and Componation (2009: 22) found "a wide range of approaches and a discipline in its infancy". Gordon et al. (2009: 309) were more critical and stated that "discussions of ERM are generally devoid of any specifics on how to quantitatively measure the concept". With reference to such criticisms of ERM measurement, also as outlined in Sect. 2, the methodological design of this literature review considered several key aspects of the articles with regards to ERM measurement, including the methodology of the studies i.e. qualitative or quantitative, and for the latter whether they are based on primary or secondary data.

Almost ten years after the criticism raised by Gordon et al. (2009: 309), this study's review of the selected ERM measurement articles provides findings referring to a variety of perspectives on ERM and how to measure ERM. Both the main empirical methodologies were well represented in the articles, namely qualitatively by means of fieldwork, interviews and case studies of people and organizations, as well as quantitatively by means of empirical analysis of secondary and primary data.

4.1 Qualitative Studies on ERM

A qualitative methodology was represented in 10 (approximately 20%) of the 51 selected articles, with one article selecting a mixed methodology. In one of the seminal qualitative studies, Mikes (2011) explored the effect of culture in ERM measurement. She homed in on several case studies, and presented a comprehensive discussion of the effect of organizational culture on ERM, specifically investigating, measuring and reporting on the concept of calculative cultures in the banking sector. In summary, some banks feature "quantitative enthusiasts" who enjoy "risk management by the numbers", and others are comprised of "quantitative sceptics," in other words managers who favor "softer instrumentation" and risk management that is qualitative and "holistic" in nature. According to Mikes (2011: 230), "risk management has its own cultural cartographers. Some draw the boundaries of risk management to encompass only 'measurable' risks, others make claim on the control of uncertainties for which reliable measurements do not exist and may never be found."

With regard to ERM playing a role in influencing the organization, its decision-making, and thus its overall culture, Meidell and Kaarbøe (2017: 40) "understand the ERM function as sense-givers that vertically and horizontally influence meaning construction among decision-makers in the organization". As is sometimes alluded to in the business and management sciences literature, there can be within organizations a strategic battle for the center, or control, of the organization. Not only do risk practitioners in positions such as Chief Risk Officer (CRO) attempt to influence organizational strategy, but "risk managers, like many other occupational groups, particularly those wishing to be seen as 'professions' therefore can be expected to engage in ideological rhetoric and boundary-work, in order to stake claims over particular kinds of work" (Mikes 2011: 229). These examples evidence that it is critical to measure the *values* of executives, managers and employees of the organization with regard to these ERM implementation issues.

Another article featuring a qualitative methodology and introducing the study of practice to examine ERM implementation was Arena et al. (2011: 792), who presented the concept of maturity levels of ERM—these being labelled as "responsive, discursive and prospective". Arena et al. (2011) also provided a strong discussion wherein the authors referred to the potential downside or limitations of a case study research methodology to study the phenomenon of ERM, and noted that in future, surveys and industry-specific in-depth studies would be useful around ERM implementation.

In conclusion, with regards to qualitative ERM measurement research, the literature review provided examples investigating risk management practices that contribute to the measurement of ERM and indicated that ERM incorporates a variety of implementation variables (Woods 2009), dynamics (Arena et al. 2010), and systematic variances and cultures (Mikes 2009). These articles followed different ERM research streams, examining practical examples and case studies of ERM implementation in firms in qualitative studies providing strong practical insights.

4.2 *Quantitative Studies on ERM*

With reference to empirical quantitative studies, the bulk of the 51 studies, 34, were quantitative, of which about half, 16, relied on secondary data alone. There are studies that promulgate a mixed methodology. More than half of the contributions identified through the literature review adopt a very simple approach and proxy ERM by looking at the appointment of specific subjects within the corporate governance system. Thus, they adopt a monistic approach to ERM measurement and normally use binary variables as independent variables in regression models.

Selected ERM indicators refer to the presence of a CRO or the Risk Committee because "firms choosing to adopt an ERM strategy need a person or group of persons responsible for the coordination of the ERM program and the communication of goals and results to the board" (Liebenberg and Hoyt 2003: 41–42). These studies underline that the CRO normally represents high technical expertise, in that (s)he takes the responsibility to implement the ERM program and oversees relevant risks. The appointment of a CRO is thus considered a sign of aggregated risk management (Liebenberg and Hoyt 2003; Beasley et al. 2008; Pagach and Warr 2011). One study (Aebi et al. 2012) also focuses on the CRO characteristics, for example their participation in the executive board and whether they report directly to the board of directors (i.e. more power) or to the Chief Executive Officer (i.e. less power and conflicting interests).

The presence of the Risk Committee, defined as "a dedicated committee solely charged with monitoring and managing the risk management efforts" (Aebi et al. 2012: 3215), is another corporate governance-related body assumed as a proxy for ERM in quantitative studies based on secondary data. A dedicated Risk Committee is considered a distinctive element compared to an Audit Committee that takes responsibility (also) for risk management. When present, the Risk Committee is described in its specific features, like the number of meetings in the same year, the number of directors and the percentage of independent directors pertaining to it. These are all proxies for ERM.

A recent stream of literature searches for ERM activities with a broader view compared to just looking at the appointment of a CRO or the Risk Committee. In this case, the studies perform a keyword search on public databases, company websites and even Google, by considering a broad range of words, such as enterprise/strategic/consolidated/holistic/integrated risk management, chief risk officer, and risk committee (Gordon et al. 2009; Hoyt and Liebenberg 2011; Lin et al. 2012; Eckles et al. 2014). Intuitively, these studies admit that ERM may be structured differently in different companies and may be more or less institutionalized (Mikes and Kaplan 2015). Thus, these studies allow for research overcome this concern by looking at any signal of ERM implementation.

In the attempt to holistically measure ERM, Andersen (2008) and Eckles et al. (2014) assume an indirect approach to record for ERM adoption. Andersen (2008) uses the variability of annual net sales on the variability of economic returns to capture the firm's capability to manage risk exposure in the external environment of reference. Eckles et al. (2014) adopts predictive models to estimate the probability of a firm adopting ERM, given some firm characteristics like size and age, institutional ownership, diversification, and pressures from regulators or rating agencies. Conversely, Florio and Leoni (2017) made the effort to adopt a holistic approach to directly measure ERM by considering several ERM proxies both individually and in different combinations. More specifically, they look at governance-related ERM measures like CRO appointment, Risk Committee appointment and the frequency of reporting from the Risk Committee to the Board of Directors. They also refer to operational ERM measures in terms of risk assessment level, frequency and method. The authors then combine each set of variables to create a unique proxy to identify advanced ERM systems. Their holistic measure aims at providing "a sort of flexibility to the concept of an advanced ERM system, especially considering the limits of a 'one size fits all' approach in the implementation of ERM systems (Mikes and Kaplan 2015)" (Florio and Leoni 2017: 69).

McShane et al. (2011: 645) were the first researchers to combine secondary data from public sources and primary data from an organisation's actual ERM implementation gathered by a primary data industry measurement instrument (S&P's ERM maturity scores) and utilising it as secondary data, in research that they themselves referred to as "novel". McShane et al. (2011) point out that S&P's developed a comprehensive risk management rating as a component of its overall rating of insurance and banking companies since 2006. After a careful analysis, McShane et al. (2011: 642) conclude that S&P's rating "is a sophisticated and comprehensive index that assesses the risk management culture, systems, processes, and practice". A similar approach was followed by Lin et al. (2012) and Baxter et al. (2013) in order to investigate determinants and consequences of ERM program quality. Baxter et al. (2013: 1264) underline that the criteria used by S&P's to rate ERM quality "relate to effective communication of strategy throughout the enterprise, appropriate project selection, improvement of accounting-based returns and risk-adjusted market returns". S&P's

assigns each company a rating over four categories (i.e. weak, adequate, strong and excellent), which allows creation of categorical variables able to grade ERM according to its intensity. Baxter et al. (2013) further refine the ERM grading of sampled companies with adequate ERM by considering the narrative provided into the analyst's report. Finally, Nair et al. (2014) adopt the S&P's rating to proxy for ERM as a dynamic capability, and examine whether it allows to respond to financial crises effectively.

Another example of using a primary data industry rating as secondary data is the Tillinghast Towers Perrin ERM survey submitted to Chief Financial Officers, chief actuaries, and CROs of life and nonlife insurers. Grace et al. (2015) use the results of this survey to create a set of ERM variables regarding economic capital models, by capturing their adoption per se and their maturity.

An example of a seminal study featuring a quantitative direct primary data collection methodology, of which there are 18 of the 51 in the literature reviewed, is Altuntas et al. (2011), who provided an ERM measurement model which incorporates an additional perspective on a direction towards capturing aspects of ERM in so-called dimensions or constructs, which impact on ERM implementation i.e. an organisational culture of 'Risk Awareness'. According to Altuntas et al. (2011: 417), ERM consists of the following five dimensions critical to implementation from a conceptual perspective:

(i) Processes to identify all relevant risk categories and exposures;
(ii) Quantitative models to measure and evaluate these risks;
(iii) Tools, like risk limits, to manage them efficiently;
(iv) An organisational culture of risk awareness; and
(v) A management approach that integrates ERM and all its components into operational and strategic decision-making.

Altuntas et al. (2011: 419) also explored the concept of linking within ERM implementation a strong element of culture and company success, whereby national culture, risk culture, corporate culture, organisational culture etc. all play a role in determining an organisation's culture. Culture is comprised of the values of the directors, managers and employees of an organisation. In the Altuntas et al. (2011) study, 44 percent of firms said they had a strategy to address a risk management culture in the organisation. It is critical to note, that Altuntas et al. (2011: 433) actually proposed a construct for risk management culture with six manifest variables exploring issues such as employee training and consideration of risk management in decision-making.

Further examples of quantitative studies incorporating a primary data methodology are by Kimbrough and Componation (2009) who collected primary data on ERM practices and an organizational culture scale to test for relationships between the two variables, and Lundqvist (2014), an exploratory study providing a measure based on the pillars of ERM. In summary, there are to date only a limited number of academic studies identified in the literature review (Gates et al. 2012; Kimbrough and Componation 2009; McShane et al. 2011), which are based on primary data collected for empirical investigation of ERM practices, and many of these studies demonstrate possible limitations in that researchers either utilize the data as secondary data (i.e. the researchers did not collect the data themselves), or they did not follow the full 'classical' management sciences scale and construct development process, for example, as proposed by Churchill (1979) and MacKenzie et al. (2011).

5 Concluding Remarks

5.1 Originality and Value of the Study

This paper provides a systematic and comprehensive literature review of ERM across academic disciplines, focusing on measurement of ERM and detailing the three possible empirical ERM measurement streams, i.e. qualitative, quantitative based on secondary data and quantitative based on primary data. It highlights the need for further developments of academic, empirically tested primary data measures for ERM.

5.2 Limitations of the Study

The literature offers a variety of perspectives on ERM and its measurement; the articles are much cited and come from highly rated peer reviewed journals. Within this ERM landscape, there are, however, several academic disciplines represented, which are not completely aligned on the definition of the theoretical ERM construct and how to measure it. This study presents a rigorous methodology where a holistic and comprehensive literature review incorporates the key aspects of the research questions, for example, whether ERM measured in the literature and if so, how. Whilst having a considerable body of knowledge in the academic literature spanning decades, ERM is still a relatively new topic and will continue to gain from contributions—in particular around its measurement.

5.3 Future Research Directions

There are many debates about measurement of ERM, the efficacy of ERM, its perceived cost and how best to implement it in practice. This study suggests that further development of ERM measurement scales based on primary data will be a step towards enabling scientifically robust investigation of these issues. A key advantage of a methodology centered on primary data, is that these data are observed or collected directly from first-hand experience, following careful operationalization of variables and using carefully chosen procedures. Consideration is given to what is being gathered in terms of data so that they are reflecting 'real life' practices in the organizations. Operationalizing the scale for primary data collection is done so that it represents precisely what is to be measured in terms of validity and reliability. In general, methodology utilizing primary data demonstrates greater validity because the study is designed and carried out explicitly for the main purpose of the research. This study contributes to the literature that clearly highlighted the need for a robust academically-validated measurement instruments that will provide ERM measurement scales comprising items and constructs that can act as variables for empirical studies (Lim et al. 2017).

However, this exercise is not purely an academic one. More than 50 years after Drucker's (1959) work, Bromiley et al. (2015: 273) observed, "practitioners need to understand how different individuals and groups within organization define risk, potential biases in risk assessment, and challenges in implementing risk management initiatives". They also pointed out that practitioners and academics must collaborate on the development of the ERM body of knowledge, in order to extend the depth and breadth of the theoretical matter, whilst remaining relevant to organizations and their managers. The discussion of the findings from the literature review on existing ERM measures, and the reasoning towards the need for measurement scales using primary data, may thus inspire further reflections by both academics and practitioners.

Furthermore, constructs derived from a primary data measurement scale can ultimately act to help predict work attitudes and behaviors, which is a significant contribution to the business and management sciences from both an academic and practitioner standpoint. The main thrust of the future research directions from this study is to further expand this concept of developing primary data scales and the resultant constructs to act as an ERM measurement instruments that can be utilized to assess ERM behaviors, attitudes, and practices. This will provide valid and reliable outputs for management sciences research and practice in a variety of domains and ultimately lead to ERM living up to its paradigm of a formalized risk management process, namely one that provides both resilience and opportunity for organizations in the face of uncertainty.

In the review of the ERM literature, it was evident that the majority of studies measuring ERM either relied on statistical analysis of secondary data (such as evidence of a CRO), or were qualitative investigations featuring case studies of organizations, with some primary data-based quantitative studies. One possible future research direction emanating out of the literature review is to combine methodologies in order to provide more robust empirical measurements of ERM. Such a study would require a great amount of coordination, but could give a deeper and valuable understanding of ERM values and practices in organizations. Which in turn, would ultimately contribute to the management sciences by providing insights into a potential means of enabling an organization to achieve its objectives and improve organizational value.

References

Aebi, V., Sabato, G., Schmid, M.: Risk management, corporate governance, and bank performance in the financial crisis. J. Bank. Finance **36**(12), 3213–3226 (2012)

Altuntas, M., Berry-Stölzle, T.R., Hoyt, R.E.: Implementation of enterprise risk management: evidence from the German property-liability insurance industry. Geneva Pap. Risk Insur. Issues Pract. **36**(3), 414–439 (2011)

Andersen, T.J.: The performance relationship of effective risk management: exploring the firm-specific investment rationale. Long Range Plan. **41**, 155–176 (2008)

Arena, M., Arnaboldi, M., Azzone, G.: The organizational dynamics of enterprise risk management. Acc. Organ. Soc. **35**(7), 659–675 (2010)

Arena, M., Arnaboldi, M., Azzone, G.: Is enterprise risk management real? J. Risk Res. **14**(7), 779–797 (2011)

Baxter, R., Bedard, J.C., Hoitash, R., Yezegel, A.: Enterprise risk management program quality: determinants, value relevance, and the financial crisis. Contemp. Acc. Res. **30**(4), 1264–1295 (2013)

Beasley, M.S., Clune, R., Hermanson, D.R.: Enterprise risk management: an empirical analysis of factors associated with the extent of implementation. J. Acc. Public Policy **24**(6), 521–531 (2005)

Beasley, M., Pagach, D., Warr, D.: Information conveyed in hiring announcements of senior executives overseeing enterprise-wide risk management processes. J. Acc. Auditing Finance **23**(3), 311–332 (2008)

Bromiley, P., McShane, M., Nair, A., Rustambekov, E.: Enterprise risk management: review, critique, and research directions. Long Range Plan. **48**(4), 265–276 (2015)

Churchill Jr., G.A.: A paradigm for developing better measures of marketing constructs. J. Mark. Res. **16**(1), 64–73 (1979)

COSO: Enterprise risk management (2004). Available on the internet at http://www.coso.org. Last accessed 18 Sept 2017

COSO: Enterprise Risk Management—Integrating with Strategy and Performance (2017). Available on the internet at http://www.coso.org. Last accessed 21 June 2018

Dickinson, G.: Enterprise risk management: its origins and conceptual foundation. Geneva Pap. Risk Insur. Issues Pract. **26**(3), 360–366 (2001)

Drucker, P.F.: Long-range planning: challenge to management science management science, vol. 5, no. 3, pp. 238–249 (1959), April 1959

Eckles, D.L., Hoyt, R.E., Miller, S.M.: The impact of enterprise risk management on the marginal cost of reducing risk: evidence from the insurance industry. J. Bank. Finance **43**, 247–261 (2014)

Florio, C., Leoni, G.: Enterprise risk management and firm performance: the Italian case. Br. Acc. Rev. **49**(1), 56–74 (2017)

Fraser, J., Simkins, B.: Enterprise risk management: today's leading research and best practices for tomorrow's executives, vol. 3. Wiley, Hoboken (2010)

Gates, S., Nicolas, J.-L., Walker, P.L.: Enterprise risk management: a process for enhanced management and improved performance. Manage. Acc. Q. **13**(3), 28–38 (2012)

Gordon, L.A., Loeb, M.P., Tseng, C.: Enterprise risk management and firm performance: a contingency perspective. J. Acc. Public Policy **28**, 301–327 (2009)

Grace, M.F., Leverty, J.T., Phillips, R.D., Shimpi, P.: The value of investing in enterprise risk management. J. Risk Insur. **82**(2), 289–316 (2015)

Hoyt, R.E., Liebenberg, A.P.: The value of enterprise risk management. J. Risk Insur. **78**(4), 795–822 (2011)

International Standards Organization (ISO). 31000: 2009 Risk management – Principles and guidelines. International Organization for Standardization, Geneva, Switzerland (2009)

ISO: Risk management—guidelines (2018). Available on the internet at https://www.iso.org/obp/ui#iso:std:iso:31000:ed-2:v1:en. Last accessed 10 Sept 2018

Kaplan, R.S.: Accounting scholarship that advances professional knowledge and practice. Acc. Rev. **86**(2), 367–383 (2011)

Kimbrough, R.L., Componation, P.J.: The relationship between organizational culture and enterprise risk management. Eng. Manage. J. **21**(2), 18–26 (2009)
Liebenberg, A.P., Hoyt, R.E.: The determinants of enterprise risk management: evidence from the appointment of chief risk officers. Risk Manage. Insur. Rev. **6**(1), 37–52 (2003)
Lin, Y., Wen, M., Yu, J.: Enterprise risk management. N. Am. Actuarial J. **16**(1), 1–28 (2012)
Lim, C.Y., Woods, M., Humphrey, C., Seow, J.L.: The paradoxes of risk management in the banking sector. Brit. Acc. Rev. **49**(1), 75–90 (2017)
Lundqvist, S.A.: An exploratory study of enterprise risk management. J. Acc. Audit. Financ. **29**(3), 393–429 (2014)
MacKenzie, S.B., Podsakoff, P.M., Podsakoff, N.P.: Construct measurement and validation procedures in MIS and behavioral research: integrating new and existing techniques. MIS Q. **35**(2), 293–334 (2011)
Massaro, M., Dumay, J., Guthrie, J.: On the shoulders of giants: undertaking a structured literature review in accounting. Acc. Auditing Accountability J. **29**(5), 767–801 (2016)
McShane, M.K., Nair, A., Rustambekov, E.: Does enterprise risk management increase firm value? J. Acc. Auditing Finance **26**(4), 641–658 (2011)
Meidell, A., Kaarbøe, K.: How the enterprise risk management function influences decision-making in the organization—a field study of a large, global oil and gas company. Br. Acc. Rev. **49**, 39–55 (2017)
Mikes, A.: Risk management and calculative cultures. Manage. Acc. Res. **20**(1), 18–40 (2009)
Mikes, A.: From counting risk to making risk count: Boundary-work in risk management. Acc. Organ. Soc. **36**, 226–245 (2011)
Mikes, A., Kaplan, R.S.: When one size doesn't fit all: evolving directions in the research and practice of enterprise risk management. J. Appl. Corp. Finance **27**(1), 37–40 (2015)
Nair, A., Rustambekovb, E., McShane, M., Fainshmidta, S.: Enterprise risk management as a dynamic capability: a test of its effectiveness during a crisis. Manag. Decis. Econ. **35**, 555–566 (2014)
Oliva, F.L.: A maturity model for enterprise risk management. Int. J. Prod. Econ. **173**, 66–79 (2016)
Paape, L., Speklé, R.F.: The adoption and design of enterprise risk management practices: an empirical study. Eur. Acc. Rev. **21**(3), 533–564 (2012)
Pagach, D., Warr, R.: The characteristics of firms that hire chief risk officers. J. Risk Insur. **78**(1), 185–211 (2011)
Power, M.: The risk management of nothing. Acc. Organ. Soc. **34**(6), 849–855 (2009)
South Africa's King IV Report (2017) available on the internet at https://c.ymcdn.com/sites/www.iodsa.co.za/resource/resmgr/king_iv/King_IV_Report/IoDSA_King_IV_Report_-_WebVe.pdf. Last accessed 10 Sept 2018
UK Corporate Governance Code (2018) available on the internet at https://www.frc.org.uk/getattachment/88bd8c45-50ea-4841-95b0-d2f4f48069a2/2018-UK-Corporate-Governance-Code-FINAL.PDF. Last accessed 10 Sept 2018
Woods, M.: A contingency theory perspective on the risk management control system within Birmingham city council. Manage. Acc. Res. **20**(1), 69–81 (2009)

Accounting, Soci(et)al Risks, and Public Reason: Governmental Risk Discourses About the ILVA Steel Plant in Taranto (Italy)

Alessandro Lai, Silvia Panfilo and Riccardo Stacchezzini

Abstract The case of the ILVA steel plant in Taranto represents an example of contrasting, incommensurable sustainability issues, explored in terms of "social" and "societal" risks (Asenova et al. in Managing the risks of public spending cuts in Scotland, 2013; Redistribution of social and societal risk: the impact on individuals, their networks and communities, 2015) [Asenova et al. (2015) refer to social risks as the risks of unemployment, and to societal risks as environmental and health risks.]. The case of ILVA has received significant attention for the great amount of dangerous pollutants spread in the environment, as well as the evidence of higher illness and mortality rates in the districts nearest to the plant. In July 2012, the Italian Judiciary halted activity in the steel plant. Four months after, the Italian Government declared the steel plant site as a "Strategic National Interest Site", and allowed the company to restart its activity. Drawing on governmentality (Foucault in Questions of method, 1991), the paper aims to explore the role of accounting—here broadly intended as calculative practices (Miller in Soc Res 68:379–396, 2001)—in moulding ministerial discourse to support decisions when the governance of contrasting risks is needed to safeguard public interest. Supported by discourse analysis of governmental speech, the research shows that the Italian Government based its decision on various experts' risk appraisals: accounting shaped governmental discourse by giving more visibility and relevance to "social" risks (i.e. unemployment, economic development, productivity and competitiveness risks), while silencing "societal" ones (i.e. environmental and health risks). Focusing on a case of incommensurable contrasting issues, the findings contribute to show that accounting concurrently plays a significant role in government decisions legitimizing the business continuity through the creation of a specific risk discourse.

Keywords Social and societal risks · Risk governance · Governmentality · ILVA s.p.a.

A. Lai · R. Stacchezzini
University of Verona, Via Cantarane 24, Verona, Italy

S. Panfilo (✉)
Ca' Foscari University of Venice, Cannaregio 873, Venice, Italy
e-mail: silvia.panfilo@unive.it

P. Linsley et al. (eds.), *Multiple Perspectives in Risk and Risk Management*, Springer Proceedings in Business and Economics,
https://doi.org/10.1007/978-3-030-16045-6_3

1 Introduction

At global level there is an increasing call for business sustainability (Hart 1997; UN Principles for Responsible Management Education 2007; UN Sustainable development goals 2017), which is referred to three pillars: economic, social and natural (Dyllick and Hockerts 2002). Nevertheless, the governance of sustainability issues is not always easy because governing a single pillar may lead to neglecting the others. Prior research has not yet investigated situations where such a paradox takes place. Our analysis of the ILVA steel plant in Taranto aims at investigating how accounting is mobilized within ministerial discourses to support decision-making when the governance of contrasting risks is needed to safeguard public interest.

The case of the ILVA steel plant has received significant attention from EU institutions, and has echoed worldwide because of the size and the amount of pollution that the factory has produced (Pooler and Politi 2017). It attests to the political and legal complexities involved in addressing a case of environmental non-compliance in a factory whose economic significance extends beyond local level. With the employment of about 12,000 people and a capacity of producing 10 million tons of steel annually, the ILVA steel plant in Taranto is the largest steel factory in the EU (European Parliament 2015). The pollution resulting from the activities has determined a higher than average incidence of some diseases as well as a number of deaths in areas close to the plant. Such a sensitive condition was highlighted by the halt provision of the steel plant ordered by the Italian Judiciary. This stop was justified by many factors: a level of pollution above the limits, the evidence of causality between dioxins emitted by the plant and found in the blood of sheep grazing around it, and higher illness and mortality rates in the districts nearest to the steel plant. However, four months after the Judiciary's decision, the Government decided for allowing ILVA to continue business activities by declaring the company as a "Strategic National Interest site".

In arguing its decision, the Italian Government drew on the technical documentation prepared by several "experts" (e.g. chemical experts, environmental experts, epidemiologists, economists, experts of industrial associations, accountants, etc.). This documentation, as well as the speeches of the Government's representatives, relied on a wide plethora of calculative practices, mobilized to provide evidences of the environmental, health and economic risks associated with the (dis)continuity of ILVA.

The government decision and the assessment process of the 'social and societal risks' shed light on the paradoxical situation in which the goal of contrasting societal risks through the adoption of new technologies is not aligned with the social risks (e.g. unemployment due to the crisis of the steel industry) nor with the timing and kind of business activities (in that it would take several months to turn off the plant). The Government had indeed to decide on allowing the steel plant to continue its activities, reducing the rate of unemployment in the region and increasing Italian industrial competitiveness, while implying the risks of increasing environmental pollution and the death of employees and people of the local community, or vice versa. Furthermore, all these risks were measured but remained largely incommensurable because calculated and expressed through different standards/measures (average daily concentrations of pollutants; toxicological and epidemiological data; cancer rates; stochastic causality for risk estimation; rates of unemployment; financial values, etc.). Such a situation feeds interest in understanding how accounting—here broadly intended as calculative practices (Miller 2001; Jeacle 2017)—has been mobilized by the Italian Government in facing a decision involving contrasting and incommensurable sustainability issues.

Specifically, while previous studies predominantly focus on the role of accounting in measuring distinct environmental, economic, or health risks, the current research investigates the mobilization of accounting in the governmental creation of discourses on contrasting (environmental, economic and health) risks. Accounting is here intended not (only) as a "technical tool" adopted to quantify risks and rationally orientate decision-making, but also for its capacity to shape social reality by participating in the construction of "political truths" (Burchell et al. 1980; March 1987; Hopwood 1992; Carruthers 1995). In this respect, we take into great consideration the argument that accounting may participate in the "construction of an appearance of rationality" as it helps shaping the "rationale for decisions" (Carruthers 1995: 313–322). The analysis focuses on the "soci(et)al risks" attributed to the ILVA plant in governmental speeches and technical documentation prepared by the "experts" involved in the investigation of the environmental, occupational and health impacts.

The sociological studies on risk based on the Foucauldian Governmentality framework (Ewald 1991; Dean 1998, 1999; Lupton 2006; Gephart et al. 2009; O'Malley 2009, 2012) support the interpretation of accounting as a technology through which governmental risk discourses are created. According to this framework, government of risks becomes possible only through "discursive mechanisms that represent the domain to be governed as an intelligible field" (Miller and Rose 1990: 6), and accounting represents a form of "scientific" knowledge that provide rationales for risk discourses to be considered as "true" (Dean 1998). The present paper also benefits from the work of Jasanoff (1990, 2012) on how politicians construct "public reason", i.e. "what emerges when states act so as to appear reasonable" (1990: 5). She argues that modern Governments, in claiming legitimacy, draw on a number of practices, discourses, techniques and instruments that help to cope with countless risks and manage them for citizens (Jasanoff 2012). In constructing "public reason", governors are required to face trade-off between risks to health or the environment and the economic issues (Jasanoff 1990: 3), and they produce their arguments by drawing on the technical knowledge produced by "science advisors" (i.e. experts in the field).

Such theorization is expected to produce an understanding of how accounting is mobilized by governmental authorities when a decision must be made to safeguard public interest while contrasting and incommensurable social and societal risks have to be governed.

2 Accounting, Risks and Public Reason: Prior Research

Seminal accounting studies on the role of accounting in organizations and society (e.g. Hopwood 1973, 1983; Burchell et al. 1980, 1985) have figured out the relationships between accounting and decision-making. Going beyond a fully rational interpretation of the decision-making procedures, such studies assert the idea of accounting as "machinery" to be mobilized under conditions of uncertainty. Under these conditions, accounting often enacts complexity, ambiguity, and politics (March 1987; Carruthers 1995) as it cannot offer strict answers. Yet it may provide "learning" for judging complex situations, "ammunition" for "interested parties seeking to promote their own particular interests", or serve as a "rationalization machine" for parties that need to "justify actions that already have been decided upon" (Burchell et al. 1980: 14–15).

Decision-making on risks falls within a "non-consequentialistic logics" (Mouritsen and Kreiner 2016: 21), as it entails the consideration of uncertainty over the "patterns of causation which determine the consequences of action" (Burchell et al. 1980: 14). The situation is considered to be even more complex when there is uncertainty [or disagreement] over the objectives of action [ibidem], as can happen when contrasting risks are simultaneously at play, and there is no agreed interpretation of the "best" objective to achieve and/or of the most proper way to commensurate various calculations (Samiolo 2012).

In this vein, Broadbent (2002) and Broadbent et al. (2008) has elucidated the role of accounting as a "steering device" apt for adjudicating social conflict in the case of a controversial initiative: "the visibilities that are created (by accounting) become resources to justify the particular approach that is required by the institutional steering bodies (in this case the government)" (Broadbent 2002: 443). The studies show the dominance of "accounting logic" in making certain kinds of risk visible and legitimizing the public decision process. Indeed, a "privileged position" has been given to quantitative risk estimation based on accounting, with the result of "silencing" qualitative uncertainties intrinsically connected to decision-making. In brief, they show the role of accounting in shaping and constraining the nature of the decision criteria, and in turn the legitimization of (risk) government.

Other studies point out that accounting can even create risks, or reinforce and redistribute existing ones. With a focus on "social and societal risks", Asenova et al. (2013, 2015) show that the UK Government austerity measures towards Scottish local authorities have finished by mostly affecting disadvantaged, vulnerable people exposed to risks of health and unemployment. Hastings et al. (2015), in analysing the impact of the cost of funding cuts on English and Scottish local governments, identified the implication of accounting in the rising levels of social inequality: State governmental measures, enacted through the intermediate level of local governments and inspired by accounting considerations, put poorest people at higher social risk. Further, as Beck et al. (2005) show in their study of the UK bovine spongiform encephalopathy crisis, accounting considerations that are made possible by the involvement of experts, are deemed to be of limited value for governmental decision-making when accounting cannot precisely quantify relevant health and safety risks.

Considered as a whole, these studies show that accounting is intrinsically involved in pondering, emphasizing or silencing risks associated to public interest. Indeed, State and local governors continuously draw on accounting expertise to make certain risks visible and affirm "public reason" (Jasanoff 1990). This is proven to happen when some risks can be quantified and other risks remain unquantified (see Broadbent 2002; Broadbent et al. 2008) as well as when most of the risks remain unquantified (Beck et al. 2005). What previous studies have failed to highlight is how accounting is mobilized when a State government has to deal with contrasting risks—i.e. risks that suggest opposite decisions—and such risks are quantifiable but incommensurable. To what extent and how is accounting mobilized in governmental discourses on contrasting incommensurable risks to support decision-making and public reason? The present research tries to answer this question.

3 Theoretical Framework

Sociological inquiries in the past decades have been vastly attracted by the concept of risk (Lupton 2006). Such inquiries have gone beyond the interpretation of risk as a "straightforward matter, measurable and calculable" (Gephart et al. 2009: 141). Rejecting the idea of risk as objective, socio-cultural perspectives neglect the idea that risk pre-exists in nature: "it all depends on how one analyses the danger, considers the event" (Ewald 1991: 199). Risk therefore is considered to be part of shared cultural understanding of society (Douglas 1986), as well as a matter that increasingly involves late modern societies (Beck 1992).

In line with a socio-cultural interpretation of society and its institutions, the Governmentality framework depicted by Foucault (1991) offers a unique basis for discussing the role of risk in regulating societies (Ewald 1991; Dean 1999) which may fill the gap identified in the literature. According to Governmentality, risk is created through discourse, strategies and practices that the governors draw upon to manage citizens (Lupton 2006). What is crucial about risk "is not risk itself but what risk gets attached to" (Dean 1999: 131). Government of risk thus becomes possible only through "discursive mechanisms that represent the domain to be governed as an intelligible field" (Miller and Rose 1990: 6). Notions of risk are mobilized to render reality in such a form as to make it amenable to types of action and intervention" (Dean 1999: 132). Further, risk is not considered to be "intrinsically real, but as a particular way in which problems are viewed or 'imagined' and dealt with" (O'Malley 2009: 5).

To make risk "thinkable" and then "governable" to the governors' eyes, several forms of knowledge are mobilized: "from statistics, sociology and epidemiology, to management and accounting" (Dean 1999: 131) all are forms of "scientific" knowledge that provide rationales for risk discourse to be considered as "true". Discourse produce "truths" on risks that are then the basis for action (Lupton 2013: 113).

With her work on how politicians construct "public reason", Jasanoff (1990, 2012) strengthens the Governmentality perspective. She argues that modern Governments, in claiming legitimacy, draw on a number of practices, discourse, techniques and instruments that help to cope with countless risks and manage them for citizens (Jasanoff 2012). In constructing "public reason", governors are required to face "explicit trade-off between risks to health or the environment and the economic and social costs of regulation" (Jasanoff 1990: 3), and they produce "true" and "relevant" arguments by drawing on technical knowledge produced by "science advisors". Governmental legitimization thus relies on "invoking science" (Jasanoff 1990) in support of the governors' planned actions. It follows that the rationality ascribed to expertise is "never natural but always achieved, through institutionalized rules of the game that admit or preclude particular modes of asserting expertise" (Jasanoff 1990: 12). Jasanoff adds that experts and political authorities should commit to accuracy and evidence, but underlines that the former are more focused on the accuracy of their representation of nature, while the latter are more interested offering a "persuasive demonstration of causality and relevance (evidence)" (Jasanoff 1990: 15).

As argued by Dean (1999: 132), accounting participates in the constitution of risk discourse and public reason, being one of the "practices, techniques and rationales that seek to make the incalculable calculable". Critical and interpretative accounting research has provided insightful interpretations of accounting as constitutive of organizational and social life (Burchell et al. 1980; Hopwood and Miller 1994), thus opening the possibility of exploring the role of accounting in the governing of risk.

Following the Governmentality perspective, accounting can be constitutive of risk when it contributes to the construction of discourse around it. The condition for accounting to be constitutive of risk relies on the participation of accounting in the unfolding of risk discourse, allowing risk to be calculated. According to Foucault, discourse not only relies on knowledge, but is also productive of knowledge in the sense that it establishes the basis for determining which statements count as true or false (Hardy and Maguire 2016: 84). Thus, accounting can be constitutive of risk when it supports the "truth" that governors are trying to assert. In this respect, and in line with Jasanoff's arguments on public reason, we should expect the marginalization of the use of accounting in the constitution of risk where it does not allow supporting discourses contingently accepted as "true". In brief, to be constitutive of risk, accounting should participate in the making of discourse by making the latter both possible and legitimate: accounting should make risk visible by creating discourse around it, but at the same time such a role is conditioned by the necessity that accounting supports governmental discourse by creating an aura of rationality around it.

4 Methodology

In order to support our analysis of how accounting informs the construction of governmental risk discourses on ILVA, this research develops a discourse analysis of the Italian Government's official speeches in relation to the technical documentation produced by experts as a result of their risk assessments of ILVA activities.

Our focus is on how the Italian Government supports its claims by drawing on the accounting calculations that the "experts" made visible in their social and societal risk assessment. This means that we do not regard accounting only as a technique of risk assessment, but also as a "machine" (Burchell et al. 1980) that legitimates the construction of a specific risk discourse. In this sense, we recognize the rhetorical dimension of accounting discourse (Burchell et al. 1980; March 1987; Carruthers 1995; see also Zhang and Andrew 2016).

The seminal work by Foucault (1972, 1977, 1982) offers a basis for developing our analysis. We have also taken into consideration extant studies adopting such a Foucauldian technique (e.g. Bacchi and Bonham 2014). Foucault argues that a discourse contains discursive practices and that a discourse should be analyzed for its capability in "ordering the world in a particular way" such as to create truth around it. In other words, Foucault calls on us to investigate the discursive processes through which knowledge about particular objects is formed and defines what should be considered as true. In their analysis of the potential of the Foucauldian concept of discursive practice, Bacchi and Bonham (2014) explain that "the term 'discursive practices' describes those practices of knowledge formation by focusing on how specific knowledge ('discourse') operate and the work they do. Hence discursive practices are the practices of discourse". Foucault requires exploring the "set of regularities" on which the discourse is based. This means that we are required to detect the rules governing the emergence of "true" knowledge within the discourse (Bacchi and Bonham 2014: 180). Further, Foucault (1972: 229) asks us to "recognize the activity of cutting-out and rarefaction of a discourse", paying attention to how the discourse normalizes certain subjects/objects and excludes others. As "comparing", "ranking", "classifying", "hierarchizing" are considered as techniques of normalization and exclusion, we investigate how accounting plays this role. Further, we take inspiration from Lemke's (1995: 29) interpretation of Foucault's concept of discourse as a "general theory of intertextuality for the purposes of history", to inspect how the risk discourse created by the Italian Government refers to other texts (i.e. those of the experts) in order to construct its truth. We are interested in detecting how the Italian Government refers to the experts' texts to construct its risk discourse, and in particular to highlighting how the experts' accounting calculations are part of these (inter)textuality processes.

From a procedural point of view, the analysis started with the search for public sources about the case of the ILVA steel plant in Taranto (technical documentation produced by "experts", Governmental speeches and decisional acts, Judiciary decisions, European Union reports, company communications and financial statements, magazines and newspapers, etc.). This stage allowed us to reach a comprehensive understanding of the main issues and the related risks ascribed to ILVA by the various parties involved in the debate about the (dis)continuity of ILVA's activities. According to our research aim, we decided to develop the discourse analysis by taking into consideration both the Italian Government's public speech in the Italian Parliament and the technical documentation produced by experts in the period from 2010 to 2012. The time span covers the period from the initial Judiciary inquiries to the final Italian Government decisions to allow the ILVA steel plant to restart its full activities.

We sorted the sources into three categories: the "technical texts", the "parliamentary debate texts", and the "decisional texts". The "technical texts" refer to the scientific reports produced by experts: they are chemical and epidemiological appraisals as well as other reports cited by the Judiciary and the Italian Government as sources. The "Parliamentary debate texts" report the Italian Government Ministers' speeches in Parliament. It is through such debates that discourse took form at the governmental level. Lastly, the "decisional texts" include the collection of the Italian Government's decisions together with the texts of the Judiciary's interventions. These last texts are very concise and do not offer possibility for developing a discourse analysis directly concerning them: they are considered to reveal both the Italian Judiciary and the Italian Government's decisions. Further details are reported in Table 1.

The analysis of the "technical texts" permitted highlighting how calculative practices were mobilized within the process of risk assessment developed by the "experts". Operatively, we looked for numbers (e.g. benchmarks, target values, rates, averages, etc.) ascribable to the assessment of the social and societal risks. We underline how the accounting calculations offer visibility to the social and societal risks. The focus lies on the risk measures, their actual values, and the descriptive details offered in the experts' reports.

We then focused on the "Parliamentary debate texts" in order to inspect the rhetorical dimension of accounting discourse. Relying on Foucault's interest in the rules that determine which statements are accepted as "true", we investigated the "themes", "practices", and "strategies" moulding risk discourse within Italian government speeches. First, we identified the focus of the "risk discourse", distinguishing between social and societal risks in each single statement. Second, we identified what are the "themes" emerging from the governmental statements. Themes are intended as the discourse summary emerging from each minister's statement. Third, to investigate the "practices" used by the government per each focus of risk discourse (social/societal), we verify the intertextuality (Lemke 1995) process associated to the use of accounting. That is, in which way accounting is referred to the same texts or of others according to the different social or societal risk discourse. Finally, we identified the emerging "strategies" as conveyed by "set of regularities" (Foucault 1972) in the governmental use of the practices. Specifically, we are interested in identifying a regular use of accounting in shaping broader (social and societal) risk discourses.

The analysis reveals how the governmental public reason on the risks posed by ILVA is constructed by discursively referring to accounting calculations developed by the experts. In this sense, we investigate the "practices" of textual and intertextual processes used through which accounting is mobilized within the discourse. This

Table 1 Official documents covered by the discourse analysis

	Institution	Document name (and our coding)	Date of publication
Technical texts	Regional Environmental Protection Agency (ARPA)	Environmental data relation about Taranto's area 2009 [T1] Benzoapyrene (BaP) analysis 2010 [T2] Environment and safety analysis 2011 [T3] Technical report for the analysis of pollution in the Tamburi district 2012 [T4] Dioxin emissions from E312 stack [T5] ILVA agglomeration plants emissions chronology [T6] Technical report following NOE inspection [T7] Health damage assessment SENTIERI project 2012 [T8]	2010, 2011 and 2012
	Lecce's NOE (Police Environmental Operative Unit)	Note prot. 41/10 [T9]	2-Jul-2011
	Chemical and epidemiological experts	Chemical appraisal conclusions [T10] Epidemiological appraisal conclusions [T11]	2012
	Superior Institute for the Environmental Protection and Research together with the Integrated Pollution Prevention and Control National Investigation Commission	Decisive opinion [T12]	Oct-2012
	Inquiry Parliamentary Commission about waste cycle illegal activities	Regional relation: Doc. XXIII n.10 [T13] Regional relation: Doc. XXIII n.12 [T14]	20-Jun-2012 17-Oct-2012
	Eurofer—European steel industry association	European Steel in Figures 2007–2011 [T15] EUROFER Annual Report 2011 [T16]	2007, 2008, 2009, 2010 and 2011
	ILVA	Separate and consolidated Financial statements [T17] Financial trends [T18]	2010 and 2011 2007–2011

(continued)

Table 1 (continued)

	Institution	Document name (and our coding)	Date of publication
Parliamentary debates texts	Government	Senate 782a public audition of the Environment Minister [P1] Senate 788 public audition of the Economic Development and Environment Ministers [P2]	1-Aug-2012 5-Sep-2012
Decisional texts	Judiciary	Ilva stop production measure [D1]	07/26/2012
	Government	Protocol agreement on financial public resources for urgent environmental recovery and retraining measures for the Taranto area [D2]	07/26/2012
	Government	Environment Ministry Decree. Re-examination of the Integrated Environmental Authorization n. DVA/DEC/2011/450 released for the ILVA steel plant of Taranto [D3]	Oct-2012
	Judiciary	Production's requisition measure [D4]	Nov-2012
	Government	Law-Decree n.207 converted into law n.231/2012: Urgent provisions to protect health, employment levels, in the event of a crisis of industrial plants of National Strategic Interest [D5]	24-Dec-2012

permits detecting the overall "strategies" through which knowledge of social and societal risks is created and made "true".

5 Findings

5.1 The Italian Judiciary's Intervention and the Experts' Appraisals

At the end of 2009, the regional administrative authorities (that is. the Regional Environmental Protection Agency and the Taranto Local Health Agency) ordered 14 flocks of sheep to be put down. The decision was taken after the animals were found to have three times the legal limit of dioxin in their blood. All the flocks belonged to farms operating in the Taranto industrial area and, for that reason, a ban on grazing within a twenty kilometers range from the area was issued and it is still in place.

The Judiciary immediately requested consultation in order to understand which kind of dioxin contaminated the animals and where it came from. Two kinds of analysis were run: a *chemical appraisal* to verify if there was any kind of pollutant inside and outside the industrial area and, if identified, to establish its source; and an *epidemiological appraisal* to inspect the local citizens' past, present and future potential health damage due to environmental pollution.

The Parliamentary Inquiry Commission on waste cycle illegal activities requested counsel from the Superior Health Institute (*Istituto Superiore della Sanità*) about beryllium and benzopyrene pollution levels in the Tamburi area. The result of this counsel was a report called "SENTIERI study".

In September 2010, the Italian Government approved a decree to extend the dioxin legal limit. According to this decree, even if a company had dioxin levels over the legal emissions benchmark in force up to that moment, the dioxin emissions would still have been considered as compliant to regulations for an additional period of three years. By means of this law, the ILVA steel plant was not prosecuted due to its dioxin emission level at that time. However, in the same year, in accordance with European Union standards, a new Integrated Environmental Authorization (the so-called "*Autorizzazione Integrata Ambientale*", labeled as "A.I.A.") was introduced in Italy. This authorization is based on hundreds of technological and environmental prescriptions that companies have to adopt. Verification of such adoption is carried out by the Integrated Pollution Prevention and Control national commission. On the basis of the conclusions reach by this commission, the national Environment Ministry approves authorization. Concession of such an authorization is crucial as it decides about the (dis)continuity of business activities.

In 2010 the Ecological Operative Police Unit (the so called "Nucleo Operativo Ecologico", labeled as "NOE") also started its investigation into ILVA. The results were revealed in a note [prot. N.41/10] which highlighted many irregularities concerning emissions into the air detected within the ILVA Taranto plant.

Following the NOE note, an inspection within the ILVA plant was requested by the Puglia Region's Environmental Quality Department. The Environmental Protection Regional Agency (the so called "Agenzia Regionale per la Protezione Ambientale", labeled as "ARPA") was in charge of data collection. As a technical-scientific body within the Puglia Region, it has the tasks of prevention, control, and monitoring. ARPA indeed released many reports on environmental data concerning the Taranto area (document T1 in Table 1), Benzo[a]pyrene analysis (document T2 in Table 1), environmental and safety analysis [T3] and pollution in the Tamburi district [T4]. ARPA was also in charge of data collection related to concentration levels, benchmark, range, average and pollutant quantities published in the reports about dioxin emissions from the ILVA E312 stack [T5], the ILVA agglomeration plants emissions chronology [T6], and technical results following the NOE note [T7]. Those technical results in particular report that almost 38% of the produced gas during the blowing operation is flared. Therefore confirming the NOE findings [T9] on the ILVA "slopping phenomena"—out of control emissions—and its huge environmental impact evaluated at almost 442,172,900 Nm^3 of gas emissions spread in the air.[1]

Despite the NOE and ARPA "results", the A.I.A. was granted to ILVA with a governmental decree (August, 4th 2011), thereby authorizing its activities while prescribing that the functioning of the plant had to remain within in the interventions and emissions' limit values indicated or requested in the measure itself. However, a few months later (in March 2012), the European Commission defined the steel industry "Best Available Technologies" that all the European steel companies have to adopt. This upgrade urged the Italian Environment Ministry to update the A.I.A.'s requirements and prescriptions, and to review the entire ILVA A.I.A. granting procedure.

The results of the chemical and epidemiological appraisals requested by the public prosecutors were revealed in July 2012. The findings of the chemical appraisal attested dangerous and out of control emissions, unloading powders, and toxic waste in contact with the aquifer [T10]. Epidemiological results estimated deaths attributable to exceeding of the limit for the annual average concentration of PM10 but also pointed out the limits of the study and the "great uncertainty in the estimations" [T11].

On the 26th July 2012, immediately after the revelation of both the chemical and epidemiological appraisals' findings, the Judiciary intervened with the measure to stop ILVA's production [D1]: "*functional to the protection of preventive-protective needs indicated in the law [omissis] and in particular about the serious and current situation of environmental and health emergency suffered by the Taranto's territory, attributed to the pollutant emissions by Ilva factory*".

[1] ARPA was also requested to collect and collate data for the publication of this document in 2012. However, it was only released in 2013. Therefore, it is not cited the Parliamentary debate about ILVA made by Government and is not considered within the scope of this research.

5.2 *The Emergence of the Social and Societal Risks in the Experts' Appraisals*

The experts' appraisals allowed for the identification of the major risks surrounding the ILVA's (dis)continuity. Indeed, the experts' reports make the risk measures and values computed by the experts "visible", as well as the related descriptive information (Table 2).

The major focus of the experts' appraisals is on the "societal" risks, and environmental and health risks in particular. The risk assessment developed by the experts permitted revealing several risk measures and values regarding the chemical pollutants and the epidemiological risk data. As a technique of risk assessment, accounting permitted evaluation of many risk measures: the daily or annual average concentration; a comparison of the concentrations with legal limits; a geographical comparison; the computation of mortality, diseases and hospitalization rates; etc.

The assessment of the risks is primarily aimed at verifying both a potential non-compliance with legal limits and a possible association of such risks to a specific source, i.e. the ILVA plant.

The experts' appraisals identify and measure the environmental risk attributable to ILVA, highlighting that its IPA emissions' level corresponds to almost 95% of the national level, and identifying the pollutants deriving from its production as the main source of many legal overruns (Benzo[a]pyrene, PM10, NO_2, Polycyclic aromatic hydrocarbons). Other kinds of pollutants (such as PCDD/PCDF) instead are compliant to the limits. Further, a time span comparison shows a decreasing trend of the risk. The current pollution level is under the limits while previous data showed their overrun.

The geographical comparison between the average data of health in Taranto and in the nearest districts to the plant shows higher health risks in the latter. In particular, Borgo and Tamburi districts are the most affected with higher cancer rates, higher mortality rates, higher estimated deaths due to excess of pollutants concentration and higher risk of hospitalization.

The documentation produced at the "technical" level also refers to "social" risks. Such documentation is produced by the European steel associations [T15; T16], and by ILVA itself, in ILVA financial statements and trends [T17; T18].

The social risk measures refer to specific company statistics like the number of employees and financial costs deriving from their employment, and the trend of its revenues. The technical economic value of the steel industry at the international level in terms of production and employment units is also presented.

Descriptive details on social risks refer to geographical and temporal comparisons highlighting the significant role of the steel industry for Italy. Results indeed show that Italy is the second highest country in Europe for market share and employment level in this industry. Financial data about ILVA, instead, are about the contribution of the plant accounting for 40% of the national steel production, with a disclosure of the almost 20,000 (direct and indirect) employees in the Taranto area, the total

Table 2 Examples of risk measures and values related to the social and societal risks, as reported in the experts' appraisals

Source (see Table 1)	Risk category	Risk measures	Values	Legal parameters and terms for comparison	Descriptive details
T1	Environmental risk	PM10, NO_2 pollutants	In 2008 59 days of PM10 concentration over 50 $\mu g/m^3$ NO_2 annual average concentration [$\mu g/m^3$]: 49 in 2007, 39 in 2008, 32 in 2009 [first semester]	35 days/year with greater PM10 daily concentration of 50 $\mu g/m^3$ NO_2 annual average concentration limit 40 $\mu g/m^3$ Geographical comparison	Despite a positive trend, the limit on daily PM10 concentrations, continues to report exceedance in respect to the daily legal threshold
T2	Environmental risk	Polycyclic aromatic hydrocarbons emissions	IPA 25.84 tons/year 93% of the total national emission PAHs in air of 18.82 tons/year	Large industrial sources with pollutants emissions above 50 kg/year	In 2005 ILVA polluting emissions' levels are equal to the 93% of the total national emissions
T2	Environmental risk	Benzo(a)pyrene	1.31 Ng/m^3	1 ng/m^3	The predominant emission source of the legal overrun consists of the production processes conducted in the ILVA steelwork's hot area
T8	Environmental risk	Benzo(a)pyrene	1.8 Ng/m^3 annual average concentration	1 ng/m^3	In 2010, there is a significant excess of the target value of 1 ng/m^3 indicated by Legislative Decree 155/2010

(continued)

Table 2 (continued)

Source (see Table 1)	Risk category	Risk measures	Values	Legal parameters and terms for comparison	Descriptive details
T8	Health risk	Cancer mortality	10 and 13% cancer rate	Geographical comparisons	The geographical comparison shows an excess of cancer rates around the steel plant
T8	Health risk	Polycyclic aromatic hydrocarbons pollutant	25% of workers had levels above 2.3 microMol/Molcreat	2.3 microMol/Molcreat	Data shows higher limits compared to the 2.3 microMol/Molcreat guideline
T10	Environmental risk	PCDD/PCDF pollutants	0.27 ng I-TEQ/Nm3	0.40 ng I-TEQ/Nm3	Pollutants values are below the limit according the Regional Decree no. 44 of 19/Dec./2008
T11	Health risk	Increase of PM10 and hospitalization rates	0.8% risk of hospitalization due to increments of 10 mg/m3 of PM10 8.3% vp risk of hospitalization for respiratory diseases in Tamburi district 5.83% vp risk of hospitalization for respiratory diseases in Taranto	Geographical comparison	The analysis on residents in the nearest districts shows an association with mortality from all causes higher than for the Taranto city

(continued)

Table 2 (continued)

Source (see Table 1)	Risk category	Risk measures	Values	Legal parameters and terms for comparison	Descriptive details
T11	Health risk	PM10, estimated deaths	83 attributable deaths in Taranto due to PM10 exceedance of 20 micrograms per m^3. 91 estimated deaths for Borgo and Tamburi districts	20 micrograms per m^3 Geographical comparison	Estimated deaths nearer the plant are attributable to the exceedance of the PM10 concentrations legal limit
T13	Health risk	PM10, NO_2	0.84% increment of death risk for PM10. 0.60% increment of death risk for NO_2	Geographical comparison	There is an increase in the risk of death due to increments of PM10 and NO_2. Results show higher levels of risk in the area around the plant
T15	Occupational risk	Employees units	An average of 14,790 employees, 11,586 of which located in Taranto. Euro 634,400 for cost of labor	Geographical comparison between business units and with the previous year	In 2011 most of the ILVA employees are located in Taranto and the labor cost is increased compared to the previous year
T15	Economical risk	Revenues	Increase of revenues equal to €/000 1,046,333 (from 4,619,903 to 6,026,236)	Comparison with the previous year	Despite, the crisis, the revenues increased between 2010 and 2011

(continued)

Table 2 (continued)

Source (see Table 1)	Risk category	Risk measures	Values	Legal parameters and terms for comparison	Descriptive details
T16	Economical risk	Metric tons	2007: 31,553 2008: 30,590 2009: 19,848 2010: 25,750 2011: 28,726 (metric tons) 16.2% Italian market share; 25% German market share	International comparison and with previous years	In 2011, in line with the European market, Italy has an increasing trend of crude steel output and with the 16.2% of the European market share it represents the second country for production after Germany
T17	Occupational risk	Employment	36,898 employment units in the Italian steel industry 90,645 employment units in the German steel industry	International comparison	In 2010 Italy represents the second country (after Germany) for number of employees in the EU steel industry

cost for labor, and the amount and increasing trend of revenues despite the start of an industrial crisis at international level.

Overall, the "*technical texts*" give visibility to several "societal" and "social" risks.

5.3 The Italian Government's Decision on ILVA's Activities

On the same day of the Judiciary stop measure (26-July-2012), the Italian Government signed a protocol agreement [D2], to establish financial public resources for urgent environmental recovery and retraining measures for the Taranto area.

In the following months, the Italian Government, in the persons of the Environment and Economic Development Ministers, made speeches in Parliament in the debate about the events related to ILVA [P1 and P2].

On the 26th October 2012 the Environment Minister signed the A.I.A. review for ILVA, allowing the continuity of business through a ministerial decree [D3]. With such a decree the Government's decision on ILVA's future seemed established. However, on November 26th, the Judiciary published a new measure under which the company's finished and semi-finished products were seized [D4].

In response to the latter measure, a new governmental decree-law, dated December 3rd 2012, followed. The ILVA steel plant was declared a "*National Strategic Interest Site*" ensuring its business continuity. Finally, on the 24th December 2012, this decree became law and the steel plant could definitively continue to run its activities:

> In the case of a national strategic interest factory, identified with a Premier's decree, when it employs a number of no fewer than 200 subordinated employees for at least one year, if there is the absolute need to safeguard employment and production, at the moment of the review of the integrated environmental authorization, the Environment Ministry can authorize, business continuity for a determined period of no more than 36 months and conditional on compliance with the prescriptions contained in the measure of such an authorization, according to the procedures and the indicated timing, with the aim of guaranteeing the most adequate environmental and health protection utilising the best available techniques [D5].

5.4 The Construction of Risk Discourse by the Italian Government

Some months before the final decision [D5], the Italian Government made its speech in Parliament [P1 and P2]. This speech gives information on both the "social" and the "societal" risks. The first refer to unemployment risks, local development risks, productivity and to international competitiveness risks. The latter refer to environmental and health risks. Details about the two categories of risks are provided in a very different manner (Table 3).

Table 3 The governmental speech: example of risk discourses' focus, themes, practices and emerging strategies

Source (see Table 1)	Authority	Statements	Risk discourse's focus/Themes	Practices: Textual or inter-textual references to risk measures	Emerging strategies
P1	Environment Minister	1. "Therefore, part of the problems detected, for example, by epidemiological surveys that have been carried out on behalf of the Judiciary, but also from those which were made by the Higher Institute of Health, give an account of the population health status, with evident excess mortality, which presumably refers to environmental contamination derived from plants that were operating in accordance with laws of that time. Evident environmental impacts and likely health impacts, which however need to be correlated with the standards of that time and with the authorizations that over time these plants have received, as for all the technologies and plants operating in Europe over the last fifty years"	Societal risks – Environmental risk – Health risk Themes: Health status and causality with environmental contamination from the plant	Intertextual reference to epidemiological measures	To marginalize the societal risk discourse
P1	Environment Minister	2. "The analysis has shown that there is a broader spectrum, both in women and child population, which does not exclude that there is a relationship between environmental risks and damage to health; but this requires a more complex investigation"	Societal risks – Environmental risk – Health risk Themes: Conceivable relationship between environmental risks and health damages	Intertextual reference to epidemiological measures	To marginalize the societal risk discourse

(continued)

Table 3 (continued)

Source (see Table 1)	Authority	Statements	Risk discourse's focus/Themes	Practices: Textual or inter-textual references to risk measures	Emerging strategies
P1	Environment Minister	3. "Nevertheless, what also it emerges from the inquiry that was carried out by Taranto Judiciary experts, is that we are in the presence of data that refer to diseases which, however, have the characteristic of long evolution course, and they have the characteristic of chronicity, when they are not tumors. In other words, these data are based on diseases that are manifested in the course of time and, in the event that it would be detected a relationship between the environment and these pathologies, among the environmental risks and these diseases, we must consider that the environmental risks are those of past decades, while it might be more difficult to identify a direct relationship of cause and effect with the current situation of the Ilva plant in Taranto which, as a result of the measures imposed by the environmental authorization, due to regional laws and national laws, however, has evolved"	Societal risks – Environmental risk – Health risk Themes: Difficulty to establish a direct cause-effect relationship between the environment, diseases and the current situation of the ILVA plant	Intertextual reference to epidemiological measures by experts	To marginalize the societal risk discourse

(continued)

Table 3 (continued)

Source (see Table 1)	Authority	Statements	Risk discourse's focus/Themes	Practices: Textual or inter-textual references to risk measures	Emerging strategies
P1	Environment Minister	4. "ILVA is currently the largest European steelwork, one of the largest in the world, and the hot area of the Ilva Taranto plant is the first step of the all domestic steel industry production cycle. That is, it is from Taranto that semi-products depart to the various sites and steel industry plants of our country. It must be said that Ilva of Taranto represents the 75% of the gross domestic product of the Taranto province and the 76% of the harbor activities"	Social risks – Competitiveness risk – Local development risk Themes: Important role of ILVA at the local, national and EU levels	Textual reference to percentage of the gross domestic product covered by the company at the local level	To provide visibility and relevance to social risk discourse
P2	Economic Develop-ment Minister	5. "Overall, it [business closure] would result in a negative impact, which has been estimated at over 8 billion euro per year, attributable to approximately 6 billion euro to the imports' growth, 1.2 billion euro to income support and lower revenue for the public administration, and for about 500 million euro in terms of reduced spending power for the directly affected area"	Social risks – International competitiveness risk – Productivity risk Themes: Impressive costs related to the ILVA's discontinuity	Textual reference to the costs of the ILVA closure	To provide visibility and relevance to social risk discourse

(continued)

Table 3 (continued)

Source (see Table 1)	Authority	Statements	Risk discourse's focus/Themes	Practices: Textual or inter-textual references to risk measures	Emerging strategies
P2	Economic Develop-ment Minister	6. "The Taranto pole is one of the main European steel poles, with a production capacity of about 10 million tons per year, equivalent to more than 40% of national steel production. In the field of flat rolled production Taranto covers more than 60% of domestic demand, contributing decisively to the supply of strategic sectors for the Italian industry, such as household appliances, shipbuilding, automotive and mechanics. In occupation, Ilva employs more than 11,600 workers directly employed, to which must be added a closely related induced on the vertical plane, which brings direct employment to nearly 15,400 units. To this figure must add up 9200 units linked to indirect industries"	Social risks – Productivity risk – International competitiveness risk – Unemployment risk Themes: Very high production capacity and employment levels of the company	Textual reference to production values, percentages of the steel production and national demand, and number of direct and indirect employees	To provide visibility and relevance to social risk discourse

(continued)

Table 3 (continued)

Source (see Table 1)	Authority	Statements	Risk discourse's focus/Themes	Practices: Textual or inter-textual references to risk measures	Emerging strategies
P2	Environment Minister	7. "This is not a conflictual approach with the business continuity, but is intended to make sure that industrial activities - through technological innovations aiming at protecting the environment—acquire better productive capacity and thus enhance its competitiveness. Because the European target is to make sure that the European economy's competitiveness is driven by interventions that improve environmental quality. This is the aim that we have too"	Social risks – Competitiveness risk – Environmental risk Themes: Technological innovations for both protecting the environment and enhancing competitiveness	Intertextual reference to economic and environmental measures	To marginalize the risk discourse
P2	Economic Development Minister	8. "The company's commitment about the investments during these years was important, as evidence of a shareholder genuine interest to remain in the industry and in the area. Altogether, since it was acquired in 1995 until 2011, the Riva Group has invested more than 4.5 billion euro in the Taranto factory, concentrating in it almost the 72% of the investments made in the whole Ilva Group, in Italy and abroad. In the same period, the share of investment devoted to environmental protection accounted for 24% [approximately 1.1 billion euro] of the total invested in the Taranto plant"	Societal risks – Environmental risk Themes: Relevant corporate investments in the area and for the environmental protection	Textual reference to the costs for environmental protection investments supported by the company	To attach a "social" connotation to the societal risk discourse

(continued)

Table 3 (continued)

Source (see Table 1)	Authority	Statements	Risk discourse's focus/Themes	Practices: Textual or inter-textual references to risk measures	Emerging strategies
P2	Economic Develop-ment Minister	9. "However, those findings cannot justify the serious situations of environmental damage and risk to health which remain despite the investments supported by the Riva Group: for this reason, a Protocol agreement was signed and 396 million euro have been allocated for environmental adjustments, adaptation of the harbor area [which recently entered into a strategic network of European harbors and it is affected by material infrastructure projects] and industrial upgrading"	Societal risks – Environmental risk – Health risk Themes: Governmental money allocation for enhancing environmental conditions	Textual reference to the costs for environmental protection investments allocated by the State	To attach a "social" connotation to the societal risk discourse
P2	Environment Minister	10. "There was, that is, an upgrade of technology; from the point of view of the technological performance, there have been significant results in terms of reducing emissions. In particular, dioxin emissions have been cut down drastically, but there was also a significant reduction of dust emissions, of the hot cycle emissions, also with regard to polycyclic aromatic hydrocarbon compounds"	Societal risks – Environmental risk Themes: Decreasing emissions trends	Intertextual reference to chemical measures	To marginalize the societal risk discourse

Firstly, the discourse associated with the societal risks describe a situation of decreasing emissions trends, in particular related to a dramatic reduction in dioxin thanks to technological upgrades (see statement 10, Table 3). Such discourse suggests a decreasing relevance of the environmental risks. The Government indeed underlines the many investments that ILVA's owner has undertaken, since the acquisition of the company, and the high amount set aside for environmental protection, representing almost one fourth out of the total investments made for the Taranto plant (see statement 8). In addition, according to the Minister charged with dealing with environmental risks a different practice is identified. Themes on environmental risks discussed by the Environment Minister adopt an intertextual reference to chemical measures. Whereas, when such themes are discussed by the Economic Development Minister a textual reference to the costs for environmental protection supported by the company is underlined. This latter practice suggests the attachment of an economic connotation (costs) to societal risks (environmental protection).

Secondly, the discourse on health risks are always present in association with environmental risks (see statements 1, 2, 3 and 9). The discourse analysis highlights the research into a causality relationship between environmental contamination, health damages and the plant activities. Intertextual references to epidemiological measures computed by experts highlighted the evident excess of mortality, presumably referring to environmental contamination deriving from the plant, which however was operating in accordance with the laws at that time. Governors highlight the impacts on the environment and the likely diseases presenting a long evolution path (statement 3). The difficulty of establishing a direct cause-effect relationship implies an uncertain attribution of causality with the current ILVA activity (statements 1, 2 and 3) and such uncertainty suggests need for more complex investigation (statement 2). Furthermore, it emerges that despite the investments made by the ILVA's owner, a serious situation of environmental damage and health risk remains and with the aim of environmental adjustments the Government decided to sign a Protocol Agreement. To highlight such risks a textual reference to the costs sustained by the State has been adopted (statement 9).

Thirdly, the discourse on unemployment risks tends to underline the very high employment levels within the company. A textual reference to both directly and indirectly involved employees (statement 6) is adopted to give relevance to such risks.

Fourthly, the Governmental discourse underlines that ILVA has a very high production capacity, equivalent to almost half of the national steel production, covering a third of the domestic demand (statement 6). By mentioning the gross domestic product, the productive capacity and the domestic demand covered by the company, ministers underlined its key economic role not only for the Taranto area, but also for the national economy as a whole. There are textual references to the percentage of the gross domestic product covered by the company at the local level, to production measures, and to percentages of the steel production and the national demand (statements 4 and 5).

Finally, discourse on international competitiveness risks highlight that ILVA is currently the largest European steelwork and among the largest in the world, and that its business closure would result in negative impacts on import growth, income support, and lower revenue for the public administration as well as in terms of reduced spending power for the Taranto area. The emerging themes therefore highlight the importance of the company at international level and the impressive costs related to the ILVA closure (statements 4, 5 and 6). Discourse on competitiveness risk adopt a textual reference to costs and production values.

Furthermore, focusing just on the Environment Minister's speeches, the fact emerges that, despite his professional skills, he tends to speak about economic aspects a lot. For instance, he underlines the possibility of taking advantage of the environmental crisis and the mandatory adoption of new technologies to transform it into an economic development opportunity for the area, giving also the opportunity of increasing employment levels (statement 4). In his speech, the Environment Minister offers an economic perspective on the environmental issues. For instance, he speaks about "environmental *performance*", "*financial resources* for environmental adjustments" or "environmental best available technologies at lower *cost*". This discourse, linking environmental vocabulary to an economic meaning, appear to lead attention to the social side of the debate giving societal risks 'objects' a "social risk connotation".

To sum up, the governmental discourse about occupational, productivity, economic development, and international competitiveness risks was based on textual reference to their measures, making them "visible" and "relevant". On the other hand, relying on *intertextual* reference to societal risk measures, the governmental discourse emphasizes a decreasing environmental risk while recognizing its direct association to ILVA's past activities. In the meantime, the *intertextual* reference revealed that a direct association between diseases and current ILVA activity is difficult to identify, thus downsizing the relevance of the current environmental risks and the ILVA association with health risks.

Overall, this discourse allows the Government to feed the social risk "truth" through strategies diversified according to the focus of risk discourses. The adoption of textual reference, in particular, conferred great relevance on social risks, thus supporting a discourse oriented to silencing societal risks while arguing for business continuity. The adoption of intertextual reference allowed the marginalization of the societal risks without excluding their assessment. Confirmation of such conclusions are found into the Governmental law attesting the "absolute need to *safeguard employment and production*" however conditional to the adoption of the best available technologies "with the aim of guaranteeing the most adequate environmental and health protection" [D5].

6 Discussion and Conclusions

The sociological studies on risk informed by the Foucauldian Governmentality framework reject the idea of risk as objective, and argue that risk is created through discourse, strategies and practices that the governors draw upon to manage citizens.

Government of risk is made possible through discursive mechanisms that allow representing the risk domain to be governed. To make risk "thinkable" and then "governable", several forms of knowledge are mobilized to provide rationales for risk discourse. As a form of technical/scientific knowledge, accounting participates in the construction of risk discourse by making this latter "possible" and "legitimate". As underlined by Jasanoff (1990, 2012), the construction of governmental discourse is more and more based on the technical knowledge produced by "science advisors": these latter offer politicians the possibility of producing "true" and "relevant" arguments while constructing "public reason".

The present paper has drawn on this body of literature to investigate how the Italian Government has constructed its risk discourse in the case of the ILVA steel plant in Taranto, where various and contrasting risks were associated to its (dis)continuity. The technical texts give evidence of environmental and health risks (i.e. the "societal" risks) as well as to unemployment and economic development risks (i.e. the "social" risks). Thus, accounting provides the Italian Government and other authorities (e.g. the Judiciary) with a great number of risk measures and assessments. Citing the seminal work of Burchell et al. (1980: 14), we can say that accounting—mobilized in conditions of "uncertainty over the patterns of causation which determine the consequences of action"—supported governmental decision-making by clarifying the specific risk conditions. Government was indeed called to a decision on ILVA's destiny drawing on the experts' risk appraisals which identify measurable but incommensurable risks. Such a condition highlights the paradox regarding the governing of health and environment risks not aligned with the social risks. That is, the obligation for ILVA of achieving environmental standards and investing in new technologies as soon as possible does not match with the long period needed for the business reconversion and involves, due to the steel industry crisis, the loss of thousands of jobs in the poorest Italian area.

Thus, in the case under investigation the role of accounting extended beyond its capability to act as a "learning machine" (Burchell et al. 1980). Indeed, accounting was also mobilized to inform the risk discourse that the Italian Government produced in order to shape "public reason" on such decision. The risk discourse produced by the Italian Government—made "visible" by mean of the "Parliamentary debate texts"—draws on risk measured based on accounting calculations in various ways. The discourse analysis developed on these texts allows for detecting the governmental practices used to make the discourse as "true". We find that the Government broadly adopts the following practices:

1. When the statements present arguments inherent to the "societal" risks (e.g. health status and causality with environmental contamination from the plant; conceivable relationship between environmental risks and health damages; decreasing emissions trends, etc.), there is an *intertextual* reference to the experts' appraisal, while the statements do not report any specific risk measures. In other words, there is an *implicit* reference to the experts' risk assessment, but without any disclosure about the specific risk measure. The citation of the experts' risk assessment

allows legitimating the Governmental discourse as true, but there no explicit visibility of the measure of the "societal" risks;

2. Diversely, when the statements present arguments inherent to the "social" risks (e.g. very high production capacity and employment levels of the company; impressive economic and social costs related to the ILVA's discontinuity; relevance of the ILVA's activities at the local, national and EU, etc.), such statements also explicitly report specific risk measures or at least some calculation inherent to the situation and the context. In other words, there is a *textual* citation of the specific measures assessed by the experts in their risk assessment processes. The disclosure of the risk measures offers visibility to this category of risks.

This "set of regularities" (Foucault 1972) on which the discursive practices of the Italian Government are based, highlights the governmental strategy of emphasizing the relevance of the "social" risks while silencing the "societal" ones. While "social" risks measures are made "visible" within the discourse (Lupton 2013), "societal" risks are not.

Another emerging strategy corroborates our argument: the "societal" risks are often displayed in governmental discourse by referring to economic calculations. In such a way, the Italian Government does not explicitly say that the "societal" risks are not relevant, but it emphasizes the efforts made by the Government itself in financial terms and by ILVA to safeguard the environment and consequently reduce health risks. Thus corroborating previous research (e.g. Broadbent 2002; Broadbent et al. 2008) that has highlighted the dominance of the "accounting logic" in making visible certain kinds of risks, while silencing other risks.

The Government has created its discourse without explicitly explaining how the comparison between the "social" and the "societal" risks and the following decision-making took place: there is no evidence of commensuration between them. However, the characterization of both the "social" and the "societal" risks from an economic point of view creates an aura of commensuration around the two categories of risks. The previous studies that have highlighted the rhetorical dimension of accounting (Burchell et al. 1980; March 1987; Carruthers 1995) offer a basis for the interpretation of this finding. We can say that the Italian Government used the experts' calculations as an "ammunition machine" in order "to promote [its] own particular position" (Burchell et al. 1980: 15).

Further, while the Italian Government offered its public speeches in Parliament in August and September 2012, its first intervention can be dated 26th July 2012, when it signed the environmental Protocol agreement. This means that the speeches followed its first intervention about the environmental matter. Thus, we can interpret accounting even as a "rationalization machine", used to "legitimize and justify actions that already have been decided upon" (Burchell et al. 1980: 5). To summarize, accounting can play different roles concurrently, as the seminal work of Burchell et al. (1980) has called on to investigate but the majority of studies has largely neglected (Mouritsen and Kreiner 2016).

Prior studies that have explored the relationships between accounting and soci(et)al risks, advocate that accounting can create risks, or reinforce and redistribute existing ones (Asenova et al. 2013, 2015; Beck et al. 2005; Hastings et al. 2015). We enrich this body of literature by showing how this role is mediated by the mobilization of accounting itself within a risk discourse.

According to Jasanoff's body of research on the construction of public reason, the construction of a "credible" and "relevant" discourse strongly relies on technical knowledge ascribable to experts (Jasanoff 1990: 11). The present study shows the fundamental role of experts in legitimizing/rationalizing the governmental public reason. Further, the present research shows the different "work" done by the experts and the politicians. The former offered an accurate representation of the social and societal risks by detailing several risk measures. Differently, the latter constructed a discourse by omitting part of the risk measures but continuously referring to the experts' appraisals. These textual and intertextual practices permitted persuasive demonstration of the "relevance" of the social risks in comparison with the societal ones.

The attribution of "relevance" to the social risks rather than to the societal ones supporting the decision for business continuity while recognizing the need for an environmental transformation of the company reflects this: 'the idea of sustainability has undergone a significant change of meaning, now connoting "sustainable development", with the emphasis on sustaining economies rather than nature (Pfaller and Lerch 2005: 205).

Our research has a number of limiting factors. First, we deliberately chose to inspect some texts and to exclude others in order to concentrate the attention on the experts' risk appraisals commissioned by both the Judiciary and Italian Government. Further, given the aim of approaching the governmental discourse by focusing only on its official speech, the discourse analysis does not consider the comments of the Italian Government's representatives within newspapers, TV and other media. Despite these limitations, we believe that the paper contributes to critical and interpretative accounting research by depicting how accounting can be mobilized when a State government has to deal with *contrasting risks*, quantifiable but *incommensurable*. The paper shows that accounting played several roles: it worked as a learning machine to reduce uncertainty and allowed the governors to take their decision on ILVA's destiny on the basis of the risk measured highlighted by the experts. Further, accounting also served as an "ammunition" and "rationalization" machine to create an "elusive link" between information and decision-making (March 1987). Thus, accounting participated in the governance of risk as it allowed for the construction of a discourse by making this latter "credible" and "relevant".

Acknowledgements The authors are grateful to the editors and the reviewers for their insightful comments and the support provided during the review process. In its earlier version, the article benefited from the feedback provided by the attendees at ERRN 8th European Risk Conference, Katowice, Poland, 20–21 September 2018. While the paper is the result of a joint effort of the authors, Alessandro Lai wrote Sections 5.1 and 6, Silvia Panfilo wrote Sections 1, 4, 5.3 and 5.4, and Riccardo Stacchezzini wrote Sections 2, 3 and 5.2.

References

ARPA: Relazione sui dati ambientali dell'area di Taranto (Environmental data relation about Taranto's area) (2009)
ARPA: Benzo(a)pirene aerodisperso presso la stazione di monitoraggio della qualità dell'aria di Via Macchiavelli a Taranto – attribuzione alle sorgenti emissive – relazione tecnica preliminare (Benzoapyrene (BaP) analysis at the air quality monitoring station in Macchiavelli street in Taranto - preliminary technical report on the emission sources) (2010)
ARPA: Rapporto Ambiente e Sicurezza 2011 – ILVA Taranto (Environmental and safety analysis) (2011)
ARPA: Emissioni di diossine dal camino E 312: Il risultato della campagna di monitoraggio 2011 (Dioxin emissions from E312 stack: results of the monitoring campaign) (2012a)
ARPA: Cronologia emissioni da impianti agglomerazione ILVA 1994–2011 (ILVA agglomeration plants emissions chronology) (2012b)
ARPA: Relazione tecnica: Analisi delle tendenze di inquinanti nel quartiere Tamburi di Taranto per il 2012 (Technical report for the analysis of pollution in the Tamburi district in 2012) (2012c)
ARPA: Relazione tecnica a seguito di sopralluogo del 2/08/2011 nello stabilimento siderurgico ILVA di Taranto effettuato a seguito di nota del NOE di Lecce prot. N.41/2010 del 2/07/2011 trasmesso da Regione Puglia con nota prot. N. AOO_169_0000412 (Technical report following NOE inspection on 08/02/2011) (2012c)
ARPA et al.: Valutazione del Danno Sanitario Stabilimento ILVA di Taranto ai sensi della LR 21/2012 - Scenari emissivi pre-AIA (anno 2010) e post-AIA (anno 2016) (Health damage assessment so called SENTIERI project - ILVA emission scenarios pre- and post-Integrated Environmental Authorization (year 2010 and year 2016)) (2012)
Asenova, D., Bailey, S.J., McCann, C.: Managing the Risks of Public Spending Cuts in Scotland (2013). http://www.jrf.org.uk/sites/files/jrf/public-spending-cuts-scotland-full.pdf
Asenova, D., McKendrick, J., McCann, C., Reynolds, R.: Redistribution of Social and Societal risk: The Impact on Individuals, their Networks and Communities (2015). http://www.jrf.org.uk/sites/files/jrf/social-societal-risk-full.pdf
Bacchi, C., Bonham, J.: Reclaiming discursive practices as an analytic focus: political implications. Foucault Stud. **17**, 179–192 (2014)
Beck, U.: Risk Society: Towards a New Modernity, vol. 17. Sage, Thousand Oaks (1992)
Beck, M., Asenova, D., Dickson, G.: Public administration, science, and risk assessment: a case study of the U.K. bovine spongiform encephalopathy crisis. Publ. Adm. Rev. **65**(4), 396–408 (2005)
Biggeri, A., Forastiere, F., Triass, M.: Conclusione della perizia epidemiologica (Epidemiological appraisal conclusions) (2012)
Broadbent, J.: Critical accounting research: a view from England. Crit. Perspect. Acc. **13**(4), 433–449 (2002)
Broadbent, J., Gill, J., Laughlin, R.: Identifying and controlling risk: the problem of uncertainty in the private finance initiative in the UK's National Health Service. Crit. Perspect. Acc. **19**(1), 40–78 (2008)
Burchell, S., Clubb, C., Hopwood, A.G.: Accounting in its social context: towards a history of value added in the United Kingdom. Acc. Organ. Soc. **10**(4), 381–413 (1985)
Burchell, S., Clubb, C., Hopwood, A., Hughes, J., Nahapiet, J.: The roles of accounting in organizations and society. Acc. Organ. Soc. **5**(1), 5–27 (1980)
Carruthers, B.G.: Accounting, ambiguity, and the new institutionalism. Acc. Organ. Soc. **20**(4), 313–328 (1995)
Dean, M.: Risk, calculable and incalculable. Soziale Welt **49**, 25–42 (1998)
Dean, M.: Risk, calculable and incalculable. In: Lupton, D. (ed.) Risk and Sociocultural Theory: New directions and Perspectives, pp. 131–159. Cambridge University Press, Cambridge (1999)
Decreto - Legge 3 dicembre 2012, n. 207, convertito in legge 24 dicembre 2012, n. 231: Disposizioni urgenti a tutela della salute, dell'ambiente e dei livelli di occupazione, in caso di crisi

di stabilimenti industriali di Interesse Strategico Nazionale (Law-decree 3rd December 2012, n.207, converted into law on the 24th December 2012, n.231: Urgent provisions to protect health, employment levels, in the event of a crisis of industrial plants of National Strategic Interest) (2012)
Douglas, M.: Risk Acceptability According to the Social Sciences (Vol. 11). Russell Sage Foundation (1986)
Dyllick, T., Hockerts, K.: Beyond the business case for corporate sustainability. Bus. Strategy Environ. **11**(2), 130–141 (2002)
Environment Minister decree: Riesame dell'autorizzazione integrata ambientale n. DVA/DEC/2011/450 del 4/8/2011 rilasciata per l'esercizio dello stabilimento siderurgico della società ILVA S.p.A. ubicato nel comune di Taranto (Re-examination of the Integrated Environmental Authorization n. DVA/DEC/2011/450 released for the ILVA steel plant of Taranto) (26th October 2012)
EUROFER: European steel in figures 2007–2011 (2011a)
EUROFER: Annual report 2011 (2011b)
European Parliament: The ILVA Industrial Site in Taranto, report produced by the Directorate-General for Internal Policies—Policy Department Economic and Scientific Policy A (2015). http://www.europarl.europa.eu/RegData/etudes/IDAN/2015/563471/IPOL_IDA(2015)563471_EN.pdf
Ewald, F.: Insurance and risk. In: Burchell, G., Gordon, C., Miller, P. (eds.) The Foucault Effect: Studies in Governmentality. Hemel Hempstead, Harvester Wheatsheaf (1991)
Foucault, M.: The Archeology of Knowledge and the Discourse on Language. Pantheon books, New York (1972)
Foucault, M.: Discipline and Punishment. Allen Lane, London (1977)
Foucault, M.: The subject and power. Crit. Inq. **8**(4), 777–795 (1982)
Foucault, M.: Questions of method. In: Burchell, G., Gordon, C., Miller, P. (eds.) The Foucault Effect: Studies in Governmentality. Hemel Hempstead, Harvester Wheatsheaf (1991)
Gephart Jr., R.P., van Maanen, J., Oberlechner, T.: Organizations and risk in late modernity. Organ. Stud. **30**(2/3), 141–155 (2009)
Hardy, C., Maguire, S.: Organizing risk: discourse, power, and "riskification". Acad. Manag. Rev. **41**(1), 80–108 (2016)
Hart, S.L.: Beyond greening: strategies for a sustainable world. Harvard Bus. Rev. **75**(1), 66–77 (1997)
Hastings, A., Bailey, N., Bramley, G., Gannon, M., Watkins, D.: The Cost of the Cuts: The Impact on Local Government and Poorer Comunities. Joseph Rowntree Foundation Report, New York (2015)
Hopwood, A.G.: An Accounting System and Managerial Behaviour. Saxon House and Lexington (1973)
Hopwood, A.G.: On trying to study accounting in the contexts in which it operates. Acc. Organ. Soc. **8**(213), 287–305 (1983)
Hopwood, A.G.: Accounting calculation and the shifting sphere of the economic. Eur. Acc. Rev. **1**(1), 125–143 (1992)
Hopwood, A.G., Miller, P.: Accounting as Social and Institutional Practice, vol. 24. Cambridge University Press, Cambridge (1994)
ILVA: Bilancio annuale e consolidato (Separate and consolidated financial statement) (2010)
ILVA: Bilancio annuale e consolidato (Separate and consolidated financial statement) (2011)
ILVA: Trend finanziari 2007–2011 (Financial trends 2007–2011) (2011)
Inquiry Parliamentary Commission about waste cycle illegal activities: Relazione territoriale sulle attività illecite connesso al ciclo rifiuti della Regione Puglia. Doc. XXIII 10 (Regional relation on the illegal activities about waste cycle Doc. XXIII 10) (2012a)
Inquiry Parliamentary Commission about waste cycle illegal activities: Relazione territoriale sulle attività illecite connesso al ciclo rifiuti della Regione Puglia. Doc. XXIII n.12 (Regional relation on the illegal activities about waste cycle Doc. XXIII 12) (2012b)

Italian Government: Protocollo di intesa per interventi urgenti di bonifica, ambientalizzazione e riqualificazione di Taranto (Protocol agreement on financial public resources for urgent environmental recovery and retraining measures for the Taranto area) (2012, 26th July)
Jasanoff, S.: American exceptionalism and the political acknowledgment of risk. Daedalus **119**, 61–81 (1990)
Jasanoff, S.: Reason in practice. In: Science and Public Reason. Routledge, Milton Park, UK (2012)
Jeacle, I.: The popular pursuit of DIY: exploring the role of calculative technologies in an actor network. Manag. Acc. Res. **35**, 99–109 (2017)
Judge for the preliminary inquiries: Ordinanza di fermo della produzione e sequestro prodotti ILVA S.p.A. (Production's requisition measure) (2012a)
Judge for the preliminary inquiries: Ordinanza di chiusura di ILVA S.p.A. (Ilva stop production measure) (2012b, 26th July)
Lemke, J.L.: Intertextuality and text semantics. Adv. Discourse Processes **50**, 85–114 (1995)
Lupton, D.: Sociology and risk. In: Beyond the Risk Society: Critical Reflections on Risk and Human Security, pp. 11–24 (2006)
Lupton, D.: Risk, 2nd edn. Routledge, Milton Park, UK (2013)
March, J.G.: Ambiguity and accounting: the elusive link between information and decision making. Acc. Organ. Soc. **12**(2), 153–168 (1987)
Miller, P.: Governing by numbers: why calculative practices matter. Soc. Res. **68**, 379–396 (2001)
Miller, P., Rose, N.: Governing economic life. Econ. Soc. **19**(1), 1–31 (1990)
Mouritsen, J., Kreiner, K.: Accounting, decisions and promises. Acc. Organ. Soc. **49**, 21–31 (2016)
NOE of Lecce: Nota prot. N.41/2010 (Note prot. N.41/2010) (2011)
O'Malley, P.: Governmentality and risk. In: Zinn, J. (ed.) Social Theories of Risk and Uncertainty, pp. 52–75. Blackwell Publishing, Oxford (2008). Sydney Law School Research Paper No. 09/98 (2009). Available at SSRN: https://ssrn.com/abstract=1478289
O'Malley, P.: Risk, Uncertainty and Government. Routledge, Milton Park, UK (2012)
Pfaller A., Lerch M.: Challenges of globalization: new trends. In: International Politics and Society. Transaction Publishers, NJ (2005)
Pooler, M., Politi, J.: Bidding Race to Win Europe's Biggest Steel Plant Heats up. Financial Times, 5 March 2017 (2017). https://www.ft.com/content/24c73c76-ff6f-11e6-8d8e-a5e3738f9ae4
Samiolo, R.: Commensuration and styles of reasoning: Venice, cost-benefit, and the defence of place. Acc. Organ. Soc. **37**(6), 382–402 (2012)
Sanna, M., Monguzzi, R., Santili, N., Felici, R.: Conclusione perizia chimica (Chemical appraisal conclusions) (2012a)
Senate 782ª public audition (antimeridian): Informativa del Ministro dell'ambiente e della tutela del territorio e del mare sull'ILVA di Taranto (Environment Minister audition on Taranto's ILVA) (2012, 1st August)
Senate 788ª public audition: Informativa del Ministro dello sviluppo economico e delle infrastrutture e dei trasporti e del Ministro dell'ambiente e della tutela del territorio e del mare sui più recenti sviluppi della vicenda dell'Ilva di Taranto (Economic Development and Environment Ministers auditions on the newest developments on Taranto's ILVA) (2012, 5th September)
Superior Institute for the Environmental Protection and Research together with the Integrated Pollution Prevention and Control National Investigation Commission: Opinione decisiva (Decisive opinion) (2012, October)
United Nation: Principles for Responsible Management Education (2007). http://www.unprme.org/index.php
United Nation: Developing program: Sustainable Development goals (2017). http://www.undp.org/content/undp/en/home/ourwork/sustainable-development/overview.html
Zhang, E., Andrew, J.: Rethinking China: discourse, converge and fair value accounting. Crit. Perspect. Acc. **36**, 1–21 (2016)

(In)Consistency Between Private and Public Disclosure on Enterprise Risk Management and Its Determinants

Silvia Panfilo

Abstract Worldwide governance organizations and regulators have recently called for more enhanced disclosures about how organizations manage risks. Enterprise Risk Management (ERM) is recognized as a value-contributing best practice even when legal standards do not require it (Whitman in Risk Manag Insur Rev 18(2):161–197, 2015), but public disclosure on such a process is not generally mandatory. In Italy emphasis on risk disclosure started in 2008 but it was the 2011 revision of the Corporate Governance (CG) code for listed companies to ask for the board commitment in disclosing, within the CG report, about the main internal control and risk management system's characteristics (Borsa Italiana in Codice di Autodisciplina, 2011). Given the proprietary nature of risk information in addition to the Italian capital market characteristics (small capitalization and presence of a dominant shareholder) and the lack of any mandate for what specific aspects board should disclose, the study aims at investigating a potential variation between private and public disclosure on ERM. Relying on the ERM concepts provided by the COSO framework (2004) the author submitted a survey seeking information about ERM practices within Italian listed companies. Such a private information is compared to public CG reports released by the same companies. The comparison shows companies tend to privately reveal a more effective ERM process than the one they publicly disclose. An examination of CG and firm's risk variables potentially determining higher variation—i.e. information inconsistency—supports proprietary costs theory rather than agency theory expectations. Thus showing the limits of voluntary disclosure dealing with risk management systems. The study might have international policy implications.

Keywords Enterprise risk management (ERM) · Private disclosure · Public disclosure · Information (in)consistency · Determinants

S. Panfilo (✉)
Ca' Foscari University of Venice, Cannaregio, Venice 873, Italy
e-mail: silvia.panfilo@unive.it

P. Linsley et al. (eds.), *Multiple Perspectives in Risk and Risk Management*, Springer Proceedings in Business and Economics,
https://doi.org/10.1007/978-3-030-16045-6_4

1 Introduction

Worldwide, a number of corporate governance-focused entities have issued calls for effective risk management processes within organizations including the introduction of specific corporate governance (CG) bodies, such as Chief Risk Officers (CRO) and/or risk committees (Brown et al. 2009).

The European Directive 2001/65/EC on "transparency" introduced in Europe new requirements for management reporting including disclosure on risk. Further, the obligation in directive 2006/46/CE to describe the risk management systems requires also the explanation of risk management functions, policies, structures, and procedures. European financial companies are also required to have some risk process standards. Large banks, for instance, have to comply with the international regulatory framework Basel III (Directive 2013/36/EU and Regulation (EU) No. 575/2013). Likewise, insurance companies are subject to Solvency II (Directive 2009/138/CE) and they must complete their "Own Risk and Solvency Assessment (ORSA)" for filing with state insurance regulators. Those initiatives require to implement an effective and integrated risk management process and to report focusing on the enterprise risk management effectiveness. Further, other international voluntary disclosure initiatives ask for information relates to risk and risk management process [see for all the content elements of the Integrated Reporting framework (IIRC 2013)].

Enterprise Risk Management (ERM) definition in the current paper relies on the Enterprise Risk Management—Integrated Framework issued by Committee of Sponsoring Organizations of the Treadway Commission. It is the most adopted framework (Hayne and Free 2014) providing guidance about the key elements of an effective, top-down, enterprise-wide approach to risk management and defining ERM as "a process, effected by an entity's board of directors, management and other personnel, applied in strategy setting and across the enterprise, designed to identify potential events that may affect the entity, and manage risk to be within its risk appetite, to provide reasonable assurance regarding the achievement of the entity's objectives" (COSO 2004).

In response to so much international attention and push on ERM as part of good corporate governance, risk management information is expected to be increasingly sought by the firm's stakeholders and information users (Lajili and Zeghal 2005). Nevertheless, previous literature on risk disclosure has limited its focus on risk factors (Beretta and Bozzolan 2004; Linsley and Shrives 2005, 2006) rather than exploring the disclosure of ERM practices.

In Italy, emphasis on risk disclosure stems from a consultative document that was issued in 2008 by the Council of Italian Chartered Accountants (IRDCEC 2008) to assist entities with implementing the new directives' requirements (Elshandidy and Neri 2015). Specifically, since the 2011 revision of the CG code for listed companies it follows the board commitment in disclosing, within the CG report, about the main internal control and risk management system's characteristics (Borsa Italiana 2011; art. 7.C.1.d; see Table 1). Further, the 2015 review of the CG code compulsorily enhances the disclosure on the risk management process.

Table 1 Risk management duties according to the 2011 Italian CG code

Subject	Duties
Board of Directors (BoD)	– Lead the internal control and risk management (ICRM) system to favour the identification, measurement, management, and control of risks in the company and its subsidiaries, according to its risk appetite and its strategy – Evaluate, at least yearly, the suitability and the effectiveness of the ICRM system according to the characteristics of the company and its risk appetite – Endorse, at least yearly, the IC program, consulting the Board of Statutory Auditors (BoSA) and the ICR officer – Describe in the CG report the main features and the suitability of the ICRM system – Assess, in accordance with the BoSA, the results of the external audit – Appoint and overrule the internal audit manager, ensure the availability of his resources, and define his remuneration according to the company's policies
Internal Control and Risk (ICR) committee	– Evaluate, in collaboration with the chief financial officer, the external auditor, and the BoSA, the accuracy of the use of accounting principles – Give opinions about the approach to the identification of the firm's risks – Study the reports provided by the ICRM system and the internal audit function – Check the independency, suitability, effectiveness, and efficacy of the internal audit function – Report to the BoD, at least biyearly, about its activity and the suitability of the ICRM system
Internal Control and Risk (ICR) officer	– Identify the company's risks, with reference to the of the business, and report timely on risks to the BoD – Carry out the guidelines provided by the BoD, programming, executing, and managing the ICRM system, maintaining constant control of its suitability and effectiveness – Accomplish the coordination of the ICRM system with the operating and regulatory conditions – Ask for verifications from the internal audit function regarding compliance with rules and strategy, reporting to the BoD, the ICR committee, and the BoSA – Report timely to the ICR committee (in case of absence to the BoD) about identified critical issues

Source Florio and Leoni (2017)

The relationship between risk management disclosure and corporate governance is of interest to regulators because less concentrated ownership and independent directors are expected to reduce agency problems, and thus reduce the need for regulatory intervention in corporate reporting (Abraham and Cox 2007). Following this increasing push for transparency on ERM and considering most of accounting regulators—including corporate governance ones—do not ask for uniform and mandatory information about that, there is a call for examining this specific disclosure attempting to answer the overarching research question: To what extent are public disclosures consistent with what companies privately declare about their internal ERM process? The answer can be important especially in a setting where capital market is characterized by a dominant shareholder and expectation is that of greater information asymmetry overcame by an increasing regulatory demand for voluntary ERM disclosure (e.g. Italy).

Considering ERM is recognized as a value-contributing best practice in CG even when legal standards do not require it (Whitman 2015), this paper adopts the ERM fundamental concepts provided by COSO (2004) and operatively aims at investigating the consistency of ERM information in a setting of voluntary disclosure examining: (1) the nature and extent of variation between public disclosure compared to a private source of information on ERM practices and (2) the determinants of higher variation—interpreted as information inconsistency.

These two research questions can provide impetus to the debate in accounting regulation, here intended as including corporate governance regulations on risk management disclosure, and practice among national and international regulatory bodies as they try to harmonize their efforts. Thus, providing results which can show potential limits emerging from the practices and investigating the determinants of higher variation which may indicate the conditions under which this happens.

To answer the former research question, in line with Marshall and Weetman (2002) the author compared data collected from two disclosure sources: a private on-line survey submitted to all Italian listed companies, and the public CG reports drafted by the same respondents' companies. A score is developed for both the private and the public source of disclosure on ERM. The difference between the two scores allowed the identification of the level of disclosure variation on ERM and the investigation of the information (in)consistency.

Finally, to answer the second research question, adopting a theoretical comparative approach, the paper examines corporate governance factors (board independence and ownership's concentration) and firm's risk characteristics (leverage and market to book ratio) as determinants explaining information inconsistency about ERM practices. Therefore, the paper helps extending previous literature on risk disclosure focusing on ERM process instead of risk factors. In addition, prior research mainly analyzes entities in a non-financial setting while the current study takes into account also financial companies. Results showing how most of the companies' public reports are inconsistent with the private disclosure on the internal process shed insights that may support the need for more disclosure transparency. In particular, companies tend to not fully disclose information about ERM processes in place. That is, the private disclosure suggests more extensive ERM processes than public disclosures reveal.

The study finds that board independence, the extent of ownership's concentration, the extent of leverage, market to book ratio, companies size, financial industry, and years of ERM experience are factors associated with information inconsistency in the setting analyzed. Findings show the proprietary costs' limits of voluntary disclosure dealing with ERM systems, while supporting the decision of the Italian Corporate Governance committee to compulsorily enhance additional disclosure at the aim of improving transparency about these processes. The next section presents the prior studies on risk management disclosure that allow to motivate the need for an explicit focus on the ERM process disclosure and the theoretical background relying on managers' incentives theories used in the paper to develop the hypotheses. Sections about the research design, analysis and results are then provided. Finally, conclusions with a discussion of the key findings.

2 Theoretical Background and Hypotheses Development

Healy and Palepu (2001) claim investors view voluntary disclosures as credible information. Prior literature on risk disclosure has predominantly examined the nature and extent of risk disclosures and their influencing factors by applying content analyses to data collected from annual reports (Buckby et al. 2015). Indeed, most of the prior studies focused on the investigation of risk factors in terms of information quality (Beretta and Bozzolan 2004; Oliveira et al. 2011; Miihkinen 2012; Abraham and Shrives 2014), and their determinants (Linsley and Shrives 2005, 2006; Abraham and Cox 2007; Amran et al. 2009; Hassan 2009; Elshandidy et al. 2013; Elshandidy and Neri 2015). Differently, Buckby et al. (2015) focus on risk management practices disclosure in corporate governance reports.

Risk management information is expected to be increasingly sought by the firm's stakeholders and information users (Lajili and Zeghal 2005). The benefits of enhancing risk management disclosure could be many (Courtnage 1998). For instance, knowledge of the ERM may help investors in assessing the usefulness of financial reports in predicting future cash flows (Baxter et al. 2013). Investors in addition might incorporate risk information into their price decisions and thus improve the market liquidity by reducing information asymmetry (Campbell et al. 2014). Nevertheless, a key constraint on empirical research on management control systems is the lack of information on what corporations do internally (Zimmerman 2001).

Prior scant literature shows corporations disclose only minimal details of their risk management program (Tufano 1996; Maizatulakma et al. 2015; Buckby et al. 2015) and risk management disclosure becomes a compliance exercise (Collier et al. 2007). Further Marshall and Weetman (2002) find evidence that, even for specific risk management practices (i.e. disclosure of foreign exchange risk management) in a mandatory disclosure regime, companies persist to have information asymmetry. Specifically, companies tend to publicly disclose less information in the annual report compared to what they declare privately in a prior questionnaire.

Managers' incentives theories (agency and proprietary costs) are used in the current paper to explain potential variation in voluntary disclosures released by firms (privately vs. publicly). The most adopted agency theory proposes that in public companies the interests of managers diverge from those of the owners (Jensen and Meckling 1976). For the owners, solutions include corporate control mechanisms to counter managerial power and CG to monitor management and improve accountability (O'Sullivan 2000). In the risk literature agency theory has been widely used in the area of disclosure (Abraham and Cox 2007; Oliveira et al. 2011; Tao and Hutchinson 2013; Buckby et al. 2015) and ERM characteristics (Beasley et al. 2005, 2008).

Proprietary cost theory (Verrecchia 1983) instead focuses on the competitive disadvantage of greater disclosure. Proprietary costs indeed include not only the costs of preparing, disseminating and auditing information, but also the cost deriving from disclosing information which may be used by competitors and other parties in a way that is harmful for the reporting company (Prencipe 2004). The threat of economic disadvantage may give rise to disincentives to disclose risk information voluntarily (Dobler 2008). Proprietary cost theory argues that the incentive of disclosing information is a decreasing function of the potential costs attached to a disclosure, and that it is an increasing function of the favorableness of the news in a disclosure (Verrecchia 1983). Whether proprietary costs are higher than the benefits of full disclosure, managers have incentives to not disclose (Prencipe 2004). Abraham and Shrives (2014) adopt proprietary cost theory to explain the behavior emerging from their results, suggesting that company managers prefer providing formal rather than substantial risk disclosures.

2.1 Determinants Hypothesized to Affect Inconsistency on ERM Disclosure

A significant body of literature demonstrates that the monitoring function of corporate governance significantly influences the propensity for better voluntary disclosure (see Patelli and Prencipe 2007). Governance and ownership factors may play a vital role in firms' risk reporting because directors are accountable for the CG report prepared for shareholders. Thus, the governance arrangements of the board of directors can be expected to influence disclosure policy. In particular, relying on Patelli and Prencipe (2007), who focus on the Italian stock market which is dominated by companies characterized by the presence of a dominant shareholder, the current paper investigates two main mechanisms of CG that may affect agency costs in such a context.

First, the presence of independent directors (Abraham and Cox 2007; Lajili 2007). Independent directors are considered to enhance the quality of the board as they are expected to be more unbiased representatives of shareholders due to an assumed absence of conflicts of interest between the principal and the agent (O'Sullivan 2000). Furthermore, Chen and Jaggi (2000) argue that a board comprising more independent directors is more likely to promote high quality performance-related disclosure. Thus, agency theory claims more independent directors may provide greater information on risk and ERM to reduce agency costs, resulting in reduced information asymmetry and lower inconsistency.

Previous research identifies a positive relation between the number of independent directors and voluntary risk disclosure (Abraham and Cox 2007; Oliveira et al. 2011).

Proprietary costs theory expectations are aligned to agency theory. Accordingly, companies with higher percentages of independent directors are expected to have a lower variation between public and private source of information on the ERM process. Thus, it is expected a negative association between the number of independent directors and greater variation between public and private source of information on the ERM process—i.e. inconsistency.

Hyp 1 There is a negative association between the number of independent directors and information inconsistency about the ERM process.

Second, the nature of the specific ownership structure (Abraham and Cox 2007; Kajüter 2006; Lajili 2007). In ownership structures more closely held, agency costs are generally lower (Ball et al. 2000). High concentrated ownership indeed plays a key role in controlling and monitoring the firm mitigating agency costs. Thus, in highly concentrated ownership structure, public disclosure is less needed and proprietary costs of voluntary disclosure higher. On the contrary, in companies less closely held there is more need to monitoring managers' activities, and a greater level of public disclosure is expected given its lower proprietary costs. Therefore, the inverse relation between agency costs and proprietary costs allow to hypothesize—according to both the theories—that highly closely held companies have low agency costs but higher proprietary costs. Thus, showing greater information inconsistency.

Hyp 2 There is a positive association between highly closely held companies and information inconsistency about the ERM process.

Although a range of disclosure studies have documented the impact of various influential CG factors on the level of risk management disclosures, little prior research has addressed the possible impact of companies' risk-related factors (Buckby et al. 2015). Because risk is inherently proprietary in nature (Woods et al. 2008), proprietary cost theory would suggest that higher risky companies disclose less information not willing to attract market attention. A first risk-related factor considered is leverage. Literature on the association between risk disclosures and leverage offers mixed results. Specifically, agency theory by Jensen and Meckling (1976) argues that highly leveraged firms have higher monitoring costs. Such firms may seek to reduce these costs by disclosing more information in their annual report narratives. Nevertheless, most of empirical studies (Linsley and Shrives 2006; Abraham and Cox 2007; Amran et al. 2009; Oliveira et al. 2011) find that leverage in listed companies does not significantly affect risk disclosure. Just Elshandidy et al. (2013) find a positive association between leverage and aggregated risk disclosures.

Whereas, proprietary cost theory suggests that debt is negatively related to corporate disclosure levels: managers of companies having less risk or a better risk management process have less costs of disclosing their better ability; companies having higher risks are less prone to disclose about them because of proprietary costs such as deriving from competitive reasons. To the best of author knowledge, no prior study investigated the relation between leverage and risk disclosure according to proprietary cost theory. Further in the Italian capital market there are factors that seem to support such a theory: firms are composed by a dominant shareholder (Patelli and Prencipe 2007; Allegrini and Greco 2013) find a negative but non-significant relation between leverage and the general level of disclosure. Thus, the current paper hypothesizes a positive relationship between leverage and greater variation between public and private source of information on ERM in the analyzed context.

Hyp 3 There is a positive association between company's leverage and information inconsistency about the ERM process.

Finally, a second risk-related factor is the market to book ratio (Francis et al. 2008; Baxter et al. 2013) measured as the ratio between the firm's market capitalization and the book value of shareholder's equity. According to agency theory and consistent with Buckby et al. (2015) bigger market to book ratio indicates greater expectations about future cash flows than a lower ratio. As future cash flows are inherently uncertain, high market to book ratio firms tend to have more volatile share prices than small market to book ratio firms. Thus, companies with larger market to book ratio are expected to disclose greater amount of information.

According to proprietary cost theory only firms financially sound may be able to trade off the benefits from additional disclosure with the cost of revealing potentially damaging information (Cormier and Magnan 2003). Thus, given higher market to book ratio is interpreted as greater expectation about future cash flows, it is expected these firms are able to better bear proprietary costs despite the greater financial risk and to disclose more information. Therefore, relying on the interpretation of both agency and proprietary cost theories it is expected a negative relation between the market to book ratio factor and greater variation between public and private source of information on the ERM process.

Hyp 4 There is a negative association between company's market to book ratio and information inconsistency about the ERM process.

3 Research Design

3.1 Sample Selection and Data: The Italian Institutional Context

In Italy the debate and regulation on corporate governance emerged around the 2000s. Both financial scandals and financial crisis of those years not only affected the US, but also European countries, and Italy in particular (Florio and Leoni 2017). For this reason, several regulatory reforms took place and Italy was one of the former countries adopting a Corporate Governance (CG) Code drafted by the Italian stock exchange Corporate Governance Committee in 1999. Then reviewed in 2002, 2006, 2010, 2011, 2014 and in 2015. The code is based on the "comply or explain" principle according to which listed companies may decide whether to adopt it. If companies do not comply—fully or partially—they need to explain the reason. The changes in the Italian regulation highlight the importance of board structure and the independent directors as a means to overcome Italian market weaknesses such as the markedly concentrated ownership and the trend for large owners to expropriate minority shareholders (Elshandidy and Neri 2015).

Since the 2011 Corporate Governance revision, greatest attention has been put on risk with a specific appendix included to discuss the importance of risk management disclosure. The revision recommends the creation of an integrated system of internal control and risk management (Borsa Italiana 2011; art. 7.C.1.a). The Internal Control and Risk Management shall be integrated and treated as a unitary system focused on risks, and integrated within the overall organizational, administrative and accounting system of the firm (Florio and Leoni 2017). It follows the board commitment in disclosing, within the CG report, about the main internal control and risk management system's characteristics (Borsa Italiana 2011; art. 7.C.1.d; see Table 1).

Thus, the choice of an Italian sample may be useful from an international perspective considering the possible interest in the results by a European audience. The obligation in directive 2006/46/CE to describe the risk management systems requires the explanation of risk management functions, policies, structures, and procedures. The resulting risk governance requirements and recommendation for listed companies by each European member State reveals how the Italian context is the only one (not only at the European level) recommending and requiring through the Corporate Governance code or laws all the following:

- specific provisions describing the board responsibilities for risk management;
- the establishment of a board-level committee charged with risk management;
- the implementation of the internal control and risk management system;
- the identification of a person in charge of risk management (OECD 2014).

Further, in 2015 Risk Management duties were partially increased. Specifically, it was introduced the obligation to "transparently disclose in the Corporate Governance report the coordination among people and bodies designed to the Internal Control Risk Management System" (Borsa Italiana 2015; art. 7.C.1 lett. D). The Corporate Governance committee which approved the revised code invited the companies to apply the changes within the following year reporting. Thus, the recent 2015 review of the CG code compulsorily enhances the disclosure on the risk management process.

Furthermore, it has to point out how a mandatory description of the main risks and uncertainties is requested in the Management Discussion and Analysis (MD&A) section of the annual report since Legislative Decree no. 32/2007 that modified Article 2428 of the Civil Code (Elshandidy and Neri 2015). Therefore, managers have already to explain in detail all of the risks faced by their company during the past year, and how they have managed these risks, in their annual reports. However, the focus of the current paper is on the ERM process disclosure, thus attention is on the annual CG report.[1]

The sample is drawn from companies listed into the ordinary market of the Italian Stock Exchange at the end of the years 2013 and 2015.[2] The year selection is driven by two main reasons. First, in 2011 there was the greatest amendment of the Italian Corporate Governance code effective from 2012. The choice of the year 2013 aims at reflecting a sufficient time for listed companies to achieve compliance to the 2011 revision of the code in particular about the risk management duties. Given the partially increased duties of the risk management system in 2015, CG reports referring to this fiscal year are the last ones before the revised code. Thus representing the last year in which companies can disclosure more information on internal control and risk management system on voluntary basis. Therefore, the period selection constitutes a time frame in which there have been no institutional changes about risk management duties to disclose in the CG report. Thus helping to better investigate the voluntary disclosure on the ERM process. Second, survey methodology asks for repeating the survey after two years at the aim of increasing reliability to the analysis.

In total, the author received 75 completed surveys (32 in 2013 and additional 43 in 2015). She excluded 9 companies because of incomplete questionnaires or due to missing CG reports (4 in 2013; 5 in 2015), leaving a final sample of 66 companies for the analysis.[3]

Table 2 provides the profile of the sample. In terms of positions held by the respondents, individuals serving in high-level positions (i.e., board members, internal auditors, Chief Risk Officers and top managers) represent more than 50% of the respondents. The classification of the represented industries relies on the Italian Stock Exchange (Borsa Italiana) website. More than one third of the respondents in the sample (34.84) are industrial (manufacturing) companies, followed by financial industry (19.70%) which includes both banks and insurance companies. Public services entities—mostly utilities—represent the 12.12% of the sample. In terms of

---

[1]An analysis on MD&A section has been done as a robustness check but information about the risk management process are exclusively provided in the CG reports.

[2]In line with prior studies to assure homogeneity of listing requirements, those companies listed in the Star Segment and the Nuovo Mercato Segment have been excluded from the analysis (see Beretta and Bozzolan 2004; Florio and Leoni 2017).

[3]The sample size depends on different reasons. First, the high difficulty of data access in Italy and to set data on this context given the small size of the Italian stock market. Second, the complexity of collecting data on internal processes as already highlighted by prior studies (Zimmerman 2001). Nevertheless, the overall response rate reflects about the 30% of the total number of Italian listed companies (on average 255 in the main Italian market in the considered time span excluding those companies not compliant to the CG code). In addition, the response rate is higher than previous studies adopting the survey methodology (see Beasley et al. 2005; Paape and Speklé 2012). Further, there are many prior studies on risk disclosure with a similar sample size (see for instance, Beretta and Bozzolan 2004; Allini et al. 2016). Finally, considering Italy is the 8th largest country in the world based on GDP and it has an advance environment in terms of risk management disclosure since 2011, the data collected represent the ERM practices of a large part of the Italian market capitalization (about the 40% of the total market capitalization in the years of analysis).

revenues size, almost 50% of the companies range between €25 million and €500 million. Only a few companies have revenues lower than €25 million. In addition, more than half of respondents (56.06%) indicate their organizations have adopted an enterprise risk management process for at least 3 years. Therefore, it is expected that ERM process as described both in the survey and in the CG reports is quite developed.

4 Three-Stage Approach

The analysis is based on a three-stage approach. First, to investigate the ERM internal practices, an online survey tool consisting of 30 questions has been structured relying on the ERM definition developed by the Committee of Sponsoring Organizations of the Treadway Commission (COSO) in the 2004 framework[4] and its fundamental concepts.[5]

The ERM definition reflects certain fundamental concepts, which are highlighted explicitly in the COSO framework, according to which "Enterprise risk management is:

1. A process, ongoing and flowing through an entity;
2. Effected by people at every level of an organization;
3. Applied in strategy setting;
4. Applied across the enterprise, at every level and unit, and includes taking an entity-level portfolio view of risk;
5. Designed to identify potential events that, if they occur, will affect the entity and to manage risk within its risk appetite;
6. Able to provide reasonable assurance to an entity's management and board of directors;
7. Geared to achievement of objectives in one or more separate but overlapping categories."

From the operational point of view, most of the survey's questions require a five-point scale response developed according to prior literature (see details in the Appendix). The two highest options are considered to represent an ERM implementation according to the COSO (2004) definition, while the three lowest options are not considered to be reflective of an ERM component. Survey data are coded according to the score obtained by respondents; a value of 0 is attributed in case of no answer to the items of interest related to each of the seven fundamental concepts.

[4]The author is aware of the changed ERM definition according to the recent COSO draft (2016) which states the following: *The culture, capabilities, and practices, integrated with strategy-setting and its execution, that organizations rely on to manage risk in creating, preserving, and realizing value.* However, given the intention to investigate the level of ERM implementation in the Italian setting the author choices to rely on the most adopted framework (Hayne and Free 2014; and as supported by results) at the period of analysis.

[5]Enterprise Risk Management—Integrated Framework Executive summary (2004).

Table 2 Profile of the sample

	2013	2015	Total number of respondents	% number of respondents
Respondents position held				
Board member	–	2	2	3.03
Chief risk officer	6	4	10	15.15
Internal auditor	6	3	9	13.64
Top manager (CEO/CFO)	4	10	14	21.21
Middle manager	10	17	27	40.91
Not available	2	2	4	6.06
N	28	38	66	100
Industry represented				
Chemical and basic material	–	1	1	1.52
Consumer goods	4	6	10	15.15
Consumer services	–	3	3	4.55
Financial	6	7	13	19.70
Health care	–	1	1	1.52
Industrial	10	13	23	34.84
IT	4	1	5	7.57
Oil and gas	–	2	2	3.03
Public services	4	4	8	12.12
Revenues				
€0 ≤ x ≤ €5 million	2	7	9	13.64
€5 million ≤ x ≤ €25 million	1	1	2	3.03
€25 million ≤ x ≤ €100 million	8	8	16	24.24
€100 million ≤ x ≤ €500 million	6	11	17	25.75
€500 million ≤ x ≤ €1 billion	3	8	11	16.67
x > €1 billion	8	3	11	16.67
Year of ERM adoption				
Less than 6 months	5	12	17	25.76
At least 1 year	3	9	12	18.18
At least 3 years	6	11	17	25.76
At least 5 years	12	5	17	25.75
10 years	2	1	3	4.55

The second stage of the analysis is based on the hand collection of respondents CG reports related to the year of survey collection (i.e. 2013 survey matched with 2013 CG report and 2015 survey with 2015 CG report). A thematic content analysis (Buckby et al. 2015) has been done on the CG reports section regarding the internal control and risk management system. Specifically, information has been categorized according to themes corresponding to the seven ERM fundamental concepts and related items of interest (see Table 3). Data have been categorized as categorical variables ranging from 0 to 5 to investigate public disclosure as well, where the value of 0 reflects no disclosure on the specific item.

Finally, once coded both the survey and the report for each company, the author summed up the scores attributed to each item to define an ERM score ranging from 0 to 53 for both the disclosure sources (private and public). To verify the level of ERM disclosure variation the author computes the difference between the scores attributed respectively to the report and the survey, specifically as:

$$ERM\_Variation\_Index = ERM\_Report\ Score - ERM\_Survey\ Score \quad (1)$$

ERM_Variation_Index if positive is interpreted as an overstatement in the public disclosure; vice versa, if negative, as an understatement of the ERM process in the public voluntary disclosure. To better analyze the extent of ERM_Variation_Index and its determinants, such a score is distinguished into two sets (high vs. low) representing the level of information INCONSISTENCY between the sources of disclosures. It amounts to the dummy dependent variable on which the hypothesized CG and firm's risk characteristics are regressed (as outlined below).

4.1 Research Model for Testing Hypotheses

A Probit model is used to test the association between INCONSISTENCY and the hypothesized determinants[6]:

$$\begin{aligned} INCONSISTENCY = {} & \beta_0 + \beta_1 BOARD + \beta_2 OWNERSHIP \\ & + \beta_3 LEVERAGE + \beta_4 MTB\_RATIO \\ & + \beta_5 CONTROL\ VARIABLES + \varepsilon \quad (2) \end{aligned}$$

Control variables are justified as following. First, based on agency theory, high-quality risk disclosure is needed for large firms to satisfy the requests of a larger group of stakeholders (Amran et al. 2009). In addition, larger companies have an incentive to improve investors' confidence and reduce political sensitivities by providing higher quality risk disclosure (Hassan 2009). Previous studies reveal a positive association between firm size and risk disclosure quantity (Linsley and Shrives 2005,

[6]A detailed definition of each variable is provided at Table 5.

Table 3 Description of report and survey coding

COSO ERM fundamental concepts	ERM items of interest	Description	Report (n = 66)		Survey (n = 66)		Test of difference	
			Mean	S.d.	Mean	S.d.	T-test of means (two-sided)	Test of median Wilcoxon test
1. A process, ongoing and flowing through an entity	1	Extent of ERM implementation	1.575758	2.327499	3.924242	1.256498	−8.8959***	−5.929***
2. Effected by people at every level of an organization	2a	Training activities about risk and risk management	0.1363636	0.7822328	3.318182	1.266845	−17.625***	−7.025***
	2b	Business plan resource allocation for ERM	1.69697	2.183643	2.969697	1.380855	−3.9513***	−3.557***
3. Applied in strategy setting	3	ERM relation with strategic planning	2.712121	2.021158	3.469697	1.349868	−3.0417**	−2.368**
4. Applied across the enterprise, at every level and unit, and includes taking an entity-level portfolio view of risk	4a	Identification and prioritization of risks	2.484848	2.451012	4.727273	0.5696275	−7.8719***	−5.687***
	4b	Methodology used for risk prioritization	1.060606	0.5038315	1.666667	0.4750169	−5.5177***	−4.588***
	4c	Extent of integration in risk prioritization	1.30303	1.968754	3.939394	0.8923398	−11.556***	−6.605***

(continued)

Table 3 (continued)

COSO ERM fundamental concepts	ERM items of interest	Description	Report (n = 66)		Survey (n = 66)		Test of difference	
			Mean	S.d.	Mean	S.d.	T-test of means (two-sided)	Test of median Wilcoxon test
5. Designed to identify potential events that, if they occur, will affect the entity and to manage risk within its risk appetite	5a	Frequency of risk reporting	1.363636	2.027779	3.636364	1.260481	−8.9105***	−6.096***
	5b	Temporal orientation of risk reporting	0.1818182	0.5793655	1.712121	0.4562439	−17.598***	−7.171***
6. Able to provide reasonable assurance to an entity's management and board of directors	6a	ERM process accountable person	1.742424	1.791524	2.484848	1.243351	−3.3193**	−3.169**
	6b	Frequency of ERM managers meetings	4.242424	1.627273	3.575758	1.489043	2.7690**	3.267**
7. Geared to achievement of objectives in one or more of separated but overlapping categories	7	Level of comprehensiveness (range) of risks considered	2.757576	2.411897	3.924242	1.206528	−3.9771***	−2.743**
Overall average score			21.29 out of 53		30.12 out of 53			

2006; Abraham and Cox 2007; Dobler et al. 2011; Elshandidy et al. 2013). In addition, larger companies also have the expertise and resources to cover the cost of producing high-quality disclosure (Miihkinen 2012). Proprietary cost theory indeed would suggest that managers in large firms will disclose more risk information than those in small firms having larger competitive disadvantage. Thus, both the theories support a negative relation between size and information inconsistency about the ERM process.

Second, literature also supported the relationship between performance measures and levels of disclosures. To investigate such relation, the current study analyzes the Tobin's Q ratio measuring the firm's performance on the capital market (Gordon et al. 2009; Hoyt and Liebenberg 2011; McShane et al. 2011). The higher Tobin's Q is, the better is the judgment expressed by the financial market about the company representing a measure of future investors' expectations (Florio and Leoni 2017). Agency theory suggests that managers disclose information for promoting personal interests as a number of prior studies documented the relation between managers' stock-based compensation and extent of disclosures (for all Murphy 1996). Proprietary cost theory would suggest that more profitable companies have lower costs of disclosing information, even if evidence show mixed results (Leuz 1999; Giner et al. 1997). Both the theories therefore suggest a negative relationship between profitability and information inconsistency about the ERM process.

Third, different industries may provide different risk and risk management process disclosure because of industry specific characteristics and regulations. Beretta and Bozzolan (2004) find no relation between industry and risk disclosure. Hassan (2009) instead find a significant relation with variation in corporate risk disclosure. Further, financial industry is quite specific operating under a greater layer of increased regulation and scrutiny (see Basel III; Solvency II; ORSA). As the financial companies constitute the 20% of the total sample, the current study controls for industry effects by including the financial industry as a control variable (Amran et al. 2009). In particular, financial companies being enforced of greater disclosure on risk management effectiveness are expected to signal a lower information inconsistency about the ERM process.

Finally, another factor that can affect ERM disclosure and specifically the (in)consistency between private and public disclosure is for how long the companies have adopted the process (defined as ERM experience). On one side, agency theory would suggest that companies implementing the ERM process for a longer time would be more willing to disclose about it. On the other side, companies having an ERM process for a longer period could incur in higher proprietary costs and therefore are expecting having a greater variation between private and public disclosure. As best of the author's knowledge no prior literature has examined such a relation.

5 Results and Analysis

5.1 Nature and Extent of ERM Disclosures Variation (RQ1)

Findings reveal that companies tend to give more information on their ERM process through the private source (survey) rather than in their public disclosure (CG report). Data provided by the on-line surveys about the internal ERM process are self-reported and cannot be independently verified. Nevertheless, all respondents indicate the company name and their e-mail contact (voluntary option). The author is not aware of any reason why a survey participant would willfully falsify their responses and she believes the responses obtained provide an opportunity to explore information about their internal ERM process. As a way of assurance and to find confirmation about the reliability of the answers, after the analysis, fifteen respondents have been randomly interviewed to better understand how the risk management disclosure process works and if they were in charge of it. The results of this "triangulation" check (Routhbauer 2008) confirmed their high knowledge of the risk management process and their key role in the preparation of the CG report section related to the disclosure of the Internal Control Risk Management System. Thus, assuring the reliability of the data collected through the survey.

Table 3 shows the mean and standard deviation values of each ERM item examined both in the survey and in the report. Additionally, it presents the results of a test of difference in mean and median. Results in detail show that the extent of ERM implementation (item 1) is one of the item most privately disclosed. On average it takes value of 3.9242, while in the public reports its extent is described on average with a value of 1.5758. The most highly privately disclosed item relates to the information about the identification and prioritization of risks (item 4a) with an average value near to the maximum of 5. Whereas, on the voluntary public disclosure side, it is disclosed for a value on average equal to 2.48. Among the most highly privately disclosed items there are also the ones referring to the extent of integration in risk prioritization (item 4c) and to the level of comprehensiveness of risks considered (item 7).

Looking at the public reports, the most highly disclosed factors are the ones referring to the application in the strategy setting (item 3) and to the frequency of risk managers' meetings (item 6b). Specifically, companies on average publicly disclose to link their ERM process to the strategic planning with a value of almost 3 out of the 5 scale, even if privately such a value results higher. The highest value corresponding to the item about the frequency of risk reporting is publicly declared higher than 4, that is at least annually; while in the private disclosure source companies on average declare a value lower than 4.

Overall, from what directly emerge from the surveys, companies on average indicated the presence of 39.12 out of the maximum 53 values that ERM survey score can assume. In contrast, their public CG reports revealed the presence of 21.29 out of the 53 values of the ERM report score. This suggests that while there may be a high degree of ERM maturity (Beasley et al. 2015) within companies, those entities on average are not so willing to voluntary public disclose of it.

The test of difference (two-sided) in means reveals a significant univariate difference for all the twelve items of interest examined. Specifically, the mean is highly negative significantly different ($p < 0.001$) for the items related to: the extent of implementation, the training activities about risk and risk management, the business plan resource allocation for the ERM process, the identification and prioritization of risks, the methodology used for risk prioritization, the extent of integration in risk prioritization, the frequency of risk reporting, the temporal orientation of risk reporting and the level of comprehensiveness. With the exemption of the item related to the frequency of ERM managers' meetings presenting a positive significant difference in mean ($p < 0.05$), the remaining items related to the ERM relation with strategic planning and to the ERM process accountable person show a negative difference in mean ($p < 0.05$). Thus, with the exclusion of the frequency of ERM managers' meetings, all the items present a higher mean for data obtained from a private source of information compared to the public disclosure. Such results are also confirmed by the Wilcoxon test of difference in median.

Given these findings, the author further dug into the ERM voluntary disclosure and the differences between information privately obtained by the companies and publicly available. Figure 1 shows the distribution of the companies per each level of ERM_Variation_Index. The companies of the sample are normally distributed in a range from −40 to +7. With the exemption of the positive extreme of the range, all companies' ERM_Variation_Index present negative sign, stressing the lower level of public disclosure on ERM rather than that obtained from the private channel. The mean of the distribution (−17.86) is considered as the threshold to distinguish firms into two sets: high versus low ERM_Variation_Index (see Table 4). A low variation is considered to be in those firms falling in the interval [−17.86;

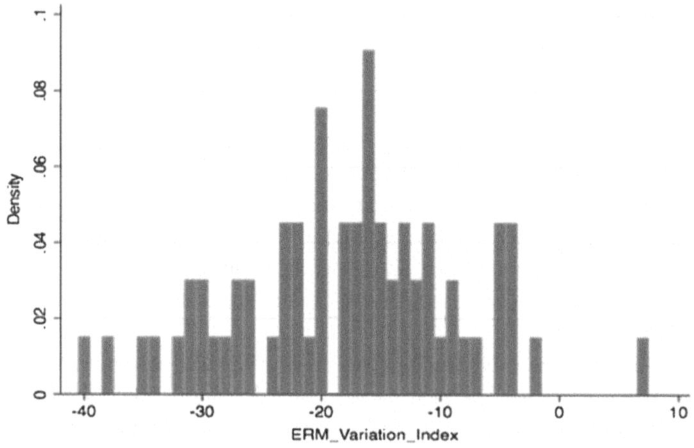

Fig. 1 Distribution of the companies per each level of ERM_Variation_Index

Table 4 ERM disclosure (in)consistency: high versus low variation

ERM_Variation_Index	# Companies	(In)consistency
−40	1	High variation/inconsistency
−38	1	
−35	1	
−34	1	
−32	1	
−31	2	
−30	2	
−29	1	
−28	1	
−27	2	
−26	2	
−24	1	
−23	3	
−22	3	
−21	1	
−20	5	
−18	3	
−17	3	Low variation/consistency
−16	6	
−15	3	
−14	2	
−13	3	
−12	2	
−11	3	
−10	1	
−9	2	
−8	1	
−7	1	
−5	3	
−4	3	
−2	1	
7	1	

+7] and it is interpreted as a higher level of information consistency. Vice versa, results external to such interval are considered to be representative of information inconsistency. According to such a distinction about half of the companies (35 out of 66) are consistent in term of ERM disclosure, while 31 are not. Thus, it follows the aim of the second research question of understanding which are the determinants of the ERM disclosure (in)consistency comparing the two opposite sets (high vs. low variation).

5.2 Determinants of Inconsistency Between Private Source of Information and Public Disclosure on ERM (RQ2)

Descriptive Statistics and Correlation Analysis. Descriptive statistics in Table 5 show the dependent (dummy) variable mean equals to 0.4696 meaning almost 47% of the companies tend to have high disclosure variation. Thereby, on the opposite side 53% of the companies have a low disclosure variation demonstrating relatively consistent private and public disclosures. Corporate governance factor such as board independence variable shows on average boards are composed by 44.48% of independent directors, representing less than half of the board. Companies for the 57.57% are owned by a single person controlling more than the 50% of the shares.[7] The accounting literature generally defines a company as dominated by a controlling shareholder when there is at least one owner who has 10% or more of the voting rights. It must be pointed out that Italian companies, even when listed on an official securities market, are in most cases family controlled. This means that even when a large portion of a company's equity is widespread among investors on the market, there is no real separation between owners and managers (Prencipe 2004).

For what concern firms' risk characteristics, the average amount of leverage is 61.27% showing Italian listed companies mostly rely on debt as tool for financing their activities. The systematic risk of the company on average is pretty high having a mean of 0.7552 (not shown in the Table). Market to book ratio has a mean of 2.831 interpreted as a pretty high undervaluation of stocks in the market. The average of the natural logarithm of revenues is equal to 12; for a better understanding of the amount of companies' revenues see details in Table 2. The market profitability of the companies is on average equals to 0.1083, confirming the undervaluation of the stocks value. Financial companies represent almost the 20% of the sample. Finally, regarding the years of ERM experience, companies on average declare to have implemented the process for a period ranging between 3 and 5 years.

The results of the Spearman rank correlation are presented in Table 6. They show a correlation at 10% level of market to book ratio and the control variable ERM experience with the dependent variable (INCONSISTENCY). Thus, suggesting potential associations also in the regression analysis. Few correlations among independent

[7] Additional descriptive statistics not inserted in Table 5a show ownership concentration in the sample is on average 47.86%.

Table 5 Descriptive statistics

Heading level	Mean	S.d.	Min.	Max.
Dependent variable				
Inconsistency	0.469697	0.5029053	0.00	1.00
Independent variables				
Board	0.4448	0.1582446	0.1538	0.8947
Concentration	0.5757576	0.4980147	0.00	1.00
Leverage	0.6127	0.2098272	0.00055	1.109
Market_to_book	2.831	4.422469	0.07895	26.33
Size_revenue	12.67	2.48213	8.16	23.24
TobinQ	0.1083272	0.5017228	0.0001009	2.901489
Financial	0.197	0.4007569	0.00	1.00
ERM_experience	2.651515	1.24644	1.00	5.00

Notes Variables are described as following: INCONSISTENCY = equal to 1 if ERM_Variation_Index is high, that is negatively beyond the mean (equals to −17. 86364), 0 otherwise (see Table 5). BOARD = number of independent directors out of the total number of directors; OWNERSHIP = a dummy variable equals to 1 if the highest percentage of shares owned by a single shareholder is over the 50%, 0 otherwise. LEVERAGE = defined as the ratio between total liabilities and total assets (sourced by Compustat database); MTB_RATIO = market to book ratio, measured as the market capitalization over the book value of shareholder's equity at the end of the year (Compustat database). SIZE_REVENUE = the natural logarithm of the total revenues (Compustat database); TOBINQ = performance on the capital market at the end of the year, measured as market value of equity plus book value of liabilities divided by the book value of assets (sourced by Compustat database). FINANCIAL = a dummy variable equals to 1 if the company belongs to the financial industry as classified by Borsa Italiana; ERM_experience = how long the companies declare to have adopted the risk management process [1 = less than 6 months; 2 = at least 1 year; 3 = at least 3 years; 4 = at least 5 years; 5 = at least 10 years]

variables are also found. Tests on multicollinearity and endogeneity suggest data do not present such issues.[8]

Inconsistency between Private and Public Disclosure: Determinants. Table 7 presents the results of the empirical Probit model developed to answer the second research question.

Results of the probit model show both the corporate governance characteristics are significantly associated to information inconsistency on ERM. Either the proxy for board independence and the variable related to the percentage of control present the expected sign. Results indeed show the number of independent directors has a negative significant impact on the information inconsistency about the ERM process ($p < 0.05$), while higher levels of ownership concentration positively affect such information inconsistency ($p < 0.1$). Hypotheses 1 and 2 are therefore supported.

[8]Multicollinearity was checked by the variance inflation factor (VIF) test. VIF value of 1.22 for this model ruled out a multicollinearity problem. IVprobit test for endogeneity displays no endogenous variables.

Table 6 Spearman rank correlation analysis

	INCONS.	Board	Owner.	Lev.	Mtb_ratio	Size_rev.	TobinQ	Fin.	ERM_exp
INCONS.	1.000								
Board	−0.080	1.000							
Ownership	0.132	0.111	1.000						
Leverage	0.192	0.204*	−0.082	1.000					
Mtb_ratio	−0.302*	0.012	−0.024	−0.084	1.000				
Size_revenue	0.025	−0.029	0.013	0.184	−0.211*	1.000			
TobinQ	−0.173	0.210*	−0.034	−0.127	0.139	0.139	1.000		
Financial	−0.008	0.176	−0.192	0.363*	−0.281*	−0.021	0.103	1.000	
ERM_exp	0.213*	0.188	−0.046	0.106	−0.154	0.203	0.154	−0.023	1.000

Notes *Correlation is significant at the 0.10 level (two-tailed)

Table 7 Probit model results

Inconsistency	Coefficient
Board	−0.0285908** (0.036)
Ownership	−0.7044636* (0.064)
Leverage	2.525829** (0.020)
Mtb_ratio	−0.1451485** (0.013)
Size_revenue	−0.1461361* (0.071)
TobinQ	6.501505 (0.154)
Financial	−0.9844539* (0.094)
ERM_experience	0.2729999* (0.086)
Constant	0.6978686 (0.579)
No. of observations 66 Prob > Chi^2 0.0025 Pseudo-R^2 0.2602	

Notes Amounts in parentheses are p-values. ***, **, * indicate significance at the 1%, 5%, 10% level, respectively

For what concern firm risk characteristics, a positive and significant result ($p < 0.05$) is found for leverage thus supporting the association stated in hypothesis 3 and contributing to prior mixed results. Results show firms more leveraged are generally less forthcoming in public disclosures about their ERM processes. A significant association ($p < 0.05$) is also found for the market to book ratio variable. In contrast to findings related to leverage, the relation with such a firm risk characteristic is negative. It indicates more consistent information on the ERM process at the companies' financial risk increase. Hypothesis 4 is also supported.

Among control variables companies size and industry have a negative significant association with the dependent variable ($p < 0.1$). This shows that bigger companies have more consistent disclosures supporting expectations. The variable related to industry shows that financial companies are negatively significant related to inconsistency, again supporting expectations. That is, given financial companies have different characteristics, and in particular stronger regulations about risk management it is expected they have greater disclosure consistency. Further, contrary to expectations market firm profitability is not associated to information inconsistency about the ERM process. Finally, interestingly the variable proxying for firm's ERM experience is positively significant associated ($p < 0.1$) to inconsistency; at the enhancement of

Table 8 Probit model on companies having lower versus greater ERM_experience

Inconsistency	Panel A Coefficient	Panel B Coefficient
Board	−0.0266093 (0.429)	−0.0315463* (0.074)
Ownership	0.4272366 (0.718)	1.027232** (0.047)
Leverage	4.977333** (0.025)	2.404916 (0.140)
Mtb_ratio	−1.08703 (0.045)**	0.0575061 (0.601)
Size_revenue	−0.0245758 (0.952)	−0.0912594 (0.288)
TobinQ	−18.4437 (0.541)	5.433301 (0.385)
Financial	−2.183997* (0.067)	0.1258688 (0.882)
ERM_experience	0.1982419 (0.962)	0.4190353 (0.785)
Constant	−0.0266093 (0.429)	−0.0315463* (0.074)
No. of observations	29	37
Prob > Chi^2	0.0024	0.1099
Pseudo-R^2	0.5740	0.2297

Notes PANEL A. Probit model on companies having lower ERM experience (ERM_experience < 3); PANEL B. Probit model on companies having greater ERM experience (ERM_experience ≥ 3)

ERM experience, measured in term of years of adoption, it is found greater information inconsistency about the process.

The tested model has an explanatory power with a pseudo-R^2 equal to 0.2602. Overall, results show that highest levels of disclosure variation on ERM are either associated to CG characteristics and to firm's risk characteristics.

Given the significance of the variable ERM experience, further investigation is requested on this aspect. At this aim the model is tested splitting companies into two sets: those having a shorter experience (less than 3 years of adoption) and those having a longer experience of ERM adoption (equal or longer than 3 years). Results are shown in Table 8 panel A and B, respectively.

Table 8 (panel A) shows how the explanatory power of the model increases to a pseudo-R^2 of 0.5740. Findings reflect a situation in which just firm's risk factors affect information inconsistency on ERM, supporting hypotheses 3 and 4. Specifically, leverage maintains a positive significant association ($p < 0.05$) and market to book ratio a negative significant association ($p < 0.05$) with inconsistency. Whereas, both the CG variables lose their association with the dependent variable. Among the control variables just financial industry ($p < 0.1$) confirm prior results.

Examining data for companies declaring to adopt ERM for longer, Table 8 (panel B) shows instead just CG variables significantly affect ERM information inconsistency, supporting hypotheses 1 and 2. However, no other variable of the model appears affecting the dependent variable in this set.

To summarize, findings of the complete model reveal how both CG variables (board independence and ownership's concentration) and firm's risk factors (leverage and market to book ratio) affect information inconsistency on the ERM process. Nevertheless, controlling for the level of ERM process' experience, interestingly it emerges how in companies adopting the process in recently time the disclosure inconsistency is driven by firm's risk factors, while for companies more mature in terms of ERM adoption the inconsistency is driven just by CG characteristics.

Sensitivity Analysis. A sensitivity analysis on an identical model has been run using an alternative variable to the dummy related to the ownership concentration. Specifically, the highest percentage of shares owned by a single shareholder has been adopted. Results (not shown in the paper) confirm the significant association with the independent variables (hypotheses 1, 2, 3 and 4 are supported). Specifically, it shows a negative and significant relation between board independence, market to book ratio and inconsistency. Whereas, it shows a positive and significant association between ownership concentration and leverage with inconsistency. Among control variable just size maintains the significance.

The slight significance of financial companies' variable in the findings represented in Table 6 would suggest for further investigation. However, given impossibility to run the same model either on non-financial and financial companies because of the small sample of the latter ($n = 13$), Table 9 aims at showing the results of the model just on non-financial companies. Findings confirm the role of both risk factors in the association with information inconsistency (both hypothesis 3 and 4 are supported). CG variables play a partial role in the association with inconsistency: only board independence is found negatively significant (hypothesis 1 is supported; hypothesis 2 is not). Among control variables just size maintains its significance.

Finally, given six of the respondent companies participated to the survey both the years 2013 and 2015, an additional analysis has been run not considering the 2015 data for those companies. In such a way the sample for the two years become more homogeneous with 28 companies in 2013 and 32 in 2015. Results confirm all the hypotheses. Significant associations between CG variables (board independence and ownership concentration at $p < 0.05$) and firm's risk variables (leverage and market to book ratio at $p < 0.05$) are found. The control variables too are confirmed significant as in the original model: companies' size, financial companies and ERM experience (Table 10).

Table 9 Probit model on non-financial companies

Inconsistency	Coefficient
Board	−0.0391189** (0.012)
Ownership	0.5777792 (0.175)
Leverage	3.216437** (0.011)
Mtb_ratio	−0.1362497** (0.037)
Size_revenue	−0. 151717* (0.081)
TobinQ	1.272287 (0.411)
Financial	0.1420315 (0.141)
ERM_experience	1.235772 (0.397)
Constant	−0.0391189** (0.012)
No. of observations 53 Prob > Chi^2 0.0047 Pseudo-R^2 0.2789	

6 Discussion and Conclusions

Over the last years an increasing call has emerged at the international level for effective risk management processes within organizations and for greater transparency about that. Emerging academic research provides limited evidence about the ERM implementation around the world while still little is known about how companies publicly disclose information related to their ERM process. The current paper contributes to prior research offering meaningful insights about which factors companies disclose both publicly and privately, finding some variation between these two sources.

Variation determined as difference between information obtained from CG report and the submitted survey respectively, underlines how companies even if adopting an effective ERM process according to COSO (2004) are sometimes less willing to voluntary disclose of it. Specifically, companies tend to understate information about: the extent of their ERM process implementation; the training activities about risk and risk management put in place; the business plan resources allocated for the ERM process; the ERM relation with the strategic planning; the identification and prioritization of risks; the methodology used for risk prioritization; the extent of integration in risk prioritization; the frequency of risk reporting and its temporal orientation; the ERM process accountable person; and, the level of comprehensive-

Table 10 Probit model with no data 2015 for those companies answering both the survey's years

Inconsistency	Coefficient
Board	−0.0415123** (0.013)
Ownership	1.024538** (0.022)
Leverage	2.73705** (0.018)
Mtb_ratio	−0.1603119** (0.012)
Size_revenue	−0.1725365** (0.050)
TobinQ	6.833866 (0.161)
Financial	−1.040656* (0.097)
ERM_experience	0.4379525** (0.026)
Constant	1.015507 (0.444)
No. of observations 60 Prob > Chi^2 0.0020 Pseudo-R^2 0.2925	

ness of risks considered. These results support previous findings about the company managers' preference of providing risk related disclosure that are formal rather than substantial (Abraham and Shrives 2014; Tufano 1996) understating their effective ERM process.

On the contrary, companies tend to overstate information related to the frequency of ERM managers' meetings. This latter result may be explained by the risk management duties requested by the CG code. Specifically, the need to report to the board at least biyearly (see Table 1). Thus, suggesting potential "boiler plate" information (Woods et al. 2008). It follows, the study additionally investigates which are the determinants of ERM disclosure inconsistency identifying both CG and firms' risk characteristics as significant drivers of it. Among corporate governance characteristics, the association with board independence is stronger than the one between ownership's concentration and ERM disclosure inconsistency. The study also finds that firm's risk characteristics such as leverage and market to book ratio are significantly associated to ERM disclosure inconsistency, even if according to opposite signs. Companies having a greater level of debt tend to be more inconsistent on ERM disclosure supporting the results by Elshandidy et al. (2013) which identify leverage as a determinant of risk voluntary disclosure; while, companies having greater market to book ratio present a negative sign of the association, showing greater consistency. Both results support proprietary cost theory expectations. These findings may contribute to prior results and to a still understudied relation between firm's risk characteristics and ERM process disclosure (Buckby et al. 2015).

Among control variables, firm size and financial industry have a light negative significant influence on ERM disclosure inconsistency. This in line with the expected sign according to both the tested theories. The latter finding about financial companies, in particular, suggests that the greater specific regulations requested for those firms—including also disclosure on ERM—is not so much reflected into their CG reports. In addition, it is found a positive and slightly significant relation with the so called ERM experience—the years of ERM adoption the companies declared. Such a positive relation appears to support proprietary cost theory according to which companies limit voluntary disclosure when proprietary costs emerge from it. Information on the ERM process is perceived proprietary in nature, mainly at the beginning of the companies ERM experience, thus affecting the decision by the firms to not fully disclose about it. Indeed, a deeper investigation shows this variable has an impact on results when the sample of companies is split according to a shorter or longer ERM experience. Such additional investigation helps to verify that for companies with lower ERM experience the greater disclosure inconsistency on the process is driven by firm's risk factors. In contrast, for those companies having greater ERM experience the drivers of disclosure inconsistency are corporate governance variables, in particular the fact of being closely held by a single owner, condition pretty common in the context analyzed. In line with the results by Buckby et al. (2015) which find that board independence does not impact on the level of risk management disclosure in the Australian context, the additional test finds that this factor does not affect so much inconsistency between public and private source of information on ERM. Thus suggesting that board independence acts just partially as control mechanisms of information asymmetry on such a topic. The relationship between ERM and CG is of interest to regulators because less concentrated ownership and independent directors are expected to reduce agency problems (Abraham and Cox 2007). Therefore, the results of the current study demand for carrying on the international reflection about the need for reducing regulatory intervention on corporate reporting.

Thus, all together the findings mainly support proprietary cost interpretation, the additional analysis based on the distinction of shorter versus longer ERM experience helps to orient even more towards such an interpretation in contrast to the agency one.

The paper has both theoretical and practical implications. First, from a theoretical point of view, it contributes to literature on risk disclosure focusing on risk management practices instead of risk factors. Second, the paper originally contributes to the literature benefiting of private information on the internal ERM process and comparing such information to public disclosure of it. In addition, the study investigates a new variable (ERM experience) which is found to affect the ERM process disclosure and that asks for future investigations. Third, prior research mainly analyzes non-financial setting while the current study takes into account also financial companies surprisingly showing that such industry does not affect so much the analyzed relation. Finally, results contribute to the recent risk management disclosure stream of literature not focusing on the annual report but investigating other kind of public sources such as the CG reports (Buckby et al. 2015; Florio and Leoni 2017) extending prior studies focusing on the Italian context (Arena et al. 2011; Elshandidy and Neri 2015; Florio and Leoni 2017). In particular, the paper contributes to prior findings given the double perspective offered by data obtained through a survey compared to what companies publicly voluntary disclose. The resulting inconsistency between the two sources suggests a general understatement of public voluntary disclosure and a potential underestimation of the investors' benefits prior international literature identifies. Thus, due to perceived proprietary costs that companies suffer, additional research is needed to identify the potential benefits that companies might have when disclosing more informative disclosure on ERM.

From a practical point of view, the results appear to support the decision of the Italian stock exchange CG committee to increasing transparency through the compulsorily enhancement of the risk management process disclosure. In particular, given riskier companies tend to have higher variation scores, the findings would suggest not only for a mandatory disclosure regime but also for the adoption of a stricter rule-based approach instead of a principle-based approach. Indeed, just because riskier companies publicly disclose less, it is expected that if they are asked to be compliant to a principle-based approach on ERM process disclosure they continue to act in the same way (in the absence of a CG report audit). A further investigation of the same context after the year 2015 may provide empirical evidences on the superiority, or not, of a mandatory disclosure on risk management processes.

The paper's results may lead to contribute to the international increasing attention and push on Enterprise Risk Management (ERM) as part of good CG, and to the debate about the different investors' benefits from the enhancement of risk management disclosure (Baxter et al. 2013; Campbell et al. 2014). The study can shed light to understand if CG reports information content is informative to stakeholders given also the international increasing interest for the assessment of companies' "management and governance". Specifically, such assessment, with reference to the effectiveness of risk management processes, is based on information (mostly not publicly disclosed) provided by the entity to rating agencies as part of the credit evaluation process (see Standard & Poor's 2012). Therefore, finding public disclosure on ERM process is undervalued compared to the internal process described through private disclosure, the research empirically shows how—in the analyzed context—ERM public disclosure may not be informative about the effective quality of "management and governance". Thus, requiring further investigation.

Findings can also contribute to the academic call to investigate the dilemma between better and more regulation, in times where the issue of compliance and risk management becomes more important for top management (AIDEA 2017). The paper suggests the limits of voluntary disclosure regulation and the conditions under which this happened showing how companies tend to not fully disclose their effective internal ERM process. Specifically, the paper allows to identify the presence of disclosure's proprietary costs associated to CG and firm's risk characteristics, and the condition under which they became manifest—that is the years of ERM experience. These are factors the regulators should take into account when recommend information on such a topic. Finally, the study can also contribute to the current debate about the Integrated Reporting (IIRC IR 2013).

The paper however presents many limitations. First of all, the sample size associated to the specificity of a voluntary disclosure context could affect the generalizability of results in different settings. Second, the construction of the variables leave room for alternatives; sensitivity analysis attempt to mitigate such a limitation. Future research that captures potential inconsistency between private and public disclosure on ERM in different settings could enable to extend the debate. Finally, an analysis of the same context after the 2015 CG code review may help to investigate changes in the behavior of the company under a stricter disclosure regime.

Acknowledgements The author is grateful to the editors and the reviewers for their insightful comments and the support provided during the review process. In its earlier version, the article benefited from the feedback provided by the attendees at AIDEA conference, Rome, Italy, 14–15 September 2017 where the paper has been awarded as Emerging scholar colloquium—Best Paper Award and at ERRN 8th European Risk Conference, Katowice, Poland, 20–21 September 2018.

Appendix: Survey

The survey questions about an ERM process were developed using the seven fundamental concepts defining ERM from the COSO framework as a basis. Twelve questions in the survey map to the seven fundamental concepts from COSO to operationalize them. Thus, scores based on the 12 factors were created based on the survey responses and scores based on the same 12 factors were created based on the reading of the CG reports. Specifically, as summarized in Table 3, the first concept—defining ERM as a process on-going and flowing through the entity—is composed by one factor identifying the extent of ERM implementation (Paape and Speklé 2012). The second concept relates to the participation extent of people at every level of the organization. Therefore, the two factors by which it is composed respectively ask for training activities (Beasley et al. 2015) and business plan resources allocated to the ERM process (NCSU & Protiviti report 2016). Both these factors indeed aim at widening the ERM scope among people within the organization.

The third fundamental concept is about the application in the strategy setting and thereby the factor investigates the relation of ERM with strategic planning (Frigo and Anderson 2011; Beasley et al. 2015; COSO framework draft 2016). The fourth concept is composed by three factors investigating the identification and prioritization of risks, the methodology used for risk prioritization, and the extent of integration[9] in risk prioritization to verify the application of the process across the enterprise (Arena et al. 2011; Paape and Speklé 2012). In particular, Arena et al. (2011) in their study based on the Italian setting find that generally an entity's risk evaluation method comprises a combination of qualitative and quantitative techniques. Also

[9]The integration concept introduced by Arena et al. (2011) refer to how risks are governed within all levels and functions of an organization.

other studies find a combination of the two methodologies (Woods 2009; Jordan et al. 2013; Mikes 2009). Thus, for this factor based on a three-point scale and related to the methodology used for risk prioritization, it is attributed a 1 only in the case both the methodologies are applied by the company, 0 otherwise.

Then, the ERM process according to the fifth concept needs to be designed to identify potential events that, if they occur, will affect the entity and to manage risk within its risk appetite. A crucial element to identify potential events is a frequent communication in terms of risk reporting (Paape and Speklé 2012). Thus, the current study aims to investigate the frequency of risk reporting and its temporal orientation (back vs. forward-looking). Considering the proactive aim of ERM, the coding choice is to attribute a 1 if respondents answer forward-looking, 0 otherwise.

The sixth concept relates to the ERM process' ability to provide reasonable assurance to an entity's management and board of directors. Beasley et al. (2005) is the first study identifying Chief Risk Officer role (or a person having the same role but with a different title) as a good proxy for ERM effectiveness. The presence of such a person in charge for the process can provide the requested reasonable assurance of the ERM process (Baxter et al. 2013; Ellul and Yerramilli 2013). Another related factor providing assurance to the process is the frequency of risk managers' meetings. Finally, the seventh concept geared to the achievement of objectives in one or more separate but overlapping categories is operationalized in a question asking for the level of comprehensiveness (i.e. range of risks) considered (Arena et al. 2011). Risks can be classified according many overlapping categories linked to the companies' goals, such as strategic, operative, compliance and reporting (COSO 2004; AICPA & NCSU 2016). Wider and more holistic level of risks comprehensiveness considered can contribute to overcame a silo-based approach and to the companies' objectives achievement.

For a detail about the survey/report factors and corresponding five-point scale answers see the following.

Concept 1. A process, ongoing and flowing through an entity

Item 1. How much has Enterprise Risk Management (ERM) process been implemented?

1. Risk management is mainly incident-driven; no plans exist to implement ERM.
2. We actively control risk in specific areas (e.g. health & safety, financial risk); we are considering to implement a complete ERM.
3. We identify, assess and control risk in specific areas; we are planning to implement a complete ERM.
4. We identify, assess and control strategic, financial, operational and compliance risks; we are in the process of implementing a complete ERM.
5. We identify, assess and control strategic, financial, operational and compliance risks; ERM is an integral part of the (strategic) planning & control cycle.

Concept 2. Effected by people at every level of an organization

Item 2. Are training activities about risk carried out?

1. Not at all
2. Minimally
3. Somewhat
4. Mostly
5. Extensively

Item 3. Are business plan resources allocated to ERM initiatives?

1. Not at all
2. Minimally
3. Somewhat
4. Mostly
5. Extensively

Concept 3. Applied in strategy setting

Item 4. To make stronger the responsibilities is there a relation between capital allocation, budget decisions and identified risks? Namely, risk management process is related to strategic planning?

1. Not at all
2. Minimally
3. Somewhat
4. Mostly
5. Extensively

Concept 4. Applied across the enterprise, at every level and unit, and includes taking an entity-level portfolio view of risk

Item 5. Do you identify and prioritize risks?

1. No at all
2. Minimally
3. Somewhat
4. Mostly
5. Extensively

Item 6. Which kind of methodology do you use to prioritize risks:

1. Qualitative: phenomenon description;
2. Quantitative: phenomenon description in monetary terms;
3. Both

Item 7. What is the extent of integration in risk prioritization?

1. Not at all widespread
2. Uncommon
3. Spread just at top levels: board and top management
4. Spread in the majority of the organization: board, top and middle managers
5. Enterprise widespread: board, top and middle managers and operative levels

Concept 5. Designed to identify potential events that, if they occur, will affect the entity and to manage risk within its risk appetite

Item 8. What is the frequency of general risk reporting?

1. Every 3 years or never
2. Once a year
3. Every 9 months
4. Twice a year (every 6 months)
5. Every 3 months or less

Item 9. Temporal orientation of risk reporting:

1. Past-looking (overcame risks)
2. Forward-looking (expected risks)

Concept 6. Able to provide reasonable assurance to an entity's management and board of directors

Item 10. Who is accountable for ERM process?

1. CEO
2. Internal Auditor
3. Board
4. Chief Risk Officer
5. Others (specify)

Item 11. ERM managers meeting: what is their frequency?

1. Every 3 years or never
2. Once a year
3. Every 9 months
4. Every 6 months
5. Every 3 months or less

Concept 7. Geared to achievement of objectives in one or more separate but overlapping categories

Item 12. What is the level of comprehensiveness—range of risks considered (strategic, operative, compliance and reporting risks…)?

1. Not at all
2. Minimally
3. Somewhat
4. Mostly
5. Extensively

References

Abraham, S., Cox, P.: Analysing the determinants of narrative risk information in UK FTSE 100 annual reports. Br. Account. Rev. **39**(3), 227–248 (2007)

Abraham, S., Shrives, P.J.: Improving the relevance of risk factor disclosure in corporate annual reports. Br. Account. Rev. **46**(1), 91–107 (2014)

AICPA & NCSU: The State of Risk Oversight: An Overview of Enterprise Risk Management Practices. Available at: https://erm.ncsu.edu/az/erm/i/chan/library/AICPA_ERM_Research_Study_2016.pdf (2016)

AIDEA: "New Trends" in Business Economics and Management Studies Rewriting the Relationship between Business and Society. http://www.accademiaaidea.it/wpaidea/wp-content/uploads/2016/12/CFP-AIDEA-2017-ENG1.pdf (2017)

Allegrini, M., Greco, G.: Corporate boards, audit committees and voluntary disclosure: evidence from Italian listed companies. J. Manage. Governance **17**(1), 187–216 (2013)

Allini, A., Manes Rossi, F., Hussainey, K.: The Board's Role in Risk Disclosure: An Exploratory Study of Italian Listed State-Owned Enterprises. Public Money and Management (2016). http://dx.doi.org/10.1080/09540962.2016.1118935

Amran, A., Bin, A.M.R., Hassan, B.C.H.M.: Risk reporting: an exploratory study on risk management disclosure in Malaysian annual reports. Manag. Audit. J. **24**(1), 39–57 (2009)

Arena, M., Arnaboldi, M., Azzone, G.: Is enterprise risk management real? J. Risk Res. **14**(7), 779–797 (2011)

Ball, R., Kothari, S.P., Robin, A.: The effect of international institutional factors on properties of accounting earnings. J. Account. Econ. **29**(1), 1–51 (2000)

Baxter, R., et al.: Enterprise risk management program quality: determinants, value relevance, and the financial crisis. Contemp. Account. Res. **30**(4), 1264–1295 (2013)

Beasley, M., Branson, B., Pagach, D.: An analysis of the maturity and strategic impact of investments in ERM. J. Account. Public Policy **34**(3), 219–243 (2015)

Beasley, M.S., Clune, R., Hermanson, D.R.: Enterprise risk management: an empirical analysis of factors associated with the extent of implementation. J. Account. Public Policy **24**(6), 521–531 (2005)

Beasley, M., Pagach, D., Warr, R.: Information conveyed in hiring announcements of senior executives overseeing enterprise-wide risk management processes. J. Account. Audit. Financ. **23**(3), 311–332 (2008)

Beretta, S., Bozzolan, S.: A framework for the analysis of firm risk communication. Int. J. Account. **39**(3), 265–288 (2004)

Borsa Italiana: Codice di Autodisciplina. Available at: http://www.borsaitaliana.it/comitato-corporate-governance/codice/2011.pdf (2011)

Borsa Italiana: Codice di Autodisciplina. Available at: http://www.borsaitaliana.it/comitato-corporate-governance/codice/2015clean.pdf (2015)

Brown, I., Steen, A., Foreman, J.: Risk management in corporate governance: a review and proposal. Corp. Gov.: Int. Rev. **17**(5), 546–558 (2009)

Buckby, S., Gallery, G., Ma, J.: An analysis of risk management disclosures: Australian evidence. Manag. Audit. J. **30**(8/9), 812–869 (2015)

Campbell, J.L., et al.: The information content of mandatory risk factor disclosures in corporate filings. Rev. Account. Stud. **19**(1), 396–455 (2014)

Chen, C.J.P., Jaggi, B.: Association between independent non-executive directors, family control and financial disclosures in Hong Kong. J. Account. Public Policy **19**, 285–310 (2000)

Collier, P.M., Berry, A.J., Burke, G.T.: Risk and Management Accounting: Best Practice Guidelines for Enterprise-Wide Internal Control Procedures, vol. 2. No. 11. Elsevier (2007)

Cormier, D., Magnan, M.: Environmental reporting management: a continental European perspective. J. Account. Public Policy **22**(1), 43–62 (2003)

COSO: Enterprise risk management—Aligning Risk with Strategy and Performance. Available on the internet at http://www.coso.org (2016)

COSO: Enterprise risk management. Available on the internet at http://www.coso.org (2004)
Courtnage, S.: Financial reporting of risk. Tolley's Pract. Audit. Account. **9**(6), 61–63 (1998)
Dobler, M.: Incentives for risk reporting: a discretionary disclosure and cheap talk approach. Int. J. Account. **43**(2), 184–206 (2008)
Dobler, M., Lajili, K., Zéghal, D.: Attributes of corporate risk disclosure: an international investigation in the manufacturing sector. J. Int. Account. Res. **10**(2), 1–22 (2011)
Ellul, A., Yerramilli, V.: Stronger risk controls, lower risk: evidence from U.S. bank holding companies. J. Finance **68**(5), 1757–1803 (2013)
Elshandidy, T., Neri, L.: Corporate governance, risk disclosure practices, and market liquidity: comparative evidence from the UK and Italy. Corp. Gov.: Int. Rev. **23**(4), 331–356 (2015)
Elshandidy, T., Fraser, I., Hussainey, K.: Aggregated, voluntary, and mandatory risk disclosure incentives: evidence from UK FTSE all-share companies. Int. Rev. Financ. Anal. **30**, 320–333 (2013)
EU Parliament and Council: Directive 2001/65/CE, del 27 settembre 2001, che modifica le direttive 78/660/CEE, 83/349/CEE e 86/635/CEE per quanto riguarda le regole di valutazione per i conti annuali e consolidati di taluni tipi di società nonché di banche e di altre istituzioni finanziarie (2001)
EU Parliament and Council: Directive 2006/46/CE, del 14 giugno 2006, che modifica le direttive del Consiglio 78/660/CEE, relativa ai conti annuali di taluni tipi di società, 83/349/CEE, relativa ai conti consolidati, 86/635/CEE, relativa ai conti annuali e ai conti consolidati delle banche e degli altri istituti finanziari, e 91/674/CEE, relativa ai conti annuali e ai conti consolidati delle imprese di assicurazione (2006)
EU Parliament and Council: Directive 2013/36/UE, del 26 giugno 2013, sull'accesso all'attività degli enti creditizi e sulla vigilanza prudenziale sugli enti creditizi e sulle imprese di investimento, che modifica la direttiva 2002/87/CE e abroga le direttive 2006/48/CE e 2006/49/CE (2013)
European Parliament and Council: Regulation (UE) n. 575/2013, del 26 giugno 2013, relativo ai requisiti prudenziali per gli enti creditizi e le imprese di investimento e che modifica il regolamento (UE) n. 648/2012 (2013)
European Parliament and Council: Directive 2009/138/CE, del 25 novembre 2009, in materia di accesso ed esercizio delle attività di assicurazione e di riassicurazione (solvibilità II) (2009)
Florio, C., Leoni, G.: Enterprise risk management and firm performance: the Italian case. Br. Account. Rev. **49**(1), 56–74 (2017)
Frigo, M.L., Anderson, R.J.: Strategic risk management: a foundation for improving enterprise risk management and governance. J. Corp. Account. Financ. 81–88 (2011)
Francis, J., Nanda, D.J., Olsson, P.: Voluntary disclosure, earnings quality, and cost of capital. J. Account. Res. **46**(1), 53–99 (2008)
Giner, B., Ruiz, A., Cervera, N., Arce, A.: Accounting policy choice and the disclosure of segmental information: Spanish evidence. In: Paper Presented at the 20th EAA Annual Congress, Graz, April (1997)
Gordon, L.A., Loeb, M.P., Tseng, C.: Enterprise risk management and firm performance: a contingency perspective. J. Account. Public Policy **28**(4), 301–327 (2009)
Hassan, M.K.: UAE corporations-specific characteristics and level of risk disclosure. Manag. Audit. J. **24**(7), 668–687 (2009)
Hayne, C., Free, C.: Hybridized professional groups and institutional work: COSO and the rise of enterprise risk management. Account. Organ. Soc. **39**(5), 309–330 (2014)
Healy, P., Palepu, K.: Information asymmetry, corporate disclosure, and the capital markets: a review of the empirical disclosure literature. J. Account. Econ. **31**, 405–440 (2001)
Hoyt, R.E., Liebenberg, A.P.: The value of enterprise risk management. J. Risk Insur. **78**(4), 795–822 (2011)
IIRC: The International Integrated Reporting Framework. www.theiirc.org (2013)
IRDCEC: Documento n. 1. La Relazione sulla Gestione. Alcune considerazioni. Roma: Istituto di Ricerca dei Dottori Commercialisti e degli Esperti Contabili (2008)
Jensen, M.C., Meckling, W.H.: Theory of the firm: managerial. J. Financ. Econ. **3**, 305–360 (1976)

Jordan, S., Jørgensen, L., Mitterhofer, H.: Performing risk and the project: risk maps as mediating instruments. Manag. Account. Res. **24**(2), 156–174 (2013)
Kajüter, P.: Risk disclosures of listed firms in Germany: a longitudinal study. In: 10th Financial Reporting & Business Communication Conference, July, Cardiff Business School: Unpublished (2006)
Lajili, K.: Board characteristics, ownership structure and risk disclosures: Canadian evidence. In: 30th Annual Congress of the European Accounting Association, April, Lisbon: Working Paper (2007)
Lajili, K., Zeghal, D.: A content analysis of risk management disclosures in Canadian annual reports. Can. J. Adm. Sci. **22**(2), 125–142 (2005)
Leuz, C.: Proprietary versus Non-Proprietary Disclosures: Voluntary Cash Flow Statements and Business Segment Reports in Germany. Working Paper, Department of Business and Economics, Johann Wolfgang Goethe-Universitat, Frankfurt (1999)
Linsley, P.M., Shrives, P.J.: Examining risk reporting in UK public companies. J. Risk Financ. **6**(4), 292–305 (2005)
Linsley, P.M., Shrives, P.J.: Risk reporting: a study of risk disclosures in the annual reports of UK companies. Br. Account. Rev. **38**(4), 387–404 (2006)
Marshall, A., Weetman, P.: Information asymmetry in disclosure of foreign exchange risk management: can regulation be effective? J. Econ. Bus. **54**, 31–53 (2002)
Maizatulakma, A., et al.: Risk management disclosure: a study on the effect of voluntary risk management disclosure toward firm value. J. Appl. Account. Res. **16**(3), 400–432 (2015)
McShane, M.K., Nair, A., Rustambekov, E.: Does enterprise risk management increase firm value? J. Account. Audit. Financ. **26**(4), 641–658 (2011)
Miihkinen, A.: What drives quality of firm risk disclosure? The impact of a national disclosure standard and reporting incentives under IFRS. Int. J. Account. **47**(4), 437–468 (2012)
Mikes, A.: Risk management and calculative cultures. Manag. Account. Res. **20**(1), 18–40 (2009)
Murphy, K.J.: Reporting choice and the 1992 proxy disclosure rules. J. Account. Audit. Financ. **11**(3), 497–515 (1996)
NCSU & Protiviti.: Executive Perspectives on Top Risks for 2016. Key Issues Being Discussed in the Boardroom and C-Suite. Research Conducted by North Carolina State University's ERM Initiative and Protiviti. Available at: https://www.protiviti.com/sites/default/files/united_states/insights/nc-state-protiviti-survey-top-risks-2016.pdf (2016)
OECD: Risk Management and Corporate Governance, OECD Publishing. Available at: http://dx.doi.org/10.1787/9789264208636-en (2014)
Oliveira, J., Lima Rodrigues, L., Craig, R.: Risk-related disclosures by non-finance companies. Manag. Audit. J. **26**(9), 817–839 (2011)
O'Sullivan, N.: The impact of board composition and ownership on audit quality: evidence from large UK companies. Br. Account. Rev. **32**(4), 397–414 (2000)
Paape, L., Speklé, R.F.: The adoption and design of enterprise risk management practices: an empirical study. Eur. Account. Rev. **21**(3), 533–564 (2012)
Patelli, L., Prencipe, A.: The relationship between voluntary disclosure and independent directors in the presence of a dominant shareholder. Eur. Account. Rev. **16**(1), 5–33 (2007)
Prencipe, A.: Proprietary costs and determinants of voluntary segment disclosure: evidence from Italian listed companies. Eur. Account. Rev. **13**(2), 319–340 (2004)
Rothbauer, P.: Triangulation. In: Given, L. (ed.) The SAGE Encyclopedia of Qualitative Research Methods. Sage Publications, Beverly Hills (2008)
Standard and Poor's: Methodology: Management and Governance Credit Factors for Corporate Entities and Insurers. S&P, New York (2012)
Tao, N.B., Hutchinson, M.: Corporate governance and risk management: the role of risk management and compensation committee. J. Contemp. Account. Econ. **9**, 83–99 (2013)
Tufano, P.: Who manages risk? An empirical examination of risk management practices in the gold mining industry. J. Financ. **51**(4), 1097–1137 (1996)

Whitman, A.F.: Is ERM legally required? Yes for financial and governmental institutions, no for private enterprises. Risk Manag. Insur. Rev. **18**(2), 161–197 (2015)

Woods, M.: A contingency theory perspective on the risk management control system within birmingham city council. Manag. Account. Res. **20**(1), 69–81 (2009)

Woods, M., Dowd, K., Humphrey, C.: Market risk reporting by the world's top banks: evidence on the diversity of reporting practice and the implications for international accounting harmonisation. Span. Account. Rev. **11**(2), 9–41 (2008)

Verrecchia, R.E.: Discretionary disclosure. J. Account. Econ. **5**, 179–194 (1983)

Zimmerman, J.L.: Conjectures regarding empirical managerial accounting research. J. Account. Econ. **32**(1–3), 411–427 (2001)

Forward-Looking Information Disclosure as a Risk Factor in Accounting—The Case of Poland

Ewelina Papaj-Wlisłocka and Marzena Strojek-Filus

Abstract Contemporary accounting faces a full range of challenges in addressing the growing need for information from financial statements. Non-financial information disclosures are becoming increasingly common and important. Especially for the largest Polish companies its' disclosure is a legal obligation. Among non-financial information, forward-looking disclosures might be considered crucial, as they are bound with a certain level of risk for both the entity and the recipients of the financial statement. In this paper the problem of risk in accounting will be analysed from the perspective of the forward-looking disclosures. This paper aims to investigate the relationship between the type and range of forward-looking information disclosures and the problem of risk in the accounting system, which is an emerging research area on Polish ground. The main goal of this paper is to present the general concept of forward-looking information disclosures and their associations with risk factors. The research method applied in the theoretical part of the paper is a critical analysis of the available literature and law regulations on the topic. The paper also features an empirical part which examines the forward-looking information in financial statements of companies quoted on the Warsaw Stock Exchange. There is a very limited number of studies that cover forward-looking disclosures in Poland. Therefore, a preliminary study conducted in this paper might serve as a basis for an extended research. The study bases on the content analysis method, which along with the usage of text analysis software is a widespread tool in international studies. General results indicate a relatively low level of forward-looking information disclosures, which could indicate an aversion towards risk in accounting. However, a variation of results among industries may be observed.

Keywords Risk in accounting · Non-financial information · Forward-looking information

E. Papaj-Wlisłocka (✉) · M. Strojek-Filus
University of Economics in Katowice, ul. 1 Maja 50, 40-287 Katowice, Poland
e-mail: ewelina.papaj@ue.katowice.pl

P. Linsley et al. (eds.), *Multiple Perspectives in Risk and Risk Management*, Springer Proceedings in Business and Economics,
https://doi.org/10.1007/978-3-030-16045-6_5

1 Introduction

Conducting an economic activity is inherent and commonly associated with the risk borne by entrepreneurs. Dynamic changes in business practice cause some shifts in the assessment of the scope and degree of relevance of various risk types. At the same time, economic entities face greater social awareness and wider dimension of accountability than only narrowly understood economic processes implemented by them. This, in turn, forces those entities to focus more on their image in order to reduce the risk of losing good reputation.

The accounting system plays a crucial role in the process of mitigating risk in business operations. It is the main source of information about the financial position of the entity. Sets of such information are presented by means of financial statements. However, in recent years, external users of such information are in practice increasingly interested in non-financial data, which lets them analyse the situation of entities in a broader context and identify less common areas of risk. Traditional financial information seems to be insufficient for rational decision making. Investors and other financial statement recipients require information connected to future plans of the companies. For this reason, the importance of reporting non-financial data is increasing, in particular the type, scope and way of presenting the forward-looking information. As much as risk is a hugely important concept in this area, its relationship with prospective data is not ambiguous. Forward-looking information can be a useful source of information for investors and can reduce the asymmetry of information. On the other hand however, such disclosures might inspire harmful responses from the competition and generate the risk of not fulfilling the committed plans. The research question in this article is associated with examining the scope of forward-looking information disclosures among Polish companies.

The authors would like to study and preliminarily assess the importance of forward-looking non-financial data on the example of companies quoted on the Warsaw Stock Exchange. The main aim is to analyse whether the scope of forward-looking information disclosure in Polish companies matches the level of disclosures observed in foreign studies. Empirical research was carried out on the basis of the content analysis method enhanced by text analysis software.

The conducted research constitutes the first stage of a multidimensional research evaluating the importance of forward-looking disclosures in the practice of enterprises in Poland. Main contribution of this paper is to implement idea of empirically researching the forward-looking information disclosures into Polish accounting studies. The intention of the authors is also to start the discussion around the phenomenon of prospective data disclosures in the light of the concept of risk.

2 Theoretical Background

2.1 Definition of Risk

Risk is inseparably bound to the decision-making process within various types of human activity (Renn 1998). It is often linked to the concept of uncertainty. For the first time, the distinction between these two concepts was introduced by A. H. Willett already in 1901 (Janasz 2009). Knight (1921) extended the interpretation of the terms 'risk' and 'uncertainty', emphasising the measurability of the former. Uncertainty can be defined as a state of the lack of knowledge whether a given statement about the future is true (Messiasz 2010). The concept of risk can be related to both positive and negative phenomena. However, in most cases it refers to negative consequences (Rosa 1998). Renn (1998) and Aven (2010) emphasise the diversity of approaches to the subject of risk. The literature often points to etymology of 'risicum' notion in the Latin language, translated as the probability of both positive and negative events, success or failure (Nahodko 2001; Thlon 2013). Other definitions of this concept can be indicated on the basis of law or management theory. Kelman (2003) draws attention to a certain regularity in defining risk. On the ground of exact sciences, definitions are precise and generally refer to risk measurement methods. On the contrary, social sciences consider risk in a specific context and relate it to the cultural factor. Table 1 presents exemplary risk definitions, with reference to the diversity of the approaches to define risk.

Two concepts of risk in the context of economic activity are specified in the literature: traditional concept of hazard (the classical Markowitz model) and risk concept as dispersion of outcomes (Markowitz 1952). In the first case, the risk is measured by an array of portfolio rates of return. In the second case, the risk is measured by the semi-variance from the assumed rate of return. As part of the basic risk division, the following can be distinguished: external risk, internal risk and random risk (Szczepankiewicz 2016).

From the economic entity's operations' perspective, one can indicate the following risk groups (Bizon-Górecka 2004):

- managerial,
- financial,
- organizational,
- technological,
- reputational.

The differences in the aspect of terminology are also worth remembering. Different classifications might specify the same category of risk in a different way (Kelliher et al. 2011). An important difference is that risk can be managed in contrast to uncertainty, which is not quantifiable and is a psychological category (Raczkowski and Tworek 2017). Various accounting instruments are adopted in the framework of risk management, in particular non-financial data reporting.

Table 1 Exemplary approaches to risk definitions

Approach	Definition	Author
By risk effects	Risk is a deviation from the expected value of the assumed goal	Gardner and Mills (1988: 212)
By probabilistic or statistical measures	Risk is a measurable probability of an impending event	Markowitz (1959)
By risk sources	The source of risk is inaccurate or incomplete information	Kreim (1988: 45)
By category of decisions made after completing goals	Risk is related to future events or results of decisions. The decisions made can lead to both unexpected losses and profits	Sierpińska and Jachna (1993: 232)
By the economic value	The possibility of events, or combinations of events, which can have a negative impact on the economic value of an enterprise as well as the uncertainty over the outcome of past events	Kelliher et al. (2011)
By human value	The possibility that human actions or events lead to consequences that affect the aspects of human value	Renn

2.2 *Risk in Accounting*

Risk is inherent to the decision-making process. In turn, it underlies all economic processes, particularly conducting business operations by economic entities and capital groups. Risk occurs whenever a choice is made between different actions requiring a correct analysis and assessment of multiple factors. When it comes to entities conducting economic activity, there is a two-fold analysis. The first of these is related to the assessment of the entity's situation and its prediction created by the managers of that entity. They can use all the available macro-, microeconomic and operational data sources. The management accounting system is of particular importance in this process.

As a part of the second type of analysis, external users, especially investors, assess the financial condition of the entity using primarily the data reported by it in the financial and non-financial statements. The financial statements are 'past' reports presenting the assets and financial results of operations in the reporting period. However, non-financial data may refer to both the past and current status, as well as future periods.

Entities (organisations) are perceived as a set of contracts concluded between various agents involved in the commitment and use of resources. These agents contribute negotiated resources in exchange for an entitlement to a share of resources. Sounder explains the accounting as 'a mechanism that is designed to support and sustain this system under the tensions of conflicting incentives.

Based on the accounting system, entities should identify risk factors and measure them in a timely manner. On the other hand, the functioning of the accounting system is also based on making the right choices and making decisions related to them. Therefore, the use of the accounting system is also subject to risk. Habelman (2014) draws attention to the issue of the impact of risk on the implementation of the accounting function.

Financial information disclosed in the financial statement is a crucial factor in identifying and limiting the risk for financial statements users. However, nowadays such data is insufficient and the scope of disclosures should be expanded (e.g. Cabedo and Tirado 2004). The problem of information asymmetry between internal and external users in the area of decision making process is becoming more visible (Greenwald and Stiglitz 1990). The concept of behavioral risk in companies can also be observed, which is a reaction to political, environmental and other kind of changes.

Non-financial information is of growing importance, as it allows the investor to assess the market position and entity's development possibilities. Non-financial data may relate to areas such as:

- entity's influence on the natural environment,
- employment policy, including trade union activities,
- organisation and functioning of internal control,
- top management, rotation of board members,
- cooperation with local communities,
- diversity policy.

Non-financial information fulfill a double role in accounting system. Primarily, they create an appropriate background for the analysis of financial data and enable broadening the scope of interpretation of its results. Moreover, they play an increasingly important role in identifying and reducing the risk of companies.

Altman et al. (2010) underline their importance especially for medium-sized and small non-quoted enterprises. Their research shows that non-financial information can be particularly important for creating credit risk model. Such kind of data can be effective predictors of companies' crediting possibilities.

The significance of non-financial information in reducing the risk in the area of law changing and environmental problems is also worth mentioning. Obligation to disclose data considering employment policy, diversity, as well as environmental issues might be an incentive for managers to create positive image of companies and to limit image and behavioral risk. The example of such process is implementation of obligatory disclosures concerning environmental issues (Strojek-Filus et al. 2017).

However, non-financial information can also have a negative impact as far as risk is concerned. It is mainly connected to voluntary disclosures, which might be used by managers to improve marketing image of company. The specifics of non-financial information, which is difficult to compare and easy to relativise might also lead to misleading the financial statements users. This shows the ambiguity in the connection between those disclosures and risk. Non-financial information (especially forward-looking) might reduce the risk but at the same time can cause it both for company and for reports' users. Forward-looking information might be crucial for credit institution as indicators (Bulletin of Department of Banking and Finance, Georgia 2018). Such indicators can promote the identification of emerging risks and tend to be more predictive of future performance.

2.3 Forward-Looking Disclosures

Non-financial data disclosed by the companies within the management report can be divided by their time perspective into forward-looking information and historical information, also known as backward-looking information (Hussainey 2004). Backward-looking information can be defined as a description of events related to past performance of the entity. Thus, the backward-looking information presented in the report concerns the already executed events and their results, and they are not burdened with the risk of uncertainty of their fulfilment. Forward-looking data, on the opposite, considers future activity of the entity and future forecasts (Aljifri and Hussainey 2007). It covers, inter alia, future investment activities, forecasted revenues of the entity, sales plans, planned actions in the area of improving the sales offer (Orens and Lybaert 2013). These examples mentioned are projections, which implies that they are burdened with a high degree of risk. Investors, who constitute a large group among recipients of financial statements, tend to consider the prospective data very useful in their decision-making processes (Abed et al. 2016). An unquestionable difficulty when analysing forward-looking data is the lack of their unambiguous definition (Papaj 2017).

Disclosing prospective data is sometimes faced with criticism, as it involves risk derived from the uncertainty of predicting the future. Incorrect or imprecise forecasts might impose unfavourable decisions taken by the recipients of reports and eventually leading to lawsuits (Hail 2002). Thus, the disclosure of prospective data, the use of which may prove detrimental to investors, may involve very high compensation costs in the event of lost court proceedings. Potential high costs associated with misleading forecasts are undoubtedly one of the key factors discouraging companies from disclosing prospective information (Celik et al. 2006).

An interesting solution aimed at encouraging entities to disclose forward-looking information is the safe harbour statement clause. It is a tool widely used in the United States (Baginski et al. 2004). The safe harbour clause allows to protect the company from liability for losses resulting from decisions taken under the influence of unfulfilled prospective information. In practice, the safe harbour clause is a statement of the company's management board, in which it informs that the data on future activities of the entity presented in the financial statements involves risk due to its particularity and therefore the entity is not liable for the eventual outcome of the forecasts. In addition, the management board ensures that it has made every effort to reliably inform the recipients of reports on future intentions, however, taking into account the rapid changes observed in the business environment, it will never be able to ensure their full attainment. The proposal to introduce the clause reminiscent of the safe harbour statement within Polish accounting was first proposed by Krasodomska (2014), but so far it has not become a common solution among Polish companies.

Another argument against the publication of prospective data is competition. The forward-looking data disclosed in the financial statements are an object of interest not only of investors but also of competitors. It can be exceptionally dangerous that with an easy access to forward-looking information they could gain knowledge of the investment plans of the entity and its plans for the future. This may be used against the company (Healy and Palep 2001). As a result, companies have to balance between the benefits of universal access to prospective data and the risk of harmful endeavours of the competitors.

Business activities of the 21st century cannot rely solely on historical data, effective investment decision-making must be supported by data concerning the future (Wang and Hussainey 2013). The data presented in the reports must adapt to the dynamic economic environment, which cannot be achieved basic on classic backward-looking information (Kieso and Weygandt 1995). As the research results show, investors are more willing to invest their funds in transparent companies, considering a large number of disclosures to be a determinant of their integrity, reliability and professionalism (Bujaki et al. 1999; Amir and Lev 1996). Credibility is another important feature associated with disclosing forward-looking data, as it manifests efforts to reduce the information gap and provide the recipients with high quality information. This, together with expressing the entity's focus on the future, constitutes a useful tool for building positive reputation (Hammond and Slocum 1996; Helm 2007; Francis and Schipper 1999).

All the presented considerations demonstrate that forward-looking information disclosures are a multidimensional subject and its relationship with the concept of risk is ambiguous. Taking into account the Polish perspective of forward-looking information disclosures, the scope of disclosures is not legally regulated and it depends solely on a voluntary decision of the company. At the same time it is worth mentioning that Poland implemented the assumptions of Directive 2014/95/UE into Polish accounting system which main aim is to establish a certain minimal legal requirement for the extent of the non-financial information. However, these regulations do not apply to the scope of forward-looking information disclosures. Lack of an institutional factor enhances the significance of the planned research. It aims to contribute to the Polish financial system by presenting the scope of forward-looking information disclosures among Polish companies which are associated with a certain level of risk. A particularly important subject is the freedom of disclosures which allows investigating whether the companies are willing to disclose data that could generate risk. It will be the first such research on the ground of Polish accounting. The main goal of the authors is to present general trends in forward-looking disclosures in

Poland and to start a discussion about the companies' approach to the risk associated with such disclosures.

3 Research Design and Methodology

3.1 Sample and Data Collection

Empirical studies of forward-looking information disclosures relate to the analysis of the scope of published management report, also referred to as management board commentary. As it has been emphasised in the introduction, no comprehensive empirical studies have been carried out on the scope of prospective data disclosures in Poland. The results of surveys conducted abroad indicate that within the framework of management reports, prospective data contribute to around 15–20% of the volume of the report (Bujaki 1999; Clatworthy and Jones 2003). As a part of foreign research, it has been noted that companies definitely prefer to disclose positive forward-looking information, thus increasing the number of potentially interested investors.

In our study, the research sample consisted of 63 management reports of companies quoted on the Warsaw Stock Exchange. Companies, which have been selected in research, represent the largest business sectors: chemical industry, mining and metallurgy, banks, energetics, fuel industry, pharmacy and biotechnology, IT companies and plastic industry. They were chosen for a research sample. The reporting period was the year 2016. At the time of preparing the source materials for research, this was the most up-to-date data. The acquired source materials came from the official websites of the companies and were posted in the investor relations section. Since this is the first research covering forward-looking information in Poland, it has been decided to conduct a single country research.

3.2 Content Analysis and Text Analysis Software

Empirical research covering the idea of the incentives for risk in reporting use three main methodological approaches which have been adopted in international studies (Elshandidy et al. 2018). We identified: questionnaires, disclosure indices and content analysis method (Beretta and Bozzolan 2004). The most common is manual or automated content analysis method which examines the number of sentences or words in a given report. Content analysis is a widely use research method for studying sources which might be in text, picture or audio format (Bryman and Bell 2011). The simplest and most objective form of content analysis bases on unambiguous characteristics of the text such as word frequencies or the page area devoted to one issue in the report. In European studies, the content analysis method has been used by Beretta and Bozzolan (2004), Linsley and Shrives (2006), Malafronte et al. (2016), Abraham and Cox (2007), Miihkinen (2012), Elshandidy et al. (2013, 2015). It is also worth mentioning that in the era of very fast new technologies development one could observe increasing popularity of automated content analysis over the manual content analysis. Among adoption of automated content analysis, literature differentiates three main approaches: the dictionary method, supervised learning and unsupervised learning (Bao and Datta 2014).

In the case of examining prospective data, the usage of content analysis method should start with the question about the scope of disclosures, population selection as well as the relevance of the context (Krippendorff 2004). Forward-looking disclosures as a type of voluntary narrative disclosures were measured as part of BMF's framework (Beattie et al. 2004). Forward-looking information disclosures and their connections with risk were object of a very limited number of empirical studies (Carlon et al. 2000; Robb et al. 2001; Shrives and Linsley 2002; Hussainey et al. 2003; Beretta and Bozzolan 2008). They have become an inspiration for the authors of the article to conduct a similar research in Poland. This paper utilises the dictionary method, which relies on specific key words and counting the frequency of their occurrence (Kravet and Muslu 2013; Elshandidy and Neri 2015). The research tool used in the conducted research is text analysis software. The software largely replaces the manual analysis of disclosed data, and also due to the automation of the processes, reduces the risk of errors. Foreign scientists mainly use the Nudist or NVivo programmes for this purpose (Hussainey and Walker 2003; Al-Najjar and Abed 2014). In the presented paper, the studies were automated using W-Labs Professional Report Analyzer 2.0. The application identifies and examines data disclosures in management reports by implementing natural language processing and the content analysis method.

The input taken by the software includes a list of keywords that would be the basis for searching through the reports. Due to the lack of research on the empirical verification of forward-looking disclosures within the Polish literature, the key words list has been modelled basing on the foreign literature (Breton and Taffler 2001; Walker and Tsalta 2001; Abed et al. 2016). As the reports have been presented in the Polish language, the key words had to be adapted to the specificity of the language. Every effort has been made to avoid a literal translation from original languages and at the same time to adapt key words to the principles of the Polish language. Keywords used in the study are presented in a summary in Table 2.

The keywords presented in Table 2 were used to search for forward-looking disclosures. In contrast to the research carried out by Krasodomska (2014), it was not limited to analysing the table of contents. The automation of the study using dedicated software enables the study of extensive reports, which outputs more precise results.

The program divides management reports into sentences. Next, it searches for the indicated keywords to determine in what percent of the sentences there appear references to the future activity of the entity. In order to limit the impact of repeated words in one sentence on the test result, an additional condition was introduced to the software that if a keyword appears more than once in the examined sentence, it

Table 2 List of forward-looking information

List of forward-looking questions
Anticipate, projections, expect, coming financial years, coming months, coming year, the future, future, future plans, future plans, future intentions, probable, possibilities, possible, probably, goal, future goals, forecasted goals, forecasted, forecast, to forecast, forecasts, coming, is coming, hope, intend, intentions, we intend, intention, we look ahead, looks ahead, look into the future, looks into the future, we look to the future, look into the future with hope, we look into the future with hope, in the next period, perspectives, perspective, planned, soon, in the coming years, further development, establishing cooperation

will still be counted as one. This way, the influence of frequent repetitions of words in extended sentences has been limited, as management reports are often full of such sentences.

This method of course may result in slight discrepancies between actual values and achieved results, nonetheless, the generated indices can be considered a close approximation of the substantial scope of disclosures. Moreover, it should be noted that basing on the literature, the fact of subjectivism of indices created by researchers of accounting does not eliminate the usefulness of this research method (Marston and Shrives 1991; Botosan 1997).

With reference to the calculated frequency of occurrence of prospective data, the FDI (prospective data disclosures index) has been formulated. It has been inspired by the research carried out by Aljifri and Hussainey (2007) on 46 companies quoted on the Dubai Stock Exchange. The FDI indicator used as part of the study has the form:

$$FDI = FD/TD \quad (1)$$

where: FDI—forward-looking data disclosure index in the management report (forward disclosure index); FD—sentences with prospective disclosures (forward disclosures); TD—total number of sentences in the management report (total disclosures).

Figure 1 explains the steps and procedures followed in calculation the disclosure scores.

4 Results and Discussion

The first stage of the research was volume analysis of Management Commentaries. Table 3 presents basic data related to the volume of audited reports. As it was presented in Table 3, the largest volume of reports (management reports) measured in the number of pages was characteristic for banks, companies from the fuel, energy and IT sectors. The least extensive reports were published by companies from the plastics industry and those operating within pharmacy and biotechnology. Interestingly, the smallest coefficient of variation concerns the plastics industry, in which

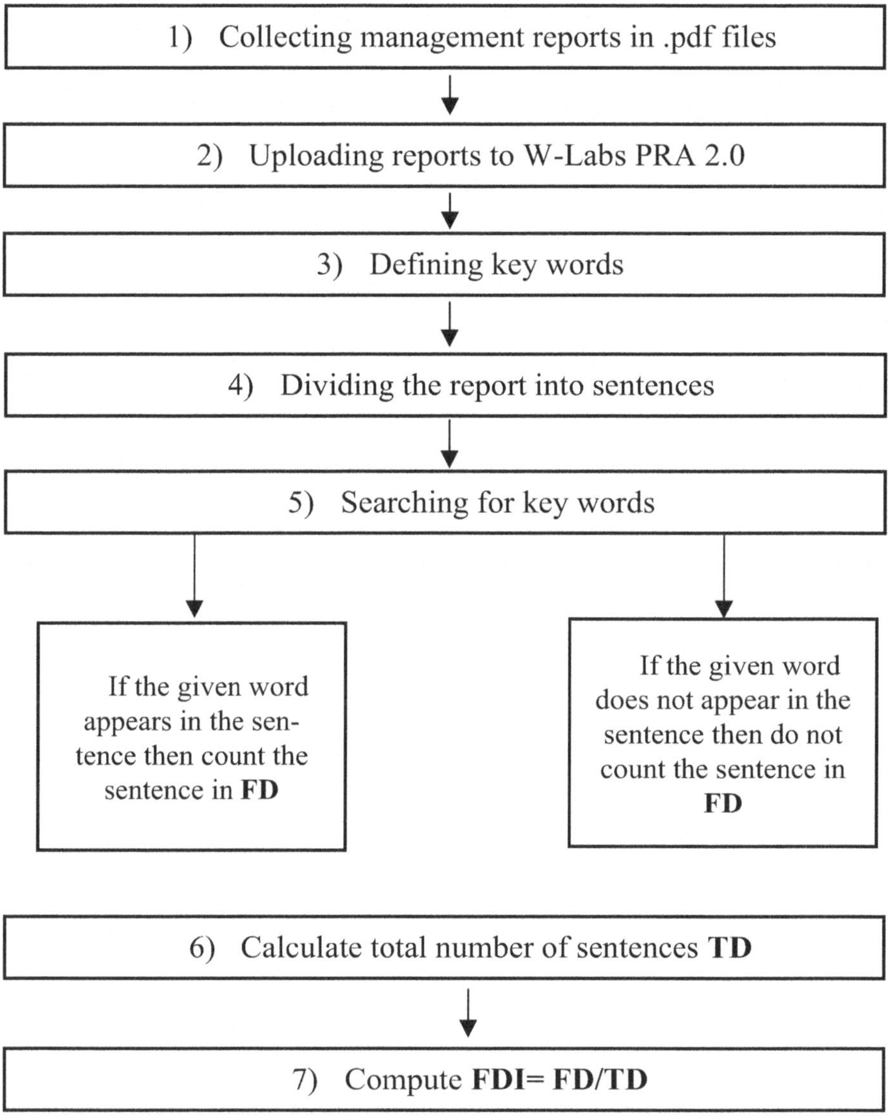

Fig. 1 Methodology for obtaining forward looking information disclosure index

Table 3 Management commentary—report volume analysis

Industry	N	Minimum	Maximum	Mean	Standard deviation	Coefficient of variation (%)
Chemical industry	6	20	104	79.50	30.31	38.13
Mining and metallurgy	7	41	124	73.00	36.46	49.95
Banks	12	49	198	107.83	40.46	37.52
Energetics	8	25	143	84.13	38.29	45.51
Fuel industry	3	58	174	126.33	60.70	48.05
Pharmacy and biotechnology	10	28	93	57.70	21.26	36.85
IT companies	10	29	141	60.50	33.87	55.98
Plastic industry	7	30	49	40.43	7.25	17.93

Table 4 Disclosure of forward-looking information

Industry	FDI disclosure	Minimum FDI	Maximum DFI	Standard deviation	Coefficient of variation
Chemical industry	7.13	2.88	8.96	2.29	32.12
Mining and metallurgy	5.91	4.10	8.93	1.75	29.61
Banks	8.33	6.66	9.77	0.96	11.52
Energetics	8.19	4.90	10.95	2.11	25.76
Fuel industry	6.78	6.33	7.45	0.59	8.70
Pharmacy and biotechnology	11.86	4.60	25.64	6.46	54.47
IT companies	7.26	4.82	11.72	2.40	33.06
Plastic industry	6.17	4.26	9.64	2.16	35.01

Notes data presented in %

the smallest volumes of reports are observed and, therefore, the smallest variability between them. The highest level of variation coefficient was observed in the IT sector.

Table 4 presents the results of the forward-looking information disclosures index (FDI) among Polish companies. The data indicate that the highest percentage of prospective disclosures occurs in the companies operating in the area of pharmacy and biotechnology. In the reports from this industry however, high coefficient of variation can be observed. This can lead to the conclusion that the high rate of disclosures does not apply to all entities under investigation.

The next industry in which a high level of prospective data disclosures has been observed are banks. What differs banks from the previously discussed companies is a low coefficient of variation. This can be explained by legislative issues. Banks as public trust institutions are subject to very restrictive reporting rules that oblige them to maintain high standards of the presented reports. Due to the fact that these regulations apply to all banks, these entities have a very similar scope of disclosures, hence the low coefficient of variation.

Similar trends can be seen in the fuel industry. The lowest coefficient of variation, demonstrating low diversity of prospective disclosures, was observed in that area, though it is characterised by low average value of prospective data (only 6.78%). The lowest scope for presenting forward-looking data was observed in case of mining and metallurgy as well as in companies related to plastics. The obtained results can be explained by conditions resulting from the particular features of those industries.

Taking into account the adjustment processes and the desire to create an ever better image, the companies from the financial sector, such as banks and technology-related companies such as pharmacy and biotechnology, IT and energy, are the leaders. On the other hand, there remain companies related to plastics, mining and metallurgy, which, due to the decrease in popularity of delivered goods and services, do not pay much attention to disclosing data related to future operations. That appears to be fully justified considering the uncertainty of the further development of these industries.

The presented research is undoubtedly of preliminary nature. In the future, both the sample and the research period will certainly need to be extended. Nevertheless, it should be noted that even a relatively small research sample gives the opportunity to make some preliminary conclusions. Firstly, the relatively low percentage of disclosed prospective data is significant (the maximum result obtained is 11.86%, whereas the international studies reported the prospective data disclosure rate at 15–20%). The low scope of prospective data disclosures in Polish companies can be explained primarily by the high risk associated with this type of disclosure (both from the point of view of possible economic losses—in case of claims caused by the lack of a safe harbour clause and taking into account the risks associated with harmful behaviour of competition), and finally, it should be taken into account that the non-financial data disclosure, in particular prospective information, is not a very popular topic in Poland. It could be said that Polish companies are just learning the principles of non-financial reporting, which may also explain the results obtained. An interesting observation was the analysis of the coefficient of variation, which may lead to a question about issues of the prospective disclosure legislation. This, as shown on the example of banks, may reduce the variability within the reports published by entities.

5 Conclusion

The disclosure of prospective data can undoubtedly be considered one of the new challenges which modern accounting faces. Despite the arguments for both disclosing them and against doing so, one can hardly disagree with the statement that a changing business environment requires an increasing amount information, emphasising the importance of informing about future intentions. A major issue related to forward-looking information is undoubtedly the aspect of risk, which has been discussed both on the theoretical level and on the example of Polish companies' practices. Arguably, the modern world's economy expects from accounting as an information system a greater 'commitment' from its current and potential tools, particularly supported by advanced technology, in the process of risk mitigation.

Changes in the reporting of both financial and non-financial data and the increase in the importance of the latter indicate the need to take into account new or less common risk areas. In the opinion of the authors of this paper, this process will intensify the evolution of the structure and scope of the accounting system. Until now, risk research and management was mainly related to insurance (risk-based and simultaneous risk-bearing) and banking operations. Currently, it is also considered with regard to entities operating in other sectors. This is a very dynamically developing area of accounting theory.

In the opinion of many theoreticians and practitioners, risk management becomes a standard that requires proper adaptation in the accounting system of economic entities. Research carried out in this paper follows this trend. As indicated in the paper, the issue worth considering is the introduction of tools aimed at mitigating risk, such as utilising the safe harbour statement clause. Another very important issue is the increase of significance of the management report as a crucial source of information about future plans of a company. Nowadays investors rely not only on traditional financial statement, but they also expect additional data—non-financial information and forward-looking information. What is more, international studies also emphasise considering other communication events, such as conference calls or seminars for investors that have the potential to provide recipients with new information in non-traditional ways (Li 2010; Mayew and Venkatachalam 2012). It is worth noting that the area of accounting under study has recently started being implemented in Poland and the intention of the authors is its in-depth analysis in the subsequent stages of the research.

References

Abed, S., Al-Najjar, B., Roberts, C.: Measuring annual report narratives disclosure. Empirical evidence from forward-looking information in the UK prior the financial crisis. Manag. Audit. J. **31**(4/5), 338 (2016)

Abraham, S., Cox, P.: Analysing the determinants of narrative risk information in UK FTSE 100 annual reports. Br. Account. Rev. **39**(3), 227 (2007)

Al-Najjar, B., Abed, S.: The association between disclosure of forward-looking information and corporate governance mechanisms: evidence from the UK before the financial crisis period. Manag. Audit. J. **29**(7), 578 (2014)

Aljifri, K., Hussaainey, K.: The determinants of forward-looking information in annual reports of UAE companies. Manag. Audit. J. **22**(9), 881 (2007)

Altman, E.I., Sabato, G., Wilson, N.: The volue of non-financial information in small and medium-sized enterprise risk management. J. Credit Risk **6**(2), 95 (2010)

Amir, E., Lev, B.: Value relevance of non-financial information: the wireless communication industry. J. Account. Econ. **22**, 3 (1996)
Aven, T.: On how to define, understand and describe risk. Reliab. Eng. Syst. Saf. **95**(6), 623 (2010)
Baginski, S.P., Hassell, J.M., Kimbrough, M.D.: Why do managers explain their earnings forecasts. J. Account. Res. **42**(1), 1 (2004)
Bao, Y., Datta, A.: Simultaneously discovering and quantifying risk types from textual risk disclosures. Manag. Sci. **60**(6), 1371 (2014)
Beretta, S., Bozzolan, S.: A framework for the analysis of firm risk communication. Int. J. Account. **39**(3), 265 (2004)
Beretta, S., Bozzolan, S.: Quality versus quantity: the case of forward-looking disclosure. J. Account. Audit. Financ. **23**(3), 333–375 (2008)
Beattie, V.A., McInnes, B., Fearnely, S.: A methodology for analysing and evaluating narratives in annual reports: a comprehensive description profile and metrics for disclosure quality attributes. In: Accounting Forum, vol. 28 (2004)
Bizon-Górecka, J.: Koszty w przedsiębiorstwie w ujęciu komplementarnym, „Rynek Terminowy" nr 2 (2004)
Botosan, C.A.: Disclosure level and the cost of equity capital. The Account. Rev. **72**(3), 323 (1997)
Breton, G., Taffler, R.J.: Accounting information and analysts stock recommendation decisions: a content analysis approach. Account. Bus. Res. **31**(2), 91 (2001)
Bujaki, M., Zeghal, D., Bozec, R.: The disclosure of future oriented information in annual reports of Canadian corporations, Working Paper No. 44, University of Ottawa (1999)
Bulletin of Department of Banking and Finance, Georgia, January (2018) https://dbf.georgia.gov/sites/dbf.georgia.gov/files/related-files/document/January2018bulletin.pdf
Bryman, A., Bell, E.: Business Research Methods, 3rd edn. Cambridge Oxford University Press (2011)
Carlon, S., Loftus, J.A., Miller, M.C.: Risk reporting: conceptual issues, regulatory approaches and voluntary disclosures. In: 23rd Annual Congress of the European Accounting Association (2000)
Cabedo, J.D., Tirado, J.M.: The disclosure of risk in financial statement. In: Accounting Forum, vol. 28, Issue 2 (2004)
Celik, O., Ecer, A., Karaback, H.: Disclosure of forward looking information: evidence from listed companies on Instanbul Stock Exchange (ISE). Invest. Manag. Financ. Innov. **3**(2), 197 (2006)
Clatworthy, M., Jones, M.J.: Financial reporting of good news and bad news: evidence from accounting narratives. Acc. Bus. Res. **33**(3) (2003)
Elshandidy, T., Neri, L.: Corporate governance, risk reporting practices, and market liquidity: comparative evidence from the UK and Italy. Corp. Gov.: Int. Rev. **23**(4), 331 (2015)
Elshandidy, T., Shrives, P.J., Bamber, M., Abraham, S.: Risk reporting: a review of the literature and implications for future research. J. Account. Lit. **40**, 54 (2018)
Elshandidy, T., Fraser, I., Hussainey, K.: Aggregated, voluntary and mandatory risk reporting incentives: evidence from FTSE all-share. Int. Rev. Financ. Anal. **30**, 320 (2013)
Elshandidy, T., Fraser, I., Hussainey, K.: What drives mandatory and voluntary risk reporting variations across Germany, UK, and US? Br. Account. Rev. **47**(4), 376 (2015)
Francis, J., Schipper, K.: Have financial statements lost their relevance? J. Account. Res. **37**, 319 (1999)
Greenwald, B.C., Stiglitz, J.E.: Asymmetric information and the new theory of the firm: financial constraints and risk behaviour, NBER Working Paper no. 3359, NBER Program: Monetary Economics (1990) www.nber.org/papers/w3359
Gardner, M.J., Mills, D.L.: Managing Financial Institutions, p. 45. He Dryden Press, Chicago (1988)
Hail, L.: The impact of voluntary corporate disclosures on the ex ante cost of capital for Swiss firms. Eur. Account. Rev. **11**(4), 741 (2002)
Hammond, S.A., Slocum, J.W.: The impact of prior firm financial performance on subsequent corporate reputation. J. Bus. Ethics **15**(2), 159 (1996)
Healy, P.M., Palepu, G.: Information asymmetry, corporate disclosure and capital markets: a review of the empirical disclosure literature. J. Account. Econ. **31**(1/3), 405 (2001)

Habelman, J.: Ocena ryzyka w rachunkowości na przykładzie Zarządu Morskich Portów Szczecin i Świnoujście SA, Zeszyty Naukowe Uniwersytetu Szczecińskiego nr 830, seria Finanse, Rynki Finansowe, Ubezpieczenia nr 70 (2014)
Helm, S.: The role of corporate reputation in determining investor satisfaction and loyalty. Corp. Reput. Rev. **10**, 22 (2007)
Hussainey, K.: A study of the ability of partial automated disclosure scores to explain the information content of annual report narratives for future earnings, Ph.D. thesis, Manchester University, Manchaster (2004)
Hussainey, K., Walker, M.: Undertaking large-scale disclosure studies when AIMR-FAF ratings are not available: the case of process leading earnings. Account. Bus. Res. (December 2003)
Janasz, K.: Ryzyko i niepewność w gospodarce – wybrane aspekty teoretyczne, Studia i Prace Wydziału Nauk Ekonomicznych i Zarządzania WNEiZ nr 14 (2009)
Kelliher, P., Wilmot, D., Vij, J., Klumpes, P.: A common risk classification system for the actuarial profession, Risk Classification Working Party, Version 3.3 (2011). www.actuaries.org.uk/.../documents/discussion-paper-v33-final(1).pdf
Kelman, I.: Defining Risk, "FloodRiskNetNewsletter", Issue 2 (2003). http://www.ilankelman.org/abstracts/kelman2003frn.pdf. 20 June 2018
Kieso, D.E., Weygandt, J.J.: Intermediate Accounting, 8th edn, p. 25. Wiley, New York (1995)
Knight, F.H.: Risk, Uncertainty, and Profit, Hart, Schaffner&Marx, Houghton, Mifflin Company. http://www.econlib.org/library/Knight/knRUP0.html
Krasodomska, J.: Informacje niefinansowe w sprawozdawczości spółek, pp. 25–50. Wydawnictwo Uniwersytetu Ekonomicznego w Krakowie, Kraków (2014)
Kravet, T., Muslu, V.: Textual risk disclosures and investors' risk perceptions. Rev. Account. Stud. **18**(4), 1088 (2013)
Kreim, E.: Zukunftsorientierte Kreditentscheidung, p. 45. Gabler, Wiesbaden (1988)
Krippendorff, K.: Content Analysis: An Introduction to Its Methodology, 2nd edn, pp. 3–25. Sage, Thousand Oaks, CA (2004)
Li, F.: Textual analysis of corporate disclosures: a survey of the literature. J. Account. Lit. **29**, 143 (2010)
Linsley, P.M., Shrives, P.J.: Risk reporting: a study of risk disclosures in the annual reports of UK companies. Br. Acc. Rev. **38**(4) (2006)
Markowitz, H.: Portfolio Selection, Efficient Diversification of Investments. Wiley, New York (1959)
Markowitz, H.: Portfolio selection. J. Finance **7** (1952)
Marston, C.L., Shrives, P.J.: The use of disclosure indices in accounting research: a review article. Br. Account. Rev. **23**(3), 195 (1991)
Malafronte, I., Porzio, C., Starita, M.G.: The nature and determinants of disclosure practises in the insurance industry: Evidence from European insurers. Int. Rev. Financ. Anal. **45** (2016)
Mayew, W.J., Venkatachalam, M.: The power of voice: Managerial affective states and future firm performance. J. Finance **67**(1), 1 (2012)
Mesjasz, Cz.: Standardy zarządzania ryzykiem w przedsiębiorstwie. In: Koncepcje zarządzania współczesnym przedsiębiorstwem, A. Stabryła (red.), Fundacja Uniwersytetu Ekonomicznego w Krakowie, pp. 145–146 (2010)
Miihkinen, A.: What drives the quality of firm risk disclosure? Int. J. Account. **47**(4), 437 (2012)
Nahodko: Ryzyko ekonomiczne w działalności gospodarczej, Oficyna Wydawnicza Ośrodka Postępu Organizacyjnego, Bydgoszcz, p. 21 (2001)
Orens, R., Lybaert, N.: Disclosure of Non-financial information: relevant to financial analysts? Rev. Bus. Econ. Lit. **58**(4) (2013)
Papaj, E.: The role of the narrative reporting in contemporary accounting, Globalization and its socio-economic consequences. In: 17th International Scientific Conference. Proceedings. Part IV (2017)
Raczkowski, K., Tworek, P.: What does risk management in an economy really mean? In: Raczkowski, K. (ed.) Risk Management in Public Administration, pp. 1–41. Palgrave McMillan, Cham (2017)

Renn, O.: Three decades of risk research: accomplishments and new challenges. J. Risk Res. **1**(1), 49 (1998)
Robb, S.W.G., Single, L.E., Zarzeski, M.T.: Non-financial disclosures across Anglo-American Countries. J. Int. Account. **10**, 71 (2001)
Rosa, E.A.: Metatheoretical foundations for post-normal risk. J. Risk Res. **1**, 15 (1998)
Shrives, P., Linsley, P.: Communicating risk to shareholders and other stakeholders: an empirical study, Copenhagen. In: 25th Annual Congress of the European Accounting Association (2002)
Sierpińska, M., Jachna, T.: Ocena przedsiębiorstwa według standardów światowych, PWN, Warszawa, p. 232 (1993)
Szczepankiewicz, E.: Wykorzystanie punktowej metody oszacowania ryzyka operacyjnego w instytucjach finansowych, Studia Ekonomiczne, Zeszyty Naukowe Uniwersytetu Ekonomicznego w Katowicach Nr 298 (2016)
Strojek-Filus, M., Tkocz-Wolny, K., Wszelaki, A.: Ecological accounting in Poland—diagnosis of good and bad practices. In: 17th International Multidisciplinary Scientific GeoConference SGEM 2017, Conference Proceedings, 29 June–5 July, 2017, vol. 17, Issue 53 (2017)
Thlon, M.: Charakterystyka i klasyfikacja ryzyka w działalności gospodarczej, Zeszyty Naukowe Uniwersytetu Ekonomicznego w Krakowie, seria Ekonomia **902** (2013)
Wang, M., Hussainey, K.: Voluntary forward-looking statements driven by corporate governance and their value relevance. J. Account. Public Policy **32**, 26 (2013)
Walker, M., Tsalta, A.: Corporate Financial Disclosure and Analyst Forecasting Activity: Preliminary Evidence for the UK, London, ACCA Research Report No. 67 (2001)

Part II
Implementation of Risk Management

Financial Slack and Company's Risk Retention Capacity

Monika Wieczorek-Kosmala and Joanna Błach

Abstract This paper addresses the buffering function of financial slack (understood as the pool of available resources) in the company from risk management perspective. The main purpose of this paper is to study the relationship between financial slack and risk retention, as one of risk management strategies. Risk retention is here considered as a risk financing method, whereby a company intentionally assumes the self-sufficient coverage of the negative financial outcomes of risk. The paper offers an original, conceptual model of the assessment of the company's risk retention capacity, as determined by the existence of financial slack. It considers more-in-depth three main strategies of risk retention: earmarked capital reserves, compensation and contingent financing and links them with the three types of financial slack: available, recoverable and potential one, respectively. The contribution of the study is manifold. Firstly, it defines and systemizes the category of a financial slack in the broad meaning, together with its measures. Secondly, it offers an original, conceptual model of the application of the financial slack measures to the assessment of the company's risk retention capacity. Finally, it provides the empirical illustration of the sector-relativity of the existence of risk retention capacity, based on the financial data of the 500 largest Polish companies. This empirical illustration is executed separately for each of the distinguished risk retention strategies and linked to the presence of a various types of financial slack.

Keywords Financial slack · Risk retention · Risk management · Corporate finance

1 Introduction

Slack is commonly associated with the pool of available resources that performs both buffering and strategic (opportunity execution) functions. A stream of academic research has examined the functions of slack, with respect to its impact on perfor-

M. Wieczorek-Kosmala (✉) · J. Błach
University of Economics in Katowice, 1 Maja 50, 40-287 Katowice, Poland
e-mail: monika.wieczorek-kosmala@ue.katowice.pl

P. Linsley et al. (eds.), *Multiple Perspectives in Risk and Risk Management*, Springer Proceedings in Business and Economics,
https://doi.org/10.1007/978-3-030-16045-6_6

mance improvement, enhancement of innovations and entrepreneurial behavior. In this study, however, we focus on the buffering function of slack, with reference to risk management process.

The main purpose of this paper is to study the relationship between financial slack and risk retention, as one of risk management strategies. In particular, the paper offers a conceptual model of the examination of company's risk retention capacity, as determined by the existence of financial slack. Risk retention is here considered as a risk financing method, whereby a company intentionally assumes the self-sufficient coverage of the negative financial outcomes of risk. As the execution of risk retention affects financial position of a company, the decision to retain risk should be preceded by the assessment of risk retention capacity. The paper considers more-in-depth three main strategies of risk retention: compensation, contingent financing and earmarked capital reserves.

The study contributes to the existing literature in several dimensions. First of all, it offers a broader look on the understanding of financial slack, going beyond the association of financial slack with the available slack reflected by the holdings of liquid assets. A second contribution is the conceptualization of the applicability of financial slack measures (in the broadened understanding) to the assessment of company's risk retention capacity prior to the decision on risk retention. The third contribution of this study is the empirical illustration of the industry-relativity of the existence of risk retention capacity. This empirical illustration is executed separately for each of the distinguished risk retention strategies and linked to the presence of a various types of financial slack.

The paper is organised as follows. In the second section it discusses the understanding and measures of slack and explains the broadened understanding of financial slack, consistent with corporate finance point of view. Third section of the paper explains the rationale behind the application of risk retention and briefly discusses the main strategies of risk retention. Additionally, this section explains the understanding of risk retention capacity and conceptualizes the estimation of risk retention capacity with the application of financial slack measures. The fourth section provides the empirical illustration of the risk retention capacity for selected industries in Poland, on average. The fifth section concludes the study.

2 Financial Slack and Its Measures

2.1 The Understanding and Functions of Slack as a Resource

Financial slack is related to the broader concept of organizational slack, which is commonly associated with the pool of available resources, in excess of company's operational needs (Nohira and Gulati 1996; Zhong 2011). The academic debate focuses on both the reasons behind holding organizational slack and on its relationship with company's performance. The importance of availability of excess resources as essential for growth was first addressed by Penrose (1959), and then advanced by Cyert and March (1963), who defined slack as the "*disparity between resources available to the organization and the payments required to maintain the coalition*". Cyert and March (1963) perceived the role of slack in behavioral context, as associated with the ability to solve intra-organisational conflicts, by providing enough resources for a wide variety of projects (Diecidue and Van de Ven 2008). Slack is also defined as the difference between the current availability of resources and the current resource demands (Child 1972; Dimmick and Murray 1978; Mishina et al. 2004). The risk-related context of slack was addressed in the definition provided by Bourgeouis (1981: 30) who defined organizational slack as "*the cushion of actual or potential resources which allows an organization to adapt successfully to internal pressures for adjustment or to external pressures for change in policy, as well to initiate changes in strategy with respect to the external environment*". This definition highlights the core functions of organizational slack, as considered from "*slack as resource*" perspective.

The first function performed by organizational slack is a cushion of excess resources that prevent disruptions in company's performance. The disruption may be caused by both endogenous (e.g. bottlenecks in the operating cycle) and exogenous forces (e.g. the negative impact of the changing environment). The second function of organizational slack as a resource is to exploit opportunities for growth. In particular, operational slack enables a company to undertake innovations (in products or in the management style) and enhances entrepreneurial behaviour. In this context, the role of slack in the execution of strategic changes remains in focus. These two main functions of slack (buffering and opportunity execution) are discussed in detail in the existing literature from many different angles, with reference to management and organization theories (for example by Bourgeois 1981; Sharman et al. 1988; Tan and Peng 2003; Greenley and Oktemgil 1998, Weinzimmer 2000; Nohria and Gulati 1996; Argote and Greve 2007; Hambrick and Snow 1977; Kim et al. 2008).

In organizational theories, slack as a resource is considered as a positive phenomenon that leads to better performance, as the company is able to response to environmental changes (Cyert and March 1963; Salancik and Pfeffer 1978; Baker and Nelson 2005; Mishina et al. 2004). However, the literature points on a contradicting view, considering "*slack as inefficiency*", which is motivated by the insights of agency theory (Jensen and Meckling 1976; Jensen 1986). The reason why slack is regarded as a negative phenomenon is that it leads to inefficiencies due to the employment of idle resources to satisfy managerial behavior. Agency theory convinces that managers and owners have conflicting goals and managers tend to engage slack resources in the projects that enhance their personal goals (e.g. prestige or empire building). Thus, agency theory suggests that slack resources should be eliminated, as slack is a costly item (Galbraith 1973; Phan and Hill 1995; Zhong 2011). The inefficiency of slack is also related to its buffering role. Slack performs a function of a safety net in managers' experimentations, thus the strategic errors in managerial decisions may remain unnoticed in comparison to the situation when little or no margin for errors is left (Laffranchini and Braun 2014). A relatively high stock of liquid assets may affect company's profitability, which is perceived as the opportunity cost of liquidity (Opler et al. 1999; Almeida et al. 2002; Eljelly 2004).

The concept of "slack as a resource" and "slack as inefficiency" was broadly researched in the context of the relationship between slack and performance and has shown contradicting results (Daniel et al. 2004; Stan et al. 2014). Some works, however, convince that there is a curvilinear relationship between slack and performance. In other words, too much and too little slack is problematic, which raises a question on the optimal level of slack (Bourgeois 1981; George 2005; Tan and Peng 2003).

The optimization of the level of slack is connected with the impact of slack on risk management decisions. As noted by Bromiley (1991) and March and Shapira (1987), if slack falls considerably below the target level, managers take risk in order to create additional slack. Alternatively, managers take few risk if slack is around the target level. In such circumstances, they perceive the performance of a company as satisfactory and continue routine operations. The slack above target levels encourages managers to innovate, assuming innovation as a form of strategic risk-taking behavior (Cyert and March 1963; MacCrimmon and Wehrung 1986; March 1981). Yasai-Ardekani (1986) argued also that too little slack leads to constraints in decision making. This view corresponds with the Cyert and March (1963) notion that appropriate level of slack helps to reduce intra-organisational conflicts, by providing enough resources for a wide variety of projects. There is also an important reciprocal causality between slack and performance relationship. The growth of slack may lead to the improved future performance, although lagged (Hambrick and D'Aveni 1988; Singh 1986; Mitchell and James 2001).

2.2 *Taxonomy and Measures of Slack Resources*

The academic literature provides some overlapping categories of slack resources, due to similarities in conceptualization and empirical operationalization (Stan et al. 2014). Dichotomous categorization of slack was proposed by Singh (1986) who distinguished between absorbed and unabsorbed slack. Absorbed slack represents irreversible commitment of resources in operating activity, whereas unabsorbed slack represents uncommitted liquid resources, easy for reconfiguration and ready for use (Kim and Bettis 2013; Thomson and Miller 2001; Wiengarten et al. 2017). Similar idea is reflected by the distinction between (b) high or low-discretionary slack (Sharfman et al. 1988), (a) generated and invested slack (Finkelstein and Hambrick 1990) or (c) immediate and deferred slack (Chakravarthy 1986; Torben 2009). High-discretionary (immediate, generated) slack reflects liquid resources, available for investment. Low-discretionary (deferred, invested) slack reflects resources already committed in operating activity. Other classifications distinguish between (a) short and long-term slack, where short-term means slack that can be committed within one year (Nohira and Gulati 1996) and (b) internal versus external slack, with reference to the availability of resources—generated internally or acquired externally (Bowen 2002; Geiger and Cashen 2002).

However, most common classification examined in numerous empirical studies is the "*easy-to recovery*" taxonomy proposed by Bourgeois and Singh (1983). This taxonomy distinguishes between (a) available, (b) recoverable and (c) potential slack. The *available slack* reflects uncommitted liquid resources, readily available for use and maintained in a form that allows immediate access. The available slack is commonly associated with a buffer of cash and marketable securities held by the company. The available slack is thus consistent with unabsorbed and high-discretionary slack. *Recoverable slack* reflects the committed resources and the recovery of these resources requires time and substantial organizational redesign. Recoverable slack refers to absorbed and low-discretionary slack. The *potential slack* represents the resources that may be obtained in the future from the external company's environment.

The distinction of available, recoverable and potential slack refers to the desired characteristics of slack: its visibility to management and employability in the future performance (Sharfman et al. 1988). For existing companies, availability of slack is a result of their performance if a company is able to generate resources in excess of its basic operating needs. For the newly established companies, however, slack is also represented by the initial capital (Firchman and Levinthal 1991; Bradley et al. 2011).

The traditional approach of measuring slack with variables obtainable from accounting-based data was initiated by Bourgeois (1981). Bourgeois assumed that better company's performance increases organization slack and thus the slack resources are reflected by the injection of funds to the company—the increase in the retained earnings (RE) or decrease in the dividend pay-out ratio (DP). The increase of general and administrative expenses (G&A) is a symptom of higher investments. Further, Bourgeois assumed that liquidity position positively influences the slack resources, which is reflected by the increase of a faster growth of working capital (WC) than the corresponding increase in sales (S). The slack resources also grow with the availability of external resources, which is reflected by both the increase in the borrowing capacity or the potential to raise equity. The borrowing capacity might be captured by the decrease of debt to equity (D/E), higher credit rating (CR) or lower interests burden (I/P).[1] The potential to raise equity was captured in Bourgeois' proposal by price to earnings ratio (P/E). Accordingly, the model of slack measure proposed by Bourgeois (1981: 38) was as follows:

$$\Delta Slack = f\Delta(RE, DP, G\&A, WC/S, D/E, CR, I/P, P/E) \tag{1}$$

Bougeois and Singh (1983) adapted this general conceptual framework to the operationalization of available, recoverable and potential slack, as the main types of slack resources. This approach was then adapted in numerous empirical works, as financial-analysis based approach provides researchers with proxies of slack resources that are easy to obtain and compare with other works. Table 1 summarizes the findings of

[1] Bourgeois proposal was to capture the relationship of short-term loan interest (I) compared to principal rate (P). Bourgeois (1981: 38).

Table 1 Common measures of slack resources in empirical works

Type of slack	Slack measures examined in empirical works	Analytical perspective
Available slack	(A.1) Current ratio (A.2) Liquidity ratio (A.3) Liquid capital	Liquidity—static approach
	(A.4) Working capital/sales (A.5) Receivables/sales (A.6) Inventory/sales	Liquidity—short-term operating cycle needs
	(A.7) Cash flows/sales	Liquidity—dynamic approach
Recoverable slack	(R.1) Expenses/sales (R.2) SGA expenses/sales *(SGA = sales+general+administrative expenses)* (R.3) Manufacturing expenses/sales (R.4) Administrative expenses/sales (R.5) Other expenses/sales (R.6) Advertising expenses/sales (R.7) R&D/sales	Efficiency and profit margin
	(R.8) Administrative expenses/costs of goods sold	
Potential slack	(P.1) Debt/equity (P.2) Equity/debt (P.3) Debt/assets (P.4) Long-term debt/assets	Capital structure and leverage
	(P.5) Interest coverage ratio (earnings before interest and taxes/interest)	Ability to cover debt obligations

Source Own study based on Daniel et al. (2004: 568–570)

meta-analysis of previous research performed by Daniel et al. (2004). The researchers commonly measure available slack by liquidity ratios or the holding of liquid assets. Recoverable slack is commonly captured by the relationship of expenses or the corresponding categories of expenses to sales revenues. The potential slack is captured by the measures that reflect the borrowing capacity: the leverage (debt to equity relationship or debt to assets relationship) or company's ability to cover interest expenses (e.g. EBIT to interest charges).

In Table 1, the right column refers to the analytical perspective in focus, with reference to the subject of financial analysis. The measures of available slack capture both static and dynamic liquidity measures, as well as the short-term operating management reflected by the working capital analysis. The measures of recoverable slack refer to the ratios measured within the efficiency and profit margin analysis, whereas the measures of potential slack capture broadly understood capital structure analysis and the ability to repay debt. However, the slack measures examined in previous works refer to one or two most distinctive ratios within a given analytical perspective and it obviously limits the analytical approach.[2]

2.3 Financial Slack in the Taxonomy of Slack Resources

Financial slack is commonly associated with available or unabsorbed slack (Bradley et al. 2011; Mishina et al. 2004; Natividad 2013). Accordingly, in the operational dimension, financial slack should be associated with the most liquid assets held by a company—the cash and cash equivalents. However, this approach seems limited from the corporate finance point of view and there are several arguments for a broader understanding of financial slack, as outlined below.

From the corporate finance management perspective, the activity of a company is related to a constant transformation of funds (cash) into assets, by the purchase of fixed assets (investments) or current assets (operating activity), followed by the transformation of assets into funds (cash), by the sale of assets (e.g. finished goods and products or divestment through the sale of fixed assets or liquidation of long-term financial assets). The effects of the constant flow of funds in a company is captured in its financial statement, as assumed in the balance-sheet model of a company (Emery et al. 2005; Baker and Powel 2005; Moles et al. 2011; Damodaran 2001). In particular, balance sheet offers a snapshot (on a balance-sheet day) of the structure of assets hold and the sources of capital used to purchase the assets. The balance-sheet captures also the ultimate effect of constant capital transformation, as expressed by the volume of the generated net profit.

Thus, from the balance-sheet model perspective, financial slack as a resource should be associated with the funds that are in company's disposal and the scale of their absorption. The scale of absorption is reflected by the liquidity of assets held by the company, and the liquidity of assets refers to the ease of assets liquidation (sale). The presentation of assets in the balance-sheet corresponds to the degree of assets' liquidity. Accordingly, fixed assets as the least-liquid assets indicate the absorbed financial slack. Current assets differ with the degree of liquidity, with inventories as least liquid current assets and cash—as most liquid assets.

From that point of view, the distinction of recoverable financial slack seems justified. The constant transformation of cash to assets and assets to cash reflects the idea of the recovery of resources, in terms of monetary dimension. In other words, through the liquidation (sale) of fixed assets or current assets other than cash, a company may recover financial slack. This approach is consistent with the general understanding of recoverable slack as a resource, as discussed above. The release of financial slack requires time and may be related to the deep organizational change. With reference

[2]Some authors examine other variables that capture similar analytical perspective. For example, Bowers et al. (2000) used NPA (net pension assets). Booth and Clearly (2006) measured financial slack with current ratio to debt ratio.

to the buffering function of slack resources, the liquidation (sale) of assets leads to the recovery of funds that will allow to overcome the existing constraints (crisis situation). With reference to the opportunity execution function, better management of current assets (e.g. lower stock of inventories or change in trade credit policy) or liquidation of inefficient or old-fashioned units (and the related divestments) release funds for new investments (Ehrhardt and Brigham 2009).

The distinction of recoverable financial slack is also justified by the common measures of available slack (as presented in Table 1). The narrowed understanding of financial slack (in accordance to Breadley et al. (2011) and Mishina et al. (2004)) associates financial slack with available slack and explains that financial slack is represented by the most liquid assets. However, among the commonly examined measures of available slack there are current and quick ratios. The current ratio assumes the relationship between all current assets and current liabilities, whereas quick ratio provides a more accurate measure of liquidity, by removing inventories from current assets, as the least liquid element of current assets. There again, this approach recalls the assets-liquidation approach, which reflects the understanding of recoverable slack.

The common association of financial slack with the available slack, reflected in the company's holdings of cash and cash equivalents, should be also considered from the cash management point of view. The cash management assumes that the volume of company's cash and cash equivalents holdings refer to the three basic motives of cash holdings, as noted by Keynes (1936): transaction, precautionary and speculative cash reserve (Bibow 1998; Han and Qiu 2007; Ehrhardt and Brigham 2009). The transaction cash reserve is the required volume of cash needed for smooth operating activity, which is established with regard to the typical volatility of cash inflows and outflows in a company (e.g. the common rules of payments for goods and services purchased or sold). Thus, the transaction reserve of cash reflects somehow absorbed financial slack. The precautionary cash reserve is hold to manage any unexpected volatilities of cash flows and thus truly reflects the buffering function of slack. The speculative cash reserve is hold to allow use the unexpected opportunities, which is consistent with the opportunity-execution function of slack. The precautionary and speculative cash holdings reflect the unabsorbed and available slack most straightforwardly. However, the balance sheet information does not allow to estimate the exact volume of each type of cash reserve, thus it could be assumed that all cash and cash equivalents held by the company refer to the available, unabsorbed financial slack.

There is also a rationale behind the distinction of potential financial slack. Potential financial slack should be associated with the company's ability to raise external funds and is determined by its current financial strength and the related borrowing capacity or market power. In corporate finance, the problem is widely disputed within the optimisation of capital structure (debt to equity relationship) and the problem of bankruptcy costs (see e.g. Kraus and Litzenberger (1973) or Titman (1984)). In the academic debate on capital structure, there are numerous theories that explain the possible internal and external forces that influence borrowing capacity or rationale

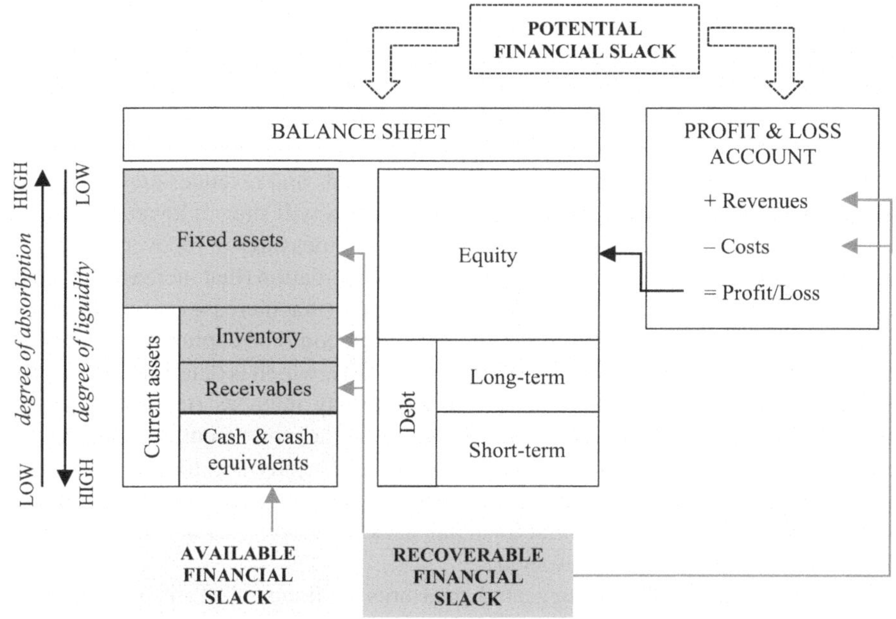

Fig. 1 Types of financial slack framed within the balance-sheet model of a company

behind the increase of equity.[3] In general, these theories indicate that the company's ability and flexibility to raise funds (and to increase the potential financial slack) is related not only to the existing debt-to-equity or interest coverage ratio, but primarily to the ability to maintain the long-term financial balance and creation of market value. In particular, the potential financial slack is low in terms of emerging or existing financial constraints. This view is consistent with Cleary (1999) approach who associated the good financial status of a company with adequate levels of financial slack, measured as the change in debt relative to net fixed assets over a given year. The importance of long-term financial balance (as the symptom of financially unconstrained firm) for the inducement of financial slack was also studied by Kaplan and Zingales (2000), Fizzari et al. (2000, 1988) and Cleary (2005).

The proposed model of the broadened understanding of financial slack, consistent with corporate finance approach, as captured by the balance-sheet model of a company, is presented in Fig. 1.

The model presented in Fig. 1 indicates the directions of measuring the distinguished types of financial slack. The available slack corresponds to the most liquid assets, thus the recommended measures are the share of cash and cash holdings in

[3]With reference to the seminal work of Miller and Modigliani, the empirical works have led to the justification of static trade-off theory of leverage, agency trade-off theory, signaling theory, pecking-order theory and market-timing theory. An overview of the premises of these theories was provided by e.g. Ehrhardt and Brigham (2009), Eldomiaty (2008), Myers (2001), Ross (1977), Baker and Wurgler (2002).

total assets (or alternatively current assets). The commonly used liquidity ratios are applicable if indicate over-liquidity (the liquidity ratio above the threshold) and the over-liquidity is not caused by high levels of receivables or inventory. The recoverable financial slack could be captured by the relationship of current assets to fixed assets, that reflects the relative flexibility in assets liquidation. Alternatively, the common measures reflecting the relationship between overheads and revenues are also applicable, as the companies with high level of fixed assets will show a lower efficiency, due to high burden of fixed costs. Cost/revenue-based measures of recoverable financial slack allow also to capture the effects of assets liquidation (that increase revenues and release financial slack) relative to assets purchase (that increase costs and absorb financial slack). Finally, the potential financial slack could be captured by plenty of measures that allow to monitor the borrowing capacity, which is determined not only by the capital structure (debt/equity) or ability to pay interests (interest coverage ratios), but also by the financial balance, reflected by the adjustment of capital structure to the existing assets structure (e.g. fixed assets/ equity and long-term debt or current ratio). From the financial analysis point of view, numerous measures capture available, recoverable and potential financial slack. However, in Table 2 the selected most common measures are presented.

The conceptualization of suggested measures of financial slack, presented in Table 2, indicates not only the expected sign of a given ratio as financial slack contributor (consistent with Bourgeois 1981 approach), but additionally the assessment of ratio relative to the benchmark. In other words, the existence of financial slack is confirmed if a situation of a company is better than the industry average or well-established benchmark. A pure increase or decrease of a given ratio should not be judged as the confirmation of the existence of financial slack (e.g. the improvement of current ratio from very poor to poor).

The proposed approach follows the idea of the distinction of the components of slack, that refer to various types of resources. For example, Voss et al. (2008) distinguished financial slack as a separate component of organizational slack, apart from operational slack, human resource slack and customer relations slack (with reference to company's resource diversity). In this context, financial slack is perceived as the financial resource and thus we may consider various types of financial slack, from the "*easy-to recovery*" taxonomy point of view. This concept was outlined in Fig. 2, with reference to other types of slack resources that emerge in slack taxonomies. As financial slack is perceived as a type of organizational slack, other dichotomous taxonomies are also applicable (time-perspective, absorption or availability of resources).

Table 2 Proposition of the selected measures of financial slack as a resource

Type of financial slack	Measures	Financial slack is detected if:	
		Δ[a]	Benchmark[b] relative
Available financial slack	(AF.1) Current ratio *alternatively* (AF.2) Quick ratio	↑	Ratio is above the benchmark
	(AF.3) Cash ratio	↑	Ratio is above the benchmark
	(AF.4) Cash and cash equivalents/current assets *alternatively* (AF.5) Cash and cash equivalents/assets in total	↑	Ratio is above the benchmark
Recoverable financial slack	(RF.1) Current assets/fixed assets	↑	Ratio is above the benchmark
	(RF.2) Overheads/revenues	↓	Ratio is below the benchmark
Potential financial slack	(PF.1) Debt/equity	↓	Ratio is below the benchmark
	(PF.2) Interest coverage ratio	↑	Ratio is above the benchmark
	(PF.3) Long-term solvency ratio	↑	Ratio is above the benchmark; industries other than trade—must be >1

[a]Δ refers to the desired direction of change; ↑ means slack stimulant (an increase in the indicator signals a corresponding increase in financial slack); ↓ means slack destimulants (a decline in the indicator signals a corresponding increase in financial slack)
[b]benchmark should be determined as the level of ratio on average for companies operating in a given industry (sector), or alternatively for the market leaders or leading competitors

3 Determination of Company's Risk Retention Capacity with the Financial Slack Approach

Facing the negative, financial outcomes of risk occurrence, a company needs funds to restore and continue operations. These funds may be provided externally, by the arrangement of risk transfer agreements (insurance in particular). Alternatively, a company may cover the losses from own funds (internally), which reflects the idea of retaining the consequences of risk. These two mechanisms of risk financing (or financial risk control) are considered within the spectrum of risk management techniques, alongside physical risk control tools, such as risk prevention or risk repression (Vaughan and Vaughan 2003; Rejda 2001; Culp 2006; Williams and Heins 1989).

A certain level of risk retention is inevitable. Due to the dynamic changes of the company's business environment and the constant emergence of new risks, a

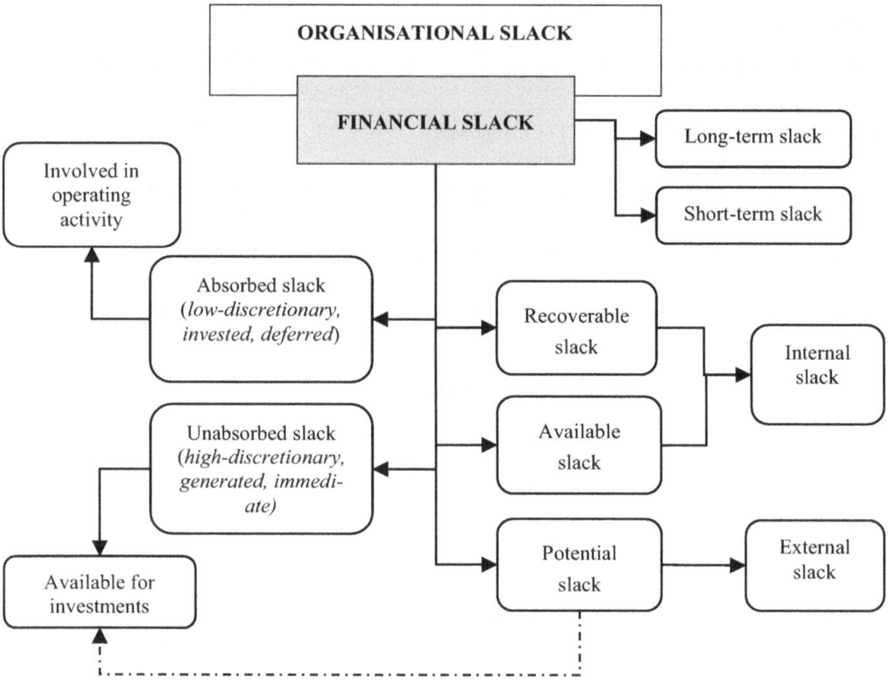

Fig. 2 Financial slack in the taxonomy of slack resources

company may not be able to identify and manage all risk exposures. In addition, errors and omissions in risk identification or the estimation of risk-severity may lead to risk exposures that remain unmanaged or managed partially (e.g. appropriate risk management techniques were not implemented or implemented with delay). It places risk retention among residual (also referred to as default) risk management techniques, which means that any risk exposure that is not avoided, transferred or reduced is automatically retained. In such circumstances, the risk retention is perceived as unconscious or unplanned. The conscious and planned risk retention means the implementation of risk retention is intentional and preceded by the thoughtful consideration of the consequences of risk retention and the detailed analysis of the justification for its applicability. In particular, from corporate finance point of view, a decision-maker should be aware that the retained risk ultimately is born by the owners (shareholders) of a company. Thus, the scale of the implementation of risk retention influences company's financial position.

However, if we assume risk management as an intentional process, the planned, conscious retention remain in focus (with its impact on decision-making process). Within the planned retention we may distinguish several strategies: (i) earmarked capital reserves (ii) compensation or (iii) contingent financing.

Earmarked capital reserves refer to the intentional accumulation of funds, either formal or informal. Ideally, a company should create a separate account which is periodically credited and debited due to the compensation of a loss. The effective implementation of earmarked capital reserves postulates that the reserves should be reflected in holdings of liquid or semi-liquid assets (cash and marketable securities, as cash equivalents). According to the accounting rules, companies may formally create capital reserves for risk. In any case, however, a company may create an informal reserve in a form of excess liquid assets. In the literature, self-insurance is often considered as an example of risk retention as a capital reserve (and a substitute of traditional insurance risk transfer). Thus, the use of term "self-insurance" is justified only if a company intentionally rejects the use of insurance and safeguards itself against the loss by creating and managing cash reserves. In this case, the computation of the volume of the desired capital reserves, as well as the amounts of periodical contributions to the account, should be proceeded similarly as by the professional insurance company. The risk exposure subject to self-insurance should allow an adequate prediction of loss frequency and loss severity (Vaughan and Vaughan 2003; Rejda 2001; Williams and Heins 1989; Holzheu et al. 2003). An important limitation of earmarked capital reserves is, however, the "cookie jar" effect—if financially constrained, a company may use the earmarked funds for purposes other than initially planned. Another limitation is the alternative cost of funds tied in liquid assets (which are considered to be less productive in comparison to operating assets). Thus, a decision on retaining risk with earmarked capital reserves needs a careful cost-benefit analysis, as compared to the cost of alternative methods (e.g. insurance). Finally, the collection of adequate volume of the capital reserve is time consuming. There is a risk that loss may emerge before the required level of funds is earmarked. Thus, a conscious application of retention with earmarked capital reserves needs the conjunction with other methods, until the required level of funds is collected and safeguarded.

Compensation is related to the current inclusion of the losses in the profit and loss account, as additional costs related to operating activity. This approach is applicable for high-frequency but low-severity losses that are somehow related to the processing methods or delivery system of goods or services and thus could be adequately estimated. This strategy of risk retention requires a careful judgement in terms of cost-revenues trade-off and is applicable only if the company is able to generate revenues in excess of costs[4] (Williams and Heins 1989).

Contingent financing is a strategy of risk retention whereby a company agrees terms and conditions of obtaining additional funds (both debt or equity), prior to the risk occurrence. The simplest example of this strategy is an open credit line in a bank, which is usually aimed at the injection of cash in any tensions of liquidity that may emerge from short-term cash flow volatility, caused by distortions in operating cycle (e.g. delay of the payment of trade credit by the customer). However, nowadays companies (the large ones in particular) reached access to more sophisticated solutions that fit the idea of contingent financing. A company may undergo an agreement (usually the long-term agreement) that allow to issue debt (bonds), equity (shares) or hybrid instruments if a predefined circumstances occur. These circumstances are

[4]Alternatively, risk compensation capabilities could be analysed from the cash flow perspective: as a relationship between cash outflows to cash inflows.

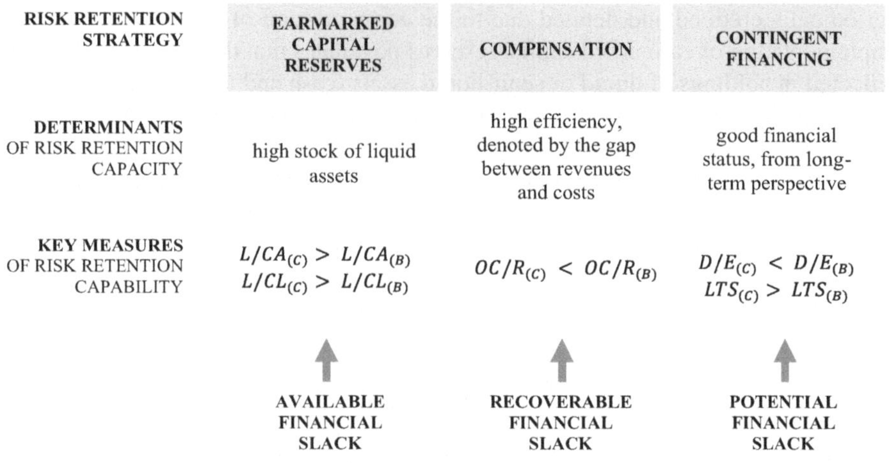

Subtraction denoted with (C) means the ratio for the analysed company; substation denoted with (B) means the benchmark (e.g. industry average); L/CA – the share of liquid assets in current assets; L/CL – liquid assets to current liabilities (cash ratio); D/E – debt to equity; OC/R – operating costs to revenues; LTS – long-term solvency ratio (equity and long-term debt to fixed assets)

Fig. 3 A conceptual framework of the assessment of risk retention capacity

linked to the distortion of company's financial performance in effect of a predefined risk occurrence. The contingent financing could be thus compared to a purchase of a put option on future issuance of debt or equity and the execution of this option is dependent on a predefined consequences of risk occurrence (Culp 2009; Weber 2011; Banks 2004).

An overview of the available and possible risk retention strategies leads to the conclusion that a company may induce both a pre-loss funding approach (as in the case of earmarked capital reserves) or a post-loss funding approach (as in the case of compensation or contingent funding).

From a corporate finance management point of view, the application of risk retention requires a conscious analysis of a broad spectrum of its consequences for the maintenance of financial balance, liquidity and efficiency. These decisions could be supported by the initial evaluation of company's risk retention capacity. *Risk retention capacity are here defined as the initial terms and conditions that allow to consider retention as risk management tool and the existence of risk retention capacity is determined by the existence of financial slack in its buffering function*. Accordingly, the methodology of the assessment of risk retention capacity is consistent with the methodology of the assessment of financial slack, as framed in Table 2. A conceptual map that links the strategies of risk retention with the types of financial slack is outlined in Fig. 3.

As presented in Fig. 3, the immediate ability to retain risk is determined by the existence of earmarked capital reserves, that correspond with the existence of available financial slack. The dimension of risk retention capacity are reflected by high share of liquid assets in current assets. Additionally, it is recommended to capture the relationship between liquid assets and current liabilities. For both measures, risk retention capacity should be judged in the industry-relative context, to capture the possible transaction motives behind high cash holdings.

The ability to retain risk by compensation is related to the existence of recoverable financial slack. In this case, the recovery of funds is reflected by the capabilities to bear additional costs (that will in turn affect the profits). Thus, a possible measure of risk retention capacity with the recoverable slack could be the relationship between costs and revenues. The lower the ratio, the higher risk retention capacity. This relationship should be judged against the industry benchmark, to capture the impact of risk retention capacity on the feasible reduction of profitability.

The ability to retain risk with the application of contingent financing is determined by the existence of potential financial slack. This could be assessed by the examination of company's borrowing capacity, traditionally reflected by debt to equity relationship. As previous research proved that capital structure is industry-specific feature (e.g. Breadley et al. 1984; Gaver and Gaver 1993 or Hovakimian et al. 2001), it is recommended to judge this ratio against the industry benchmark. A good measure of potential financial slack is also the long-term solvency ratio, which allows to assess the adjustment of capital structure to the structure of assets (as determined by the operating activity). The higher the ratio, the better is the borrowing capacity and the ratio should be higher than 1 as a benchmark. Accordingly, the lower debt to equity and the higher long-term solvency, the better risk retention capacity (regardless the industry context).

4 Illustration of the Assessment of Risk Retention Capacity with Reference to Sector Benchmarks

4.1 Research Design and Method

In the empirical illustration, we employ the market data to provide an insight on how to assess the company's risk capacity, with reference to the methodology of the financial slack measurement. The selected companies' financial data (items of balance sheet and income statement) were extracted from the EMIS data base. We have obtained data for 500 largest Polish companies active in 5-year time span (2013–2017). Although the study remains single-country oriented, it should be noted that Poland is considered as leader in Central and Eastern Europe. Poland is currently the sixth strongest market in the European Union, the largest economy among other CEE countries, and it continues to perform strongly (The World Bank 2018).[5]

---

[5]Recently, Poland has also been promoted to developed market status run by FTSE Russel and Stoxx, although it remains in the emerging-market category for MSCI (Martin 2018).

For the sampled companies we have further computed the measures of financial slack (available, recoverable and potential slack), as conceptually outlined in Fig. 2. For a given measure of financial slack, we computed the annual benchmarks as mean values for the entire sample (total 500 companies). In a cross-sector dimension, we proceeded similarly—we computed the mean values of a given slack measure for a given sector. With reference to the entries on companies activities (consistent with PKD codes),[6] we extracted 4 sub-samples of companies, with reference to their sector affiliation: (a) production, (b) trade, (c) energy, and (d) construction. It should be noted that companies analysed within sector sub-samples do not conform the whole sample. Thus, the mean values (benchmarks) obtained for the sector sub-samples do not reflect a decomposed mean value for the whole sample (as there was a set of other companies that were not assigned to one of the sectors in focus).

Our aim was to demonstrate that the risk retention capacity is sector relevant and thus it should be always analyzed in the context of sector benchmarks. We executed the analysis separately for each of the conceptually distinguished risk retention strategy. It was discussed with reference to the various types of financial slack.

4.2 Findings and Discussion

Available Financial Slack and the Ability to Retain Risk with Earmarked Capital Reserves The risk retention strategy based on the earmarked capital reserves refers to the available financial slack (Fig. 3). Thus, the company's ability to use capital reserves can be detected by the analysis of the measures based on the most liquid part of assets i.e. cash and cash equivalents.

The first of employed ratios illustrates the share of cash and cash equivalents in the current assets (*L/CA*). As presented in Fig. 4, the mean value of this ratio for all 500 companies in the analysed sample were remaining at quite stable level in the analyzed period. It indicates that cash and cash equivalents represented approx. 18–19% of current assets. The results for trading and production companies were below this benchmark (approx. 10–11%), while for the energy sector—above the benchmark, with the increasing tendency and the highest results of 29% in 2016 and 27% in 2017. The dynamic fluctuations of the ratio were observed in construction sector, with the lowest level at 10% in 2013 and the highest at 25% in 2015.

In order to confirm these findings, we analyzed additionally cash liquidity ratio that illustrates the ability to cover short-term liabilities with liquid assets (*L/CL*). In

[6]The PDK (Polish Industrial Classification) system is consistent with NACE rev. 2 (Statistical Classification of Economic Activities in the European Community) and uses digit coding with very detailed explanation of the areas of company's operating activity. Thus companies could be easily classified into larger sectors (in this case production, trade, energy and construction). The sector related sub-samples examined in this study are regarded as the key sectors in the Polish economy. According to national statistics data for 2017, companies operating in the four sectors included in our study, represent c.a. 70% of the Polish economy (GUS 2017).

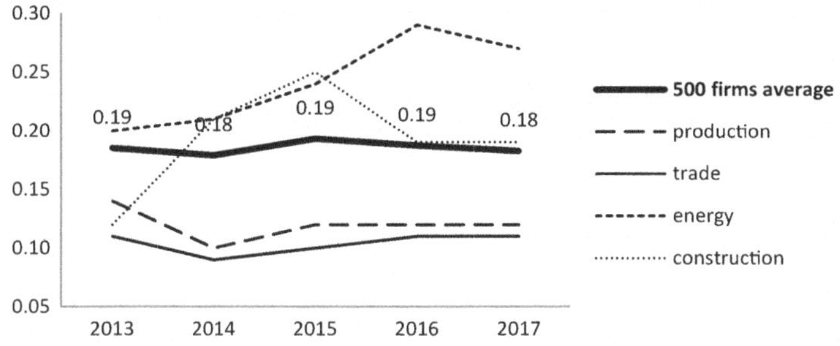

Fig. 4 Mean values of cash level ratio (L/CA) for the examined sample

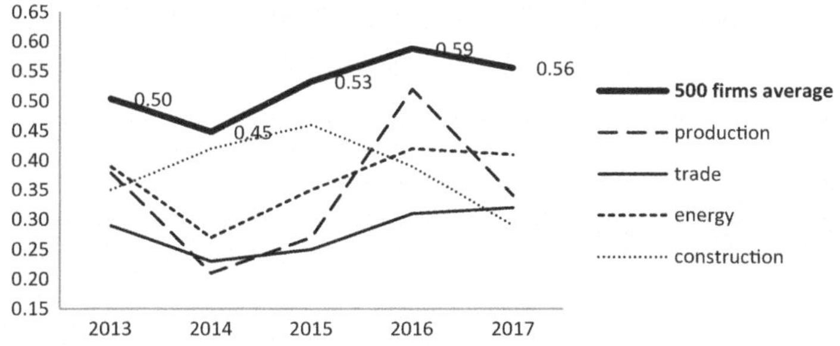

Fig. 5 Mean values of cash liquidity ratio (L/CL) for the examined sample

the analyzed period, the benchmarks (as mean values) for the whole sample (total 500 companies) were relatively high, fluctuating from 45 to 59%. As illustrated in Fig. 5, the mean values of this ratio for the analysed sectors were below the benchmark, ranging from 21% (in 2014 for production) to 52% (in 2016 also for production sector). The results for the production, trade and energy companies display similar pattern of changes in the analyzed period, with the highest values observed in 2013 and in 2016. A different pattern was observed for trade, with the peak value in 2015. Although below benchmarks, the highest average results were achieved by the construction and energy companies, which confirm our earlier observations.

Based on these two measures illustrating the available financial slack, we may assume that the energy and construction sectors are potentially capable to use earmarked capital reserves, as a risk retention strategy. A relatively lower level of the available financial slack was observed in production and trade, which indicates lower capabilities to retain risk.

Recoverable Financial Slack and the Ability to Retain Risk with Compensation As the second risk retention strategy we distinguished compensation, which is determined by the recoverable financial slack. To capture recoverable financial slack, we evaluated the ratio that indicates the gap between total operating costs and total revenues (*OC/R*). As presented in Fig. 6., the benchmark for the whole sample was decreasing from 97% in 2013 to 90% in 2017. It indicates a continuous improvement

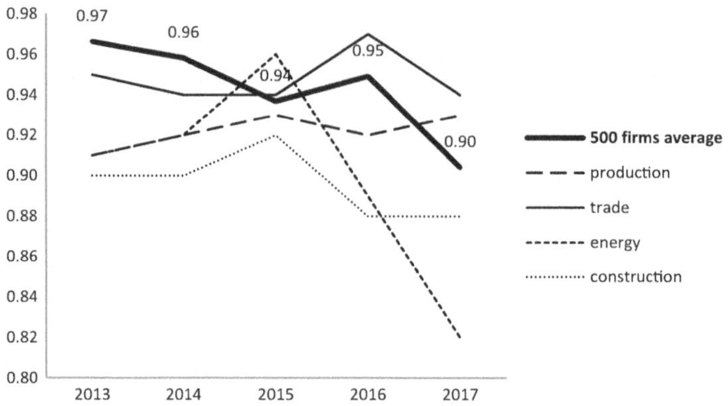

Fig. 6 Mean values of operating costs to total revenues (OC/R) for the examined sample

of the capability to compensate risk outcomes. The results for the production and construction sectors were below the benchmark in the entire analyzed period, which points out relatively higher recoverable financial slack and higher capabilities of risk compensation. High fluctuations were observed in energy sector (with the peak values above the benchmark (96%) in 2015). The worst situation was observed in trade sector (with the mean ratio above the benchmark). With reference to these data we may conclude that trade sector was of lowest ability to apply risk compensation as a risk retention strategy. Construction, energy and production sector showed greater capabilities to compensate risk, due to higher level of recoverable slack.

Potential Financial Slack and the Ability to Retain Risk with Contingent Financing. To evaluate the capabilities to retain risk with contingent financing, we employ two measures to detect the level of potential financial slack (Fig. 3): (1) capital structure ratio computed as debt-to-equity ratio (D/E) and (2) long-term solvency ratio computed as the long-term capital to fixed assets ratio (*LTS*).

Figure 7 presents the benchmarks of debt-to-equity ratio (mean values for the whole sample) and the mean values in cross sector dimension. The benchmark declined in the analyzed period from 1.68 in 2013 to 1.17 in 2017. It indicates the improved capital structure (lower levels of debt relative to equity) and greater potential financial slack, due to greater borrowing capacity. The mean values below the benchmark were observed in production and energy sectors. The construction sector was characterized by highest level of D/E ratios (reaching over 2.2 in 2017).

Data presented in Fig. 8 refer the mean values of long-term solvency ratio (*LTS*). The benchmarks (reflecting mean values for the whole sample) were relatively high, but with a visible downward tendency (from 3.02 in 2013 and ending with 2.55 in 2017). For construction sector, the mean values of LTS were above the benchmark. In 2017, after 4 years of augmentation, also the trade sector reached the benchmark. The lowest values (however above required 1.0) were observed in the production

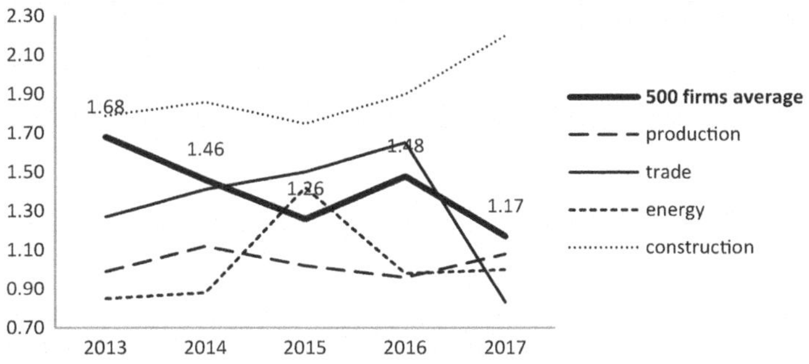

Fig. 7 Mean values of debt-to-equity ratio (D/E) for the examined sample

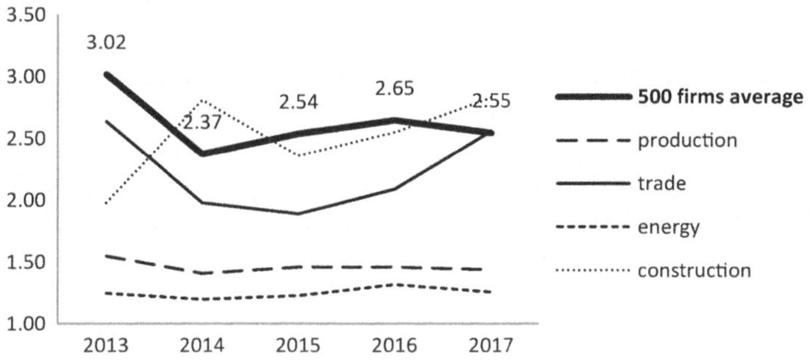

Fig. 8 Mean values of long-term solvency ratio (LTS) for the examined sample

and energy companies, which is related to their huge investments in the plant and equipment.

The data indicate, that with reference to debt capacity (D/E) the highest potential financial slack was observed in construction sector. However, if we consider additionally the maintenance of long term solvency (LTS), relatively high potential financial slack was observed in production companies. Thus, within the potential to apply contingent financing as a risk retention strategy, the results are not consistent.

Brief Summary of the Results The above presented empirical illustration confirms that the level of financial slack and the related risk retention capacity is sector-relevant. It is observable within the simple trend analysis of sub-samples related to sector affiliation (production, trade, energy and construction). A brief summary of the obtained results is presented in Table 3.

The construction sector seems to be the most flexible in shaping risk retention strategy, as the data indicated the potential to implement various solutions. This view is supported by the observed mean values of ratios reflecting available, recoverable and potential slack—these values were better than the benchmark in most of the cases. Similar flexibility is observable in the energy sector. Data for production sector indicate the ability to consider two risk retention strategies: compensation and

Table 3 Summary of the results

Sector results compared to benchmark	Available slack		Recoverable slack	Potential slack	
	L/CA	L/CL	OC/R	D/E	LTS
Production	−/↓	−/↓	+/↓	+/↓	−/↓
Trade	−/↑	−/↑	−/↓	+/↑	+/↓
Energy	+/↑	−/↑	+/↑	+/↓	−/↓
Construction	+/↑	−/↓	+/↑	−/↓	+/↑
Risk retention strategy	Earmarked capital reserves		Compensation	Contingent financing	

Where: + results better than benchmark; −results worse than benchmark; ↑ increasing financial slack; ↓ decreasing financial slack

earmarked capital reserves. In trade sector risk retention capacity seems the most limited: low levels of available and recoverable financial slack indicate the limitation of risk retention capabilities to contingent financing.

With regard to the types of financial slack, it is interesting to notice, that the results indicate the highest availability of potential financial slack, which is related to the consideration of contingent financing as a risk retention strategy. Simultaneously, the results obtained for the analysed sample of companies indicate the limited level of the available financial slack, and thus limited capabilities of using earmarked capital reserves as a risk retention strategy.

5 Conclusions

Financial slack is understood as the pool of available resources that may perform in the company both buffering and strategic functions. In this study we analyze the financial slack from the risk management perspective, placing in the center the buffering function of slack. In particular, we discuss the relationship between financial slack and company's risk retention capabilities. To explain this relationship, we developed a conceptual model that links the assessment of company's risk retention capabilities with the existence of financial slack. In this conceptual model, we distinguish between the types of risk retention strategies: earmarked capital reserves, compensation and contingent financing. Each of these strategies are linked to one type of financial slack—available, recoverable and potential slack, respectively. With reference to the previous literature on financial slack measures, we indicate the proxies for measuring each type of financial slack. The conceptual model is then employed in the simple empirical illustration that indicated the cross-sector differences within the capabilities to retain risk, as denoted by the observable levels of financial slack.

The contribution of our study is manifold. First of all, it explains and systemizes the category of the financial slack (in the broad meaning), together with its measures. Secondly, it offers a conceptual model of the application of financial slack measures to the assessment of company's risk retention capacity. The third contribution of this study is the simple empirical illustration of the sector-relativity of the existence of the risk retention capacity in the company. This empirical illustration is executed separately for each of the distinguished risk retention strategies and linked to the presence of a various types of financial slack.

As this paper offers a first conceptual insight on the possible contribution of the study and examination of financial slack in risk management context, there is an obvious plentiness of the directions of further research. Similarly to sector-relevance context, other factors and companies' characteristics could be examined. In this stream of research, the findings of previous studies related to the financial slack determinants should be taken into consideration as well. However, a more demanding, but potentially more informative direction of further research could be a deeper exploration of the relationship between the observed financial slack and the real risk retention strategies executed in the companies. In this study we assumed that the symptoms of a given type of financial slack reflect the potential to employ a given risk type of risk retention strategy. However, this should be confirmed with the real risk management policies executed by the companies.

References

Almeida, H., Campello, M., Weisbach, M.S.: Corporate demand for liquidity. NBER Working Paper No. 9253, 1–44. https://doi.org/10.3386/w9253 (2002)

Argote, L., Greve, H.: A behavioral theory of the firm—40 years and counting: introduction and impact. Organ. Sci. **18**(3), 337–349 (2007). https://doi.org/10.1287/orsc.1070.0280

Baker, K.A., Powell, G.E.: Understanding Financial Management. Blackwell Publishing, Oxford (2005)

Baker, M., Wurgler, J.: Market timing and capital structure. J. Financ. **57**(1), 1–32 (2002). https://doi.org/10.1111/1540-6261.00414

Baker, T., Nelson, R.: Creating something from nothing: resource construction through entrepreneurial bricolage. Adm. Sci. Q. **50**, 329–366 (2005). 0001-8392/05/5003-0329/$3.00

Banks, E.: Alternative risk transfer, reinsurance and the capital markets, integrated risk management through insurance. Wiley, Chichester (2004)

Bibow, J.: On keynesian theories of liquidity preference. The Manchester School **66**(2), 238–273 (1998). https://doi.org/10.1111/1467-9957.00099

Booth, L., Cleary, S.: Cash flow volatility, financial slack and investment decision, EFMA 2006 Madrid Meetings Paper, pp. 1–30. http://cicfconf.org/past/cicf2006/cicf2006paper/20060127044832.pdf (2006)

Bourgeois, L.J.III: On the measurement of organizational slack. Acad. Manag. Rev. **6**(1), 29–39. https://doi.org/10.2307/257138 (1981)

Bourgeois, L., Singh. J.: Organizational slack and political behaviour among top management teams. Acad. Manag. Proc. (1), 43–47. https://doi.org/10.5465/ambpp.1983.4976315 (1983)

Bowen, F.E.: Organizational slack and corporate greening: broadening the debate. Br. J. Manag. **13**(4), 305–316. https://doi.org/10.1111/1467-8551.00248 (2002)

Bowers, H.M., Moore, N.H., Maurice Tse, K.S.: Signaling, financial slack and corporate acquisitions. Rev. Quant. Financ. Acc. **15**(3), 195–216 (2000). https://doi.org/10.1023/A:1008373205675

Breadley, M., Jarrell, G., Kim, E.H.: On the existence of an optimal capital structure: theory and evidence. J. Financ. **39**(2), 857–878 (1984). https://doi.org/10.2307/2327950
Breadley, S.W., Shepherd, D.A., Wiklund, J.: Te importance of slack for new organisations facing 'Tough' environments. J. Manage. Stud. **48**(5), 1071–1097 (2011). https://doi.org/10.1111/j.1467-6486.2009.00906.x
Bromiley, P.: Testing a causal model for corporate risk taking and performance. Acad. Manag. J. **34**(1), 37–59 (1991). https://doi.org/10.2307/2327950
Chakravarthy, B.: Measuring strategic performance. Strateg. Manag. J. **7**(5), 437–458 (1986). https://doi.org/10.1002/smj.4250070505
Child, J.: Organisational structure, environment and performance: the role of strategic choice. Sociology **6**(1), 2–22 (1972). https://doi.org/10.1177%2F003803857200600101.
Cleary, S.: Corporate investment and financial slack: international evidence. Int. J. Manag. Financ. **1**(3), 140–163 (2005). https://doi.org/10.1108/17439130510619613
Cleary, S.: The relationship between firm investment and financial status. J. Financ. **54**, 673–692 (1999). https://doi.org/10.1111/0022-1082.00121
Culp, C.: Structured finance and insurance. The ART of managing capital and risk. Wiley, Hoboken (2006)
Culp, C.: Contingent capital versus contingent reverse convertibles for banks and insurance companies. J. Appl. Corp. Financ. **21**(4), 17–27 (2009). https://doi.org/10.1111/j.1745-6622.2009.00247.x
Cyert, R.M., March, J.G.: A Behavioral Theory of the Firm. Prentice Hall, Englewood Cliffs, New York (1963)
Damodaran, A.: Corporate Finance. Theory and Practice. Wiley, Hoboken (2001)
Daniel, F., Lohrke, F.T., Formaciari, C.J., Turner, R.: Slack resources and firm performance: a meta-analysis. J. J. Bus. Res. **57**(6), 565–574. https://aquila.usm.edu/fac_pubs/3109 (2004)
Diecidue, E., van de Ven, J.: Aspiration level, probability of success and failure and expected utility. Int. Econ. Rev. **49**(2), 683–700 (2008). https://doi.org/10.1111/j.1468-2354.2008.00494.x
Dimmick, D.E., Murray, V.V.: Correlates of substantive policy decisions in organisations: the case of human resource management. Acad. Manag. J. **21**(4), 611–623 (1978). https://doi.org/10.5465/255703
Ehrhardt, M.C., Brigham, E.F.: Corporate finance. A focused approach. South Western CENGAGE Learning, Mason, USA (2009)
Eldomiaty, T.I.: Determinants of corporate capital structure: evidence from emerging economy. Int. J. Commer. Manag. **17**(1/2), 25–43 (2008). https://doi.org/10.1108/10569210710774730
Eljelly, A.M.A.: Liquidity—profitability tradeoff: An empirical investigation in an emerging market. Int. J. Commer. Manag., **14**(2), 48–61. https://doi.org/10.1108/10569210480000179 (2004)
Emery, R.D., Finnerty, J.D., Stowe, J.D: Corporate Financial Management. Pearson/Prentice Hall, Upper Saddle River (2005)
Fichman, M., Levinthal, D.A.: Honeymoons and the liability of adolescence: a new perspective on duration dependence in social and organizational relationships. Acad. Manag. Rev. **16**(2), 442–468 (1991). https://doi.org/10.5465/amr.1991.4278962
Finkelstein, S., Hambrick, D.C.: Top-management-team tenure and organizational outcomes: the moderating role of managerial discretion. Adm. Sci. Q. **35**(3), 484–503 (1990)
Fizzari, S., Hubbard, R.G., Petersen, B.: Investment –cash flow sensitivities are useful: a comment on Kaplan and Zingales. Quart. J. Econ. **115**(2), 695–705 (2000). https://doi.org/10.1162/003355300554773
Fizzari, S., Hubbard, R.G., Petersen, B.: Financing constraints and corporate investment. Brook. Pap. Econ. Act. **1**, 141–206 (1988). https://doi.org/10.2307/2534426
Galbraith, J.: Designing complex organizations. Addison-Wesley, Reading Mss. (1973)
Gaver, J., Gaver, K.: Additional evidence on the association between the investment opportunity set and corporate financing, dividend, and compensation policies. J. Account. Econ. **16**(1–3), 125–160 (1993). https://doi.org/10.1016/0165-4101(93)90007-3

Geiger, S.W., Cashen, L.H.: A Multidimensional Examination Of Slack And Its Impact On Innovation. J. Manag. Issues **14**(1), 68–84. https://www.jstor.org/stable/40604374 (2002)
George, G.: Slack resources and the performance of privately held firms. Acad. Manage. J. **48**(4), 661–676 (2005)
Greenley, G.E., Oktemgil, M.: A comparison of slack resources in high and low performing british companies. J. Manage. Stud. **35**(3), 377–398 (1998). https://doi.org/10.1111/1467-6486.00098
GUS: Podmioty gospodarcze według rodzajów i miejsc prowadzenia działalności w 2017 roku. https://stat.gov.pl/obszary-tematyczne/podmioty-gospodarcze-wyniki-finansowe/przedsiebiorstwa-niefinansowe/podmioty-gospodarcze-wedlug-rodzajow-i-miejsc-prowadzenia-dzialalnosci-w-2017-roku,7,12.html. Last Accessed 19 Nov 2018
Hambrick, D.C., D'Aveni, R.: Large corporate failures and downward spirals. Adm. Sci. Q. **33**(1), 1–23 (1988). https://doi.org/10.2307/2392853
Hambrick, D.C., Snow, C.C.: A contextual model of strategic decisions making in organizations. Acad. Manag. Proc. **1**, 109–112 (1977). https://doi.org/10.5465/ambpp.1977.4977040
Han, S., Qiu, J.: Corporate precautionary cash holdings. J. Corp. Financ. **13**(1), 43–57 (2007). https://doi.org/10.1016/j.jcorpfin.2006.05.002
Holzheu, T., Karl, K., Raturi, M.: The Picture of Art. Sigma 1, Swiss Re, Zurich (2003)
Hovakimian, A., Opler, T., Titman, S.: The debt-equity choice. J. Financ. Quant. Anal. **36**(1), 1–24 (2001). https://doi.org/10.2307/2676195
Jensen, M.C.: Agency costs of free cash flows, corporate finance and takeovers. Am. Econ. Rev. **76**(2), 323–329. https://www.jstor.org/stable/1818789 (1986)
Jensen, M.C., Meckling, W.H.: Theory of the firm managerial behavior, agency costs and ownership structure. J. Financ. Econ. **3**(4), 305–360 (1976). https://doi.org/10.1016/0304-405X(76)90026-X3
Kaplan, S.N., Zingales, L.: Investment cash flow sensitivities are not valid measures of financing constraints. Quart. J. Econ. **115**(2), 707–712 (2000). https://doi.org/10.1162/003355300554782
Keynes, J.M.: The General Theory of Employment. Interest and Money. McMillan, London (1936)
Kim, C., Bettis, R.: Cash is surprisingly valuable as a strategic asset. Strateg. Manag. J. **35**(13), 2053–2063 (2013). https://doi.org/10.1002/smj.2205
Kim, H., Kim. H., Lee P.M.: Ownership structure and the relationship between financial slack and R&D investments: evidence from Korean firms. Organ. Sci. 19(3), 404–418. https://doi.org/10.1287/orsc.1080.0360 (2008)
Kraus, A, Litzenberger, R.H.: A state-preference model of optimal financial leverage. J. Finance **28**(4), 911–922 (1973)
Laffranchini, G., Braun, M.: Slack in family firms: evidence from Italy (2006–2010). J. Fam. Bus. Manag. **4**(2), 171–193 (2014). https://doi.org/10.1108/JFBM-04-2013-0011
MacCrimmon, K.R., Wehrung, D.A.: Taking risks: the management of uncertainty. Free Press, New York (1986)
March, J.G.: Decisions in organizations and theories of choice. In: A.H., Vand de Ven, W.F., Joyce (eds.) Perspectives on Organizational Design and Adaptive Aspirations. Journal of Economics Behavior and Organisations vol.9, pp. 5–24 (1981)
March, J.G., Shapira, Z.: Managerial perspectives on risk and risk taking. Manage. Sci. **33**, 1404–1418 (1987). https://doi.org/10.1287/mnsc.33.11.1404
Martin, K.: Poland upgraded to developed market status by FTSE Russell, Financial Times, September 24, 2018. https://www.ft.com/content/0e4eabc2-bfd1-11e8-8d55-54197280d3f7. Last Accessed 18 Nov 2018
Mishina, Y., Pollock, T.G., Porac, J.F.: Are more resources always better for growth? Resource stickiness in market and product expansion. Strateg. Manag. J. **25**(2), 1179–1197 (2004). https://doi.org/10.1002/smj.424
Mitchell, T.R., James, L.R.: Building better theory: time and the specification of when things happen. Acad. Manag. Rev. **26**(4), 530–547 (2001). https://doi.org/10.5465/amr.2001.5393889
Moles, P., Parrino, R., Kidwell, D.: Corporate Finance. Wiley, Hoboken (2011)

Myers, S.C.: Capital structure. J. Econ. Perspect. **15**(2), 81–102 (2001). https://doi.org/10.1257/jep.15.2.81

Natividad, G.: Financial slack, strategy and competition in movie distribution. Organ. Sci. **24**(3), 846–864 (2013). https://doi.org/10.1287/orsc.1120.0765

Nohira, N., Gulati, R.: Is slack good or bad for innovation? Acad. Manag. J. **39**(5), 1245–1264 (1996). https://doi.org/10.2307/256998

Opler, T., Pinkowitz, L., Stulz, R., Williamson, R.: The determinants and implications of corporate cash holdings. J. Financ. Econ. **52**(1), 3–46 (1999). https://doi.org/10.1016/S0304-405X(99)00003-3

Penrose, E.: The theory of the Growth of the Firm. Wiley, New York (1959)

Phan, P., Hill, C.: Organizational restructuring and economic performance in leveraged buyouts: an ex post study. Acad. Manag. J. **38**(3), 704–739 (1995). https://doi.org/10.2307/256743

Rejda, G.E.: Principles of Risk Management and Insurance. Addison Wesley Longman, International Ed. (2001)

Ross, S.A.: The determination of financial structure: the incentive-signaling approach. Bell J. Econ. **8**(1), 23–40 (1977). https://doi.org/10.2307/3003485

Salancik, G., Pfeffer, J.: A social information processing approach to job attitudes and task design. Adm. Sci. Q. **23**(2), 224–253. https://doi.org/10.2307/2392563 (1978)

Sharfman, M., Wolf, G., Chase, R., Tansik, D.: Antecedents of organizational slack. Acad. Manag. Rev. **13**(4), 601–614 (1988). https://doi.org/10.5465/amr.1988.4307484

Stan, C.V., Peng, M.W., Bruton, G.D.: Slack and the performance of state-owned enterprises. Asia Pac. J. Manag. **31**, 473–495 (2014). https://doi.org/10.1007/s10490-013-9347-7

Singh, J.: Performance, slack and risk taking in organisational decision making. Acad. Manag. J. **29**(3), 562–585 (1986). https://doi.org/10.2307/256224

Tan, J., Peng, M.: Organizational slack and firm performance during economic transitions: two studies from and emerging economy. Strateg. Manag. J. **24**, 1249–1263 (2003). https://doi.org/10.1002/smj.351

The World Bank: Country overview—Poland. https://www.worldbank.org/en/country/poland/overview#4. Last Accessed 18 Nov 2018

Thomson, N., Millar, C.: The role of slack in transforming organisations: a comparative analysis of east german and slovenian companies. Int. Stud. Manag. Organ. **31**(2), 65–83. https://doi.org/10.1080/00208825.2001.11656815 (2001)

Titman, S.: The effects of capital structure on a firms liquidation decision. J. Financ. Econ. **13**(1), 137–151 (1984). https://doi.org/10.1016/0304-405X(84)90035-7

Torben, J.A.: Effective risk management outcomes: exploring effects of innovation and capital structure. J. Strat. Manag. **2**(4), 352–379 (2009). https://doi.org/10.1108/17554250911003845

Vaughan, E., Vaughan, T.: Fundamentals of risk and insurance. Wiley, Hoboken (2003)

Voss, G.B., Sirdeshmukh, D., Voss, Z.G.: The effects of slack resources and environmental threat on product exploration and exploitation. Acad. Manag. J. **51**(1), 147–164 (2008). https://doi.org/10.5465/amj.2008.30767373

Weber, C.: Insurance linked securities. The role of the banks. Gabler Verlag, Wiesbaden (2011)

Weinzimmer, L.G.: A replication and extension of organisational growth determinants. J. Bus. Res. **48**(1), 35–41 (2000). https://doi.org/10.1016/S0148-2963(98)00073-3

Wiengarten, F., Fan, D., Lo., C., Pagell, M.: The differing impacts of operational and financial slack on occupational safety in varying market conditions. J. Oper. Manag. **17**, 30–45. https://doi.org/10.1016/j.jom.2016.12.001 (2017)

Williams, C.A., Heins, R.M.: Risk Management and Insurance. McGraw-Hill, New York (1989)

Yasai-Ardekani, M.: Structural adaptations to environments. Acad. Manag. Rev. **11**(1), 9–21. https://doi.org/10.5465/amr.1986.4282607 (1986)

Zhong, H.: The relationship between slack resources and performance: an empirical study from China. Int. J. Mod. Educ. Comput. Sci. **1**, 1–8 (2011)

Agent-Based Model of Risk Assessment: A Distributed Cognition Approach

Clemens Harten

Abstract To better understand where and why errors happen in risk assessment, we propose a model of the risk assessment process as a distributed cognitive task for a group of agents. This model provides the foundation for an agent-based simulation that allows a systematic investigation of the risk assessment process in a controlled setting. Building on a perspective of sensemaking and cognition on risk analysis, we present a new approach to assess a whole class of group decision-making problems by building generalized constraint satisfaction networks as a starting point for a randomized agent-based simulation.

Keywords Constraint satisfaction networks · Agent-Based modeling · Group decision making

1 Introduction

Risk assessment is an integral part of Enterprise Risk Management (ERM). Organizations rely on effective risk assessment to inform their actions. However, risk assessment relies on notorious incomplete and uncertain information. Increasingly, risk decisions under large uncertainty, that cannot be modeled in simple probabilistic terms, are a focus of interest, as they call for new methods and approached towards risk analysis (Aven 2016). Moreover, information is often spread between a group of agents who must work together to come to a useful risk assessment. Naturally, this process is prone to produce errors and inaccuracies with potentially large implications for organizations. Recently, it has been suggested that our approach to risk management should be widened to account for the sensemaking of decision-makers regarding risks, instead of viewing risk analysis only as a scientific, technical task (Taarup-Esbensen 2018).

C. Harten (✉)
Hamburg University of Technology, Hamburg, Germany
e-mail: c.harten@tuhh.de

P. Linsley et al. (eds.), *Multiple Perspectives in Risk and Risk Management*, Springer Proceedings in Business and Economics,
https://doi.org/10.1007/978-3-030-16045-6_7

Based on this understanding of risk assessment as sensemaking, we want to investigate how the quality of risk analysis is influenced by the imperfections of human cognition and interaction.

However, it is difficult to evaluate the success of risk assessment in the field, as there is no known perfect risk assessment to benchmark against. Ex-post we know what happened, but what would have happened without risk mitigating measures? What other outcomes would have been equally likely to happen?

To fully assess the quality of risk assessment practice, we must analyze not only the actual outcome of a situation, but also alternative outcomes that could have happened, but didn't. This is possible with a simulation that models the risk environment and the risk assessment process, and that identifies many alternative outcomes of a situation. Because risk assessment is often performed not by an individual, but by a group of people, the simulation must account for the interaction between these individuals. Thus, the simulation must combine a simulation of individual cognition of the participants with a simulation of the participants' interaction. Such a simulation allows us to investigate why and how risk assessments succeed or fail to provide a good understanding of future events.

We propose a model of the risk assessment process as a distributed cognitive task, which will, going forward, allow us to understand where and why typical errors appear within risk assessment, what their consequences are, and how they depend on the procedures used in the organization.

We model the group work in the risk assessment task as an instance of distributed cognition, a cognitive task distributed between a group of individuals (Hutchins 2000). The model combines agent-based simulation for simulating the interaction of several agents during the risk assessment, with Constraint Satisfaction Networks (CSN) to simulate the cognition of the individual agents: Agent-based simulation provides means to investigate complex human interactions, and to analyze these interactions in a fully controlled setting (Gilbert and Troitzsch 2005).

In order to do this, we rely on the ECHO (Explanatory Coherence by Harmany [sic] Optimization) model, as detailed in (Thagard 1989, 1992). ECHO provides a CSN that describes cognitive processes as the alignment of conflicting or reinforcing units, that represent ideas or observations of reality. It has, for example, been successfully applied to describe the reasoning about conflicting concepts or interpretations in science and judiciary (e.g. Nowak and Thagard 1992; Thagard 2004).

While initially developed to describe the cognitive negotiation of conflicting explanations for given observations of reality, the model can and has been used to describe decision-making tasks (e.g. Thagard 2004; Frigotto and Rossi 2015).

An ECHO network models the cognition of a single individual. The cooperation of multiple individuals in performing a (distributed) cognitive task can be modeled by introducing exchange between the individual networks. This can either be done by connecting all individual networks to one, shared network (as done by Hutchins in (Hutchins 2000) for a similar CSN) or by allowing the actors to communicate with each other and updating their individual networks afterward (e.g. Thagard 2000; Frigotto and Rossi 2012).

This new approach of simulating risk assessment as distributed cognition aims to contribute to the risk research literature by allowing new insights, that cannot be obtained by empirical research.

2 Modeling Risk Assessment

To learn about the risk assessment practice and its shortcomings with a simulation, all relevant components need to be modeled. In this chapter, we propose a model of risk assessment based on an understanding of risk assessment as sensemaking. First, we describe the understanding of risk assessment that underlies the model (Sect. 2.1). Second, the real-world practice of risk assessment is described as a combination of individual cognition and interaction between agents (Sect. 2.2). Finally, the technical implementation of the simulation is detailed in Sects. 2.3 and 2.4.

2.1 Risk Assessment as Sensemaking

Sensemaking is a perspective in organization studies that refers to processes "by which people seek plausibly to understand ambiguous, equivocal or confusing issues or events" (Brown et al. 2015). Pioneered by Karl Weick (Weick 1995), it has a significant following in management and organization studies (Brown et al. 2015).

Sensemaking turns out to be a valuable perspective to study risk analysis in organizations: Many important risks are difficult to quantify and decision-makers have to rely on judgment for their risk assessment (Mikes 2009). Thus, we can improve risk assessment by understanding how managers think about the causes of risks (Bromiley et al. 2014).

Recently it has been argued that, as risk management increasingly focuses on evermore complex risks, a shift is taking place in risk management research and practice from a "techno-scientific" perspective, where managers assess risks with scientific techniques as an unknown probability, towards a perspective of "risk sensemaking", where risk managers "engages with the social and physical environment with the aim of acquiring cues that could indicate how future events will unfold" (Taarup-Esbensen 2018). For successful risk management, both the analytical understanding of risks and the affective, emotional perspective have to be integrated (Slovic et al. 2004).

This perspective of risk as sensemaking suggests that risk assessment can be understood as a distributed cognitive task: A group of people collect their information and ideas ("cues" Taarup-Esbensen 2018) into a "common pool of knowledge" and, by interacting, create a collective "representation of the world" that goes beyond the individual understanding of any of the group members (Taylor and Van Every 1999).

2.2 Risk Assessment Process Model

This study aims to provide a model of the risk assessment process, as it is performed in organizations. The exact meaning of risk assessment and its role in risk management is not agreed upon (Aven 2012). We use the ISO definition that describes risk assessment as the overall process of identifying, analyzing and evaluating risks (ISO—The International Organization for Standardization 2009). At the center of the model is the process of risk analysis, that is the consideration of factors that impact the meaning of a risk for the organization and deducting an assessment of the risks consequences, their likelihood and impact (ISO—The International Organization for Standardization 2009).

Risk analysis can be described as a process of judgment and decision-making, that is based on knowledge about a risk. The knowledge is derived from evidence relating to a risk that is available to the decision-maker, as well as a broader, general understanding of the subject at hand, that goes beyond the risk itself (Hansson and Aven 2014).

The Risk Assessment Process. Risk assessment is usually a task that is performed distributed within a group or team. Every participant of the group might have some information or perspective that is relevant for a proper analysis of the risk. The risk assessment process should enable the organization to achieve the best possible analysis of a given risk, in order to make a valid assessment of a risk's consequences and to derive appropriate measures.

Within the process, participants can communicate their individual knowledge, ideas and understandings to collectively reach a better assessment of the risk at hand.

To model this interactive risk assessment process, we need to provide a model of both the individual participants' cognition as well as for the exchange between the participants.

The Individual Cognition. The agents' internal reasoning process is modeled as the interplay of three layers: The layer of knowledge, the layer of hypotheses, and the layer of assessment (see Fig. 1).

The layer of knowledge represents an agent's memory of facts that can be used to assess a risk. The facts are modeled as a pool of information concerning a risk's potential impact or probability of occurrence.

The layer of hypotheses represents the actor's cognitive activity in assessing the available information. A number of hypotheses about the correct way to interpret a given risk are activated to a varying degree by the available information. All hypotheses are connected to each other by positive or negative relationships, e.g. the activation of one hypothesis conflicts with the activation of another hypothesis because they are representing opposing ideas of how to assess a given risk. These relationships lead to tensions in the initial pattern of activation. In the simulation phase, the tensions can be (partly) resolved by the CSN. Each agent ends the reasoning about available information in a stable state of beliefs about the given risk, with a remaining element of inconsistency in its internal beliefs.

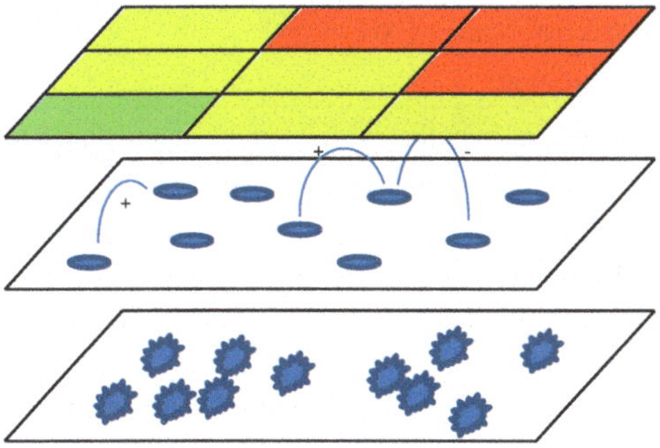

Fig. 1 The three layers of the agent's cognitive model for assessing a risk

The layer of assessment is the final stage of the agent's reasoning about the assessment of the given risk: The classification of the risk regarding its severity, as expressed by its assumed impact and probability. The final pattern of activation of hypotheses is translated into a score towards the different possible assessments of a risk, e.g. "this risk has a low probability of occurrence and would have a medium impact".

The details of the model of the individual's cognition are described in Sect. 2.3.

Model of Communication. The communication between different agents can happen on all three layers: Depending on the rules of interaction, agents can communicate their overall assessment of a risk, their opinion towards hypotheses about a risk or they can exchange information available to them. The modeling of these interactions is, depending on the layer, informed by principles of opinion dynamics in agent-based simulation (Hegselmann and Krause 2002; Xia et al. 2010) and group decision-making theory.

The regime of communication and interaction between the agents can be modeled according to the established practice in ERM, reproducing prototypical settings of hierarchy, group structure and information exchange (e.g. the Delphi method Linstone and Turoff 1975).

2.3 Constraint Satisfaction Network

The individual cognition is implemented as a Constraint Satisfaction Network. The implementation relies on the connectionist ECHO model, introduced by Paul Thagard (Thagard 1989).

There are two main approaches in cognitive science to model cognitive architecture: Rule-based systems and connectionism (Thagard 2012). While rule-based systems build upon explicit if-then statements, that are connected and combined to describe complex cognitive tasks, connectionist systems rely on a network of neuron-like units to represent elements of the cognitive task. The units are insofar

Table 1 Parameters for a generalized risk assessment CSN

Parameter	Value	Description
Nr_hypotheses	20	Number of hypotheses-units in the complete CSN
Nr_facts	20	Number of fact-units in the complete CSN
H_con	0.3	The probability of two hypotheses to be connected to each other
F_con	0.3	The probability of a hypothesis and a fact to be connected to each other
H_con_pos	0.7	The rate of connections between hypotheses that are explanatory (as opposed to contradictory)
F_con_pos	0.7	The rate of connections between hypotheses and facts that are explanatory (as opposed to contradictory)

neuron-like, as they have an individual degree of activation and are connected with each other by excitatory and inhibitory links (Thagard 2012).

For this model, a connectionist approach is chosen for the cognitive architecture of the agents. This is suitable because the rules by which a decision maker makes their risk assessment are not well known or defined. The decision maker takes many (conflicting) ideas, information, and interpretations into consideration, and aggregates them into an overall assessment. This process cannot be broken down into clear rules but must account for the imprecision and ad-hoc character of the decision-making process. Thus, a connectionist approach is better suited to model the cognitive architecture of a decision maker performing a risk assessment for this study.

Both knowledge and hypotheses are nodes or "units" in the network. Units can be "activated" in a specific range, e.g. $[-1;1]$. The higher the activation of a unit, the stronger the belief in the associated hypothesis or fact. If for example, an individual has an activation of 0.8 for the hypotheses-unit $H_{strike\text{-}customer}$: 'a strike in our plant would negatively impact the relationship to our customers', this is a belief the individual holds rather strongly. If, on the other hand, the activation for the fact-unit F_{vote}: 'our workers have voted to strike' is -0.2, the individual has a weak opinion that it is not true that workers have voted to strike.

A Generic Risk Assessment CSN. As we want to look at the general process of risk assessment, as opposed to a single specific case, we generate random networks that show the 3-layered structure detailed above: A certain number of hypotheses relevant to assessing a risk, a certain number of facts, supporting the assessment, and logical connections between the hypotheses, as well as between facts and hypotheses (e.g. "If I think F_{vote}: 'our workers have voted to strike' is true, I also believe $H_{dissatisfied}$: 'our workers are dissatisfied with the status quo'").

The parameters we used to configure the generalized networks are documented in Table 1. They were derived from building exemplary networks for prototypical risk scenarios.

The constraint satisfaction of the network is modeled along the algorithms and parameter provided in (Thagard 1989).

Table 2 Parameters for the ECHO CSN

Parameter	Value	Description
min	−1	Minimum activation of a unit
max	1	Maximum activation of a unit
θ	0.1	Decay parameter
a_{Start}	0.01	Initial activation of all units
Default_expl	0.05	Default weight of an explanatory connection
Default_contr	−0.2	Default weight of a contradiction connection

The network is described by three different possible relationships between units: Explanation, Contradiction, and Data.

Explanation. Explanations express positive relationships between units. If hypothesis a is logically consistent with hypothesis b, this is represented by an explanatory connection. For our network, a causal relationship between both hypotheses is not necessary—only consistency is. The naming of the relationships was chosen to be consistent with the algorithms presented in (Thagard 1989).

Contradiction. Contradictions express negative relationships between units. If a belief in hypothesis A is not logically consistent with a belief in hypothesis B, both units are connected by a contradiction connection.

Data. A "data" relationship is established between all fact-units in the network and a special purpose unit that is always fully activated. This relationship is supposed to make sure that stable networks must incorporate (known) facts, as they are (other than hypotheses) constantly reinforced by factual evidence supporting them.

A CSN is fully described by its units and the connections between them. Once a networked is described, all units in the network are given an initial activation. Now, the activation a of each unit is adjusted according to formula (1), until a stable state is reached (Thagard 1992):

$$a_j(t+1) = a_j(t)(1-\theta) + \begin{cases} net_j\left(max - a_j(t)\right) & if net_j > 0 \\ net_j\left(a_j(t) - min\right) & otherwise \end{cases} \quad (1)$$

The formula uses the decay parameter θ to reduce the current activation of the unit (see Table 2 for the default parameter of the ECHO network). *max* and *min* are the maximum and minimum activation of a unit (−1 and +1), net_j is the net input from connected units to unit j:

$$net_j = \sum_i w_{ij} a_i(t) \quad (2)$$

Here, w_{ij} is the strength of the connection between unit i and j.

Before we look at the cognition of individual agents, we generate a generic network that we assume to be a complete understanding of the risk at hand, that is, a network containing all relevant knowledge, all relevant hypotheses, and their interconnections.

This is the perspective of the risk at hand an all-knowing individual would have. To judge the quality of an agent's risk assessment, we compare their assessment (that is, the pattern of unit-activation) against the assessment of an all-knowing agent. Thus, we have a benchmark for the risk assessment task, something that is hard to come by outside a simulation.

To translate the agents' settled CSN into risk assessment decisions, we introduce two special hypotheses-units into all networks:

$\boldsymbol{H_{specialP}}$: "The risk is highly likely to materialize".

$\boldsymbol{H_{specialI}}$: "The risk will have a major impact, if it materializes".

The activations of $H_{specialP}$ and $H_{specialI}$ can be interpreted as the agent's assessment of the risk at hand, e.g. $H_{specialP} = 0.4$ is approximately equivalent to the assessment "the risk has a medium probability of materializing".

The limited understanding and knowledge of agents about a risk are modeled by removing random hypotheses and facts from their individual network (similar to (Frigotto and Rossi 2012), where heterogeneous agents are created by removing connections from the agents' networks).

2.4 Agent Interaction

After creating an individual CSN for all agents, we can allow agents to interact with each other. To model the communication, we follow a regime of a series of 1-on-1 meetings of two agents, where both agents can evolve their individual understanding by considering information shared by the other agent (c.f. Thagard 2000; Hegselmann and Krause 2002). From the way the individual cognition is modeled, we can distinguish two different types of exchange: Exchange of units and exchange of activations.

Exchange of Units. As described earlier, in the beginning, each agent has only limited knowledge and understanding of a risk, that is, their individual network does not contain all relevant hypothesis-units and fact-units. When two agents communicate, it is possible for them to include units into their network, that are unknown to them, but available to their communication partner. This type of communication can be interpreted as the exchange of information or ideas.

Exchange of Activations. The activation of units represents the agent's belief in the underlying hypotheses and facts. When a hypothesis or fact is known to both communicating agents, they can exchange their activations and evolve their own activation accordingly. This type of exchange closely resembles the exchange of opinions in opinion dynamics models, e.g. (Hegselmann and Krause 2002). The most basic form of adapting to the activation of the communication partner is as follows:

$$a_{Aj}(t+1) = a_{Aj}(t)(1-\vartheta) + a_{Bj}(t)\vartheta \tag{3}$$

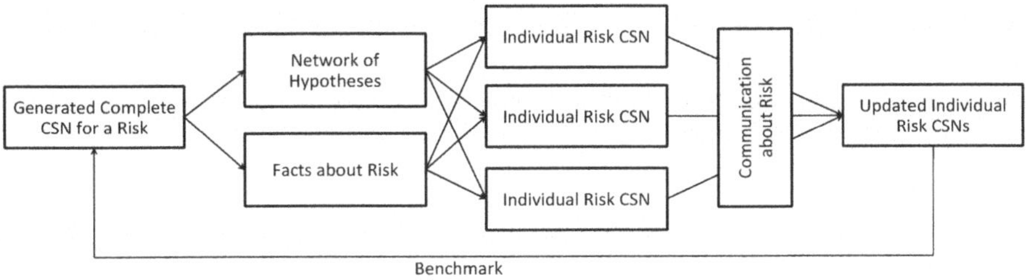

Fig. 2 The process of risk assessment in the model

Here, a_{Aj} is the activation of unit j for agent A, who meets agent B, and ϑ is a parameter for the openness of an agent to adjust to other agents' views.

After agents have updated their individual network (by adding units or adjusting unit activation), their network will be stabilized again, to reach a coherent interpretation of the risk at hand. This process can be repeated until the risk assessments of the individual agents are similar enough to each other to assume a group consensus on how to assess the risk at hand.

A whole simulation cycle is displayed in Fig. 2: It begins by randomly generating a CSN that describes the cognitive model that an all-knowing individual would have to assess a risk. Out of the complete model, the individual agents' cognitive models are generated by removing a certain number of units. Afterward, the agents communicate with each other until a consensus is reached on the risk assessment. This consensus can be benchmarked against the risk assessment by the theoretical, all-knowing agent.

By repeating this simulation cycle many times, and varying parameters of the model, like the number of agents involved, the initial distribution of knowledge, the communication behavior of the agents or the acceptance of other agents' views, we can quantify the influence of these factors on the quality of the risk assessment.

3 Discussion and Conclusion

We describe an approach to model the risk assessment in organizations as an agent-based model of distributed cognition. To our knowledge, this is the first model to use generalized CSN to describe a class of group decision-making problems.

The model will allow us to systematically simulate cognition in teams that deal with complex decisions. Moving forward, the model allows us to investigate how factors like the distribution of information, group size, hierarchy and individual traits like confidence or risk aversion influence the quality of a risk assessment.

By using a simulation to investigate the risk assessment process, we have the benefit of being able to compare results against a benchmark that provides the best possible assessment. This is difficult to do in empirical studies, where we only know one course of events, but can never say for certain what alternative courses of events would have been equally possible. Thus, a general agent-based model of the risk assessment process built on CSN will provide an interesting new perspective on the drivers of quality of risk assessment practice.

References

Aven, T.: Foundational issues in risk assessment and risk management. Risk Anal. **32**(10), 1647–1656 (2012)

Aven, T.: Risk assessment and risk management: Review of recent advances on their foundation. Eur. J. Oper. Res. **253**(1), 1–13 (2016)

Bromiley, P., McShane, M., Nair, A., Rustambekov, E.: Enterprise risk management: review, critique, and research directions. Long Range Plan. **48**(4), 265–276 (2014)

Brown, A.D., Colville, I., Pye, A.: Making sense of sensemaking in organization studies. Organ. Stud. **36**(2), 265–277 (2015)

Frigotto, M.L., Rossi, A.: Diversity and communication in teams: improving problem-solving or creating confusion? Group Decis. Negot. **21**(6), 791–820 (2012)

Frigotto, M.L., Rossi, A.: An explanatory coherence model of decision making in ill-structured problems. Mind Soc. **14**(1), 35–55 (2015)

Gilbert, N., Troitzsch, K.G.: Simulation for the Social Scientist. Open University Press, Berkshire (2005)

Hansson, S.O., Aven, T.: Is Risk Analysis Scientific? Risk Anal. **34**(7), 1173–1183 (2014)

Hegselmann, R., Krause, U.: Opinion dynamics and bounded confidence models, analysis, and simulation. Journal of Artificial Societies and Social Simulation 5(3) (2002)

Hutchins, E.: Cognition in the wild. MIT Press, Cambridge, Massachusetts (2000)

ISO—The International Organization for Standardization: ISO 31000:2009—Risk management—Principles and guidelines (2009)

Linstone, H.A., Turoff, M.: The delphi method. Addison-Wesley, Reading, MA (1975)

Mikes, A.: Risk management and calculative cultures. Manag. Account. Res. **20**, 18–40 (2009)

Nowak, G., Thagard, P.: Newton, Descartes, and explanatory coherence. In: Duschl, R.A., Hamilton, R.J. (eds.) Philosophy of Science, Cognitive Psychology and Educational Theory and Practice, pp. 69–115. State University of New York Press, Albany, New York (1992)

Slovic, P., Finucane, M.L., Peters, E., MacGregor, D.G.: Risk as analysis and risk as feelings: some thoughts about affect, reason, risk, and rationality. Risk Anal. **24**(2), 311–322 (2004)

Taarup-Esbensen, J.: Making sense of risk—a sociological perspective on the management of risk. Risk Anal. (2018)

Taylor, J.R., Van Every, E.J.: The emergent organization: communication as its site and surface. Routledge (1999)

Thagard, P.: Explanatory coherence. Behav. Brain Sci. **12**(3), 435–467 (1989)

Thagard, P.: Conceptual Revolutions. Princeton University Press, Princeton, New Jersey (1992)

Thagard, P.: Coherence in thought and action. MIT Press, Cambridge, Mass (2000)

Thagard, P.: Causal inference in legal decision making: explanatory coherence versus Bayesian networks. Appl. Artif. Intell. **18**(3–4), 231–249 (2004)

Thagard, P.: Cognitive architectures. In: Frankish, K., Ramsey, W.M. (eds.) The Cambridge handbook of cognitive science, pp. 50–70. Cambridge University Press, Cambridge, UK (2012)

Weick, K.E.: Sensemaking in organizations. Sage, Thousand Oaks, CA (1995)

Xia, H., Wang, H., Xuan, Z.: Opinion dynamics: disciplinary origins, recent developments, and a view on future trends. Phys. Rev. **18**(5), 35–39 (2010)

Small & Medium-Sized Enterprise Risk Monitoring Based on Financial Analysis Results

Tomasz Jastrząb and Artur Łopata

Abstract In the paper, we discuss the problem of risk monitoring in small and medium-sized enterprises (SMEs). To this aim, we propose to use the results of the analysis of enterprise financial standing. We indicate the crucial groups of financial ratios as well as the most important financial ratios themselves, that should be taken into account in the process of continuous risk monitoring in an enterprise. We also present the features of eanaliza.pl online service, which can be helpful in calculating the up-to-date information on enterprise financial situation. Using the service we investigate the possible risk factors for a hypothetical small-sized enterprise. We conclude the paper by stating that the use of IT tools, such as the eanaliza.pl service, can bring important benefits to the SMEs in the context of risk management.

Keywords Risk monitoring · Financial analysis · eanaliza.pl

1 Introduction

Risk monitoring, being the subject of this paper, is one of the eight elements of Enterprise Risk Management (ERM) as given by the Committee of Sponsoring Organizations of the Treadway Commission (COSO) (*Enterprise Risk Management*... 2004). It is also indicated as one of the crucial ERM elements in (D'Arcy and Brogan 2001). In the general sense, it denotes the activities and processes allowing to assess the risks in an enterprise (*Enterprise Risk Management*... 2004).

Risk management is crucial for the proper and successful operation of any enterprise. It can take different forms, from avoidance through reduction and transfer, to acceptance of the risk "as is" (Olson and Wu 2015). The ERM is especially concerned with risk reduction, which if handled properly may even lead to gaining additional

T. Jastrząb (✉)
Silesian University of Technology, Akademicka 16, 44-100 Gliwice, Poland
e-mail: tomasz.jastrzab@polsl.pl

A. Łopata
Technicenter Sp. z o.o., Tatrzańska 2, 41-907 Bytom, Poland

P. Linsley et al. (eds.), *Multiple Perspectives in Risk and Risk Management*, Springer Proceedings in Business and Economics,
https://doi.org/10.1007/978-3-030-16045-6_8

profits. According to Lam, ERM aims at answering the following four fundamental questions (Lam 2000):

1. Is taking the risk worth it?
2. Are we prepared well enough to minimize the risks?
3. Do we have the right tools to measure and handle the risks?
4. Do we have the right people and knowledge to manage the risks?

To help in answering some of the questions put forth by Lam, we propose to use the results of the financial analysis to assess the risks related to enterprise operation. To this aim, we show a semi-automatic method of risk monitoring based on the eanaliza.pl system—an online service performing the financial analysis. The semi-automatism of the method stems from the fact that after providing the financial documents, the system automatically extracts the data and calculates the financial ratios. The interpretation of the results is so far left to the service user.

Although the results of the financial analysis are valid for any type of enterprise, regardless of its size, we focus here on Small and Medium-sized Enterprises (SMEs). The reason behind the approach taken in this paper is that SMEs are in need for intuitive, easy-to-use, and, most importantly, affordable tools supporting their functioning, including risk management. As discussed in the next section, the lack of sufficient funding and very limited knowledge are the two main problems related to risk management in SMEs. Therefore, we would like to point out to the SME managers that they can use the results of the financial analysis, provided by eanaliza.pl service, to easily monitor the possible risks they may face.

The paper is organized into 5 sections. In Sect. 2 we present a brief literature review pertaining to the risk management in small & medium-sized enterprises. In Sect. 3 we discuss the eanaliza.pl online service in the context of risk monitoring. In Sect. 4 we analyze the risks revealed by the financial analysis of the sample enterprise. In Sect. 5 we summarize the paper and outline future research perspectives.

2 Literature Review

Enterprise risk management is a complex process due to the number and variety of factors affecting the enterprise. The differences between the subjective view of the identified risk, and its objective value, as well as the underestimations of actual risks, add to the difficulty of ERM (Bromiley et al. 2015). Furthermore, the clearly positive effects of ERM implementation, including the employment of Chief Risk Officers, are not always confirmed in the literature, which may be discouraging for the SME managers (Callahan and Soileau 2017; Gordon et al. 2009; Hoyt and Liebenberg 2011; McShane et al. 2011; Nocco and Stulz 2006; Quon et al. 2012; Smithson and Simkins 2005). Although the research results typically show positive associations between the enterprise value and the implementation of ERM, they are mainly based on the analysis of large enterprises. But the approach towards ERM taken by a big corporation might not be suitable for a smaller enterprise, due to its limited resources. Therefore, in our literature review, we focus on the solutions pertaining particularly to the SMEs.

In terms of official regulation or best practice guides towards risk management in small & medium-size enterprises, one may find the ISO 31000 document (*ISO 31000 Risk*… 2018). The document provides guidance as to the prerequisites and ways of implementing the risk management framework in enterprises. A review of existing literature pertaining to the subject of risk management in SMEs was given in (Falkner and Hiebl 2015). The authors point out the different risk types the enterprises face, such as the changes in interest rates of loans, technological risks, management risks, and others. They also discuss the different approaches taken by SMEs to deal with the risks they encounter, distinguishing two major solutions—a defensive and informal approach (Gao et al. 2013) or a proactive, formalized approach (Brustbauer 2014). A key element of risk management in SMEs is the influence of personal characteristics on the attitude towards ERM (Falkner and Hiebl 2015; Belás et al. 2015; Kozubíková et al. 2015).

From the perspective of the Polish sector of SMEs, it was pointed out that the typical approach towards risk management is based on risk insurance (Mikulska 2010, 2012; Wierzbicka 2015). As stated by Wierzbicka, the eagerness to buy an insurance depends on the size of the enterprise, with larger enterprises being more willing to insure their business (Wierzbicka 2015). The survey conducted by Spiżyk has shown that the entrepreneurs usually have moderate knowledge about the risks they may face and hence either do nothing to prevent the risks or act intuitively, choosing an insurance strategy as the most popular solution to risk reduction (Spiżyk 2015). A similar study conducted by Gaschi-Uciecha has shown, that micro-, small and medium-sized enterprises usually do not apply any risk management strategies (67–82% of questionnaire respondents answered negatively to the question of whether they employ any ERM strategies) (Gaschi-Uciecha 2016). The reasons for such an attitude is the problem with access to the financing sources and the lack of reserves in SMEs. This point is also confirmed by the study of SMEs in the Czech Republic and Slovakia (Virglerová et al. 2016). The works closest to ours, in the sense that they also use the financial analysis results or the balance sheet information to assess the risks, are the ones by Diaz and Sanchez (2016) or Błach (2010). However, they use different ratios that we do, and obviously, they do not use the eanaliza.pl system to calculate them.

In terms of existing software aiding the implementation of ERM processes the annual RiskTech100 report is a great source of information on the currently trending applications (*RiskTech100*… 2017). As given by Mejssner, the ERM solutions are focused on applying the Big Data techniques, provided typically in the cloud environment and possibly based on the open-source solutions (Mejssner 2018). The top-rated systems provide the users with access from various devices, through mobile, web or desktop applications (*Risk Software Report* 2017).

3 eanaliza.pl as a Risk Monitoring Tool

The eanaliza.pl system, available at https://eanaliza.pl/, is an online service developed by Technicenter Sp. z o.o. in cooperation with the University of Economics in Katowice, Poland. The service allows to perform the ratio-based analysis of the enterprise's situation based on the balance sheet and the profit and loss statement, supplemented with additional information on the short- and long-term loans taken (Jastrząb et al. 2017).

The analysis is performed over the number of periods determined on the basis of the contents of the provided documents or defined manually within the service. Depending on the user's choices the analysis can be performed over past, current or future periods, provided that relevant data is made available to the system. Taking into account the fact that the analysis can be performed retrospectively as well as prospectively, it is possible to continuously monitor the financial situation of the enterprise. It should be also understood, that whenever we speak about the assessment of the financial situation of the enterprise, we also indirectly mean the financial risk assessment, which can be performed by applying proper interpretations to the calculated values of the ratios (Jastrząb et al. 2017). Furthermore, the risk analysis can also be performed by observing the trends of ratio values' changes or by comparing them to the industry benchmarks, theoretical reference values or assumed expected values (Cowen and Hoffer 1982). Note, however, that the ratios are often highly correlated with each other (Pinches et al. 1975) and they suffer from certain limitations (Baruch and Shyam 1979). Therefore to make valid interpretations of the observed values and their changes over time, one should have a proper understanding of their meaning.

The eanaliza.pl service allows to conduct financial analysis in three major aspects:

1. Through the set of analytical ratios, divided into the following groups (Błach et al. 2013; Fabozzi and Peterson 2003):

   a. financial liquidity,
   b. debt management,
   c. efficiency (activity),
   d. profitability,
   e. general performance.

2. By means of percentage structure analysis, including the following subgroups:

   a. assets,
   b. liabilities,
   c. costs,
   d. revenues.

3. By means of dynamics analysis, containing the following subgroups:

   a. assets,
   b. liabilities,
   c. profit and loss statement.

Table 1 An overview of the groups of ratios available in eanaliza.pl service

Group name	# Basic ratios	# Additional ratios	Total
Analytical financial ratios			
Financial liquidity	6	3	9
Debt management	10	2	12
Efficiency (activity)	7	5	12
Profitability	5	2	7
General performance	6	1	7
Percentage composition			
Assets	29	0	29
Liabilities	31	0	31
Costs	12	0	12
Revenues	8	0	8
Dynamics			
Assets	29	0	29
Liabilities	31	0	31
Profit and loss statement	24	0	24

Let us also note that within the groups of analytical ratios, the service distinguishes the sets of basic and additional ratios, with the latter group allowing to perform a more detailed analysis of enterprise's financial situation (Błach et al. 2015; Gorczyńska and Wieczorek-Kosmala 2015). The numbers of elements available in each of the groups of ratios are summarized in Table 1.

Since the analytical ratios provide the best information on the enterprise's standing and consequently possible financial risks related to its operation, in the remainder of this paper we will focus on these ratios only. To provide some better understanding of how the financial ratios can be used in the context of risk monitoring and risk management let us consider what type of information regarding the potential threats is carried by the respective groups of analytical ratios mentioned before.

The group of financial liquidity ratios (liquidity ratios, in short) provides the information on the alignment between the liquid assets, which can be relatively easily converted to cash, and short-term liabilities of the enterprise. If the volume of liquid assets is not large enough to cover the current liabilities, the enterprise may easily run into the liquidity risk. Hence, the monitoring of the liquidity ratios is the key element of risk monitoring that should be performed by SME managers (Jastrząb et al. 2017; Błach et al. 2015; Gorczyńska and Wieczorek-Kosmala 2015). Taking into account the particular ratios present in this group, it should be noted that they allow monitoring the levels of risk resulting both from the insufficient liquidity as well as the excess liquidity. The former problem may lead to bankruptcy since the enterprise will not be able to cover its short-term liabilities with the use of the liquid assets. The latter issue may in turn negatively impact the profitability and efficiency, as the level of the liquid assets is too large for the enterprise's needs. For a discussion of how the changes in the liquidity and profitability levels depend on each other see also (Zygmunt 2013; Kumar and Upreti 2018) and their references.

The debt management ratios, including the indebtedness-related ratios and debt coverage ratios, allow having a look at the capital structure. They are very useful in assessing the creditworthiness of the enterprise, meaning the ability to pay its debts on time, or conversely, the probability that the enterprise defaults (Iyer et al. 2009), which means it will not manage to meet the debt liabilities on time (bankruptcy risk). Furthermore, the ratios such as the cash flow coverage ratio or the fixed assets to long-term debt ratio allow assessing the debt capacity of the enterprise, being the estimate of the amount of debt the enterprise can take and repay. From the risk monitoring perspective, the ratios are crucial not only for the enterprise managers but also for external parties, such as banks or money lenders. The latter can, for example, assess whether they can safely lend the money to the given enterprise. The enterprise owners, in turn, can observe if increasing the level of debt improves (deteriorates) the profitability by means of the positive (negative) financial leverage effect (Sojda 2015; Worzała 2015).

The activity analysis can be used to assess the efficiency of enterprise assets management, the proportion of costs in the level of revenues from sales and the turnover ratios (Jastrząb et al. 2017; Ehrhardt and Brigham 2011). The costs proportions, both operating and financial, can become serious signals of taking unprofitable actions, or of incurring excessive costs resulting from interest rates. The analysis of turnover ratios can, in turn, indicate the negative effects related to inventory management policy, the problems with receivables recoverability and trade credit policy, or the threats to liquidity resulting from the inability to pay the short-term liabilities on time. The cash conversion cycle is also a crucial indicator of potential risks, such as the excessive engagement of current liabilities in financing the current activities (Gorczyńska and Wieczorek-Kosmala 2015; Garanina and Petrova 2015; Richards and Laughlin 1980].

The profitability ratios relate the selected profit (gross, or more commonly the net profit) to various factors such as the levels of sales (ROS), assets (ROA) or equity (ROE) (Megginson and Smart 2006). The worse the profitability, indicated by the lower values of selected ratios, the greater the risk of bankruptcy in the long run. One of the important risk indicators is the Basic Earnings Power ratio, which defines the maximum interest rate value that can be allowed before the negative financial leverage effects arise.

Finally, the general performance ratios give an overview of the enterprise's financial stability and general standing. The ratios assess the risks of the loss of financial stability, deteriorated solvency and creditworthiness or unsatisfactory overall standing of the enterprise. The analysis of assets structure ratio may also indicate insufficient production capabilities (if the amount of fixed assets is much lower than the amount of current assets), or reduced flexibility related to operating risk, and consequently profitability (if the fixed assets base is excessively large). To monitor the risk of financial stability loss, the golden balance and financial rule ratios should be controlled.

As can be seen from the description presented above, each group of analytical ratios carries some information on possible risks related to the enterprise's operation. However, since the number of available ratios is quite large (47 ratios in total), only selected ratios are usually used to preliminarily assess the financial situation of the enterprise. For example, Kościelniak proposes to use a synthetic ratio calculated as a weighted sum of selected ratios including among others: the return on sales, the return on equity, the basic earnings power ratio and the current ratio (Kościelniak 2010). Nowak, in turn, points out that in the sector of micro-enterprises, only some part of the available ratios can be calculated due to the simplifications of their financial statements (Nowak 2017). However, the author concludes that even the simplified balance sheet, as well as the profit and loss statement, provide sufficient information to reliably assess the situation of the enterprise, e.g. by means of the selected profitability or efficiency ratios.

Taking into account the above considerations we decided, for the purposes of this paper, to include in the risk monitoring process the following analytical ratios:

- current ratio
- quick ratio
- debt-to-equity ratio
- inventories cycle
- receivables cycle
- liabilities cycle
- return on sales
- return on assets
- return on equity
- long-term solvency ratio based on equity coverage (golden balance rule)
- long-term solvency ratio based on fixed capital coverage (golden financial rule).

The selection of the ratios presented above was motivated by two purposes. The first purpose was to cover all groups of financial ratios discussed before. The second reason was that the chosen ratios are well-suited to indicate the potential risks related to the current financial situation of the enterprise and to its standing in the long run.

4 Risk Monitoring in Practice—A Sample Study

Let us now consider a risk monitoring scenario for enterprise X belonging to the small & medium-sized enterprises sector. The scenario has been conducted with the use of eanaliza.pl service, based on the balance sheet and profit and loss statement prepared using the document templates available in the service. The document templates were consistent with the current Accounting Act (*Ustawa z dnia*… 1994).

Table 2 Selected elements of the financial statements of enterprise X

Element	2014	2015	2016	2017
Balance sheet				
Fixed assets	6,626,388.40	7,901,434.70	5,686,687.14	4,720,905.73
Current assets	7,342,137.06	5,866,954.07	2,536,791.49	1,184,637.30
Inventory	638,328.85	630,341.55	452,827.71	457,224.75
Short-term receivables	1,507,882.02	1,448,186.18	1,077,492.92	708,547.43
Short-term prepayments	0.00	0.00	9,650.96	15,810.06
Total assets	13,968,525.46	13,768,388.77	8,223,478.63	5,905,543.03
Equity	7,579,612.51	6,225,788.03	2,661,854.53	1,782,796.73
Net profit (loss)	2,817,878.69	2,551,242.97	879,603.80	503,669.37
Liabilities and provisions for liabilities	6,388,912.95	7,542,600.74	5,561,624.10	4,122,746.30
Short-term liabilities	1,837,270.42	1,970,077.85	1,899,835.82	1,968,439.03
Total liabilities	13,968,525.46	13,768,388.77	8,223,478.63	5,905,543.03
Profit and loss statement				
Net revenues from sales	19,573,136.44	18,506,298.32	10,118,315.47	9,161,080.33
Net profit (loss)	2,817,878.69	2,551,242.97	879,603.80	503,669.37
Additional information				
Long-term loans	0.00	450,000.00	0.00	100,000.00
Short-term loans	0.00	150,000.00	150,000.00	30,000.00

The enterprise was assessed over the period 2014–2017, with the assumption that each yearly period has 360 days.[1] The key elements of the balance sheet and the profit and loss statement, from the perspective of the aforementioned financial ratios calculation, are shown in Table 2. It can be observed that both the short- and long-term loans were taken during this period of time.

Based on the data shown in Table 2, the values of financial ratios were calculated and visualized in the eanaliza.pl service. The values of ratios belonging to the groups of liquidity ratios (current and quick ratio), efficiency ratios (turnover ratios), and profitability ratios (returns on sales, assets, and equity) are shown in Figs. 1, 2 and 3, respectively. The values of the selected ratios are also given in Table 3. From the analysis of the presented ratios, it follows that there are several risks threatening the proper and efficient operation of enterprise X.

First of all, based on the liquidity ratios we can observe that the enterprise moved from the periods of excess liquidity (in years 2014 and 2015) to the period of financial liquidity loss in the year 2017. However, the loss of financial liquidity should be expected from the results obtained in 2016, when the value of the current ratio was hovering near the limiting value indicating proper liquidity level. Furthermore, the

[1] The information is crucial for the calculation of the turnover ratios (i.e. the inventories, receivables and liabilities cycles).

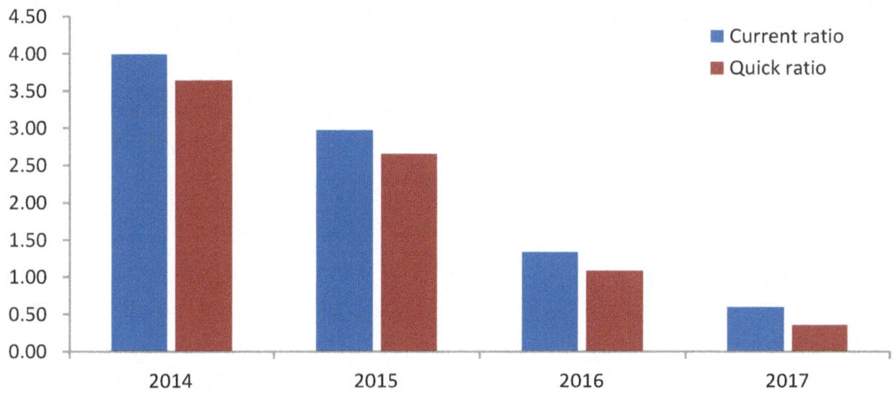

Fig. 1 The comparison of current and quick ratio for enterprise X

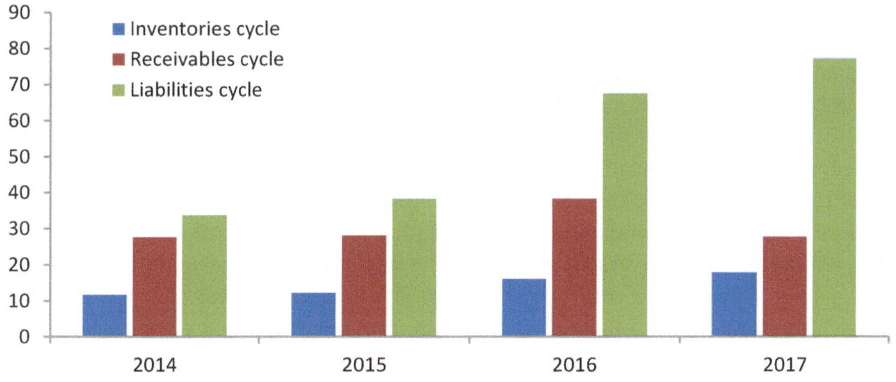

Fig. 2 The comparison of selected efficiency ratios for enterprise X

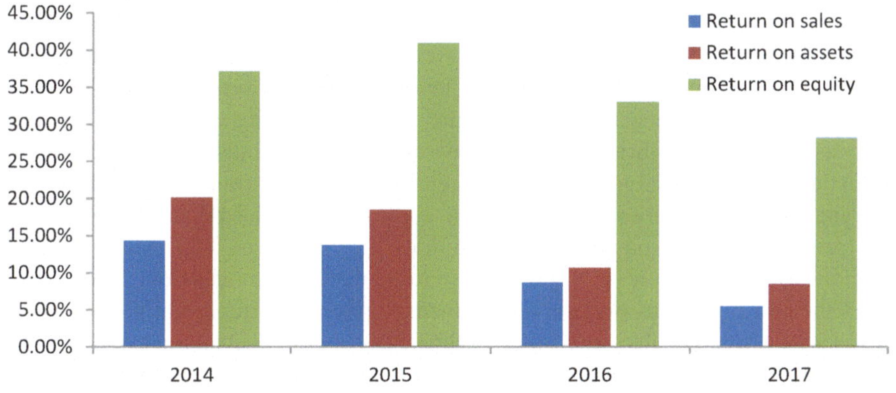

Fig. 3 The comparison of selected profitability ratios for enterprise X

Table 3 Financial ratios values for enterprise X

Ratio	2014	2015	2016	2017
Current ratio	4.00	2.98	1.34	0.60
Quick ratio	3.65	2.66	1.09	0.36
Debt-to-equity ratio (%)	84.29	121.15	208.94	231.25
Inventories cycle	12	12	16	18
Receivables cycle	28	28	38	28
Liabilities cycle	34	38	68	77
Return on sales (%)	14.40	13.79	8.69	5.50
Return on assets (%)	20.17	18.53	10.70	8.53
Return on equity (%)	37.18	40.98	33.04	28.25
Long-term solvency ratio based on equity coverage	1.14	0.79	0.47	0.38
Long-term solvency ratio based on fixed capital coverage	1.32	0.99	0.60	0.55

constantly decreasing trend of the liquidity ratios should serve as a clear indicator of the probable risk of financial liquidity loss (the industry benchmarks should be also consulted to see whether the trend is not common for the whole industry).

Secondly, the amount of debt capital corresponding to a unit value of equity is large. In particular, since in years 2016 and 2017, the debt is over twice as large as the equity, the latter element can no longer play the role of a sufficient warrant of company's liabilities coverage. However, the observed effect is mainly due to the diminishing value of the equity, and not the significantly increased levels of debt. Taking this into account, together with the values of the financial leverage effect ratio calculated by the eanaliza.pl service, which are hovering around 2 for all the periods, we can conclude that the debt-to-equity ratio is not that alarming as it seemed at the first glance.

Thirdly, the values of inventories, receivables, and liabilities cycles are more important indicators of negative effects taking place in the enterprise. Namely, the increasing value of the inventory turnover ratio in days, combined with the relatively constant level of inventory and decreasing level of revenues from sales shows the risk of stockpiling, which negatively impacts the financial liquidity and profitability. The analysis of receivables turnover ratio in days does not bring much useful information about the possible risks since except for the change in 2016, the ratio remains constant. The increase of liabilities cycle length is typically considered positive since the enterprise is allowed to pay its current liabilities later. However, in the analyzed case, the elongation of the cycle is caused by the reduction of net revenues from sales, which poses the risk of not meeting the requirement to pay the current liabilities on time. This negative trend is also confirmed by the negative cash conversion cycle in 2016 and 2017, which suggests risky engagement of current liabilities in the financing of enterprise operation, and increased probability of the existence of overdue liabilities.

Moreover, from the analysis of the selected profitability ratios, it can be concluded that all three aspects, namely the sales, assets, and equity, show a declining trend of profitability. Since the rate at which the net profit is decreasing is much larger than the rates of sales, assets and equity value reduction, it should be treated as an important signal of the risk of unprofitability of the business.[2]

Finally, it is clearly visible that the enterprise has lost the financial stability in 2015 and has not regained it since. Both the golden balance rule and the golden financial rule are not satisfied as the ratio values are below the expected value of 1. The decreasing trend of ratios values should serve as an alarming indicator of serious problems the enterprise has and might have in the future.

To sum up the conducted analysis, we would like to underline that by the analysis of just a few financial ratios we were able to detect several risks threatening the future operation of enterprise X. It should be also stated, that a more in-depth analysis is also possible, with the use of the eanaliza.pl system, which provided us with the discussed ratio values.

5 Conclusions

In the paper, we have shown that the results of the financial analysis can be useful in risk monitoring tasks for small & medium-sized enterprises. We have presented the capabilities of eanaliza.pl system related to the task at hand and conducted an analysis of a sample enterprise X. Based on the analysis of proposed, selected ratios, we were able to indicate possible risks affecting the operation of the enterprise. Therefore, we believe that applying the approach towards risk management we can provide the answers to the Lam's questions cited in the introduction (Lam 2000). By analyzing the calculated ratio values, we can determine whether taking the risk brings sufficient return, and by using eanaliza.pl system we can provide the managers with the right tools and knowledge about the possible threats they may face in the future.

We believe that to make the analysis more complete it could be supplemented with the analysis of industry benchmarks of the selected ratios. Currently, such ratios are available for instance by means of the wskaznikibranzowe.pl service (available at https://wskaznikibranzowe.pl/), developed by Technicenter Sp. z o.o. The benchmarks published by means of the service are calculated based on the financial data provided by the Central Statistical Office of Poland. Since 2019, the information provided by the wskaznikibranzowe.pl service is also incorporated in the eanaliza.pl system.

[2]The reduction of the net profit between 2014 and 2017 is over five-fold, while the reductions of the net revenues from sales, the total assets and the equity are approximately equal to 2.1, 2.4, and 4.3.

References

Baruch, L., Shyam, S.: Methodological issues in the use of financial ratios. J. Acc. Econ. **1**(3), 187–210 (1979)
Belás, J., Ključnikov, A., Vojtovič, S., Sobeková-Májková, M.: Approach of the SME entrepreneurs to financial risk management in relation to gender and level of education. Econ. Sociol. **8**(4), 32–42 (2015)
Błach J.: Financial risk identification based on the balance sheet information. In: Managing and Modeling of Financial Risks, pp. 10–19. Technical University of Ostrava, Ostrava, Czech Republic (2010)
Błach, J., Gorczyńska, M., Wieczorek-Kosmala, M.: Sytuacja finansowa śląskich przedsiębiorstw w dobie kryzysu. CeDeWu, Warszawa (2013)
Błach, J., Gorczyńska, M., Wieczorek-Kosmala, M.: Expert ratios, Katowice (2015), priv. comm
Bromiley, P., McShane, M., Nair, A., Rustambekov, E.: Enterprise risk management: review, critique, and research directions. Long Range Plan. **48**, 265–276 (2015)
Brustbauer, J.: Enterprise risk management in SMEs: towards a structural model. Int. Small Bus. J. **34**(1), 70–85 (2014)
Callahan, C., Soileau, J.: Does enterprise risk management enhance operating performance? Adv. Acc. **37**, 122–139 (2017)
Continuity Insurance & Risk (CIR): Risk Software Report (2017). http://www.cirmagazine.com/pdfs/RiskSoftwareReport2017.pdf. Last accessed 01 Mar 2018
Cowen, S.S., Hoffer, J.A.: Usefulness of financial ratios in a single industry. J. Bus. Res. **10**(1), 103–118 (1982)
D'Arcy, S.P., Brogan, J.C.: Enterprise risk management. J. Risk Manage. Korea **12**(1), 207–228 (2001)
Diaz, J.T., Sanchez, J.H.P.: Analysis of financial risk in SMEs in the City of Armenia—new empirical evidence. J. Econ. Dev. Stud. **4**(2), 75–86 (2016)
Ehrhardt, M.C., Brigham, E.F.: Corporate Finance. A Focused Approach. South-Western, Mason (2011)
Enterprise Risk Management—Integrated Framework. Committee of Sponsoring Organizations of the Treadway Commission (2004)
Fabozzi, F.J., Peterson, P.P.: Financial Management & Analysis. Wiley, Hoboken (2003)
Falkner, E.M., Hiebl, M.R.W.: Risk management in SMEs: a systematic review of available evidence. J. Risk Finan. **16**(2), 122–144 (2015)
Gao, S.S., Sung, M.C., Zhang, J.: Risk management capability building in SMEs: a social capital perspective. Int. Small Bus. J. **31**(6), 677–700 (2013)
Garanina, T., Petrova, O.: Liquidity, cash conversion cycle and financial performance: case of Russian companies. Investment Manage. Finan. Innov. **12**(1), 90–100 (2015)
Gaschi-Uciecha, A.: Badanie stopnia wdrożenia zarządzania ryzykiem w małych i średnich przedsiębiorstwach – wyniki badań. Zeszyty Naukowe Politechniki Śląskiej: Organizacja i Zarządzanie **89**, 123–133 (2016)
Gorczyńska, M., Wieczorek-Kosmala, M.: Analytical ratios, Katowice (2015), priv. comm
Gordon, L.A., Loeb, M.P., Tseng, C.-Y.: Enterprise risk management and firm performance: a contingency perspective. J. Acc. Public Policy **28**(4), 301–327 (2009)
Hoyt, R.E., Liebenberg, A.P.: The value of enterprise risk management. J. Risk Insur. **78**(4), 795–822 (2011)
ISO 31000 Risk Management—A Practical Guide for SMEs. International Organization for Standardization, Switzerland (2018)
Iyer, R., Khwaja, A.I., Luttmer, E.F.P., Shue, K.: Screening in new credit markets: can individual lenders infer borrower creditworthiness in peer-to-peer lending? In: NBER Working Paper Series, NBER Working Paper No. 15242, pp. 1–43. National Bureau of Economic Research, Cambridge, MA, USA (2009)

Jastrząb, T., Wieczorek-Kosmala, M., Błach, J., Kwiatkowski, G.: eanaliza.pl—A new online service for financial analysis. In: Zgrzywa, A., Choroś, K., Siemiński, A. (eds.) Multimedia and Network Information Systems 2017, AISC, vol. 506, pp. 343–355. Springer, Cham (2017)
Kościelniak, H.: Monitoring finansowy przedsiębiorstw w ujęciu sektorowym. Organizacja i Zarządzanie: kwartalnik naukowy **3**(11), 43–55 (2010)
Kozubíková, L., Belás, J., Bilan, Y., Bartoš, P.: Personal characteristics of entrepreneurs in the context of perception and management of business risk in the SME segment. Econ. Sociol. **8**(1), 41–54 (2015)
Kumar, G., Upreti, M.: Liquidity and profitability tradeoff (a study of Idea Cellular Limited). In: Kumar, A., Agarval, S. (eds.) International Conference on Recent Innovation in Management, Engineering, Science and Technology 2018, pp. 150–156. A.R. Research Publication, India (2018)
Lam, J.C.: Enterprise Risk Management, Enterprise Risk Solutions (2000)
McShane, M.K., Nair, A., Rustambekov, E.: Does enterprise risk management increase firm value? J. Acc. Auditing Finan. **26**, 641–658 (2011)
Megginson, W.L., Smart, S.B.: Introduction to Corporate Finance. South-Western, Mason (2006)
Mejssner, B.: ERM—systemy na straży ryzyka. ComputerWorld (2018)
Mikulska, A.: Rola ubezpieczeń w zarządzaniu ryzykiem na poziomie MSP. In: Prusak, B. (ed.) Przedsiębiorstwo w czasach kryzysu, pp. 57–68 (2012)
Mikulska, A.: Zarządzanie ryzykiem jako czynnik sprzyjający wzrostowi MSP. Współczesne Zarządzanie: Kwartalnik Środowisk Naukowych i Liderów Biznesu **4**, 75–83 (2010)
Nocco, B.W., Stulz, R.M.: Enterprise risk management: theory and practice. J. Appl. Corp. Finan. **18**(4), 8–20 (2006)
Nowak, E.: Problemy oceny sytuacji finansowej jednostek mikro. Prace Naukowe Uniwersytetu Ekonomicznego we Wrocławiu **471**, 327–335 (2017)
Olson, D.L., Wu, D.D.: Enterprise Risk Management, 2nd ed. World Scientific Publishing Co. Pte. Ltd., Singapore (2015)
Pinches, G.E., Eubank, A.A., Mingo, K.A., Caruthers, J.K.: The hierarchical classification of financial ratios. J. Bus. Res. **3**(4), 295–310 (1975)
Quon, T.K., Zeghal, D., Maingot, M.: Enterprise risk management and firm performance. Proc.-Soc. Behav. Sci. **62**, 263–267 (2012)
Richards, V.D., Laughlin, E.J.: A cash conversion cycle approach to liquidity analysis. Finan. Manage. **9**(1), 32–38 (1980)
RiskTech100 2018 Report, Chartis Research Ltd. (2017)
Smithson, C., Simkins, B.J.: Does risk management add value? A survey of the evidence. J. Appl. Corp. Finan. **17**(3), 8–17 (2005)
Sojda, A.: Dźwignia finansowa a struktura kapitału przedsiębiorstw górniczych w Polsce. Zeszyty Naukowe Wyższej Szkoły Bankowej we Wrocławiu **15**(5), 707–714 (2015)
Spiżyk, J.: Zarządzanie ryzykiem w firmach z sektora MSP. Studia Ekonomiczne Regionu Łódzkiego **18**, 73–87 (2015)
Ustawa z dnia 29 września 1994 r. o rachunkowości. J. Law 1994 no. 121 pos. 591, Sejm RP, Poland (1994)
Virglerová, Z., Kozubíková, L., Vojtovič, S.: Influence of selected factors on financial risk management in SMEs in the Czech Republic. Montenegrin J. Econ. **12**(1), 21–36 (2016)
Wierzbicka, E.: Ryzyko małych i średnich przedsiębiorstw i możliwości jego ubezpieczenia. Zeszyty Naukowe PWSZ w Płocku: Nauki Ekonomiczne **22**, 75–82 (2015)
Worzała, W.: Wybór źródeł finansowania przedsiębiorstwa na przykładzie projektu inwestycyjnego. Organizacja i Zarządzanie: kwartalnik naukowy **2015**(3), 149–166 (2015)
Zygmunt, J.: Does liquidity impact on profitability? In: Matiaško, K., Lieskovský, A., Mokryš, M. (eds.) 2nd International Conference of Informatics and Management Sciences 2013, pp. 247–251. EDIS–Publishing Institution of the University of Zilina, Slovakia (2013)

Risk Management in German Leasing SMEs—A Qualitative Study

Christian Glaser

Abstract Although the majority of German companies in general and leasing companies in particular are small and medium-sized enterprises (SMEs) and even though risk management is gaining more and more practical as well as academic relevance, there are only very few studies focusing on risk management in SMEs. This paper aims to fill this gap by presenting a comprehensive approach to the topic and presenting a framework tailored for leasing SMEs. Research was based on 40 semi-structured in-depth interviews, thereof 35 SMEs and 5 large German leasing companies. This represents about 25% of the whole German leasing market in terms of annual sales volume and number of active leasing firms. Based on the interviews, a framework on enterprise-wide risk management was developed with a grounded theory approach and also a scoring of interviewees was undertaken. The scoring was based on the Miles and Snow typology (Miles et al., Acad Manage Rev 3(3):546–562, 1978). It was found that a clear size effect exists. Smaller and owner-managed companies tend more often to have a passive and simplistic approach to risk management, whereas larger and non-owner-managed firms have more active, sometimes also enterprise-wide approaches to risk management in place.

Keywords Risk management · Small and medium-sized enterprises · SMEs · Leasing · Germany · Financial service firms

1 Introduction

Although SMEs are of great importance for the German economy in general and the German leasing industry in particular, they have been neglected in empirical investigations so far. The present paper aims to fill this gap by presenting an empirical approach to risk management in German small and medium-sized enterprises (SMEs)

C. Glaser (✉)
University of Portsmouth, Portsmouth P013AH, UK
e-mail: christian.glaser@myport.ac.uk

P. Linsley et al. (eds.), *Multiple Perspectives in Risk and Risk Management*, Springer Proceedings in Business and Economics,
https://doi.org/10.1007/978-3-030-16045-6_9

Table 1 EU definition for small and medium-sized enterprises

Company-category	Number-of-employees	Annual-turnover-(EUR-m)	Balance-sheet-total (EUR-m)
Medium-sized	<250	≤50	≤43
Small	<50	≤10	≤10
Micro	<10	≤2	≤2

Source The Commission of the European Communities (2003)

in the leasing industry and by answering the research question "How can German leasing SMEs develop more effective risk management".

The German finance leasing market has been regulated by the banking supervision since the end of 2009. Similar to credit institutions, finance leasing companies (in the following, simply called "leasing companies") also have to comply with the "minimum requirements for risk management" [MaRisk] and the "German Banking Act" [KWG]. The focus of regulation is mainly on risk governance and factors like risk organisation and risk appetite as well as risk culture (Gontarek 2016). In general, these regulations are applicable independent of the company's size, although some specific rules of the KWG are not applicable for leasing companies. Consequently, a persistent practical need for and research interest in effective risk management for leasing companies can be identified.

Studies in the subject pointed out that leasing is a comparably low-risk business (Deloitte 2013; Pirotte and Vaessen 2008; Schmit 2004). Deloitte analysed 1.5 million leasing contracts of ten European leasing companies with exclusively small and medium-sized customers between 2005 and 2011 and found that default rates are comparably low. Especially when comparing to credit portfolios of banks, these numbers are significantly lower. A similar picture can be seen when looking at the incurred losses (Deloitte 2013; Grunert and Weber 2005; Pfingsten et al. 2016). One often mentioned reason for this comparably low risk profile is the fact that leasing companies usually have a good asset know-how and most of the companies are specialists operating only in a very narrow market niche (BDL 2015; Deloitte 2013). Furthermore, older leasing contracts often show only low remaining exposures or even gains due to market prices that exceed obligations (De Laurentis and Riani 2005; Hartmann-Wendels and Elbracht 2010; Pfingsten et al. 2016; Pirotte and Vaessen 2008; Schmit 2004).

As the leasing industry is greatly shaped by SMEs (BDL 2015), a special focus on these firms is of great importance. Risk management in small and medium-sized German leasing companies therefore seems to be a highly significant topic that is worth being researched. In the following, the term SME is applied according to the EU definition in Table 1.

When comparing international research, one can find major differences in the inclusion criterion "number of employees" for SMEs. While in the UK or the EU, companies with less than 250 employees are considered to be SMEs, in the USA the number of employees of SMEs covers firms with up to 500 employees (Dana 2006: 3). Therefore, to ensure comparability with other research results, the EU size class definition of SMEs was chosen. Additionally, each research was carefully selected and the inclusion criteria checked.

2 Theoretical Background

A literature review conducted on the risk management practice in German leasing SMEs has revealed that only little is known about the present level of risk management. In general, there are only very few national and international studies and academic reports on the risk management practice of SMEs, no matter if it is in the German (Arnsfeld et al. 2007; Gleißner et al. 2004; Henschel 2010; Kirchner 2002) or the international context (CPA Ireland 2005). In particular, it is not clear which methods and procedures are used, to what extent enterprise-wide approaches to risk management are implemented or how the connection with strategic planning is created. The most common explanation on this situation is the comparably young discipline of risk management as a branch of business management (e.g. Alquier and Tignol 2006: 277; Hoitsch et al. 2006: 69).

In the following, an enterprise-wide, sometimes also called "holistic" or "integrated" approach to risk management is adopted. It is a widely held view that enterprise-wide risk management is closely related to management behaviour, performance measurement systems, like for example the balanced scorecard, as well as strategic planning. As there is not just one major theory or standard on the question what is to be understood by enterprise-wide or holistic risk management, this figure is derived from major contributions to this topic (e.g. RIMS 2005; Henschel 2007: 23; Smallman 1996: 15; Spikin 2013: 101) based on empirical studies in a German as well as international context. The presented linkage of the major management subsystems that are frequently discussed and researched with risk management will help answering the research question as well as achieving the research objectives of the present inquiry in the following literature review.

Furthermore, the literature review revealed that the attitude of the owner or manager is essential on risk behaviour and the so-called risk appetite. Lack of sophisticated theoretical knowledge as well as limited management techniques for strategic planning furthermore show clear room for improvement.

Figure 1 presents a research framework that was developed on the basis of the literature review. This framework formed the basis for the data analysis section as well as the targeted framework for enterprise-wide risk management appropriate for German leasing SMEs.

Until today (04/2018), there are only very few studies on risk management in the German (Hartmann-Wendels et al. 2010, 2014) or the international (De Laurentis and Riani 2005; Deloitte 2013; Gholamreza Farsad 2016; Gholamreza Farsad and Joriah Binti 2016; Pirotte and Vaessen 2008; Schmit 2004; Tot 2017; Vasiliauskaitė and Cvilikas 2008) leasing context. No study is known that focuses on SMEs following a

Fig. 1 Research framework on the basis of a recent literature review (*Source* Own illustration)

broader, enterprise-wide perspective—no matter if it is in the German or international leasing context. The main aim of the present paper is to fill this gap.

Also typologies to classify firms are common in the literature. Mainly focussing on strategy formulation and organisational behaviour, there are also some approaches to the risk management practice (Henschel 2010; Hill 2016). The present inquiry mainly develops the findings of Henschel further and researches them for the German leasing industry with a focus on SMEs.

In the following, the focus is not on psychological and behavioural aspects like for example the risk-taking behaviour of the manager. Instead, the focus of the developed typology is on the aspect of an enterprise-wide approach to risk management.

Concerning the typology development, mainly the Miles and Snow approach was of major importance (Miles et al. 1978). He distinguished four different types of managers:

- reactor,
- defender,
- prospector, and
- analyser.

This typology was consulted by several researchers and transferred to the risk management context. Besides Smallman (1996), it was mainly Henschel (2010) who has already researched selected German SMEs of different industries with this particular typology. This is also in line with Gimenez (2000) who states that this typology is particularly suitable for classifying SMEs' strategic behaviour.

3 Research Methodology

Edmondson and McManus (2007: 1156) defined four key elements of a field research project: research question and focus of the study, prior work and current state of the literature, research design and data collection, and contribution to literature as an outcome of the study. While the research question and the focus of the study as well as prior work were addressed in the two previous chapters, the following chapter will focus on the research design. In the final chapter, the focus is on the contribution to literature.

3.1 Reasons for Applying Qualitative Research

As the state of research in risk management for small- and medium-sized German leasing companies is nascent and the main domains of this research are hard to measure in a quantitative way, a qualitative research approach is chosen. In-depth expert interviews with brief background information are preferred rather than other qualitative approaches such as case studies, ethnography, or focus groups.

Research can be seen as cross-sectional, which actually means that the chosen non-random samples are taken in snapshot rather than a longitudinal mode. In building theory, the researcher relies on induction. Characteristically for research in a nascent knowledge area, the aim of this inquiry is to identify patterns that might be transferred to a resulting framework. To ensure plausibility and feasibility of the proposed framework, four additional interviews were conducted with risk managers of German leasing SMEs. Surely, this testing is not statistically representative in regards of quantitative research, but it is intended to pave the way for further research on the one hand and avoid obvious weaknesses in terms of plausibility and/or feasibility on the other hand.

3.2 Sample Selection

As it is not possible to collect and analyse all data available, a sampling strategy was used for the present research. In general, one can distinguish between probability or representative and non-probability or judgmental sampling (Saunders and Lewis 2012). As the research project does neither involve statistical analysis nor require positivistic information gathering, statistical generalisability was not a research aim. Although some basic statistics may play a role in the analysis section, they are only of minor extent. Therefore, non-statistical sample selection seems to be appropriate according to the underlying research paradigm and research objectives.

For the present research topic, non-probability sampling was applied as the samples were self-selected by the researcher. This seems to be appropriate as also no statistical inferences about the characteristics of the population were drawn. On the basis of this sample, one is still able to generalise about the population not on statistical basis (Saunders et al. 2009).

To be included in the sample, different criteria needed to be achieved. Besides others, only SMEs according to the EU definition were chosen and persons either responsible for risk management or general managers were interviewed.

4 Research Findings

4.1 Interviews with Leasing SMEs

Risk management organisation. Since 2009, leasing is regulated by the German banking supervision with strict rules also on the risk management organisation. Therefore, it is not surprising that the large majority of the interviewees stated that the banking regulation had a great influence on the risk management organisation. Nevertheless, there was a controversial discussion whether the regulative requirements are useful or rather a burden.

> The requirements of the banking regulation have no practical relevance for us. Of course, the regulative requirements with process documentations etc. are very expensive. I personally see the requirements as bothersome without any additional value. Instead, I would guess that the requirements cost us about 100 k EUR each year. [Interviewee 11]

Surprisingly, those managers who used to work in larger banks or larger leasing firms state that the treatment of the banking regulation is rather lenient and the principle of proportionality leads to several facilitations.

> My personal view is that we are treated very sympathetically by the banking regulation. Especially when I compare this with my former employers, large banks or large leasing firms which were part of banks. [Interviewee 31]

The major motivation of risk management of the interviewed SMEs is intrinsic, although the regulatory requirements increased the meaning and importance of risk management. Before 2009 (prior to regulation of leasing) many leasing SMEs focused mainly on the passive form of risk management with a large proportion of insurances and forfaiting (sale of receivables on a non-recourse basis to banks) and therefore needed only very little resources for their risk management function. This changed over the years due to two reasons: on the one hand, the regulative requirements focused on a more holistic approach of risk management and on the other hand, several stakeholders disappeared due to the subprime crisis and an increasing number of leasing firms was forced to take a more active approach to risk management. Nevertheless, SMEs are still rather conservative in their risk strategy. Avoiding losses and especially avoiding risk concentrations are the major strategies to ensure a sustainable survival of the company.

Essential risks. When researching the essential risks of SMEs, the typical “leasing risks” were present. Here, again the strong influence of the banking regulation can be seen as without any exception all companies used the vocabulary and the expressions for describing their risks that were given by the banking regulation.

By far the most essential risk for all leasing firms, no matter of their company size, was according to their estimation the counterparty risk. This seems to be plausible as the default of a lessee is the original risk of a leasing firm. Through a high forfaiting ratio, companies try to transfer this default risk to the forfaiting partner.

The second most essential risk is the market price risk. This risk type ranges from losses due to changed market prices for the leasing asset but also for commodities like interest rates, exchange rates etc. Most leasing firms try to eliminate interest rate risks through congruent terms of funding and terms of the leasing contract.

Probably the most under-estimated risk also goes along with scarce resources: dependency on key players/human resources risk (HR risk). Partly this type of risk was included in “other risks”, but it was mentioned only by three firms. When putting probing questions afterwards, most of the interviewees described “reducing dependencies of key players” and “recruiting suitable employees” as one of their major tasks in risk handling.

> Although we have a formal substitution policy in place, we are still depending strongly on key players. Shortly, our general manager was absent for some time due to health reasons. This absence could be seen in our sales figures by return. [Interviewee 24]

Operations and resources. One of the central challenges that should be considered when dealing with SMEs is the importance of informal communication and informal ways of decision-making. This can be especially seen in the different steps of the risk management process but also in informal meetings as well as informal exchange of ideas with colleagues in the leasing industry, e.g. on competition analysis but also on risk identification and fraud prevention.

> Another important role besides formal topics plays also the informal exchange of experiences. Especially lawyers, auditors or colleagues from competitors or members of the federal association of leasing firms (BDL) are an important source. [Interviewee 27]

> Informal processes play a major role for the initial identification of new risks […]. Due to the flat hierarchies, the employees get in touch with the management anyways very frequently. This ensures that the management is informed early on potential risks. [Interviewee 15]

On the one hand, the typically flat hierarchies promote informal processes and measures. On the other hand, strict rules and process descriptions put pressure on more formal processes.

> While we were able to handle things on an informal basis in the past, we are now forced more often to get processes described and created in a more formal way. [Interviewee 14]

Some SMEs are therefore afraid of losing their high degree of flexibility and refuse strict limits as they see their unique selling proposition and their fast and uncomplicated decision-making process in jeopardy otherwise.

In addition to the overwhelming influence of historic and also informal data, many SMEs also rely to a certain degree on both unstructured data and their gut feelings. This appears to be explained by two factors: firstly, a low amount of available structured data elements and secondly, a lack of management experience in collecting, generating and interpreting statistical data. In the interviews, only two medium-sized firms out of 35 SMEs (thereof 10 medium-sized firms) use statistical data, whereas all five large firms use statistical risk models.

> Especially when handling fraud risks, I rely on my experience as well as gut feeling and to a certain degree, we simply need luck/coincidence to identify a fraud case early enough. [Interviewee 1]

Besides scarcity of resources, especially in the IT environment, one explanation for the limited use of models might also be a lack of know-how of the risk managers.

Status-quo reporting. Whereas micro and small firms are often at the beginning of creating a comprehensive risk reporting, medium and large firms are more experienced and put more focus on a portfolio view.

> We currently do not have a risk reporting, especially with automated ad hoc elements respectively an integrated database due to our limited IT resources. We have hand written lists of the monthly payments, but I would not describe that as risk reporting. [Interviewee 8]

> The goal of our risk reporting is to enable conclusions on the portfolio and measures. In general, we report on a quarterly, well documented and comprehensible basis, although I am scanning several developments on a monthly basis. Especially when "traffic lights" are changing and trigger events are creating ad hoc reports. [Interviewee 34]

The major task of risk reporting seems to be a comparison of actual developments to planned events. When deciding on measures due to specific developments, there is a media discontinuity which means that SMEs normally do not work with predefined measures. Instead, it is decided individually and on a qualitative basis which measures are to be taken.

> The core of our risk reporting is quantitative in general. However, in case of changes or peaks of specific key figures for the different risk types, the measures are additionally qualitatively assessed. [Interviewee 33]

The early warning systems are differently implemented in terms of their degree of automation. Whereas smaller firms mainly operate manually, larger firms often have a more integrated approach that is also often connected to an ad hoc reporting. Besides classical early warning figures for a potential default of a customer like return debit notes, open items, deferment of payment etc., it is particularly the field of fraud which is quite far advanced with extensive measures. On the basis of constant pattern analyses of realised fraud cases, the companies try to derive early warning indicators.

> For the realised fraud cases, we could discover returning patterns: very high margins, acquired by brokers, owner-managed company, partly increased or skyrocketed inquiry counter of an information bureau like Creditreform etc. [Interviewee 8]

> We have a zero tolerance policy towards fraud indicators. In case we cannot fully eliminate any early warning signs for fraud, we decline an approval. Additionally, we have a fraud database where we enter all realised fraud cases or any declined requests and analyse them in terms of recurring patterns. [Interviewee 27]

Although fraud databases are increasing, the degree of informality is still very high and most, especially smaller, SMEs still work on an individual, single exposure basis.

> We do not have any general restrictions due to specific early warning indicators. Instead, I am screening every single case and decide on an individual basis. [Interviewee 2]

Development and budgeting. The process of strategic planning shows clear differences. The larger the firm, the more probable is it that a strategic planning is implemented. Besides the fact that very small firms more often do not plan at all, they also have a shorter planning horizon on average. Several micro and some small firms only have a one year planning in place.

The typical planning process is undertaken once a year with a detailed operative one year budget and a less granular medium-term, strategic planning on a three up to five year basis.

> Typically at the year end, we conduct a planning for the next three years. The level of detail stays constant over the years. On the basis of these plans, we derive a detailed sales planning for our sales regions and our sales reps. [Interviewee 22]

> We undertake a five year planning. The figures of the first year are extrapolated on the basis of selected scenarios for the later years. In the current year, we undertake on a monthly basis a controlling based check of the plan fulfilment and identify potential plan adjustment needs. The one year planning is the basis for the target agreement and management by objectives for the single employees. [Interviewee 33]

Especially for captives, the planning process is a little bit different as it is seen as given by the vendor partner. The plans are mainly based on the sales targets of the vendor.

> Our planning is done once a year for a three year time horizon and is based on the different regional plans of our vendor partner […]. As a captive, we strongly depend on the sales of our vendor partner. [Interviewee 12]

4.2 Development of a Framework on Enterprise-Wide Risk Management

This framework essentially carried forward the work of Henschel (2007: 23), RIMS (2005), Spikin (2013: 101), Brustbauer (2016: 81) and Smallman (1996: 15). The validity of this approach might also be seen in the fact that the Committee of Sponsoring Organizations of the Treadway Commission (COSO) updated its Enterprise Risk Management Framework in late 2017 by the parameters "performance" and "strategy" (COSO 2017).

Risk Management Organisation. The core of the framework is the risk management organisation. Aside from the business model, the shareholder structure or other resources, there are essentially the three elements of the risk strategy, the motivation as well as the essential risks that determine all subsequent requirements.

The risk strategy is the centre of all risk activities and needs to be derived directly from the general business strategy. When this connection is missing, no effective risk management is possible or at least numerous resources are necessary to harmonize the business and risk strategy during the operative actions.

The underlying motivation greatly influences the entire risk management system. Is the motivation intrinsic or maybe even to establish an enterprise-wide, economic perspective or is the main driver merely regulatory compliance? Based on this, it can be decided how many resources are needed to satisfy the motivation.

The essential risks are needed to be captured systematically, typically in a so-called risk inventory. The methods to identify them are diverse with brainstorming approaches, based on scenario analyses, or simply experience and experts' opinions.

Operations and resources.
In an enterprise-wide approach to risk management, the risk management function comprises more than just the basic risk management tasks like dunning, liquidity management and credit approval. Moreover, it includes formal policies and internal procedures, a systematic process description and a contingency planning that also considers outsourced tasks. Of major importance are also the steps of risk assessment and risk response, especially the risk culture and the compensation scheme.

Risk culture describes the actually lived standards and is therefore even more focused on the daily and operative activities than the more global risk strategy or global portfolio targets. To ensure a strong motivation for every single employee as well as to avoid the principal agent problem, risk culture and compensation scheme need to be harmonized.

Status quo reporting.
Besides risk and portfolio reporting, the core element of status quo reporting is surely the risk bearing ability that is calculated on a one year basis. In a nutshell, the risk bearing ability calculation determines whether the risk strategy is successful and whether the leasing firm is able to finance its risks (in particular the expected losses).

Besides additional back testing activities and also connections to the opportunity cost perspective when calculating alpha and beta errors, it is mainly the connection to the company's performance and the connection to risk performance measures that offers an integrated, enterprise-wide view including risk perspectives. On the basis of status quo reports and findings from risk monitoring, not only historic stress tests are created but also databases are fed and pattern recognitions are undertaken. Especially in the field of counterparty as well as external fraud risks, these analyses are comparably advanced and help to identify events in advance due to a well working early warning function.

Development and budgeting.
The core of the development and budgeting perspective is surely strategic planning and objective setting. Especially when recalling the definition of risk as "a negative

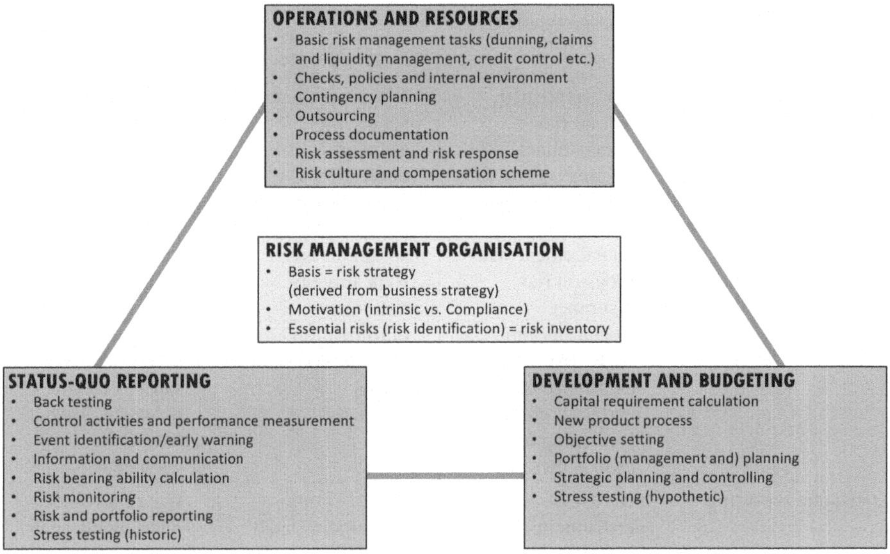

Fig. 2 Framework on enterprise risk management for leasing SMEs *Source* Own illustration

deviation from the plan" (Gleißner et al. 2016: 14; Leitch 2010), it becomes clear that risk and planning definitely need to be considered commonly. Besides the regulatory requirements of the capital requirement calculation (three to five year focus), which is essentially a prolonged risk bearing ability calculation (one year focus), scenario analyses and hypothetic stress tests as well as the new product process, especially portfolio management is of great importance in the development stage.

Figure 2 presents the derived framework on the basis of the conducted 40 interviews with 35 SMEs and 5 large firms from the German leasing industry.

4.3 Scoring of Typologies and Life Cycles

Table 2 summarises the main characteristics of the used risk management practice typologies.

Concerning the typology of risk management practice, the results of Henschel (2010) were widely confirmed although some slight differences could be seen. Especially the fact that the leasing industry is regulated by the German banking supervision can be seen as the main driver for a more advanced risk management. Especially factors on the portfolio level as well as selected tools and measures like for example stress testing, scenario analyses, the process of strategic planning etc. are more professional than they were before regulation.

Table 2 Risk management practice typologies

	Reactor	Defender/prospector	Analyser
Risk management operations and resources	– No established formal risk management system – Passive approach to risk management with focus on risk insurance (forfaiting ratio >50%) or avoidance of certain contracts (operating leasing ratio <5%)	– Focus on a narrow set of risks, although neglecting key risks like e.g. key player risks, strategic risk etc. – Risk strategy = risk return optimization instead of avoiding losses	– Risk bearing ability drilled down to single employee – Fully integrated software for the whole risk management process – Risk function fully integrated with sales to ensure a balanced, long term risk perspective
Status quo reporting	– No use of instruments such as balanced scorecard, SWOT, benchmarking, portfolio analysis etc.	– Use of simple instruments such as SWOT, portfolio reporting etc. – Risk adjusted pricing and opportunity cost considerations with alpha and beta errors	– Use of advanced instruments such as balanced scorecard, benchmarking, etc. – Full consideration of opportunity costs with alpha and beta errors etc.
Development and budgeting	– Flying blind as main option – No or only rudimentary strategic planning	– Medium-term planning horizon of 1–2 years – Little use of forecasting methods – Linkage of planning and risk management with major weaknesses	– Long-term planning horizon of 3–5 years – Planning fully integrated with risk management – Risk culture implemented and lived by all employees (also basis for each employees' compensation)

Source Own illustration

Concerning the sophistication of the risk management practice, a clear size effect can be seen. The same is true when applying the typology system with reactors, defenders/prospectors, and analysers.

Reactors who are characterized through lacks in basic requirements in the field of strategy, planning, and risk management practice do not follow any pro-active approach to risk management. Applying the size classification of Table 1, four micro firms (67%) and five small firms (26%) were classified as reactors. Additionally, the large majority of these firms are owner-managed (78%).

The defender/prospector type aims for a stable environment in a small niche within the industry and is securing its market niches with little or no product development. This management type is shaped by central control and information systems and maintains its traditional approach when facing environmental changes. The defender/prospector type can be seen mainly among all SME size classes with a larger proportion of small firms (47%) compared to micro (33%) and medium-sized (20%) firms. A similar result was also found by Henschel's research who found mainly small firms as well as some medium-sized ones in this type (Henschel 2010: 284).

The analyser type is characterized through advanced approaches of budgeting and reporting as well as performance measurement. The analyser type is found mainly with increasing company size among small (26%), medium-sized (80%) and large (100%) firms. Only a very small proportion of analysers is owner-managed (11%) and the majority of the managers of this type has an academic education. This is also in line with Henschel's findings (Henschel 2010: 287).

5 Conclusions

5.1 Status Quo of Risk Management

The research outcome was quite diverse and profound. It is widely in agreement and corresponds with the few, existing literature on risk management in SMEs, although those studies differed in design and sample. The central research outcome is summarised in the following seven theses:

1. Regulation can be seen as the central driver of risk management practice
2. Risk management decisions of SMEs are mainly based on single exposure level
3. The vast majority of SMEs does not have an integrated approach to risk management
4. Lack of know-how and a high degree of informality strongly influence the risk management practice of SMEs
5. Scarcity of resources can be seen as a driving force in every management decision of SMEs
6. Organisational learning shows clear room for improvement and is often conducted in a rather unstructured way

7. The business organisation is shaped by strong dependencies on key players and by flat hierarchies.

The scoring approach revealed that German leasing SMEs have different levels of risk management sophistication. With increasing firm size, the level of sophistication is increasing. Small firms are typically lacking know-how as well as key resources like time, money, and IT equipment. Especially compared to larger firms, it is important to state that SMEs need their own solutions and processes as they are not just "the smaller version of large firms" and their methods can therefore not be handed down to them (Shrader et al. 1989; RIMS 2005: 5).

5.2 Novelty/Contribution to Knowledge

The present inquiry takes a pioneer role and is the first study of its kind for the German leasing industry with a focus on SMEs and goes beyond pure regulative requirements. The research design explicitly considers the importance of practical as well as academic relevance.

The presented framework might serve as an assessment tool of the current risk management practice and helps each risk manager and/or owner-manager to determine which level is supposed to be achieved and which measures need to be undertaken. The three dimensions of operations and resources, status quo reporting, and development and budgeting that are arranged around the core risk management organisation need to be acknowledged by every manager willing to shift away from pure loss management/reactor to a more active and more enterprise-wide approach to risk management with an analyser type. Such a typology approach is a new contribution to the field of risk management in general and the risk management practice of leasing SMEs in particular. It intends to enable the users to increase their effectiveness of risk management.

The presented framework considered two facts that are of great importance for SMEs. Firstly, it offers a systematic guideline for structuring different tasks in the risk management system. Besides the scarce resources, mainly the lack of know-how presents a major challenge for implementing effective risk management systems. Secondly, the framework is specifically tailored for SMEs and therefore neither too abstract nor too formal like other models and tools that are already available but not often used by SMEs. The goal must be that SMEs can still keep their flexibility, which is one of their key competitive advantages. At the same time, a minimum degree of formality is also necessary to ensure an effective as well as structured procedure.

6 Limitations and Recommendations for Further Research

In terms of the chosen philosophy of critical realism, both the data analysis with the findings as well as the discussion with interpretations and generalisations depend on subjective views. At contrary to a purely positivist research, it is known that qualitative studies "generally have more validity but less reliability" (Babbie 2015: 320). Although an audit trail was carefully created in NVivo as well as a standardized interview guideline used for all interviews, it might be very difficult that two identically experienced and qualified researchers will come up with exact same results. Therefore, it might be interesting to conduct a similar research by another researcher to assess the reliability of this research.

Another critical point of risk management in general, especially when focussing on an enterprise-wide approach is the proof of concept. Although the framework explicitly includes the opportunity cost perspective and therefore balances chances and risks, it is hard to precisely quantify the influence on a firm's performance when applying an integrated approach to risk management or a risk management system compared to no risk management/no risk perception at all. Therefore, a longitudinal study of comparable samples maybe in accordance to action research might be beneficial to determine the success of risk management in general or even go further to determine precisely what the marginal benefit of achieving the next higher step is in the presented life cycle risk development model.

Two areas for further research are also influenced by the sample selection of the present inquiry. Although five large leasing companies were interviewed as well, it might be interesting to research a larger sample size of large firms to be able to draw more robust conclusions and comparisons. Additionally, it might also be interesting to compare leasing SMEs from other countries to German SMEs to determine also regional and cultural differences in the risk management approaches.

References

Alquier, B.A.M., Tignol, L.M.H.: Risk management in small-and medium-sized enterprises. Prod. Plan. Control **17**(3), 273–282 (2006)

Arnsfeld, T., Berkau, C., Frey, A.: Risikomanagement im Mittelstand: Luxus oder Notwendigkeit. Controller Magazin **32**(5), 488–493 (2007)

Babbie, E.R.: The Practice of Social Research. Nelson Education, Boston, MA (2015)

Brustbauer, J.: Enterprise risk management in SMEs: towards a structural model. Int. Small Bus. J. **34**(1), 70–85 (2016)

Bundesverband Deutscher Leasing-Unternehmen e.V. (BDL): Homepage, https://bdl.leasingverband.de/internet/downloads/Broschueren/Marktstudien/2015-marktstudie.pdf. Last accessed 27 Jun 2018

Committee of Sponsoring Organizations of the Treadway Commission (COSO) Homepage: https://www.coso.org/Documents/2017-COSO-ERM-Integrating-with-Strategy-and-Performance-Executive-Summary.pdf. Last accessed 27 Jun 2018

CPA Ireland Homepage: http://www.cpaireland.ie/docs/default-source/business-resource/icaew---risk-management-among-smes.pdf?sfvrsn=2. Last accessed 27 Jun 2018

Dana, L.-P.: Entrepreneurship and SMEs in the Euro-Zone: Towards a Theory of Symbiotic Entrepreneurship. World Scientific Books, London (2006)

De Laurentis, G., Riani, M.: Estimating LGD in the leasing industry: empirical evidence from a multivariate model. In: Altman, E., Resti, A., Sironi, A. (eds.) Recovery Risk. The Next Challenge in Credit Risk Management, pp. 143–164. Risk Books, London (2005)

Deloitte Homepage: http://www.leaseurope.org/uploads/documents/Basel%203/Implicit%20Risk%20Weights%20for%20SME%20Leasing%20in%20Europe%20-%20Key%20Findings.pdf. Last accessed 27 Jun 2018

Edmondson, A.C., McManus, S.E.: Methodological fit in management field research. Acad. Manage. Rev. **32**(4), 1246–1264 (2007)

Gholamreza Farsad, A.: The influence of external factors on the credit risk in leasing industry. Manage. Sci. Lett. **6**(3), 251–258 (2016)

Gholamreza Farsad, A., Joriah Binti, M.: The influence of micro economic factors on the default risk of leasing industry. Manage. Sci. Lett. **6**(1), 99–108 (2016)

Gimenez, F.A.: The benefits of a coherent strategy for innovation and corporate change: a study applying Miles and Snow's model in the context of small firms. Creativity Innov. Manage. **9**(4), 235–244 (2000)

Gleißner, W., Berger, T., Arnold, M.: Risikomanagement, 5th edn. Carl von Ossietzky Universität Oldenburg, Center für lebenslanges Lernen C3L, Oldenbourg (2016)

Gleißner, W., Lienhard, H., Stroeder, D.H.: Risikomanagement im Mittelstand: Planungssicherheit erhöhen, Rating verbessern, Unternehmen sichern. RKW, Eschborn (2004)

Gontarek, W.: Risk governance of financial institutions: the growing importance of risk appetite and culture. J. Risk Manage. Finan. Inst. **9**(2), 120–129 (2016)

Grunert, J., Weber, M.: Empirische Evidenz zur Prognose des Ausfallwahrscheinlichkeit und der Recovery Rate von Bankkrediten an deutsche Unternehmen. University Mannheim, Mannheim (2005)

Hartmann-Wendels, T., Elbracht, H.C.: Ermittlung und Schätzung des Loss Given Default im Leasing: Die Verlustquote als Mischverteilung. Leasing-Wissenschaft & Praxis **8**(1), 67–80 (2010)

Hartmann-Wendels, T., Miller, P., Töws, E.: Loss given default for leasing: parametric and nonparametric estimations. J. Bank. Finan. **40**(2014), 364–375 (2014)

Henschel, T.: Risk management practices in the main industries of German small to medium-sized enterprises an empirical investigation: an Empirical Investigation. Doctorate, School of Accounting, Economics and Statistics. Edinburgh Napier University, Edinburgh (2007)

Henschel, T.: Typology of risk management practices: an empirical investigation into German SMEs. Int. J. Entrepreneurship Small Bus. **9**(3), 264–294 (2010)

Hill, M.: Mind the gap—financing decisions in midcap firms. Doctorate of Business Administration, Edinburgh Napier University, Edinburgh (2016)

Hoitsch, H.-J., Winter, P., Baumann, N.: Risikocontrolling bei deutschen Kapitalgesellschaften Ergebnisse einer empirischen Untersuchung. Controlling **18**(2), 69–78 (2006)

ISO Homepage: https://www.iso.org/standard/65694.html. Last accessed 27 Jun 2018

Kirchner, M.: Risikomanagement: Problemaufriss und Umsetzungsmöglichkeiten in KMU. Zeitschrift für das gesamte Genossenschaftswesen **52**(1), 189–200 (2002)

Leitch, M.: ISO 31000: 2009—the new international standard on risk management. Risk Anal. **30**(6), 887–892 (2010)

Miles, R.E., Snow, C.C., Meyer, A.D., Coleman, H.J.: Organizational strategy, structure, and process. Acad. Manag. Rev. **3**(3), 546–562 (1978)

Pfingsten, A., Kaposty, F., Löderbusch, M.: Analyse der Verlustquoten im Leasing-Geschäft. Finanzierung Leasing Factoring **63**(3), 94–98 (2016)

Pirotte, H., Vaessen, C.: Residual value risk in the leasing industry: a European case. Eur. J. Finan. **14**(1–2), 157–177 (2008)

RIMS Homepage: https://www.rims.org/resources/ERM/Documents/Risk%20in%20Government.pdf. Last accessed 27 Jun 2018

Saunders, M., Lewis, P.: Doing Research in Business and Management: An Essential Guide to Planning Your Project. Financial Times Prentice Hall, Harlow (2012)
Saunders, M., Lewis, P., Thornhill, A.: Research Methods for Business Students, 5th edn. Financial Times Prentice Hall, Harlow (2009)
Schmit, M.: Credit risk in the leasing industry. J. Bank. Finan. **28**(4), 811–833 (2004)
Shrader, C.B., Mulford, C.L., Blackburn, V.L.: Strategic and operational planning, uncertainty, and performance in small firms. J. Small Bus. Manage. **27**(4), 45–60 (1989)
Smallman, C.: Risk and organizational behaviour: a research model. Disaster Prev. Manage. **5**(2), 12–26 (1996)
Spikin, I.C.: Risk management theory: the integrated perspective and its application in the public sector. Estado, Gobierno y Gestión Pública **2013**(21), 89–126 (2013)
The Commission of the European Communities: Commission recommendation concerning the definition of micro, small and medium-sized enterprises. Off. J. Eur. Union **46**(L124), 36–41 (2003)
Tot, I.: Residual value risk in automotive operating lease contracts. Zbornik Pravnog Fakulteta Sveučilišta u Rijeci **38**(1), 303–336 (2017)
Vasiliauskaitė, A., Cvilikas, A.: Fuzzy sets theory adoption for credit risk assessment in leasing sector. Taikomoji ekonomika: sisteminiai tyrimai **2**(1), 85–98 (2008)

What Is the Worst Scenario? Modeling Extreme Cyber Losses

Grzegorz Strupczewski

Abstract Digitalization is not only a source of development and innovation, but also carries a risk related to the growing number of threats in cyberspace—so-called cyber risk. Any significant disruption in cyberspace, whether global or local, will have an impact on the security of business transactions, a sense of security for citizens, the efficiency of public sector institutions, the course of production processes and services, and consequently on national security in general. Modeling extreme events in the area of cyber risk may be used in determining the level of capital necessary to cover financial losses resulting from low-probability high-impact (LPHI) events. We conduct an analysis of the tail distributions, using univariate extreme value theory. In particular, we adopt the peak-over-threshold (POT) by Generalized Pareto Distribution (GPD) approach for exceedances (tails). Moreover, we applied another approach to extreme risk modelling—fitting a spliced distribution. The splicing of a Mixed Erlang distribution for the body and an extreme value distribution (Pareto or GPD) for the tail as well as mixtures of gamma/log-normal/Weibull distributions with GDP are considered. This approach overcomes the subjectivity of manual threshold selection, because it can be estimated as a parameter. We compare the results of fitted distributions and draw conclusions based on VaR's estimates for each analyzed models. We found that the GPD model has proven its superiority over spliced distributions in terms of goodness-of-fit and accuracy of VaR estimations. Therefore we conclude that the GPD is the most recommended distribution to model extreme risk measures (VaR, ES). VaR and ES indicate the level of risk capital that should be carried by a company in case of LPHI cyber event.

Keywords Cyber risk · Cyber loss · Extreme value theory · EVT

This research received financial support from the resources granted to the Faculty of Finance and Law of the Cracow University of Economics as part of the subsidy for the maintenance of the research potential.

G. Strupczewski (✉)
Cracow University of Economics, 27 Rakowicka Street, 31-510 Cracow, Poland
e-mail: grzegorz.strupczewski@uek.krakow.pl

P. Linsley et al. (eds.), *Multiple Perspectives in Risk and Risk Management*, Springer Proceedings in Business and Economics,
https://doi.org/10.1007/978-3-030-16045-6_10

1 Introduction

Social and economic development is increasingly dependent on quick and unhampered access to information and its use in management, production, services and public entities. The constant development of networks and information systems impacts most areas of modern state and society. As social relations are formed by cyberspace, the Internet has become a tool for influencing the behavior of social groups, particularly in the political sphere. Any significant disruption in cyberspace, whether global or local, will have an impact on the security of business transactions, a sense of security for citizens, the efficiency of public sector institutions, the course of production processes and services, and consequently on national security in general.

Digitalization is not only a source of development and innovation, but also carries a risk related to the growing number of threats in cyberspace—so-called cyber risk. Cyber risk is defined as operational risk to information and technology assets that have consequences affecting the confidentiality, availability, or integrity of information or information systems (Cebula and Young 2010). World Economic Forum (2017) underlines the systemic character of cyber risk saying that a cyber event at an individual component of a critical infrastructure ecosystem may cause significant delay, denial, breakdown, disruption or loss, such that services are impacted not only in the originating component but consequences also cascade into related (logically and/or geographically) ecosystem components, resulting in significant adverse effects to public health or safety, economic security or national security.

Cyber losses are a material manifestation of cyber risks. Studying cyber losses is important for interconnected modern economy. According to recent research, it is becoming obvious that no firm is immune from cyber threats. Even with the best protection, detection, and correction tools in place, losses from security breaches will likely occur (Wang 2017).

Despite improvements in risk protection techniques over the last decades due to hardware, software and cryptographic methodologies, it is impossible to achieve perfect cyber security protection. Residual risk always retains (Ruan 2017). In this regard, many stakeholders have identified cyber insurance as a potential tool for effective risk management and transferring the residual cyber risk to an insurance company (Bandyopadhyay 2012). Alternatively, a company may decide to accept the risk and not transfer it outside. Risk assumption (also called risk retention) is commonly used risk management method (Vaughan and Vaughan 2013). However, it's connected with the necessity of acquiring an adequate funding in case of loss—so called risk capital.

The typical question that most managers seek to answer is: "If things go wrong, how wrong can they go?" According to the 80/20 rule, which is widely used in risk management, 20% of the largest losses is responsible for 80% of total losses (Koch 1998). It means that by focusing on minimizing the negative effects of these 20% of extreme losses, a significant effect will be obtained in terms of reducing risk exposure of a company. It justifies the application of extreme value theory in cyber risk management. Modeling extreme events in the area of cyber risk may be used by insurance carriers and other entities to determine the level of capital necessary to cover financial losses resulting from low-probability high-impact (LPHI) events. Value-at-Risk (VaR) and Expected Shortfall (ES) are measures of risk that are frequently used to calculate extreme losses and thus are able to provide approximations of risk capital (McNeil 1999). Risk capital is an equity capital of a firm against which all losses are charged and which provides financing of the effects of failures, uncertainties, and adverse circumstances. In short, risk capital supports risk (Kuritzkes 2002).

Data on actual reported costs of cyber incidents reveal the right-skewness of the dataset. It means that while the median and average cyber loss are relatively low, in some rare cases cyber incidents can cause massive losses (Romanosky 2016). It justifies the use of Extreme Value Theory to model and predict extreme cyber losses.

Extreme Value Theory is a statistical approach that allows to model the occurrence of extreme events with relatively small amounts of extreme data. EVT is most naturally developed as a theory of large losses, rather than a theory of small profits. EVT can be used in insurance to estimate the risk of extreme events that result in large insurance claims. A typical problem might be pricing or building reserves for products which offer protection against catastrophic losses, such as excess-of-loss (XL) reinsurance treaties concluded with primary insurers (McNeil 1999). The peaks-over-threshold (POT) method is the most common EVT approach (Engberg 2016). Compared to Block Maxima approach, POT uses data more efficiently. However, the conventional POT procedure, where the threshold excesses are modelled by a Generalized Pareto Distribution (GPD), suffers from some weaknesses. The number of threshold excesses are usually small but the GPD approximation relies on asymptotic results which may not be met for small samples. The validity of the GPD approximation also relies on the threshold choice, which is made subjectively and affects parameter and quantile estimates. Further, it is pointed out that the conventional POT procedure is sensitive to single influential observations (Davidson and Smith 1990). The subjectivity of manual threshold selection can be overcome by mixture models. The procedure is to fit one distribution to the non-extreme part of the data and a GPD to the tail. The threshold, representing the boundary between the two distributions, is estimated automatically as a parameter (Scarrott and MacDonald 2012).

By applying a scientific methodology—univariate Extreme Value Theory (EVT)—the aim of the paper is to find an adequate method to explain extreme cyber events. We want to obtain the statistical model of large claims by comparing goodness-of-fit of a classical GPD and some mixtures of distributions. Next we compute tail risk measures of modeled cyber losses using VaR. We compare the VaR estimations, that are based on the cyber losses distributions considered in this study, with empirical VaR based on our dataset representing historical cyber losses. Next we investigate which VaR estimation lies closest to the values of empirical VaR. Thanks to that we identify the model that explains extreme cyber events the most adequately.

This paper contributes to the existing literature in two ways. First, it identifies existing methods of modeling extreme losses and compares them empirically seeking the one that results in the best fitted model for risk management purposes. Secondly, we apply the EVT methodology to the unique cyber loss dataset. The scarcity of data on cyber risk is frequently cited reason that hinders scientific research. Our study provides empirical verification of selected EVT models and shows how the results can be used in practice.

2 Literature Review and Methodology

Extreme value theory has many applications in a variety of fields, such as hydrology [e.g. Katz et al. (2002)], climatology [e.g. Davidson and Smith (1990), Kharin et al. (2013)], insurance [e.g. Embrechts et al. (1997)] and finance [e.g. Diebold et al. (1998), McNeil (1999), Rocco (2013)]. It dates back to Fisher and Tippett (1928).

The concept of GPD is based on the assumption that maximum values of a sample of independent and identically distributed (iid) random variable would approximately follow a GPD distribution (Balkema and de Haan 1974; Pickands 1975). The cumulative distribution function of GPD can be defined by three parameters and its formal notation is:

$$F_{(\xi,\mu,\sigma)}(x) = \begin{cases} 1 - \left(1 + \frac{\xi(x-\mu)}{\sigma}\right)^{-\frac{1}{\xi}} & for \xi \neq 0, \\ 1 - \exp\left(-\frac{x-\mu}{\sigma}\right) & for \xi = 0. \end{cases} \quad (1)$$

where μ is the location parameter, $\sigma > 0$ the scale parameter and ξ is the shape parameter.

As the name suggests, the GPD simplifies to other distributions under specific conditions. For example:

- when $\xi = 0$, it simplifies to an exponential distribution,
- when $\xi > 0$, it simplifies to an ordinary Pareto distribution, and
- when $\xi < 0$, it simplifies to a Pareto type II distribution.

Choice of the threshold is critical in obtaining accurate estimates of GPD model parameters and return levels. The threshold should be chosen high enough for the excesses to be well approximated by the GPD to minimize bias, but not so high to substantially increase the variance of the estimator due to reduction in the sample size (the number of exceedances). Although many threshold selection methods are available in the literature, graphical diagnosis methods are commonly used (Scarrott and MacDonald 2012). The most useful graphical tools for threshold selection are (Engberg 2016):

- mean residual life plot (also called mean excess plot),
- parameter stability plot,
- Hill plot.

The mean residual life plot is based on the behavior of the mean of the GPD through the empirical mean excess function. Assuming that a variable X follows a GPD, the mean of X is

$$E[X] = \frac{\sigma}{1-\xi} \quad for \xi < 1 \tag{2}$$

If a GPD is appropriate for modelling the excesses over a threshold u then the conditional mean of the excesses is

$$E[X - u | X > u] = \frac{\sigma_u}{1-\xi} \tag{3}$$

According to the threshold stability property, the excesses of any higher threshold $u' > u$ also follow a GPD but with a different scale parameter. If the data follow a GPD, the mean of excesses change linearly with the threshold u'. The mean excess function can be plotted with confidence in‘tervals in a mean residual life plot with points specified by

$$\left(u', \frac{1}{n_{u'}} \sum_{i=1}^{n_{u'}} \left(x_{(i)} - u'\right)\right) \tag{4}$$

where $n_{u'}$ is the number of excesses above the threshold u'. The plot should be linear, but in practice random fluctuations in the sample will distort the linearity for areas where a GPD is appropriate. So it may be difficult to find a single threshold based only on the mean residual life plot.

Parameter stability plots are based on the threshold stability property of the GPD. The scale parameter for a GPD over a threshold u' where $u' > u$ is specified as

$$\sigma_{u'} = \sigma_u + \xi\left(u' - u\right) \tag{5}$$

The scale parameter thus changes for different values of u' for $\xi \neq 0$. To remove the scale parameters dependence on u' it is re-parameterized as

$$\sigma^* = \sigma_{u'} - \xi u' \tag{6}$$

Both parameters ξ and $\sigma*$ should be constant with respect to thresholds above an appropriate threshold u. The threshold should be set to the lowest value for which the parameter estimates are approximately constant.

Hill plot is based on the Hill estimator which is the conditional maximum likelihood estimator for the heavy-tailed distributions. Hill estimator can be seen as the estimator of slope in the upper right corner (k last points) of the Pareto QQ-plot when using constrained least squares (the regression line has to pass through the point $\left(-\log\left(\frac{k+1}{n+1}\right), \log X_{n-k}\right)$. It is given by

$$H_{k,n} = 1/k \sum_{j=1}^{k} \log X_{n-j+1,n} - \log X_{n-k,n} \tag{7}$$

Hill estimator is more robust than other methods of threshold estimation because it only depends on the shape of the distribution tail (not on the entire distribution). Simplicity of its formula is another advantage. Hill plot is effective when the distribution is Pareto or close to Pareto. Region where the estimated values are approximately constant over a range of k-values indicates what threshold value should be selected.

Maximum likelihood estimation (MLE) procedure is recommended for fitting GPD because it has the smallest variance and bias (Diebolt et al. 2007). The log-likelihood function of the GPD (if $\xi \neq 0$) is

$$l(\xi, \sigma_u; z_j) = -n_u \ln \sigma_u - \left(\frac{1}{\xi} + 1\right) \sum_{j=1}^{n_u} \ln\left(1 + \xi \frac{z_j}{\sigma_u}\right) \tag{8}$$

where $z_1, \ldots, z_{n_u}$ are excesses over a threshold u, with constraint that $\left(1 + (\xi z_j)/\sigma_u\right) > 0$.

Traditional GPD approach assumes that non-extreme data below a threshold are omitted and only those inherently extremal data are fitted by the GPD models. As the motivations for ignoring the non-extremal data are arguable (Hu 2013), recently there has been growing interests in extreme value mixture models. They provide for an automated approach for threshold estimation and use entire dataset for parameter estimation in the inference. A typical structure of a mixture model includes a model describing non-extreme data below the threshold ('bulk model') and an extreme value model, usually GPD, for the data above the threshold ('tail model').

A flexible and straightforward extreme value mixture model was developed by Behrens et al. (2004) by combining a parametric bulk model below a threshold with GPD above it. The threshold is estimated as a parameter by splicing the two distributions at this point. The bulk model might be any parametric distribution, such as gamma, Weibull or log-normal. The distribution function of the extreme value mixture model can be defined as (Hu 2013)

$$F(x|u, \theta, \sigma_u, \xi, \phi_u) = \begin{cases} H(x|\theta) & for\, x \leq u \\ H(u|\theta) + (1 - H(u|\theta)) * G(x|u, \sigma_u, \xi) & for x > u \end{cases} \tag{9}$$

where $\varphi_u = 1 - H(\cdot|\theta)$ is the proportion of data above the threshold, $H(\cdot|\theta)$ is a parametric function (gamma, Weibull or log-normal) and θ is the parameter vector of the bulk distribution. $G(\cdot|u, \sigma_u, \xi)$ represents the GPD distribution function where u is a threshold, σ_u is the scale parameter and ξ is the shape parameter.

Another extreme value mixture model applied in this study is the one based on the Erlang distribution. The Erlang distribution is a positive continuous distribution with density function

$$f(x; r, \theta) = \frac{x^{r-1} e^{-x/\theta}}{\theta^r (r-1)!} \quad for\, x > 0 \tag{10}$$

where r (a positive integer) is the shape parameter and $\theta > 0$ the scale parameter (Verbelen et al. 2015). Mixtures of Erlang distribution can be used to adequately represent any univariate distribution in a variety of applications, including actuarial science. They offer the flexibility of nonparametric density estimation and the feasibility to analytical risk quantification (Lee and Lin 2010). The formal notation of density of a mixture of M Erlang distributions is

$$f(x; \alpha, r, \theta) = \sum_{j=1}^{M} \alpha_j \frac{x^{r_j-1} e^{-x/\theta}}{\theta^{r_j} \left(r_j - 1\right)!} = \sum_{j=1}^{M} \alpha_j f\left(x; r_{j,} \theta\right) \quad for\, x > 0 \tag{11}$$

where $\theta > 0$ is a common scale parameter, the positive integers $r = (r_1, \ldots, r_M)$ are the shape parameters of the Erlang distributions and $\alpha = (\alpha_1, \ldots, \alpha_M)$ with $\sum_{j=1}^{M} \alpha_j = 1$ are the weights used in the mixture (Verbelen et al. 2015).

We also use the splicing of mixed Erlang distributions with EVT distributions (Pareto, GPD) which was proposed by Albrecher et al. (2017) and Reynkens et al. (2017). Let f_1 is the density of a mixed Erlang (ME) distribution and f_2 is the density of Pareto distribution or Generalized Pareto distribution. Their parameters are contained in the vectors θ_1 and θ_2, respectively. Consider the splicing weight $\alpha \in (0, 1)$. The spliced density is defined then as (Reynkens et al. 2017)

$$f(x|t, \alpha, \theta_1, \theta_2) = \begin{cases} \alpha f_1(x|t, \theta_1) & for\, x \le t \\ (1-\alpha) f_2(x|t, \theta_2) & for\, x > t \end{cases} \tag{12}$$

where t is the splicing point.

3 Dataset

Our dataset comes from the SAS OpRisk Global Database that is the world's largest, most comprehensive and most accurate repository of information on publicly reported operational losses in excess of US$100 k. It documents more than 32,000 events across all industries worldwide. As cyber risk is a subcategory of operational risk, we have drawn those cases that can be categorized as cyber risk. We have obtained 649 observations of cyber losses (in Millions USD). After reviewing the data collection methodology and the description of cases, four observations have been considered as mistakes (over-reported cyber risk impact, dollar amount of loss not consistent with description of the event), not being part of the distribution of interest, and they have been removed from the dataset. So the final sample counts 645 observations (see Figs. 1 and 2).

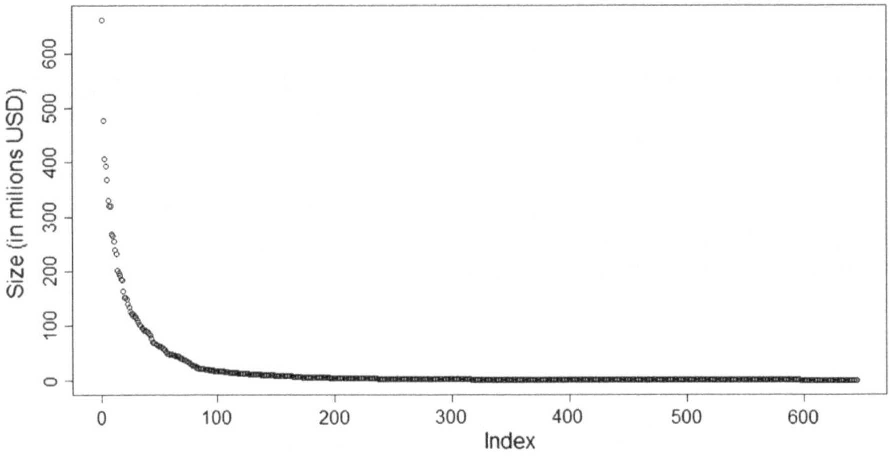

Fig. 1 The values of cyber losses (in millions USD) in our dataset

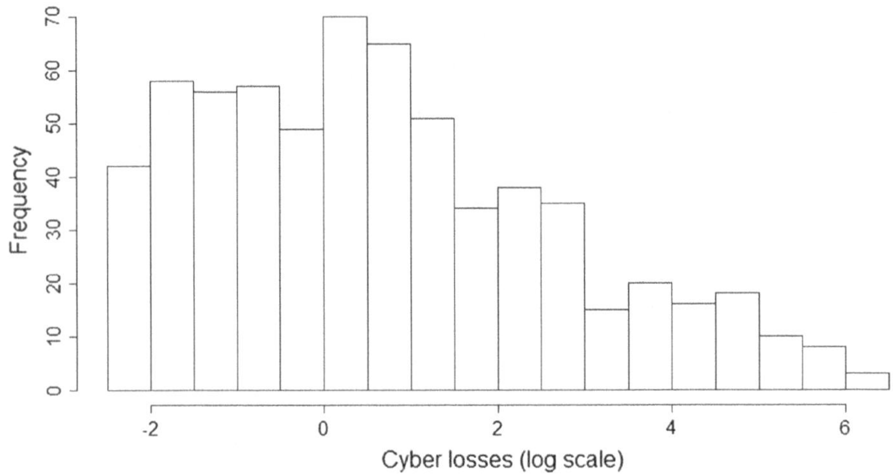

Fig. 2 Histogram of the values of cyber losses in the dataset (log scale)

Basic descriptive statistics of the dataset are presented in Table 1. The cyber losses range from USD 0.1 million to 660.55 million with an average of 18.46. However, the distribution is right-skewed. Half of observed cyber losses don't exceed USD 1.55 million, and 75% of them isn't higher than USD 7.56 million. It could be seen that the data are left truncated at 0.1 since the SAS OpRisk Global Database registers only the cases which exceed USD 0.1 million.

Table 1 Descriptive statistics of the dataset

Minimum	1st quantile	Median	Mean	3rd quantile	Maximum	Skewness	Kurtosis
0.10	0.38	1.55	18.46	7.56	660.55	5.71	41.1

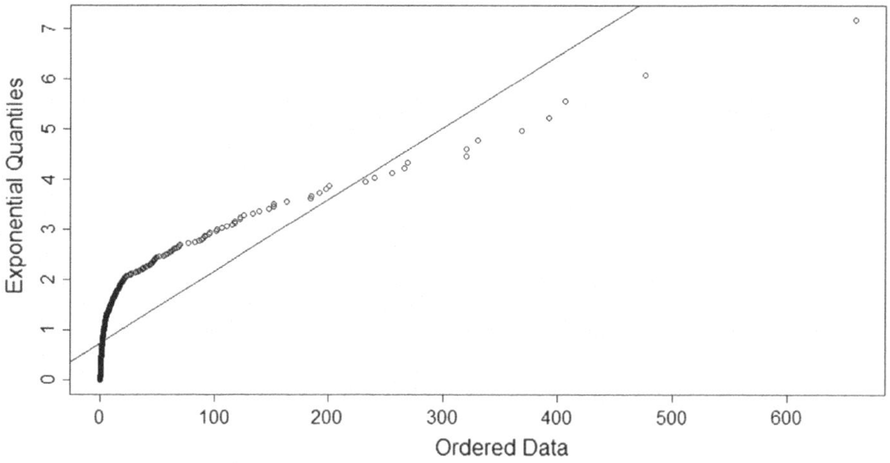

Fig. 3 The Q-Q plot against exponential distribution

4 Results and Discussion

Verifying the heavy-tailedness of the dataset. To assess if the dataset has a heavy tail and if it is reasonable to model the data with a GPD, a Q-Q plot against the exponential distribution can be used. A concave departure from the reference line indicates a heavier tail than exponential (see Fig. 3).

Pareto distribution is also confirmed by the Pareto QQ plot[1] which is not strictly linear (see Fig. 4). A concave shape of QQ plot indicates fat tail so the Pareto distribution with a $\xi > 0$ will be suitable.

Fitting GPD distribution. According to theory, a threshold u should be set sufficiently high, but not too high. Determining an appropriate threshold can be a kind of challenge, because there isn't a strict, formal method of doing this. Three common graphical techniques can help: mean residual life plot, parameter stability plot and Hill estimator plot. To overcome potential inaccuracy of the graphical techniques, we also apply a numerical approach to threshold selection based on Anderson-Darling test.

[1]It computes the empirical quantiles of the log-transform of a data vector and the theoretical quantiles of the standard exponential distribution. These quantiles are then plotted in a Pareto QQ-plot with the theoretical quantiles on the x-axis and the empirical quantiles on the y-axis. The Pareto Q-Q plot represents points $\left(-\log\left(1-\frac{i}{n+1}\right), \log X_{i,n}\right)$ for $i = 1, \ldots, n$, where $X_{i,n}$ is the ith order statistic of the data.

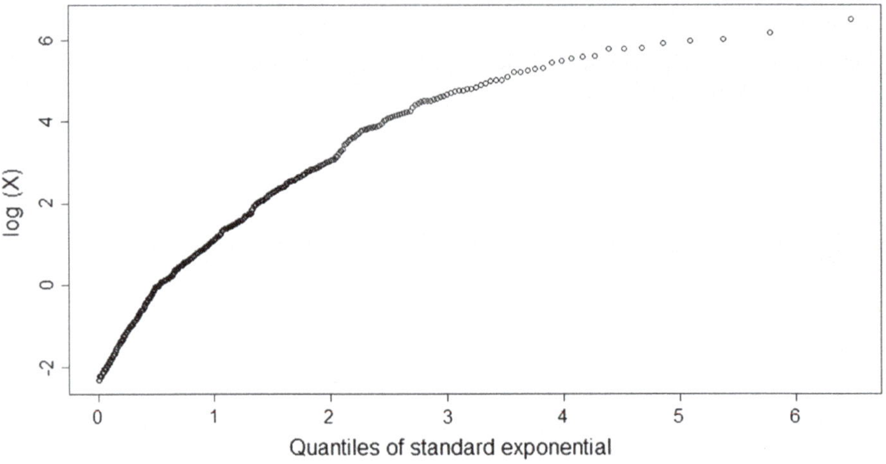

Fig. 4 The Q-Q plot against Pareto distribution

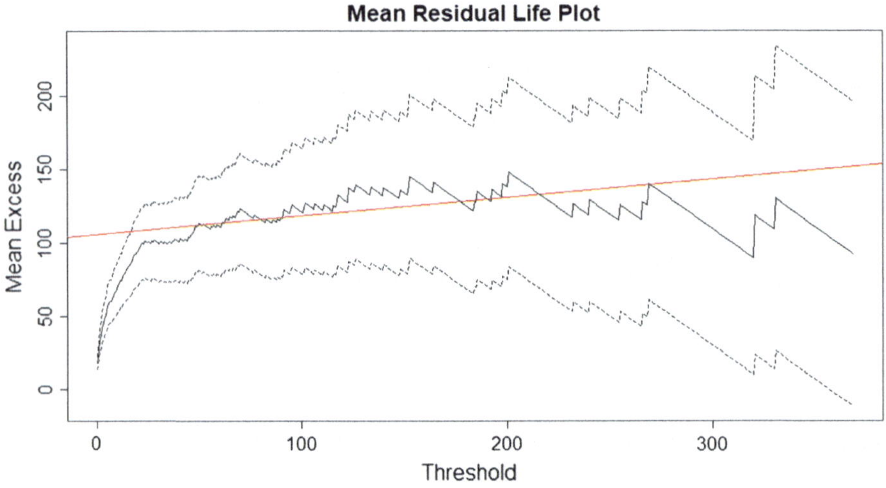

Fig. 5 Mean residual life plot

Mean residual life plot for the dataset is close to linear for thresholds higher than 22 (see Fig. 5). The red line fitted for $u \in [22, 330]$ indicates that a GPD may fit the dataset well.

Parameter stability plot for our dataset is shown on Fig. 6. The modified scale parameter shows some variation but looks stable between 22 and 47 million USD. The departures from stability at higher levels can be explained by fewer observations above higher thresholds. The shape parameter is more or less stable also from 22 million USD (see Fig. 7). So it can be concluded that the threshold should be $u = 22$.

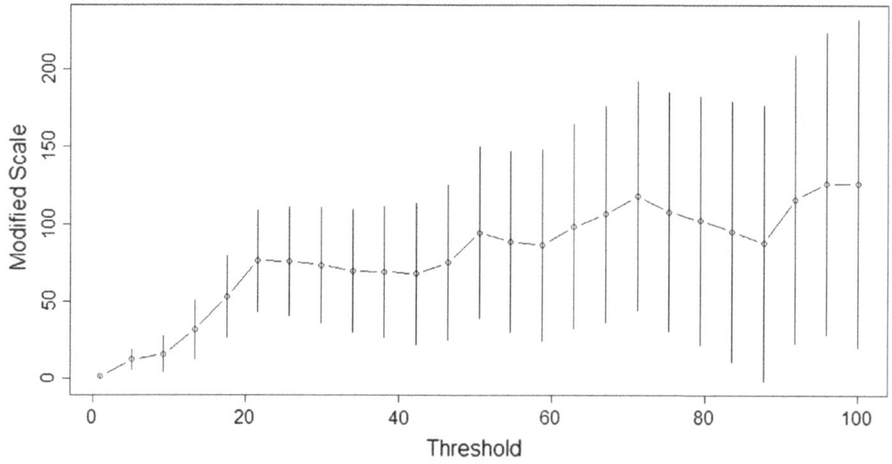

Fig. 6 Parameter stability plot—modified scale parameter

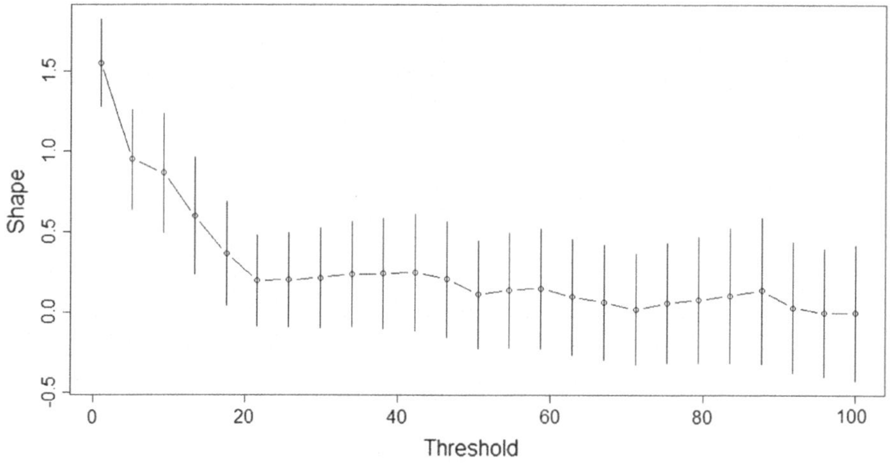

Fig. 7 Parameter stability plot—shape parameter

The above findings are verified with another approach to threshold selection that is based on Hill estimator. The vertical line on the Fig. 8 shows the right value where threshold should be chosen. It's again USD 22 million and the number of exceedances (kth order statistics) is $k = 84$. It means that our GPD model will focus on the highest 84 cases out of the entire dataset (13% of all observations).

Next, we compared the goodness-of-fit of several GPD models with the values of threshold around 22 (± 3). The data shown in Table 2 confirm our previous observation that the optimal threshold is $u = 22$. The value of the Anderson-Darling statistic is the lowest and the p-value the highest.

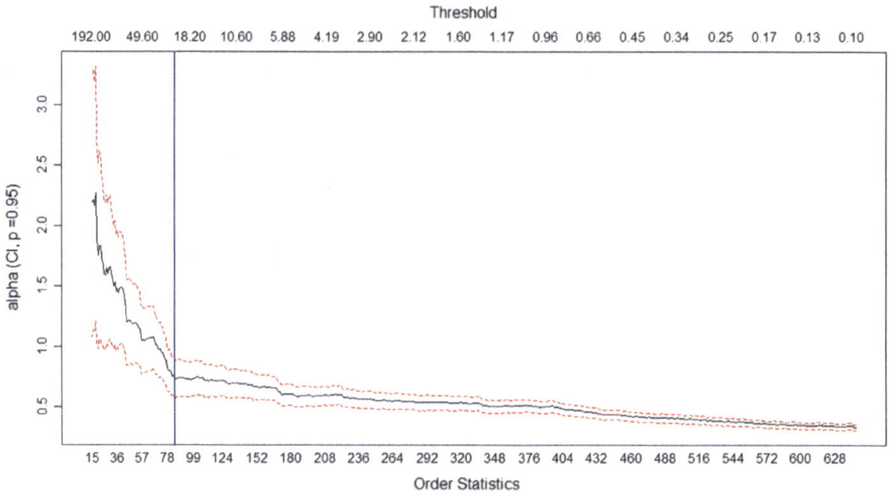

Fig. 8 Hill estimator plot

Table 2 Goodness-of-fit of GPD models with different thresholds

Threshold	*p*-values for the thresholds tested	Anderson-Darling statistic
19.0	0.1030624	0.7264453
19.5	0.1520737	0.6437679
20.0	0.1189809	0.6980991
20.5	0.2421468	0.5456814
21.0	0.3082922	0.4930371
21.5	0.5951636	0.3426686
22.0	**0.6170756**	**0.3341133**
22.5	0.5246576	0.3738521
23.0	0.5246576	0.3738521
23.5	0.5627447	0.3573693
24.0	0.5627447	0.3573693
24.5	0.5627447	0.3573693
25.0	0.5627447	0.3573693

Bold indicates the chosen threshold value (22.0)

Table 3 Estimated parameters of the GPD model

Shape (ξ)	Scale (σ_u)
0.20264 (0.13122)	79.79312 (13.50235)

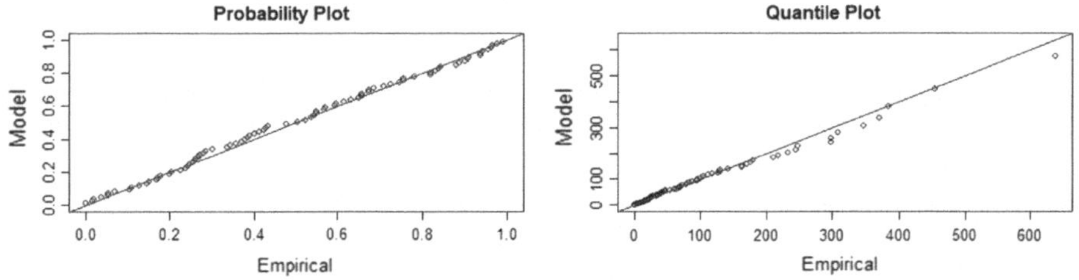

Fig. 9 Probability and quantile plots of the fitted GPD model

Once the threshold has been selected, we estimated the parameters of GPD distribution using 'eva' package of the R environment. The fitted shape and scale parameters and their respective standard errors are shown in Table 3.

Diagnostic plots illustrate very good fit of the estimated GPD model (see Fig. 9).

Fitting a spliced distribution (ME + Pa). Typical approach deals with fitting a suitable distribution for the tail of the data, nevertheless it would be useful to find a fit for the whole distribution. Reynkens (2017) proposed the splicing of a Mixed Erlang (ME) distribution for the body and an extreme value distribution (Pareto or GPD) for the tail. Mixtures of Erlang distributions have received most attention in the field of actuarial science (Verbelen et al. 2015). Our aim is to check the accuracy of a spliced model fit to empirical data and compare it to the traditional approach based on GPD.

We start with determining suitable splicing points using a mean excess plot (see Fig. 10). Linear upward pieces indicate suitability of the Pareto distribution, linear downward pieces suggest a truncated Pareto distribution. After a number of trials, we found a spliced distribution that fits best our dataset (AIC is minimal). The chosen splicing point is at 75th percentile. Its value is USD 7.49 million. The fitted spliced distribution consists of four distributions: three Erlangs and Pareto. The body of the distribution, up to the splicing point, is modeled by the mixture of three Erlangs with the common scale parameter $\theta = 0.3339$ and the following weights α and shape parameters r:

(1) $\alpha_1 = 0.5938$ and $r_1 = 1$,
(2) $\alpha_2 = 0.2715$ and $r_2 = 5$,
(3) $\alpha_3 = 0.1347$ and $r_3 = 14$.

The remaining part of the dataset, i.e. the tail, is modeled by the Pareto distribution with the gamma parameter $\gamma = 1.508$.

In order to check goodness-of-fit of the fitted distribution we use graphical method based on analysis of three plots:

- plot of the fitted survival function versus the empirical survival function (P-P plot),

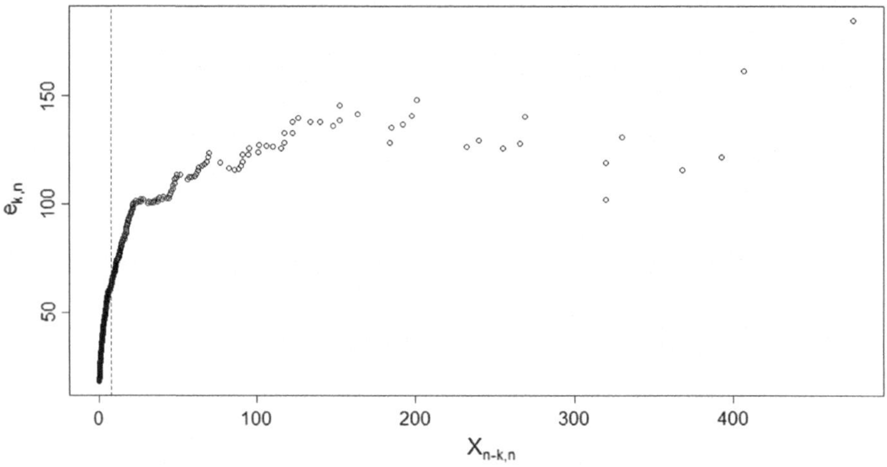

Fig. 10 Mean excess plot with the splicing point (vertical dotted line)

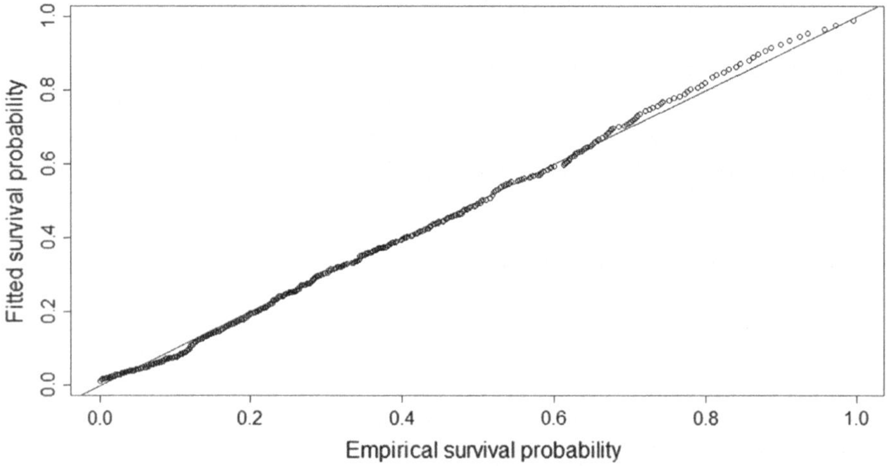

Fig. 11 Splicing P-P plot

- plot of the fitted survival function versus the empirical survival function with minus-log scale which is more informative for the tails,
- plot of the fitted quantile function versus the empirical quantile function (Q-Q plot).

We can see that the fitted spliced distribution approximates the empirical distribution not well (see Figs. 11, 12 and 13). Although most points on the plots are located close to reference line, some of them representing the highest values of cyber losses are fitted insufficiently.

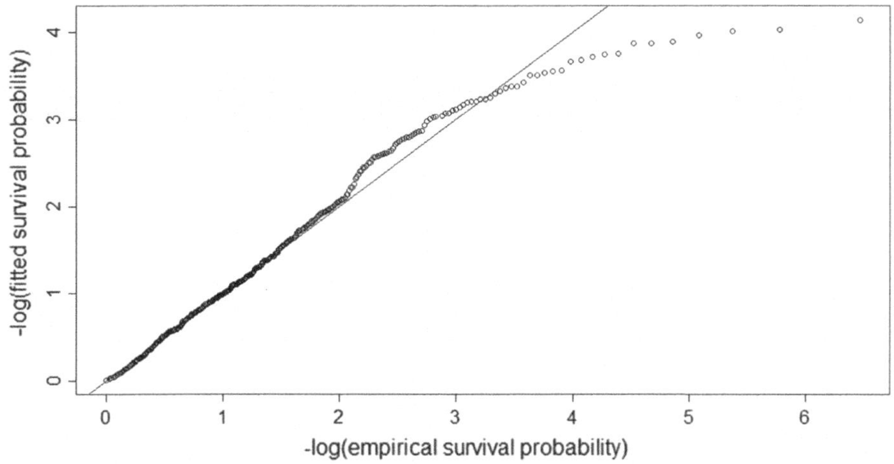

Fig. 12 Splicing P-P plot with minus-log scale

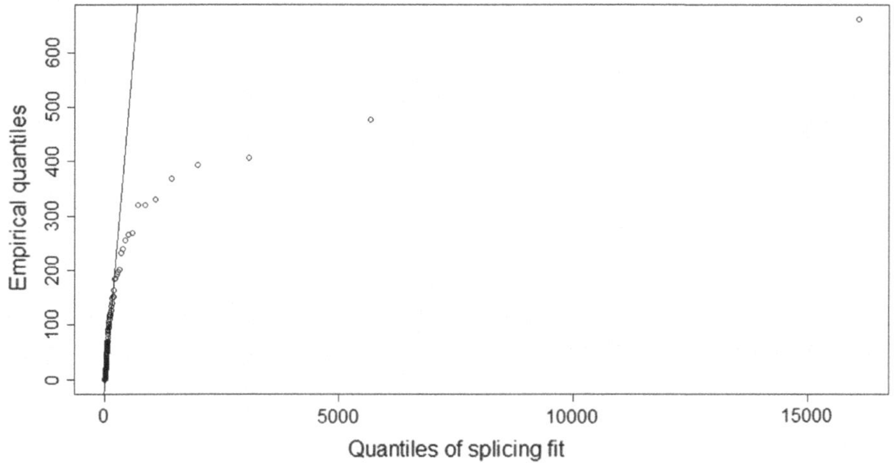

Fig. 13 Splicing Q-Q plot

Fitting a spliced distribution (ME + GPD). Similar approach has been applied to model cyber losses with a spliced distribution of mixed Erlang and GPD. We found that the most suitable splicing point is at 50th percentile representing the value of USD 1.55 million. The body of the distribution, up to the splicing point, is modeled by the mixture of two Erlangs with the common scale parameter $\theta = 0.2082$ and the following weights α and shape parameters r:

1. $\alpha_1 = 0.7177$ and $r_1 = 1$,
2. $\alpha_2 = 0.2823$ and $r_2 = 6$.

Table 4 Estimated parameters of the mixture of 7 Erlangs fitted to left-truncated cyber loss sizes

Shape (r_j)	Mixing weights (α_j)	Scale (θ)
1	0.46092	0.20289
6	0.15988	
11	0.09001	
21	0.07945	
43	0.03471	
61	0.05188	
100	0.12315	

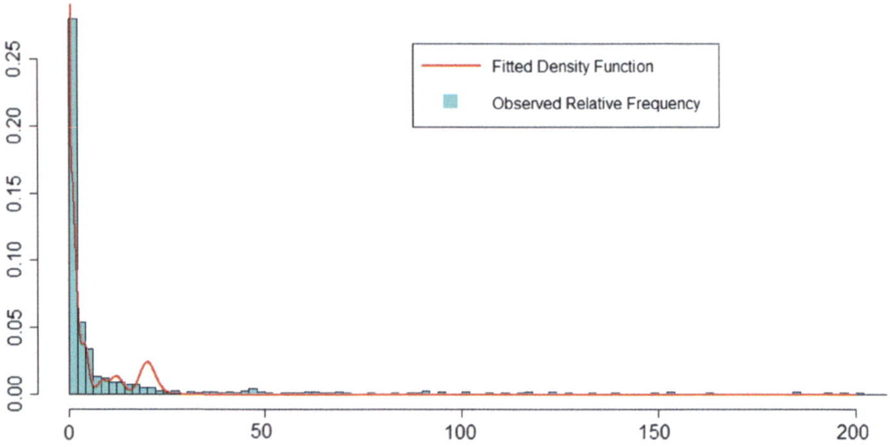

Fig. 14 Fitted mixture of Erlangs to the left-truncated cyber loss sizes (histogram)

The tail of the dataset is modeled by the Generalized Pareto distribution with the gamma parameter $\gamma = 1.449$ and sigma $\sigma = 4.468$. As the diagnostic plots look very similar to those above and indicate imperfect fit of the estimated model to empirical data, we omit them in this study.

Mixture of Erlang distributions. We used a fitting procedure implemented in R environment by Verbelen et al. (2015). It is based on minimizing information criterion AIC by seeking optimal combination of the number of Erlangs in a mixture, their shape parameters and mixing weights. It is assumed that all distributions in a mixture have the same scale. The lowest AIC value was reached for a mixture of seven Erlangs. The parameter estimates of the best-fitting mixture are shown in Table 4. The mixture is dominated by an Erlang distribution with shape 1, modeling almost the half of the data (46.09%). The remaining part of the dataset is modeled by six different Erlangs with shapes ranging from 6 to 100. Figure 14 illustrates that the fitted density coincides quite-well with histogram of the dataset.

Gamma/Log-Normal/Weibull GPD model. Next, we applied MLE method to fit three extreme value mixture models with gamma, log-normal or Weibull bulk respectively, and GPD tail. The '*evmix*' package of the R environment was used. The estimated parameters are presented in Table 5.

Table 5 Estimated parameters of the gamma/log-normal/Weibull GPD models

Parameters	Gamma GPD model	Log-normal GPD model	Weibull GPD model
Threshold (u)	19.0004	22.0204	22.0204
Tail fraction (ϕ_u)	0.1032	0.0986	0.0917
Log-likelihood	−1899.14	−1797.95	−1863.40
Bulk distribution			
Shape parameter	0.4659	1.9106	0.5551
Scale parameter	15.1479	0.6279	4.5869
Tail distribution			
Shape parameter (ξ)	0.2074	0.1964	0.2047
Scale parameter (σ)	78.2440	80.5647	79.5744

Table 6 Information criteria for the different models fitted to the cyber losses data

Model	AIC	BIC	Loglikelihood
General Pareto distribution	941.75	950.69	−468.88
Spliced distribution of mixed Erlang and Pareto distributions	3510.38	3546.13	−1747.19
Spliced distribution of mixed Erlang and GPD distributions	3485.79	3517.08	−1735.89
Mixture of 7 Erlang distributions	1801.19	1863.60	−886.59
Gamma GPD model	3806.28	3843.56	−1899.14
Log-normal GPD model	3603.89	3641.18	−1797.95
Weibull GPD model	3734.78	3772.08	−1863.40

It's worth to mention that the threshold estimations in the log-normal/GPD and the Weibull/GPD models are identical and very similar to the threshold was selected subjectively in the pure GPD model ($u = 22$). Tail fraction (ϕ_u) measures the probability of being above threshold and is close to 10% in each case. The values of log-likelihood functions indicate that the log-normal GPD model is best fitted to empirical data.

Table 6 presents a comparison of information criteria AIC and BIC for the different models fitted to the cyber loss data in this study. Despite relative complexity of mixture distributions, they haven't achieved as good fit to empirical data as the classical GPD model. The mixture of seven Erlang distributions proved to be the best fitted model among all analyzed spliced distributions which reflect the entire dataset. GPD is a type of distribution that models the tail of the data only.

Finally, we illustrate the use of the fitted GPD distribution in risk management in the context of loss modeling. Two popular risk measures have been calculated—Value-at-Risk and Expected Shortfall (see Table 7). We can compare our theoretical (or simulated) results with the standard empirically estimated quantiles from the sample, corresponding to the given probabilities. In case of the GDP

Table 7 Value-at-risk of the cyber loss data (in USD million)

p	0.900	0.950	0.990	0.995	0.999
Empirical VaR_p	44.57	101.61	319.90	387.29	541.72
GDP model VaR_p	43.66	106.31	290.62	390.46	684.19
ME + Pa model VaR_p	30.03	85.40	966.88	2749.64	31,131.70
ME + GDP model VaR_p	30.29	85.36	893.27	2441.29	25,154.25
ME model VaR_p	40.70	43.45	47.11	48.29	50.64
Log-normal GDP model VaR_p	20.75	76.83	262.84	350.05	662.23
Gamma GDP model VaR_p	21.47	81.53	269.78	355.04	649.15
Weibull GDP model VaR_p	20.68	71.84	263.50	373.66	631.51
GDP model ES	149.22	227.77	458.85	584.03	952.30

model we can see that the differences between empirical and theoretical VaR's are relatively small which is the evidence of good model fit. Other analyzed models no longer give as good VaR estimates as the GDP model. There is no single model among the mixture of distributions that would give better VaR estimates than others. It can be concluded that GDP-based models (Gamma/Weibull GDP models) give better estimates of VaR's with higher probabilities ($p = 0.99, 0.995, 0.999$), whereas ME-based models are more accurate in quantifying theoretical VaR's with lower probabilities ($p = 0.90, 0.95$). The ME model underestimates all values of VaR.

Based on the GPD model, we estimate that 90% of cyber incidents might result in a loss below USD 43.66 million, and in the cases where a claim results in a loss larger than this amount, we estimate that the expected loss will be USD 149.22 million. If we increase probability to 0.95, the estimated VaR rises more than twofold (from 43.66 to 106.31). We can also say that there is 1% chance that a loss will exceed USD 290.62 million.

5 Conclusions

Exploratory analysis of cyber losses data showed heavy-tailed distribution. It means that despite average (or median) losses appear the most often ('everyday risks'), massive cyber losses may be also expected and need to be addressed. Large losses must be analyzed separately of the rest of cases to provide more accurate estimates. McNeil (1999) argues that whenever tails of probability distributions are of interest, it is natural to consider applying the theoretically supported methods of EVT. Other methods—those based on normal distribution—might underestimate tail risk. Extreme Value Theory summarizes the scientific methodology on actuarial modelling of extremal events.

Mean Excess plot and Hill plot defined an appropriate threshold. Testing the goodness of fit provided the evidence that the threshold has been selected optimally and the Generalized Pareto Distribution as a good excess model. The estimation of the parameters gave information about the tail distribution.

However, the choice of an accurate theoretical distribution that would fit empirical data well is not an easy task. We compared the use of seven different distributions (or mixtures of distributions) and, based on AIC and BIC criteria, identified that the GPD model fits the dataset best. All the mixture of distributions taken into consideration in this study appeared to be not as well fitted to empirical data as the GPD model. Then we applied the selected distribution to calculate risk measures (VaR, ES) of potential future cyber losses. The risk measures indicate what level of risk capital should a company hold in order to be capable to maintain solvency in case of high losses, and get out of a difficult situation rather than go bankrupt (Novak 2011). Only then it can be said that a company manages risk responsibly through active (i.e. informed) risk retention.

This paper opens a new field for further research on cyber losses. In particular, the differentiation of cyber losses distributions depending on type of business, size of business or nature of threat should be investigated. The results would be highly important for cyber risk management purposes.

References

Albrecher, H., Beirlant, J., Teugels, J.: Reinsurance: Actuarial and Statistical Aspects. Wiley, Chichester (2017)

Balkema, A.A., de Haan, L.: Residual life time at great age. Ann. Probab. **2**, 792–804 (1974)

Behrens, C.N., Lopes, H.F., Gamerman, D.: Bayesian analysis of extreme events with threshold estimation. Stat. Model. **4**(3), 227–244 (2004)

Bandyopadhyay, T.: Organizational adoption of cyber insurance instruments in IT security risk management—a modeling approach. In: Proceedings of the Southern Association for Information Systems Conference, Atlanta, GA, USA, 23–24 Mar 2012. https://pdfs.semanticscholar.org/317d/6f7dfaf36abcd4c07590f696c72b785639cb.pdf. last accessed 21 Oct 2018

Cebula, J., Young, L.: A taxonomy of operational cyber security risks. In: Technical Note CMU/SEI-2010-TN-028. Carnegie Mellon University, Pittsburgh (2010). https://www.sei.cmu.edu/reports/10tn028.pdf. Last accessed 24 Feb 2017

Davidson, A.C., Smith, R.L.: Models for exceedances over high thresholds. J. Roy. Stat. Soc. **52**(3), 393–442 (1990)

Diebolt, J., Guillou, A., Ribereau, P.: Asymptotic normality of extreme quantile estimators based on the peaks-over-threshold approach. Commun. Stat.—Theor. Methods **36**(5), 869–886 (2007)

Diebold, F.X., Schuermann, T., Stroughair, J.: Pitfalls and opportunities in the use of extreme value theory in risk management. In: Refenes, A.-P.N., Moody, J.D., Burgess, A.N. (eds.) Advances in Computational Finance, pp. 3–12. Kluwer Academic Publishers, Amsterdam (1998)

Embrechts, P., Klüppelberg, C., Mikosch, T.: Modelling Extremal Events for Insurance and Finance. Springer, Berlin (1997)

Engberg, A.: An Empirical Comparison of Extreme Value Modeling Procedures for the Estimation of High Quantiles. Uppsala University, Uppsala (2016). https://www.diva-portal.org/smash/get/diva2:940749/FULLTEXT01.pdf. Last accessed 12 Apr 2018

Fisher, R.A., Tippett, L.H.C.: Limiting forms of the frequency distribution of the largest or smallest member of a sample. In: Mathematical Proceedings of the Cambridge Philosophical Society 24, pp. 180–190. Cambridge University Press, Cambridge (1928)

Hu, Y.: Extreme value mixture modelling: An R package and simulation study. M.Sc. (Hons) thesis. University of Canterbury, New Zealand (2013). http://ir.canterbury.ac.nz/simple-search?query=extreme&submit=Go. Last accessed 23 May 2018

Katz, R.W., Parlange, M.B., Naveau, P.: Statistics of extremes in hydrology. Adv. Water Resour. **25**, 1287–1304 (2002)

Kharin, V.V., Zwiers, F., Zhang, X., Wehner, M.: Changes in temperature and precipitation extremes in the CMIP5 ensemble. Clim. Change **119**, 345–357 (2013)

Koch, R.: The 80/20 Principle: The Secret of Achieving More with Less. Doubleday, New York (1998)

Kuritzkes, A.: Operational risk capital: a problem of definition. J. Risk Finan. **4**(1), 47–56 (2002). https://doi.org/10.1108/eb022954

Lee, S.C., Lin, X.S.: Modeling and evaluating insurance losses via mixtures of Erlang distributions. North Am. Actuarial J. **14**(1), 107–130 (2010)

McNeil, A.J.: Extreme value theory for risk managers. In: Internal Modelling and CAD II, pp. 93–113. RISK Books, New York (1999)

Novak, S.Y.: Extreme Value Methods with Applications to Finance. CRC Press, Boca Raton (2011)

Pickands III, J.: Statistical inference using extreme order statistics. Ann. Stat. **3**, 119–131 (1975)

Reynkens, T., Verbelen, R., Beirlant, J., Antonio, K.: Modelling censored losses using splicing: a global fit strategy with mixed Erlang and extreme value distributions. Insur.: Math. Econ. **77**, 65–77 (2017)

Reynkens, T.: Using the ReIns package. https://cran.r-project.org/web/packages/ReIns/vignettes/ReIns.html. Last accessed 06 Apr 2018

Rocco, M.: Extreme value theory in finance: a survey. J. Econ. Surv. **28**(1), 82–108 (2013)

Romanosky, S.: Examining the costs and causes of cyber incidents. J. Cybersecur. **2**(2), 121–135 (2016). https://doi.org/10.1093/cybsec/tyw001

Ruan, K.: Introducing cybernomics: a unifying economic framework for measuring cyber risk. Comput. Secur. **65**, 77–89 (2017)

Scarrott, C., MacDonald, A.: A review of extreme value threshold estimation and uncertainty quantification. Revstat Stat. J. **10**(1), 33–60 (2012)

Vaughan, E.J., Vaughan, T.M.: Fundamentals of Risk and Insurance. Wiley, Hoboken (2013)

Verbelen, R., Gong, L., Antonio, K., Badescu, A., Lin, S.: Fitting mixtures of Erlangs to censored and truncated data using the EM algorithm. KU Lueven (2015). https://lirias.kuleuven.be/bitstream/123456789/436087/3/Antonio,+K.,+Badescu,+A.,+Gong,+L.,+Sheldon,+L.+and+Verbelen,+R.+(2014).+Fitting+mixtures+of+Erlangs+to+censored+and+truncated+data+using+the+EM+algorithm.pdf. last accessed 09 June 2018

Wang, S.S.: Integrated framework for information security investment and cyber insurance. SSRN Electron. J. (2017). https://doi.org/10.2139/ssrn.2918674

WEF: The Global Risks Report 2017. World Economic Forum, Geneva (2017). http://www3.weforum.org/docs/GRR17_Report_web.pdf. Last accessed 12 Sept 2017

Risk Management in Automation of the Accounting Process

Michał Morrison

Abstract A main aim of the article is to provide complex information about risk management in areas where robotic process Automation are implemented in order to fully or partially replace manual work in various accounting systems and structures. Approach to the cost savings and quality increase forcing companies to introduce to their process RPA—Robotic Process Automation. Although a fast progress in the development of these tools could be observed in the last years, the impact is still known to be challenging because of the lack of data about the scope of the savings, risk management, quality upgrade. Risk management and cost savings are main factors of the creation tools which allowing companies to reduce need of the manual work and generate significant savings. In this study we investigate the process of the replacing manual process in accounting systems with. Article make The purpose of the research is to identify impact of the RPA solution for the risk management of global companies.

Keywords Automation · Robotic process automation · Risk management

1 Introduction

The article develops conceptual framework for companies to manage the emerging demand for savings and quality increases in their manual-accounting duties. As soon as company goes global it starts facing many challenges, one of them is growing workload which usually leads to increase in accounting costs and wages for all-around accounting staff. Once the company reached global level the amount work to do is usually counted in hundreds thousands of documents (financial and non-financial) to be processed every single working day. In this case risk of mismatching or not meeting very fixed deadlines are high. Thus, the business units are looking for alternatives to handle tasks much more efficiently and with significant savings.

M. Morrison (✉)
University of Economics in Katowice, 1 Maja 50, 40-287 Katowice, Poland
e-mail: mmichal.morrison@gmail.com

P. Linsley et al. (eds.), *Multiple Perspectives in Risk and Risk Management*, Springer Proceedings in Business and Economics,
https://doi.org/10.1007/978-3-030-16045-6_11

In this case, one of the most modern solution is Robotic Process Automation (RPA) could be implemented.

Recent studies report the benefits of the application of RPA in terms of productivity, costs, speed and error reduction are significant. As noted by Aguirre and Rodriguez (2017), "Robotic Process Automation (RPA) emerges as software based solution to automate rules-based business processes that involve routine tasks, structured data and deterministic outcomes". Explained widely by Kumar and Balaramachandran (2018) "Robotic Process Automation (RPA) is the application of technologies to configure computer software or a "robot" to capture and interpret existing applications for processing a transaction, manipulating data, triggering responses and communicating with other digital systems". RPA combines intelligence including natural language processing, machine learning, autonomics and machine vision with automation.

The increasing application of RPA changes the way of delivering services and supporting technologies for people, which leads to change in economics of service deliver, ultimately causing workforce to be less fixed and no longer being source of the risk (DeBrusk 2018).

With prediction that domestic and offshore outsourcing will continue to grow globally at between 5 and 12% a year, the key market players will seek automation as one of the way for delivery services. There is a prediction that many advisory companies will shift from advising outsourcing systems to optimizing service delivery mostly through introduction and assisting in implementation of the RPA tools (Casale 2013).

However, up to date, little attention is paid to the problem of risk in RPA implementation. The aim of this paper is to discuss the problem of risk management as one of the main factor in selecting most appropriate way to gain savings and quality improvement in various company processes. In the applicative dimension, the problem will be also highlighted by the case study of RPA implementation in the exemplary companies from automotive market. The case study indicates that the implementation of RPA solutions will not only affect specialized departments of the companies. Back offices will be most affected, as the places where the operational support systems for services are created, managed and delivered. The back offices are always under high pressure for cost savings in each industries or financial branches (for example insurances or banking). The key aspect is to ensure that cost saving will be balanced with other key performance indicators such as quality, security, compliance and flexibility (Parr et al. 1999; Mohapatra 2013).

The paper is structured as follows. The second section provides a conceptual framework of the study with reference to the idea behind the Robotic Process Automation. The third section develops a case study of the implementation of RPA, with a focus on its practical opportunities and limitations, in the risk management context. The last section summarizes and concludes the study.

2 Conceptual Framework

2.1 Robotic Process Automation (RPA)

Robotic process automation (RPA) is the application of technology that allows employees in a company to configure computer software or a "robot" to capture and interpret existing applications for processing a transaction, manipulating data, triggering responses and communicating with other digital systems. This definition, proposed by the Institute for Robotic Process Automation and Artificial Intelligence, is consistent with the definition proposed by Kumar and Balaramachandran (2018). Sometimes there are also other consideration of the RPA. For instance, Barkin (2016) provides the following definition of RPA: "RPA is any capability (software and services) that allows you to transact in any IT application or website, typically in the same way a human would, to automate complex, rule-based work." It has to be also underlined that sometimes RPA stands together with other parts of the automation. Then we should considered robotic process automation (or RPA or RPAAI) is an emerging form of clerical process automation technology based on the notion of software robots or artificial intelligence (AI) workers (DeBrusk 2018; Lacity et al. 2016).

Essentially, RPA bots are software robots that complete specific automatable activities. They are working in autonomy but it is possible to establish bots on tasks which required input from employee to proceed and finish activity (sometimes finishing activity is considered with creation of the output—here it might be report file, new file or simply issuing of invoice or registered invoice in ERP system) (Wessel 2011).

Even before RPA software, enterprises were using automation tools. Employees were automating simple processes with excel automation, macros and simple hacks. These solutions were not scalable or sustainable but they increased productivity of individual employees (Fersht and Selby 2011; Building A Center of Expertise… 2014).

First generation of RPA tools were programmable bots that required specific inputs form the users. What is important, user has to have knowledge not only related to his work duty but also relative to the IT. Cognitive or intelligent automation bots augment programmable bots with advanced functionality like Natural Language Processing, image recognition or machine learning. These bots have augmented capabilities in interacting with unstructured data and can be effective in decision making. To achieve this functionality, solution providers generally bring together services from several companies such as NLP API providers and RPA providers (Building A Center of Expertise… 2014).

Self-learning tools are being developed. These tools watch employees in action, understand processes, take over processes when they reach confidence and ask for human input if they get completely new input. However, they are mostly confined to PoCs and are not commonplace yet (Deloitte Global Report 2018).

There's an application for everything these days. Hosted in the cloud, integrated via APIs, CRM, ERP, productivity and other apps run business. Business processes need input from different tools and we have been using an increasing number of tools every year (Yao et al. 2018).

2.2 Process of Automation

Robotic process automation (RPA) software utilizes bots to automate routine tasks within software applications normally performed by a company's employees. These products are used to save time and eliminate the need for human employees to conduct time-consuming, repetitive, and tedious tasks (Lacity and Willcocks 2016).

To develop these automations, RPA solutions provide development environments for building workflows that the agents then follow. These development environments are usually codeless, drag-and-drop systems, so they are accessible enough that non-developers can build necessary processes. As an alternative method of building workflows manually, many tools also provide the ability to record actions performed by a human within a software tool that can be translated into workflows within the RPA product. The tools reperform actions following these recorded steps both with and without human supervision or interrupting of the process (Willcocks and Lacity 2016).

It is common for RPA solutions to contain some form of cognitive or artificial intelligence, usually computer vision for training the bot agents in virtual environments or general machine learning to improve bot decision-making. Additionally, products within the RPA category often contain analytics features and a central platform for maintaining and controlling all the bots deployed across a company. RPA software can be implemented in any facet of an organization where manual processes are in place, but are most commonly used in finance and operations, sales, and supply chain departments (Lacity and Willcocks 2016).

The process of identifying proper cases for implementation of the RPA software seemed most suitable where degree of process standardization and documentation, transaction volumes (invoices, accounting documents), rules-based process and process maturity is significant high (Willcocks and Lacity 2016). The other important factor is ability to transform existing process into new one with maintaining quality, cooperation with customer/supplier and correctness of the output data (if necessary to produce).

To qualify as a Robotic Process Automation tool, a product must (DeBrusk 2018):

- Deploy bots into third-party applications (for example Microsoft Office, SAP system, HFM systems, websites, databases internal and external).
- Allow users to build workflows for programs to follow, via development environments or recording capabilities. The trend is to make those workflows as much as it possible friendly-user.
- Automate tasks for employees, both with and without human intervention

Market offers various tools allowing users to develop theirs bots. Table 1 presents small comparison of the key players with advantages of these tools and disadvantages.

Table 1 RPA platforms breakdown

	UiPath	Blue prism	Automation anywhere
How will I learn?	Has a community edition/free edition available	No trial version available	Trial version is available for 30 days
Learning curve	Has a user-friendly visual designer	Has a user-friendly visual designer, easier than automation anywhere	Developers friendly but requires high programming skills
Google trends popularity	Most popular tool	More popular than automation anywhere	Least popular tool in the trio

It needs to be underlined that there are many others emerging tools which may soon become key players in case innovation, user-friendly, cost and ability to managing risks emerging from using bots as a part of ongoing companies activities.

Though these tools are extremely flexible and can automate up to 40–50% of the activities in an enterprise, they have some limitations and points to be considered (Yao et al. 2018). The first limitation is related to non-Windows environment. Most RPA vendors do not offer solutions for non-Windows operating systems such as Mac OS or Linux. This is not a major problem most of the time because a majority of human dependent company processes are conducted on Windows machines (Chang 2006). The second limitation is the reliance on programming effort. From a purely theoretical perspective, any process can be fully automated. However, as process complexity increases, programming time and cost make automation financially infeasible (Brynjolfsson and McAfee 2014).

Considerable remains reliance on programmers, while bots are relatively easy to program, they still need to be programmed by tech-savvy personnel. Enterprises solve this problem with several measures. Enterprises are founding centers of excellence (CoE) where they gather RPA talent who help departments with their automation efforts and guide them in their RPA journey (Willcocks and Lacity 2016). Sometimes enterprises outsource programming to RPA implementations specialists or other consultants. Even before RPA era, companies were using automation tools. Employees were automating simple processes and tasks with excel automation, macros and simple hacks or were using other programming languages. These solutions were not scalable or sustainable but they increased productivity of individual employees and generating savings usually called low-cost savings because resources required to prepare them were not significant or zero at all (Yao et al. 2018).

3 Case Study: RPA Tool as an Example of Supporting Company Internal Reporting Process

The subject of the case study is an example of the tool working in RPA environment, that is covering one of the key accounting area—consolidation of financial statements. The RPA tool was implemented by one of the key automotive supplier in European market. The flow chart of RPA implementation is presented in Fig. 1. Financial activities of the examined company require from finance departments to consolidate data from various plants. Data is received in digital format (the structure and fields to be filled in are the same for every single file). Once data is ready, it becomes saved in separate files for each plant individually. Before introduction of RPA tool, at this point of action a divisional controller was obliged to check each file and transform the data into consolidated file. This process was done manually and was a subject of high risk of mistakes. Currently, in the examined company, the RPA tool was implemented in section two—the tool processes data and creates final output that can be further analyzed by financial department employee or directly used as a part of external and internal reporting for examined company. The tool generates various scenarios, in accordance to monthly, quarterly and yearly reporting requirements.

The implementation of the RPA tool in the examined company significantly reduced the risk of accounting mistakes. There need of manual input of data was eliminated, and the tool performs additional control checks (in order to avoid any potential errors in data input). The examined company is currently able not only to increase quality of financial data, but also decrease the number of the errors. Thus, the company was able to achieve substantial savings both in time required to complete activity and in the number of employees engaged in these activities.

In the examined company, the implementation of RPA allowed the unit's end-users to increase scope and ability of tools. In general, this could be done in two ways—by programming (mostly performed by consulting companies) or by the companies on their own. RPA platforms offer tools that simplify the record of additional task (for

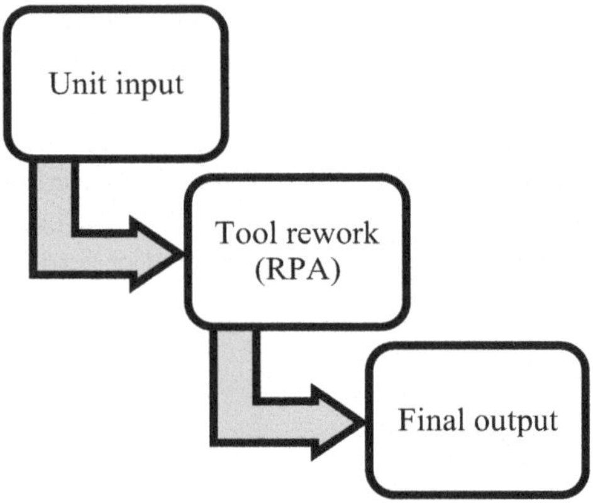

Fig. 1 Flow chart of RPA implementation

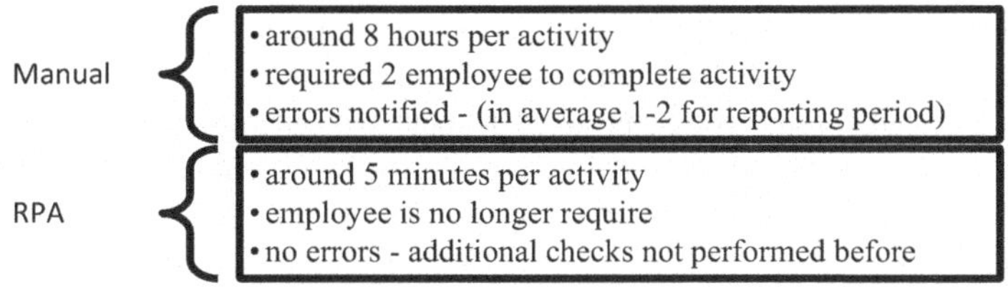

Fig. 2 Differences between manual process and RPA process

example sending an e-mail to selected employees with final output or divide the final output into pieces and send them to different locations). The significant gain in both savings and quality could be achieved immediately, and the costs of implementation are quickly covered. The RPA platform contains possibility to create more than one tool working in that same time. It allows company to plan how to combine processes in most creative and efficiency way to gain maximum savings and quality increase.

Robotic process automation offers many opportunities for companies—mostly in the area of savings and risk management. Usually highlighted are those related to the minimalization and total elimination of errors (various types from accuracy to quality), as framed in Fig. 2. RPA tools ease auditing and reporting for security and compliance purposes (granular process monitoring), focus on less, but better skilled employees (less labor dependent), which causes less FTE based project model offers ability to better align with client needs and compete in the market (scalability and flexibility).

Business processes are automated by the people who know them intimately. Important data is not lost in translation between business unit and development team. RPA processes with each year and each improvement are becoming more manageable (with positive impact on risk reduction). Seamless work without people fatigue or quality variance (continuity and tirelessness of machines) allows a company to gain additional cost efficiencies due to learning curve and potential further accumulative cost reduction of up to 20% over time. Finally, RPA tools and solutions lead to the reduction or minimize the reliance on human factor, and this is relevant if we consider the possible acts of fraud, intrusion and malpractice. All those advantages lead to the increased awareness about potential new approach to process improvement and risk management in tasks where workload is one of main factor.

4 Conclusions

The development of RPA technologies has already come a long way from the days of simple screen scraping, base macros in Excel, and RPA continues to transform how many companies approach their business activities, especially when it comes to scaling and streamlining processes and looking for savings. It's a superior technology that has made its way to the forefront for the benefits it provides and the ease at which these benefits can be obtained. Yet, the market is expected to continue to evolve even further and more innovative RPA solutions are predicted to emerge.

RPA is software-based, it can be used to perform various tasks. These include maintenance of records, queries, calculations, and transactions. Additionally, any application commonly used by your company can be operated by RPA. For example, Citrix, .NET, HTML, and Java are all technologies commonly supported by RPA. Compatible systems include Mainframe Terminals, SAP, Oracle, Blackline, and many more. Programmable automation means that RPA can be configured to perform almost any rule-based task.

Robotic process automation has gained traction as a way of automating tedious business tasks, freeing up corporate workers to tackle higher-value analysis and decision-making. But RPA requires proper design, planning and governance in order to meet companies expectations. These changes in process model have led to a significant shift in role of accountant and accounting systems as well, also impact on customers, traditional investors and shareholders is well noticed. As a result of "shift" or "new possibility" RPA is area of great risk management development and savings for global companies. What is important at this point—not only global competitors can be affected with advantages of RPA, also middle-level companies can achieve perceived savings in both financial and operation areas.

Implementation various improvements in RPA area should always leads to reasonable approach to the risk management. Risk management always should be placed in hierarchy of deciding whether choose RPA or not. RPA technology are not free from risk. Still it is technology developed by someone (it might be employee, it might by consultant of IT specialist), also external risks such as cataclysms, legal changes or technology crisis may successfully prevent RPA from complete tasks and rise unexpected issues, ultimately deciding about risks areas. Preparing for implementation forcing companies to make their internal process much more easier, transparent and clear to understand. It leads to significant decrease in areas of potentials risks. Company can not only gain additional area for bots and robots but also make compliance process easier and cheaper.

Presented case study shows how manual process can be easily transferred into automatic with usage of the RPA technology. It gives company savings, efficiency, quality increase, it is also decrease risk of fraud, manual errors (for example incorrect input to the accounting system, wrong account, incorrect value) and prevent potential malfunction in area of external reporting (RPA solution might be certified by external auditors and even produce requested by them information). RPA technology also are standardized which means that can be easily transferred from one global office to another within company without additional costs.

The limitation of the study lays mostly in branch of economy where discussed company was operating. Each branch can lead to different outcomes with better or worse impact on risk management. RPA tools are always considered as unique for each company—it is usually driven by specification of the processes and tools being under usage by entity. The quality of developed tools also should be considered as key element of the impact for the risk management.

The future of accounting and financial solutions for global companies are marked with RPA impact. Presented solutions and vision of the future is currently being implemented. There will be many areas where RPA solutions find theirs place, and many risks which will be cancelled with help of the RPA technology.

References

Aguirre, S., Rodriguez, A.: Automation of a Business Process Using Robotic Process Automation (RPA): A Case Study. Applied Computer Sciences in Engineering. WEA (2017)

Barkin, I.: RPA is Here to Stay—The Sourcing Industry Landscape Podcast (2018), https://artofprocurement.com/rpa-ian-barkin/. Last accessed: 30 Aug 2018

Brynjolfsson, E., McAfee, A.: The Second Machine Age: Work, Progress, and Prosperity in a Time of Brilliant Technologies. W. W. Norton & Company, New York (2014)

Casale, F.: Here Come the Robots: Is This the End of Outsourcing as We Know It? (2014) https://irpaai.com//wp-content/uploads/2014/01/IRPA-FC-Article-1-2014v3C.pdf. Last accessed: 20 Aug 2018

Chang, J.F.: Business Process Management Systems—Strategy and Implementation. Auerbach Publications, New York (2005)

DeBrusk, C.: Five Robotic Process Automation Risks to Avoid (2017), https://sloanreview.mit.edu/article/five-robotic-process-automation-risks-to-avoid/. Last accessed 20 Aug 2018

Deloitte Global RPA Survey (2018), https://www2.deloitte.com/bg/en/pages/technology/articles/deloitte-global-rpa-survey-2018.html. Last accessed 24 Aug 2018

Everest Global Report: Robotic Process Automation (RPA) Technology Vendor State of the Market Report. Everest Global, https://www.everestgrp.com/tag/rpa/. Last accessed: 20 Aug 2018

Fersht, P., Selby, J.R.: Robotic Automation Emerges as a Threat to Tradition Low-Cost Outsourcing. Horses for Sources, London (2012)

Forrester Research: Building A Center of Expertise To Support Robotic Automation—Preparing For The Life Cycle Of Business Change. Massachusetts, United States (2014), http://neoops.com/wp-content/uploads/2014/03/Forrester-RA-COE.pdf. Last accessed: 24 Aug 2018

Kumar, N.K., Balaramachandran, R.P.: Robotic process automation—a study of the impact on customer experience in retail banking industry. J. Internet Bank. Commer. Allied Acad. Candler (2018)

Lacity, M.C., Willcocks, L.P.: What knowledge workers stand to gain from automation. Harvard Bus. Rev. (2016) https://hbr.org/2015/06/what-knowledge-workers-stand-to-gain-from-automation. Last accessed 12 Sept 2018

Lacity, M., Willcocks, L., Craign, A.: Robotizing Global Financial Shared Services. London, United Kingdom: The Outsourcing Unit (2016), http://www.umsl.edu/~lacitym/OUWP022016Post.pdf. Last accessed: 30 Aug 2018

Mohapatra, S.: Business Process Reengineering—Automation Decision Points in Process Reengineering. Springer Science Business, New York (2013)

Parr, A.N., Shanks, G., Darke, P.: Identification of necessary factors for successful implementation of ERP systems. In: New Information Technologies in Organizational Processes, pp. 99–119. Springer, Boston (1999)

Wessel, D.: Big U.S. Firms Shift Hiring Abroad., The Wall Street Journal. Dow Jones & Company, The Wall Street Journal (2011), https://www.wsj.com/articles/SB10001424052748704821704576270783611823972. Last accessed 28 Aug 2018

Willcocks, P.L., Lacity, M.C.: Service Automation—Robots and The Future of Work 1st edn. Steve Brookes Publishing, Ashford (2016)

Yao, M., Jiy, M., Zmou, A.: Applied Artificial Intelligence—A Handbook for Business Leaders. Topbots Inc., Las Vegas (2018)

Part III
Risk as a Societal and Macro-economic Concern

The Gains and Losses Puzzle in Discounting for Long-Term Investments: Reinterpreting Ramsey Approach for Intergenerational Perspective

Monika Foltyn-Zarychta

Abstract In the appraisal of intergenerational public investments due to their extraordinary long life-cycle special attention must be given to the value of discount rate that influences greatly the net present value of a project in appraisal procedures. Of tremendous importance is the issue of including uncertainty via discounting due to the fact that intergenerational investments face high uncertainty which is coupled with the lack of unambivalent theoretical foundations and variety of empirical estimations of discount rates. The paper contributes to the discussion of social discount rate based on the Ramsey formula in the context of intergenerational allocations as well as discrepancies in treatment of costs and benefits from individual and social perspective. The reconstructed social discount rate formula that is proposed in the paper differentiates: firstly, between intra- and intergenerational frame due to discontinuity between generations, and secondly, between project's costs and benefits owing to opposite signs of risk premia and the differences in gains and losses valuation.

Keywords Intergenerational investment · Uncertainty · Social discount rate · Risk-aversion

1 Introduction

Uncertainty matters greatly in case of intergenerational projects, where effects endure for at least one generation, assuming generational switching point of 30 years. While short-term investment may be perceived as risky, while future outcomes and their probabilities are relatively well recognized, intergenerational projects face high level of uncertainty. The examples of such projects are numerous, including infrastructure like highways or railways, however the majority of such projects relate to environment, i.e. coal based and nuclear power plants, climate change mitigating activities or biodiversity protection, where effects stretch over hundreds of years. The passage

M. Foltyn-Zarychta (✉)
University of Economics in Katowice, ul. 1 Maja 50, 40-287 Katowice, Poland
e-mail: monika.foltyn-zarychta@ue.katowice.pl

P. Linsley et al. (eds.), *Multiple Perspectives in Risk and Risk Management*, Springer Proceedings in Business and Economics,
https://doi.org/10.1007/978-3-030-16045-6_12

of time combined with crossing generational border put appraisal of such long-time investments under specific threats in appraisal procedure.

There are numerous tools for dealing with uncertainty in project appraisal, i.e. expected Net Present Value (NPV) and related statistical methods, certainty equivalent approach or real option approach (cf. Pindyck 2000; Marcinek et al. 2010; Pera 2010). Discounting procedure can be used to serve this purpose as well. However, in case of intergenerational activities, especially environmental investments, one must highlight the disagreement among scholars regarding the issue of discounting distant-future events, like climate change (cf. Gollier and Weitzman 2009). These controversies arise from number of sources.

Firstly, intergenerational rate of discount is not observable on the market. The attempt to adapt market rates to intergenerational investment appraisal is limited due to relatively short maturity of majority of securities (20–30 years). That makes intergenerational intertemporal preferences unobservable on the market and justifies moving to social appraisal where social discount rate (SDR) is applied. However, the theoretical foundations of social discount rate are vague, with a number of opposite views and diverse values of rates provided by empirical works (cf. Climate change 2014; Foltyn-Zarychta 2018).

Moreover, owing to the longevity of project cycle, some ethical issues arise. One of major difficulties is the fact that the investing generation is separated in time from the people who will bear the fruits of today's activity, which is combined with inability of future people to take the decision on their own: to accept or oppose to the decision being taken by their predecessors. Future people will face certain circumstances as a consequence of a decision they cannot influence. Furthermore, substantial number of such investments influence environmental quality or quantity. These areas are especially vulnerable to uncertain effects and harm inflicting coupled with irreversibility of actions. In long-term perspective intergenerational risks may be understood as threats to future generations (Hartzell-Nichols 2012).

In view of the concerns presented above, the first issue discussed in the paper embraces the stability of theoretical foundations of discounting under uncertainty when switching the appraisal perspective from intra- to intergenerational time frame. The paper investigates components of the Ramsey formula (Ramsey 1928), which is commonly adapted approach to deliver the value of social discount rate in intergenerational time-frame as well as analyses "precautionary effect" added to the Ramsey formula and deals with risk premiums pointing to the inconsistency between lowering Ramsey discount rate in long-term perspective and adding positive risk premium during myopic analysis. Furthermore, the paper aims at redefining the Ramsey formula components to suit intergenerational time-frame. We concentrate on risk aversion that impacts the shape of utility functions, both on individual as well as social and intergenerational level. We investigate discrepancies in individual attitudes toward risky gains (risk aversion) and losses (risk seeking) and their magnitude (Kahneman and Tversky 1979). Medvecky (2012) notices there seems to be an inconsistency between theoretical assumptions and empirical evidence for treatment of cost via discount rate. This inconsistency is also visible in valuation, i.e. differences in estimations of willingness to pay (WTP) for gains and willingness to accept compensation (WTA) for losses.

The goal of the paper is to argue for the reconstructed social discount rate formula that encompasses simultaneously: (1) multiple generations and (2) discrepancies in costs and benefits perception under uncertainty.

The novelty of the study lies in elaborating a justification that differentiates: firstly, between intragenerational (individual) and intergenerational (social) frame attributable to discontinuity between generations, and secondly, between project's costs and benefits ascribed to opposite signs of risk premia and the differences in gains and losses valuation.

The methods of research included critical analysis of relevant literature sources. Logic abstraction and generalisation were used to reinterpret and develop the intergenerational social discount rate formula.

The implication of the results relates to possible facilitation of evaluation process via applying separate discount rates to negative and positive project's effects, that so far do not differentiate between gains and losses.

The paper starts with presenting an insight into social discount rate approaches that reflect uncertainty toward future effects and summarises the discrepancies in valuation of costs and benefits and risk aversion perception. Then, the reconstructed SDR formula is proposed starting with the rationale of discounting in the light of multiple-generation time-frame. The paper ends with discussion and conclusions, summarising the results.

2 Issues in Discounting for Project Appraisal Under Risk and Uncertainty

2.1 Uncertainty and Its Impact on Discount Rates: Long-Term Versus Myopic Perspective

Discount rates used by the private sector can be estimated with market-observable rates, that include inter *alia risk* premiums. These premiums are generally positive and added to a risk-free rate. It reflects assumptions behind investor's utility function comprised of return and risk (Markowitz 1952), where the increase in return boost investor's utility while increase in risk works in opposite direction pursuing investors to require higher gains for more risky outcomes.

In public projects appraisal the discounting takes place as well, however it does not have unambiguous foundations. Social discount rate can be estimated on the basis of rates of return from private investments, which are interpreted as opportunity cost of implementing public projects. It may also reflect a consumption rate of interest, based on individual intertemporal preferences observed on the markets (cf. Baumol 1968; Spash and Hanley 1994). Both—rates of return and consumption rates of discount—include risk premiums. Although it is proposed to exclude risk component from the analysis in case of public projects, due to the assumption that they form a diversified portfolio, opposite views are also present (Cropper et al. 2014; Guidelines and discount rates for benefit-cost analysis of federal programs 2016).

As an alternative to market rates, the Ramsey formula is proposed (Ramsey 1928; Cropper et al. 2014), which depends on prospects of future per capita consumption growth (g) and elasticity of marginal utility of consumption (η) coupled with pure time preference (ρ):

$$\mathrm{SDR} = \rho + \eta g \tag{1}$$

Pure time preference emerges from the fact that a person prefers to consume earlier than later or, otherwise, feels the immediate discomfort of self-denial (Frederick et al. 2002). The ηg mirrors the opportunity cost lost when the consumption is delayed. Under positive consumption growth assumption, we expect that a society will be wealthier in the future thus consumption delayed in time is worth less today due to decreasing marginal utility of each additional unit of consumption. Additionally, elasticity of marginal utility of consumption may be referred to as inequality aversion, depicting social willingness to equalize opportunities for society members (cf. Arrow et al. 2012; Freeman and Groom 2013).

When non-deterministic circumstances are taken into account, Ramsey equation is modified to include risk component by lowering its value due to uncertainty about the consumption growth rate (Arrow et al. 2012; Gollier and Weitzman 2009). The value of this reduction Arrow et al. (2012) define as "a precautionary effect": since it reduces the discount rate, the social planner will save more at present. Gollier et al. (2008) argues that it justifies decline of discount rates with time. Weitzman (1998, 2001) also introduces uncertainty via time-declining discount rates schedule. The decrease in discount rates is justified by placing much higher weights on low discount rates scenarios associated with higher present value in relation to scenarios with high discount rates (and thus low present value) (cf. Fisher 2003; Arrow et al. 2012).

Apart from time-declining discount rates, uncertainty in the Ramsey formula is included via the interpretation of elasticity of marginal utility of consumption which could be perceived as a measure of relative risk aversion. Smith states that in modelling under risk "(...) higher η implies more disutility from exposure to risk" (Smith 2011). Weitzman follows this assumption arguing that higher values of risk aversion depicted by η are associated with lower future discount rates (Weitzman 2001, 2010).

All the above proposals generally lead to decreasing values of discount rate in time, which makes present value of delayed effects higher in comparison with a situation when no uncertainty is taken into account. However, what must be pointed out is that while in long-term analysis uncertainty lowers the discount rate, the short-term rates under uncertainty are increased by risk premiums—in case of risky outcomes, investors are willing to expect higher returns to compensate for additional uncertainty they face. This discrepancy is rarely referred to directly, although the discounting basics are common both for short-term as well as long-term allocations.

2.2 *Uncertainty and Its Impact on Discount Rates: Long-Term Versus Myopic Perspective Magnitude Effects for Costs and Benefits*

A canonical, utilitarianistic approach to appraisal rests on individual utilities, which are analyzed on an individual level or aggregated when it comes to social evaluation. However, such utility functions under risk are susceptible to behavioral biases. In the paper we concentrate on risk aversion impacts in utility functions on discount rate. The roots of the problem lie in separate treatment of gain and losses in individual utility functions. There are two issues that have to be analyzed when dealing with costs and benefits.

The first one refers to preferences for risk acceptance. Under the assumption of risk aversion, an individual is willing to pay a premium to avoid uncertainty: she is willing to pay a given amount to change uncertain expected benefits into certain payoff. For a risk averse individual utility function is concave for benefits, so expected utility of risky choices is lower than utility of expected outcome and risk premium, or option value, is positive. That justifies the increase in the discount rate and inclusion of risk aversion premium as one of factors constituting SDR for project appraisal.

However, when analyzing future possible losses, an individual is in fact a risk-seeker. Kahnemann and Tversky (1979) proved that individuals show risk-averse attitude towards gains, but risk-loving preference toward losses. Assumption of risk-loving attitude toward losses and risk-aversion toward gains follows the standard discount rate estimation, where positive element exhibiting risk attitude increase the value of the discount rate and makes present value of both—costs and benefits—lower.

On the other hand, when public long-term projects are involved, some researchers indicate that risk aversion should be ascribed to losses as well. Medvecky (2012) argues that "to accurately reflect risk aversion, the part of the discount rate which reflects risk aversion in regard to future costs should be negative". Then the discounted value of future costs is higher than the same value of discounted benefits. That is confirmed by Peccoro and Nijkamp (2012), who argue that "often individuals appear to have a discount rate lower for losses than gains, exhibiting what is called the sign effect". Furthermore, taking into account "precautionary effect" that lowers the value of Ramsey discount rate, we may infer the conclusion that in case of public projects there is some willingness to ascribe risk aversion to losses as well.

Then the question arises whether to keep the discount rate uniform in both domains, reducing the present value both for gains and for losses, according to Kahneman and Tversky's findings, or whether to follow opposite assumptions keeping discount rate lower for losses, and then increasing present value in comparison to comparable future benefits.

The second issue under consideration in case of discounting under risk and separate treatment of costs and benefits emerges due to unequal valuation of gains and losses (cf. Kahneman and Tversky 1979). Pearce and Turner (1990) indicate that "people value gains and losses asymmetrically, attaching a lot more weight to a loss compared to the existing position than to a gain". It can be explained by several reasons, including pure loss aversion, or endowment effect, where people value goods which they are familiar with higher than other goods, and prospect theory, where individuals value gains and losses in comparison to some "reference point" and the negative deviations from this point (losses) are valued more than positive deviations (gains) (Kahnemann and Tversky 1979; Boardman et al. 2001).

The uneven weighting of gains and losses is also visible in contingent valuation studies, used in appraisal of public projects when non-market goods are delivered. In such cases a hypothetical market with willingness to pay (WTP) and willingness to accept compensation (WTA) is created to deliver the value of non-market effects. WTP is used to measure benefits (positive changes in quality or quantity of goods affected by the investment) while WTA serves as an illustration of a person's minimum acceptable compensation for losses (negative outcomes of the project). Whitehead and Blomquist (2006) highlight the difference in values of WTA and WTP and the general tendency in results of the contingent valuation studies showing WTA to be higher than WTP. The range of the difference can differ: Garrod and Willis (1999) indicate WTA to be higher than WTP from 2 to 5 times, while Boardman et al. (2001) suggest WTA to be higher from 4 to 15 times than WTP for the same good.

Such discrepancies in valuation may be also interpreted as a premise to diversify discount rates for gains and losses.

3 Restructuring Social Discount Rate Under Uncertainty and Intergenerational Perspective

3.1 Intergenerational Framework in Discounting: Individual, Social and Extended-Social Perspective

Apart from the vagueness in the sign and magnitude of uncertainty impact on discount rates, the issue of intergenerational time-frame makes the picture even more complex. Estimating the value of discount rate for very long-term investments is difficult due to multiple reasons.

The first obstacle is that intergenerational rate of discount is not observable on the market. While standard public investments, with life-cycles of 10, 15 or 20 years may use financial market rates as the basis of discounting, the maximum maturity dates for securities reach 20–30 years. For longer cycles some normative assumptions must be applied, whether by using Ramsey approach, or by creating intergenerational hypothetical markets to derive directly intertemporal stated preferences (cf. Drupp et al. 2018; Cropper et al. 1994).

Secondly, transition from intragenerational to intergenerational time frame creates discontinuity between the decision-makers (the present generation) and the beneficiaries of the decision (future generations). That involves irrevocably a normative judgement as well and causes some serious consequences for basic assumptions in investment decision theory, based on utilitarian individual wealth maximization.

For intergenerational perspective, the important assumption that has to be made is that the models can no longer be designed from individual perspective. Escaping from individualistic welfare is perceived as one of crucial challenges for long term projects (Sussman et al. 2014). The change of approach is needed due to the fact that for intergenerational time frame the decisions cannot be made from individual point of view, which is, inevitably, limited to the lifetime of a person that makes the decision. While public projects aim at social welfare maximization, the foundations are still utilitarianistic, meaning that this social welfare is measured by a sum of individual utilities. Therefore, any investment exceeding the expected lifetime of the decision-maker (an individual or a member of society living at present) would not be accepted, unless the expected benefits for the decision-maker herself would be greater than costs she incurs. In other words, investment decision to accept the project would be positive only when NPV *for the individuals living at a moment of taking the decision* is positive. Staying at the individualistic intra-generational models for utility maximization would lead to rejection of any investment producing positive NPV for longer, intergenerational time but negative NPV for myopic, investing-generation perspective.

Intergenerational perspective extends the appraisal to multi-generational perspective in a similar way as financial appraisal (private rates of return) is extended to the economic one (social discount rates) by switching the maximization objective from individual (maximization of the company's value, maximization of the wealth of the shareholder) to social welfare (utility maximization aggregating contemporary living individuals' welfare). The transition from an individual to society must therefore be extended to many societies appearing with the passage of time, exceeding purely utilitarianistic perspective.

Economic analysis accepts as a bottom line the simple aggregation of individual preferences (which under utilitarianistic approach aim to maximize their own utility) that in total form a social welfare function. While this view can be accepted for one-generation perspective, where the one who invests, is the one who get back all the effects (actually or potentially), this is not enough for intergenerational time frame, due to non-coexistence of the investor and the receiver. We propose then to introduce the term: *extended social approach* to reflect between-generational aggregation.

We therefore argue for a *reconstructed approach to social discount rate in intergenerational time frame*. The need for reconstructing SDR under uncertainty and intergenerational time frame arises due to the discontinuity between generations and switching from individual to extended social perspective. Aiming at elaborating a unifying approach, two issues must be considered: (1) the redefinition of components in Ramsey approach, (2) unequal treatment of gains and losses.

3.2 Redefining the Ramsey Formula Components

Since market data for long-time horizon is unobservable, the prevailing approach to estimate discount rate is the Ramsey formula. Even though for long-time frame it is adjusted to deliver time-declining discount rate schedule, lowering the rate works in opposite direction in comparison with the requirement of gaining additional compensation for risky outcome. In addition, intergenerational framework creates very specific conditions that makes the Ramsey formula's parameters highly vulnerable to normative judgements.

In the light of intergenerational discontinuity, the very issue of discounting should be interpreted differently than in intragenerational perspective. The justification starts with analysing the reasons for changing value of money in time, which are: opportunity cost, pure time preference, and risk (uncertainty). All of them are reflected in the Ramsey formula (Eq. 1), where pure time preference depicts utility discount rate (ρ), opportunity cost is reflected by consumption growth rate (g) and risk aversion is depicted by elasticity of marginal utility of consumption (η).

Opportunity cost measures what is abandoned to go on with the investment. That is true for an individual and the society comprising of aggregated individual preferences as well as for intergenerational time frame, under extended social approach. From an individual point of view, the cost of opportunities that are lost is still present, irrespectively of whether the individual is enjoying the benefits from the investment or whether the gains accrue to future people. The only doubt that should be raised is the fact, that although an individual (or society) is resigning from something today, she cannot expect any compensation since the effects (all or some) will be enjoyed by future individuals, not by herself. However, turning to extended social perspective, the discontinuity issue disappears, so it is reasonable for multigenerational society to expect the reimbursement for investments done today.

Furthermore, discussing uncertainty, we must refer first to lowering discount rate due to uncertainty about future growth, the "precautionary effect". It works both, short-term as well as long-term, with the impact lowering discount rate more and more substantial with the passage of time due to higher and higher level of uncertainty. The uncertainty of future growth reflects future outcome volatility. The precautionary element does not disappear for future generations as well. Therefore, it may be defined as *intergenerationally stable*: its justifications hold within one generation just as when crossing generational border.

While opportunity cost justification holds when switching from individual to social perspective extended intergenerationally, the pure time preference becomes controversial. The impatience makes time-distant flows value less. However, in case of intergenerational effects, that affect future people, other than those making the investments decision, pure time preference is difficult to defend. The rationale behind applying zero as pure time preference comes from the non-existence of the individual at the moment where future generations are affected by investment impacts. The excitement from immediate consumption makes it less valuable when it is delayed, however, it is still expected by the investor. In case of intergenerational investments there is no reason to expect future consumption due to the fact that it is a priori dedicated to someone else in the future. Additionally, when interpreting pure time preference as discount rate for utility, it becomes equal to zero to avoid unequal treatment of people only due to passage of time (cf. Weitzman 2010; Arrow et al. 2012; A social time preference rate for use in long-term discounting 2002). Newell and Pizer (2001) refer here to Ramsey opinion that it is ethically indefensible to discount the *utility* (i.e. well-being) of future generations, although it does not imply a zero-discount-rate for their *consumption* (e.g. measured in dollars). Opposite views suggest positive rate of utility discounting since human race faces extinction at a constant hazard rate (cf. Dasgupta 2008).

The third reason, elasticity of marginal utility of consumption (inequality aversion), need reinterpretation due to the discontinuity problem and the need of switching from individual perspective to social one. Elasticity of marginal utility of consumption should be then interpreted in intergenerational context as social aversion to inequality between generations. It follows risk aversion concept in a way that higher inequality aversion imply preference for lower but stable outcomes with passage of time instead of huge differences in consumption level between generations. Arrow et al. (2012) argue that it reflects the maximum sacrifice one generation should make to transfer income to another generation. So higher values of η imply lower inequality aversion and higher discount rates. The similar interpretation is proposed by Smith (2011), who argues that elasticity of marginal utility of consumption "(…) is equivalent to increased inequality aversion and a preference for more redistribution, both within and across generations".

Arrow et al. (2012) argue that inequality aversion can be inferred from the progressivity of the income tax structure. However, it should be noted, that such observations deliver only static inequality aversion estimates, due to the fact that they are made on the basis of present or past tax structures.

Nevertheless, since inequality aversion may only be measured by observing the preferences of contemporary generation, when it is applied for appraisal of intergenerational investments, in fact it serves as an illustration of contemporary people's ethical attitude towards future generations. The higher the inequality aversion, the lower the discount rate is and more weight is given to future people's consumption. The lower discount rate, the higher present value of future impact. As a consequence, we argue that inequality aversion reflects the willingness to equalize the weights of all generations and may be perceived as a reflection of ethical attitude, unrelated to risk attitude in myopic analyses.

Assuming this reinterpretation, and the exclusion of pure time preference for intergenerational perspective, we propose the Ramsey formula to be depicted as follows:

$$s_i = \eta g \tag{2}$$

where

s_i intergenerational social discount rate

η intergenerational inequality aversion (ethical parameter)
g projected long-run annual growth of *per capita* real consumption reflecting the opportunity cost for the investing society.

Then, Eq. 2 explains the value of intergenerational social discount rate with consumption growth rate in the future depicting opportunity cost weighted by intergenerational inequality aversion reflecting ethical stance of contemporary generation.

Equation 2 does not take into account uncertainty of future growth, which is dealt by in the Ramsey formula extensions by declining rates schedule. Since variability of *per capita* consumption growth rate in the future holds both intra- and intergenerationally, we do not refer to it directly, assuming that it will lower social discount rate with passage of time, irrespectively of crossing generational time-frame. Nonetheless, what must be looked into is the aforementioned discrepancy between positive risk premium and decline in discount rate value under uncertainty. We argue that this ambiguity may be explained by separating both issues: uncertainty over future growth rate refers to opportunities that may be lost by future people and reflect rather "precautionary effect" than simply the volatility of results, while risk premium added to the discount rate reflect compensation over possible future loses, which can be interpreted as risk aversion, positive for gains. Gollier et al. (2008) who also defines elasticity of marginal utility of consumption as inequality aversion points that it measures the curvature of the utility function, which depicts risk aversion in an individual utility function. Therefore, both may impact the value of discount rate independently from each other.

What needs to be highlighted is the fact that inequality aversion is an individual risk aversion applied in extended social perspective and illustrates the willingness of societies to equalize consumption though time. Nevertheless, the changed interpretation of elasticity of marginal utility into risk-aversion needs further investigation due to the fact that it is based on individual myopic utilitarianistic welfare maximization that does not hold in the intergenerational perspective.

3.3 *Risk Aversion in Intergenerational Framework: Sign and Scale Effects in Intergenerational Discounting*

The individual perspective of risk aversion toward gains and risk-loving attitude to losses corresponds with uniform discount rate applied for both, costs and benefits. It leads to adding positive risk premium to risk free rate that lowers benefits, for an individual with risk aversion for gains, and simultaneously lowers costs, for individual with risk-loving attitude for losses. However, this evokes a discrepancy between intergenerational justification of discounting and evaluation of investment, that must be analysed from extended social perspective. We argue that risk aversion may work as an additional element in social discount rate adjusting it to uncertainty and can be included on the basis of social attitudes toward risk instead of individual ones.

Society as a whole, in many cases exhibits preferences different from those of single individual maximizing her self-centred welfare. In case of intergenerational investments, where considerable share is devoted to environmental protection, it is depicted by a variety of concepts elaborated to provide effective pro-environmental measures and designed to suit long time perspective. The concepts like "strong sustainability", "safe minimum standard" or "precautionary principle" are adopted when human actions may cause adverse changes in environmental goods. According to them all possible *deteriorations* of environmental quality should be treated with special care (cf. Tietenberg 2006; Perman et al. 2003). Therefore, we may assume that while a consumer maximizes individual wealth and for losses may show risk-loving attitude, a citizen takes more precautious view (Perman et al. 2003). This is backed up by Sen's argument of different behaviour patterns of myopic consumer and far-sighed citizen, where the latter includes in utility functions both, consumption and non-consumption goals (Sen 1987), that may potentially comprise of future generation welfare. If a special care can be given by increasing present value of future harms, it goes in concordance with individual risk averse behaviour, although justified on aggregate social level.

Based on the above, we propose the concept of *harm aversion*. It illustrates the "precautionary effect" in regard to losses that the society is willing to take into account, separately from intergenerational inequality aversion already included in reconstructed SDR as an ethical parameter. Therefore, we may argue that while individuals as consumers follow standard behaviour for risk-aversion for gains and risk-seeking for losses, the society, as a group of citizens, in regard to intergenerational investments with possible adverse environmental effects, shows risk aversion for both: costs and benefits.

The assumption can serve as a justification of the concavity of utility functions for both—gains and losses providing separate discount rates instead of uniform value for the former and the latter (Fig. 1).

Therefore, we propose to increase discount rates by positive risk premium for benefits and to lower them by negative risk premium for costs (*harm aversion*):

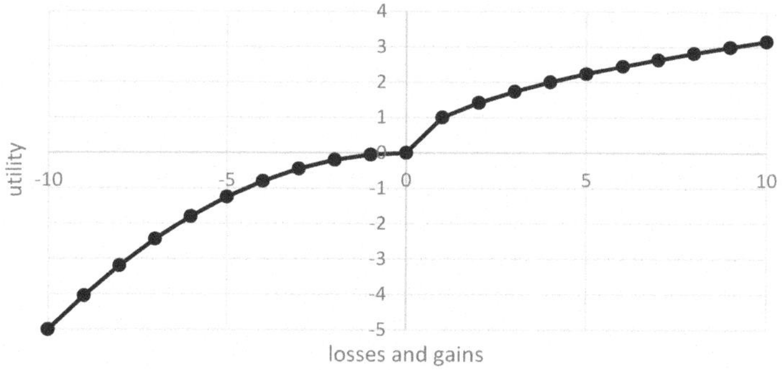

Fig. 1 A hypothetical extended social utility function for gains and losses with asymmetric valuation (losses value more) and uniform risk attitude (risk-aversion) for gains and losses

$$s_{i\,b/c} = s_i + r_{RV} = \eta g + r_{RV} \tag{3}$$

where

$s_{i\,b/c}$ social intergenerational discount rate for costs or for benefits,
s_i social intergenerational discount rate assuming indifference to risk,
r_{RV} premium for risk aversion,

and

$r_{RV} > 0$ for benefits,
$r_{RV} < 0$ for costs.

Finally, we should refer to "magnitude effect" regarding differences in valuation for gains and losses. As it was mentioned, losses are valued more, i.e. in contingent valuation studies. Looking at those discrepancies from social, intergenerational perspective, the justification may refer to irreversibility and growing scarcity of environmental goods, as it is applied in double discounting concept by i.e. Kula and Evans (2011) or Weikard and Zhu (2005). Since people put more weight on losses than gains (WTA > WTP), the unequal treatment may find its illustration in separate value of risk premiums for gains and losses which can be illustrated by the following premise: The value of negative outcomes of the project is higher than the value of positive changes of the same degree (measured in physical units) leading to higher negative discount rate premium on losses than positive premium for gains, given in absolute terms.

That is illustrated by Fig. 1, where utility functions for losses and gains reflect risk aversion and, furthermore, the change in utility for losses is faster than for gains, which justifies the higher present values placed on costs.

As a consequence, we propose two discount rate formulas, with risk aversion premiums separately estimated for costs and benefits:

$$s_{ib} = \eta g + r_{RVB} \tag{4}$$

and

$$s_{ic} = \eta g + r_{RVC} \tag{5}$$

where

s_{ib} intergenerational social discount rate for benefits,
s_{ic} intergenerational social discount rate for costs,
r_{RVC} premium for risk aversion for costs (negative),
r_{RVB} premium for risk aversion for benefits (positive)

and

$$|r_{RVC}| > r_{RVB} \tag{6}$$

Equations 4 and 5 give two separate discount rates since discount rate for costs is lower and the decrease in basic value of the discount rate s_i for costs is higher that the adequate increase for benefits. We argue that the proposed formulas resolve simultaneously:

- the issue of ethical attitudes of contemporary people to future generations, by adjusting opportunity cost given by g by a certain value of inequality aversion η defined as an ethical attitude indicator.
- the need of careful treatment of future costs, i.e. environmental resources, due to the fact that society shows a tendency for risk aversion both for costs and benefits.
- the issue of putting more weight to losses than gains due to irreversible damages and growing scarcity of environment.
- Restructuring social discount rate under uncertainty and intergenerational perspective.

4 Intergenerational Framework in Discounting: Individual, Social and Extended-Social Perspective

While discussing the results, one must turn attention to the assumption of separate risk attitudes between individuals and the society that is rooted in the criticism of utilitarianistic approach. Perman et al. (2003) highlight that individuals exist simultaneously as consumers and citizens. That is also the view presented by Sen (1987), who argues that there is essential and irreducible 'duality' in a person's considerations: "Indeed, the person himself or herself may have reasons for pursuing goals other than personal well-being or individual self-interest". He describes it as the "agency aspect" of a person, which can have some other goals than utilitarianistic well-being maximization. Taking this angle, we may further support the assumption of changing Kahneman and Tversky's (1979) "S" shape individual utility function with risk-aversion toward gains and risk-seeking toward losses as a basis that can be potentially rejected when taking social point of view, particularly in intergenerational framework, where individual perspective is cut-down to one-generation life expectancy only. This discrepancy is also noticed by Dasgupta (2008), who argues that discount rate based on discounted utility model concept suffers from a serious weakness: "(…) the formula treats differences between an individual's felicities in two periods of time in the same way as it treats differences between the felicities of two individuals in those same two periods of time. (…) It can be argued, however, that for someone to ask oneself, 'how much should I save for my children?' involves ethics that are different from those pertinent when that same person asks, 'how should I spread out my consumption over time?'(…)".

The question that should be also considered is whether the same result as proposed by Eqs. 4 and 5: positive risk premium for benefits and negative risk premium for costs, can be achieved by applying "the precautionary effect" for the Ramsey formula (cf. Gollier and Mahul 2017), which lowers the overall value of the discount rate.

We argue that there are two reasons why it cannot illustrate *harm aversion* the way as it is put forward in the paper. Firstly, it does not assume separate treatment of costs and benefits, so reduction in rate of discount due to risk inclusion, applies both for positive and negative outcomes. Secondly, the extension of the Ramsey formula is justified by the very uncertainty over the effects (consumption rate of growth or "scenarios" in Weitzman approach), not the attitude to risk itself. Therefore, we argue that uncertainty itself can be perceived a stable factor, irrespective to intra- or intergenerational perspective and the inclusion of uncertainty into the discount rate should be treated as a separate issue, due to the fact that it does not reflects individual or social risk aversion, but the variability of investment outcomes.

Furthermore, as the proposal in the paper eventually leads to applying two various discount rates, it must be contrasted with some other solutions to apply double discount rates, which emerge in case of environmental goods. It must be highlighted that such proposals do not on rest on risk aversion discrepancy in gains and losses, but they relate to the role of environment in natural and man-made resource mix. Kula and Evans (2011) as well as Weikard and Zhu (2005) indicate that the increasing scarcity in case of environmental goods should possess tremendous importance, surpassing both economic growth and diminishing marginal utility of consumption. They argue that economic growth actually undermines natural environment, and on that ground, they justify the proposal of separate discounting of environmental impacts from other costs and benefits. Another argument for separate environmental good discounting is given by Pearce and Markandya (1989), which refer to technological development and marginal productivity of capital as a source of higher relative value of environment (cf. Fisher 2003). In the light of those arguments, separate signs of both risk premia as well as magnitude effects put forward in this paper, could be applied as an extension of discount rates including the relative valuation effect, with environmental losses facing lower discount rates, than environmental gains, while man-made capital would be treated with higher discount rates for both domains.

We argue therefore that the reconstruction of social discount rate put forward in this paper can be perceived as an alternative or an extension to existing procedures, highlighting the specificity of intergenerational social framework from individual one along with differences in risk-aversion perception.

The theoretical proposal of separate discounting presented in the paper may have some implications for empirical research. Particularly, it may improve the appraisal process, particularly in case of Cost-Benefit Analysis. Majority of physical effects in economic appraisal are valued irrespectively of whether they emerge on cost of benefit side and predominant approach is to include their net value in the final analysis. In case of public goods, where contingent valuation is involved, the study may be designed from the very start to evaluate willingness to pay for gains or willingness to accept compensation for losses and then differentiating between risk premiums is not necessary as they are already included in the value of the effect. However, on a regular basis, where some secondary sources are used for valuation (cf. Guide to cost-benefit analysis of investment projects, economic appraisal tool for cohesion policy 2014–2020 2014), using the proposed intergenerational SDR may replace costly process of estimating WTP or WTA separately.

Limitations of the results should be raised as well. We may refer here first of all to the need to verify the proposed solution empirically, i.e. in respect to testing whether preferences toward intergenerational allocations are different from intragenerational in respect to risk perception. Heilmann (2013) and Ok and Masatlioglu (2007) suggest designing a questionnaire asking people about their uncertainty about the future and what is its magnitude in the discount factor which makes future flows value less at present. One must be also aware of other anomalies that may influence the intertemporal preferences. Peccoro and Nijkamp (2012) list i.e. differences in valuations between small and large changes or whether the benefits happen sooner or later than expected. Furthermore, some controversies about double discounting itself are raised (cf. Arrow et al. 2012) or giving rights to people not yet born (Spash 2002). Other controversies come from Dasgupta (2008), who argues that if consumption decrease, the rate of growth in the Ramsey formula will be negative, and then the rate of discount will turn negative as well. The paper does not reach that far in the investigation, assuming that negative inequality aversion factor is the element that decrease only the positive value of the discount rate.

5 Conclusions

Concerning the issue of reconstructing social discount rate in intergenerational projects' appraisal, on the basis of literature review and analysis done in previous sections, the general conclusions suggest the need of separation (1) between intragenerational and intergenerational time frame due to discontinuity between generations leading to failure of individual perspective for decision making, and (2) between costs and benefits of the project due to opposite signs of risk premia in the discount rate and the differences in valuation between gains and losses of the investment.

The first kind of separation involves the necessity to shift to a social point of view when investments with intergenerational perspective are analyzed. The change to social perspective is however not identical with standard cost-benefits analysis maximizing aggregated individual welfares. *The extended social approach*, the term introduced in the paper to highlight this difference, involves searching for optimum not between contemporaries, but between *generations*, and transforming reasons for change of money value in time. As a consequence of non-coexistence of the investing generation and future beneficiaries, both: pure time preference and classically defined risk aversion, cannot serve as justification for discounting of future costs and benefits. Then, the opportunity cost is the only reason for discounting that does not need redefining. However, a redefined risk aversion, which is transformed in intergenerational perspective into inequality aversion, makes the Ramsey equation risk free rate with inequality aversion reflecting ethical stance of contemporaries towards future people.

The second sort of division—between benefits and costs—assumes that the decision maker accepts "precautionary principle". It implies that for intergenerational time frame it is possible to accept risk-aversion attitude both for gains and losses (*harm aversion*), contrary to intragenerational individual perspective, where people tend to show risk-loving preference in case of losses. Furthermore, based on higher valuations of losses, estimated by willingness to accept compensation, than for gains, measured by willingness to pay, it seems reasonable to assume higher level of absolute value of risk premium in discount rate value for costs (with negative sign) than for benefits (positive sign) due to higher changes in utility for losses than for gains.

The issue of discounting coupled with uncertainty for intergenerational time frame is far too complicated to be analyzed profoundly and completely in the paper. The findings do not offer any comprehensive solution to the problem, but may add to the discussion on the issue of intergenerational allocation decision making and intergenerational justice.

References

A social time preference rate for use in long-term discounting. The Office of the Deputy Prime Minister, Department for Transport, and Department of the Environment, Food and Rural Affairs, Oxera (2002)

Arrow, K.J., Cropper, M.L., Gollier, Ch., Groom, B., Heal, G.M., Newell, R.G., Nordhaus, W.D., Pindyck, R.S., Pizer, W.A., Portney, P.R., Sterner, T., Tol, R.S.J., Weitzman, M.L.: How should benefits and costs be discounted in an intergenerational context? Resources for the Future Discussion Paper 12–53 (2012)

Baumol, W.J.: On the social rate of discount. Am. Econ. Rev. **58**(4), 788–802 (1968)

Boardman, A.E., Greenberg, D.H., Vining, A.R., Weimer, D.L.: Cost-Benefit Analysis: Concepts and Practice. Prentice Hall, Upper Saddle River, New Jersey (2001)

Climate Change 2014: Mitigation of Climate Change, Intergovernmental Panel on Climate Change. Cambridge University Press, Cambridge, New York (2014)

Cropper, M., Aydede, S., Portney, P.: Preferences for life-saving programs: how the public discounts time and age. J. Risk Uncertainty **8**, 243–265 (1994)

Cropper, M.L., Freeman, M.C., Groom, B., Pizer, W.A.: Declining discount rates. Am. Econ. Rev. **104**(5), 538–543 (2014)

Dasgupta, P.: Discounting climate change. J. Risk Uncertainty **37**, 141–169 (2008)

Drupp, M.A., Freeman, M., Groom, B., Nesje, F.: Discounting disentangled. Am. Econ. J. Econ. Policy **10**(4), 109–134 (2018)

Fisher, A.C.: Irreversibilities and catastrophic risks in climate change. In: Wesseler, J., Weikard, H.-P., Weaver, R.D. (eds.) Risk and Uncertainty in Environmental and Natural Resource Economics, pp. 9–22. Edward Elgar, Northampton (2003)

Foltyn-Zarychta, M.: Ocena inwestycji międzypokoleniowych – kryteria etyczne w ekonomicznej ocenie efektywności projektów inwestycyjnych. C.H. Beck, Warszawa (2018)

Frederick, S., Loewenstein, G., O'Donoghue, T.: Time discounting and time preference: a critical review. J. Econ. Lit. **40**(2), 351–401 (2002)

Freeman, M.C., Groom, B.: Biodiversity valuation and the discount rate problem. Acc. Auditing Accountability J. **26**(5), 715–745 (2013)

Garrod, G., Willis, K.G.: Economic Valuation of Environment: Methods and Case Studies. Edward Elgar, Cheltenham, Northampton (1999)

Gollier, C., Mahul, O.: Term structures of discount rates: an international perspective. Mimeo, Toulouse School of Economics (2017)

Gollier, C., Weitzman, M.L.: How should the distant future be discounted when discount rates are uncertain? TSE Working Paper Series, No. 09–107 (2009)

Gollier, C., Koundouri, P., Pantelidis, T.: Declining discount rates: economic justifications and implications for long-run policy. Econ. Policy **23**, 757–795 (2008)

Guide to cost-benefit analysis of investment projects, economic appraisal tool for cohesion policy 2014–2020. Directorate-General for Regional and Urban Policy, European Commission (2014)

Guidelines and discount rates for benefit-cost analysis of federal programs. Circular A-94. OMB Office (2016)

Hartzell-Nichols, L.: Intergenerational risks. In: Roeser, R.H.S. (ed.) Handbook of Risk Theory. Epistemology, Decision Theory, Ethics, and Social Implications of Risk, pp. 931–960. Springer, Dordrecht, Heidelberg, London, New York (2012)

Heilmann, C.: Time discounting functions as measures of radical uncertainty about the future? LSE Choice Group Working Paper Series 9(1) (2013)

Kahnemann, D., Tversky, A.: Prospect theory: an analysis of decision under risk. Econometrica **47**(2), 263–292 (1979)

Kula, E., Evans, D.: Dual discounting in cost-benefit analysis for environmental impacts. Environ. Impact Assess. Rev. **31**, 180–186 (2011)

Marcinek, K., Foltyn-Zarychta, M., Pera, K., Saługa, P., Tworek, P.: Ryzyko w finansowej ocenie projektów inwestycyjnych. Wybrane zagadnienia. Prace Naukowe Uniwersytetu Ekonomicznego w Katowicach, Wydawnictwo Uniwersytetu Ekonomicznego w Katowicach, Katowice (2010)

Markowitz, H.: Portfolio selection. J. Finan. **7**(1), 77–91 (1952)

Medvecky, F.: Valuing environmental costs and benefits in an uncertain future: risk aversion and discountng. Erasmus J. Philos. Econ. **5**, 1–23 (2012)

Newell, R., Pizer, W.: Discounting the benefits of climate change mitigation. In: Pew Center on Global Climate Change (2001)

Ok, E.A., Masatlioglu, Y.: A theory of (relative) discounting. J. Econ. Theor. **137**, 214–245 (2007)

Pearce, D.W., Markandya, A.: Environmental Policy Benefits: Monetary Valuation. OECD, Paris (1989)

Pearce, D.W., Turner, R.: Economics of Natural Resources and the Environment. Harvester Wheatsheaf, New York, London, Toronto, Sydney, Tokyo, Singapore (1990)

Peccoro, M., Nijkamp, P.: Estimating individual rates of discount: a meta-analysis. Appl. Econ. Lett. **16**(12), 1235–1239 (2012)

Pera, K., Zintegrowana ocena efektywności finansowej surowcowego projektu inwestycyjnego. Wydawnictwo Akademii Ekonomicznej w Katowicach, Katowice (2010)

Perman, R., Ma, Y., McGilvray, J., Common, M.: Natural Resource and Environmental Economics. Pearson Education Limited, Harlow (2003)

Pindyck, R.S.: Irreversibilities and the timing of environmental policy. Resour. Energy Econ. **22**(3), 233–259 (2000)

Ramsey, F.P.: A mathematical theory of saving. Econ. J. **38**, 543–559 (1928)

Sen, A.: On Ethics and Economics. Wiley-Blackwell, Oxford (1987)

Smith, K.: Discounting, risk and uncertainty in economic appraisals of climate change policy: comparing Nordhaus, Garnaut and Stern. Commissioned paper for the Garnaut Climate Change Review. Department of Climate Change and Energy Efficiency, Canberra (2011)

Spash, C.L.: Greenhouse Economics: Value and Ethics. Routledge, London, New York (2002)

Spash, C.L., Hanley, N.: Cost-Benefit Analysis and the Environment. Edward Elgar, Aldershot (1994)

Sussman, F., Weaver, C.P., Grambsch, A.: Challenges in applying the paradigm of welfare economics to climate change. J. Benefit Cost Anal. **5**(3), 347–376 (2014)

Tietenberg, T.: Environmental and Natural Resource Economics. Pearson International Edition, London (2006)

Weikard, P., Zhu, X.: Discounting and environmental quality: when should dual rates be used? Econ. Model. **22**, 868–878 (2005)

Weitzman, M.L.: Why the far-distant future should be discounted at its lowest possible rate. J. Environ. Econ. Manag. **36**, 201–208 (1998)

Weitzman, M.L.: Gamma discounting. Am. Econ. Rev. **91**(1), 260–271 (2001)

Weitzman, M.L.: Risk-adjusted gamma discounting. Journal of Environmental Economics and Management **60**, 1–13 (2010)
Whitehead, J.C., Blomquist, G.C.: The use of contingent valuation in benefit-cost analysis. In: Alberini, A., Kahn, J.R. (eds.) Handbook on Contingent Valuation. Edward Elgar, Cheltenham, Northampton (2006)

Relationships Between Financial Inclusion and Financial Stability and Economic Growth—The Opportunity or Threat for Monetary Policy?

Bożena Frączek

Abstract The aim of the present article is to conduct the considerations aiming at the identification and presentation of the role of financial inclusion in realization of main purposes of monetary policy—financial stability and economic growth. To achieve the aim of the paper, the reviewed articles and reports of international organizations as well as the case studies from many countries will be used. Financial inclusion is strongly connected with many other financial parameters and processes and influences the financial well-being of households, financial management in enterprises, financial stability and economy as a whole. This impact—although it is ambiguous—accompanies the monetary policy of central banks. Financial inclusion may both increase as well as decrease the efficiency of usage the different tools and channels of central bank's monetary policy in achieving the most important purposes—financial stability and economic growth. This means that many activities carried out to increase the level of financial inclusion may turn out to be risky. Complex relationships of many financial categories and processes, including financial inclusion and monetary policy require the detailed analysis to develop their coherent policy. A consideration of the financial inclusion as supporting process to monetary policy implies further research on ways of increasing the level of financial inclusion, taking into account multifaceted and bidirectional as well as direct and indirect relations between financial inclusion and monetary policy. The article presents integrated attitude to the influence of the financial inclusion on financial stability and economic growth.

Keywords Financial inclusion · Financial stability · Economic growth

---

B. Frączek (✉)
University of Economics in Katowice, 1 Maja 50, 40-287 Katowice, Poland
e-mail: b.fraczek@ue.katowice.pl

P. Linsley et al. (eds.), *Multiple Perspectives in Risk and Risk Management*, Springer Proceedings in Business and Economics,
https://doi.org/10.1007/978-3-030-16045-6_13

1 Introduction

Monetary Policy is the part of economic policy aimed at providing the price stability which usually has an impact on money supply level, exchange rate and other macroeconomic parameters as well as on various financial and economy concepts and processes. Relationships between main purposes of monetary policy and other particular parameters regarding many areas are complex and often bidirectional. The most often analysed are the relationships between monetary policy and inflation, interest rate, exchange rate, stock market, unemployment, economic growth as well as financial inclusion.

As suggested by most of the empirical literature, a price stability is the most genuine objective of monetary policy (inflation targeting, IT). This objective is typically achieved through country's money supply controlling which is usually regulated by the central bank. The most common way of conducting monetary policy for the central bank is by changing its interest rates (base rate)—simple Taylor-type rules. But the inflation targeting under the monetary policy is not always successful. There are many countries, where traditional (Keynesian) interest rate channel is weak or does not operate effectively—e.g. the MENA region (Mukherjee and Bhattacharya 2011), where adoption of IT and movements in interest rates did not affect the responsiveness of private consumption and investment behaviour. There are also promoted alternative ways of monetary policy. The results of the research show, that the substitution effect of changes in the real deposit rate becomes increasingly important as the domestic financial sector develops. This significant, positive and direct effect of financial development on investment and private consumption is direct and not through the interest rate channel. The other alternative concept under the monetary policy is "neutral money" as its purpose. The chief exponents of neutral money hold the view that monetary authority should aim at neutrality of money in the economy. The result of neutral money policy is perfectly stable quantity of money, which does not impose level of consumption and production in economy (a natural level).

Besides many different concepts of monetary policy there are various ways of realising them. For instance, under the inflation targeting concept the central banks adopt different solutions, e.g. the flexible inflation target regime and inflation stabilization (Argon and Savino 2009; Debelle 2018) or concept of inflation forecast targeting (IFT) where the repo rate decision-making process depends on the inflation fore-casts (Tura-Gawron 2017) and many others. In turn, under the concept of neutrality some economists advocated permanent interventions to ensure a constant intrinsic value of money or active cooperation among states which commit themselves to realize the same goal. Consecutively in contrary to interventionist policies more flexibility of credit is promoted that is introduced into the economy by the banking system (Chaloupek 2010; Khayat 2017).

Changes in today's reality, especially after the financial crisis and increasing risk, determine seeking the new solutions and ways of monetary policy. Contemporary proposals pay attention to and underline the meaning of monetary policy mainly to real economy. Critics of inflation targeting under monetary policy claim that many central banks are too focused on inflation and argue that monetary authorities should pay more attention just to real economy and to financial risks as well as the income imbalances. As the alternative to IT, especially when inflation is low and policy rates are at their lower bound, the level target is promoted. Using the specific parameters with determined nominal level monetary authorities specify the monetary policy target. A nominal growth target entails an implied inflation target. The most important parameter in such an alternative monetary policy is the proposed GDP (or total production) and the determined nominal GDP growth around a targeted path—may be regarded as an inflation target and a target for real GDP growth (growth rate) (Andersson and Claussen 2017).

In the aftermath of the financial crisis of 2008 and 2009 there are changes in thinking about how monetary policy should be conducted. Some argue that a price stability is not enough to achieve financial stability, and what is more, the interest rate policy is not enough to achieve financial stability (Svensson 2011). There are also known the suggestions to "rethink monetary policy along six dimensions: flexible inflation targeting, response to asset price bubbles, dichotomy between monetary policy and financial stability policy, risk management and gradualism, fiscal dominance, and forward guidance" (Mishkin 2017).

In today's world the following are worth considering: simultaneously more purposes like inflation, real economy (and sustainable economic growth) and financial stability in monetary policy deliberations. Other tools should also be considered as well as concepts and processes that may help in achieving these purposes. One of them is financial inclusion understood as the access to basic, useful and affordable financial products and services that meet their needs—delivered in a responsible and sustainable way (World Bank 2019). The financial inclusion generally refers to both individuals and business, but in the present paper it is mainly analysed from the point of view of individuals.

Regardless of the concept and details of monetary policy, current activities of monetary authorities in achieving the objectives of monetary policy are closely related to financial inclusion of individuals. The financial inclusion affects—in direct and indirect way—the household well-being and has a great impact on financial stability as well as the sustainable economic growth.

Taking into consideration the financial inclusion under monetary policy means taking into account and stressing additionally the current problems of modern finance directed to personal finance. In many academic debates, there are important questions of how to take care of individuals' well-being and financial security. There are concepts of new paradigms in finance that take into account the individuals who make financial decisions in real financial environment without too much simplification of reality and accepting assumptions detached from reality. The behaviour of financial consumer depends, on the one hand, on monetary policy, and on the other it influences the decisions of the monetary authorities.

The aim of the present article is to conduct the considerations aiming at the identification and presentation of the role of financial inclusion in realization of main purposes of monetary policy—financial stability and economic growth. To achieve the aim of the paper, the reviewed articles and reports of international organizations will be used as well as case studies and the results of previous research of the author of the present paper.

2 Financial Inclusion as the Supporting Process to Monetary Policy in the Pursuit to Financial Stability

Financial stability as the goal of monetary policy is hotly contested, because as the financial crisis, which started in 2007 confirmed that price stability as the aim of monetary policy is not sufficient for keeping financial stability. The channels through which monetary policy of central banks affects financial stability are different and they vary in particular countries, regions and circumstances.

The base rates of central banks as the main tool of monetary policy are used by banks at a lower hierarchical level (commercial banks) in deposit and credit policy, which is significant for financial stability. The quality of granted loans and accepted deposits dependent on interest rate may reflect a situation in the banking or financial sector. Therefore different aspects of credits and deposits may be used in the construction of indicators and variables used in the financial stability measurement (Gadanecz and Jayaram 2009). But the best known interest rate channel is not the only way of influence of the monetary policy on a financial stability. According to recent trends observed in many countries (especially in the group of emerging market economies, EMEs) the macroprudential tools are also used, such as the countercyclical capital buffer or surcharges for systemically important banks. Monetary policy may influence financial stability also through the monetary (price) stability channel. In most cases price stability fosters financial stability, but in rare circumstances the conflict is also possible (Issing 2003).

The next is the risk-taking channel, where monetary policy also has the potential to shape the level of the risk-taking of investors and financial institutions with further impact on financial stability (and on economic activity). These transmission mechanisms of monetary policy, which fuel risk-taking by investors and financial intermediaries can increase vulnerabilities and threaten financial stability (Caruana 2016).

In today's world in many cases the monetary policy frameworks do not give enough consideration to the build-up of financial imbalances. In such a situation the financial stability-oriented monetary policy may be supported by other processes, such as financial inclusion (Siddik and Kabiraj 2018). Financial inclusion may help in decreasing the likelihood of financial instability, not only rely on dealing with their repercussions once they occur—see Fig. 1.

In this point the areas of financial inclusion should be underlined, which should be taken into consideration. In the literature the financial inclusion is often analysed by the prism having the account in financial institutions. The meaning of financial inclusion in the context of this study is guided by a definition which described financial inclusion as the availability and equality of opportunities to access not

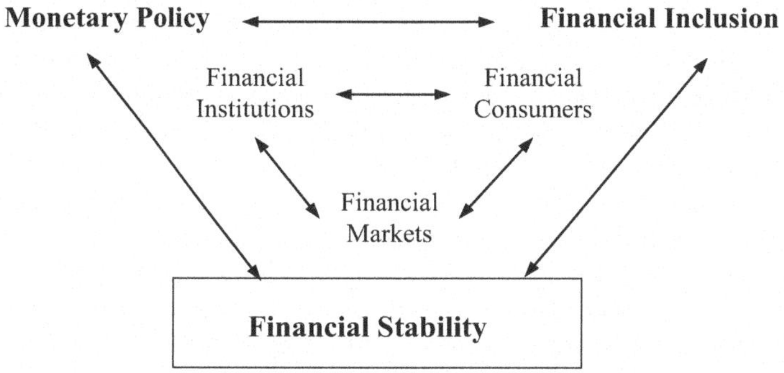

Fig. 1 Financial inclusion as the supporting process to monetary policy in achieving the financial stability

only account in financial institutions but also having savings as well as credits/loans (Frączek 2017). Such an attitude contributes to wider analyses of usage of financial inclusion policy in achieving financial stability and the economic growth under a monetary policy.

Financial inclusion of a large part of the public favors the development of the financial sector, broadening the offers of financial instruments and increasing the usage the financial offers. In addition, a financially stable and conscious financial consumer contributes to the stability of the entire sector. On the other hand financial sector stability is conducive to financial inclusion, as it encourages the use of financial services, especially to saving and investing. This relationships contributes to increasing the stability of the whole financial sector.

The financial inclusion determines the quality of sector of financial services (Chauvet and Jacolin 2017). Expanding the financial inclusion process, supported by the informed usage of financial products and services, has positive impact on the functioning and development of the financial sector in contrary to disruptions of the financial inclusion process, which have negative implications for the financial sector. The financial inclusion is extremely important for financial institutions and it is for them both the source of profits as well as a challenge to implement the concept of social responsibility (Mishra and Chauhan 2016).

On the other hand, the financial institutions (financial intermediaries) influence the level of financial inclusion by de-fining the terms and conditions of financial offers determine the scale and scope of financial products and services used. The way of doing business by financial institutions (e.g. transparency of financial offers, relationships with financial consumers) influences the consumer confidence to financial market and financial intermediaries. The level of financial institutions functionality determines the level of financial inclusion. The examples may be more or less efficient clearing systems, which represent the quality of the relationships with the financial intermediary. The quality of the relationship does not affect the mere fact of financial inclusion/exclusion, but is relevant to its level, resulting from the scale (frequency) of the operations performed.

Consumer financial behaviour (element of wide meaning of financial inclusion) is influenced by the financial market terms, such as the level and fluctuations of financial parameters, including interest rates, exchange rates, financial offers prices. The situation at the financial market may cause the panic, speculation, etc. These circumstances may cause the irrational financial decisions and subsequently the losses of financial markets participants. This may be the reason for the limited usage of financial offers or withdrawal from the market, which intensifies the phenomenon of financial contagion and panic and does not facilitate financial stability.

The presented consideration confirms, that financial inclusion can be both favourable and unfavourable in achieving financial stability—see Table 1. However, knowledge of the problems and experience of many countries and situations indicates the possibility of using financial inclusion in achieving monetary policy objectives.

Widely usage of financial offers increases the financial inclusion and generally favours financial institutions' operations, increasing their sales and resulting in higher profitability as well as creating conditions for more effective risk diversification, positively impacting stability in the financial sector (Bachas et al. 2016). A higher level of financial inclusion in the area of savings helps in providing a more stable base of retail deposits, which is very important for banks activity.

The recent global crisis has confirmed that the usage of stable financial sources in the form of retail deposits as a basis for borrowing money can significantly improve the condition and resilience of financial institutions and may limit their volatility.

The particular importance is attributed to deposits of depositors with lower and middle income, because their financial behaviour in terms of saving and lending is characterized by a high degree of stability and predictability. During systemic crises, deposits of lower middle class usually constitute a continuous and stable source of funds for financial institutions (mainly banks) (Ratnovski and Huang 2009). The lack of such deposits causes that financial institutions may find it difficult to continue

Table 1 Favourable and unfavourable impact of financial inclusion on financial stability

Favourable influence of financial inclusion on financial stability	Unfavourable influence of financial inclusion on financial stability
– Increase the financial products and services sales and enhance the profitability in financial institutions – Risk diversification at financial institutions – Ensuring a stable base of deposits – Dispersal of depositors, reducing the risk of mass withdrawals of deposits – Timely repayment of credits/retail loans – Optimize the structure of financial transactions, customers and threats (risks) – **Facilitating the implementation of monetary policy by central banks and promoting financial inclusion**	– Allocation of capital (e.g. deposits) in financial institutions threatened by bankruptcy – Fewer depositors due to slightly diversified offers of deposits – Increase of household high risk debt and deterioration in the quality of credit portfolio in the banks – Increase household indebtedness and the risk of bankruptcy (debt spiral)

lending. Deposits of low and middle income households are more fragmented, so they are less likely to be aggressively withdrawn during a crisis (Han and Melecky 2013). In addition retail deposits are usually cheaper source of funding of long-term activities of banks (Demirgüç-Kunt and Huizinga 2010; Song and Thakor 2007).

There is also plenty of evidence that low-income borrowers pay their debts on time (Hannig and Jansen 2010). There is the evidence of decreasing the level of credit risk due to increase of the credits operations accompanying the transformation process in the emerging countries of Central and Eastern Europe and the Balkans (Cottarelli et al. 2005).

The financial inclusion can also improve the performance of the mediation function between lenders and borrowers and at the same time facilitating the financial institutions' favourable change in the structure of financial transactions, changing the structure of clients using different services, changing the structure of emerging risks (new risks). Financial inclusion (especially informed financial inclusion) significantly changes the behaviour of both individual financial consumers and business entities, which are more susceptible to central banks' monetary policy.

The financial inclusion, which allows for participating in the regulated (supervised) financial system is directly influenced by monetary policy pursued by central banks in contrary to the large segment of financially excluded households and small businesses forced to use the offers of unregulated institutions, who make financial decisions independently and beyond the influence of central banks, which can significantly disrupt the implementation of monetary policy. Thus the large size of the grey economy may disrupt the transmission of monetary policy impulses and in turn the increasing level of financial inclusion (in the supervised part of financial market) may significantly improve its effectiveness (Mehrotra and Yetman 2015).

The beneficial effects of financial inclusion are more visible in the banking sectors characterized by a lower competition, where for banks with a strong market position it is easier to reduce the risk of expanding into areas that were previously neglected or excluded. It also emphasises the importance of a favourable regulatory and institutional environment that allows banks not only to ease financial constraints on vulnerable and marginalized groups, but also offers great opportunities to reduce risk and increase profitability (Ahamed and Mallick 2016).

The impact of financial inclusion on financial stability may also be unfavourable. It refers to savings, borrowing operations as well as payments (and other areas of financial inclusion). The accumulated savings may negatively influence the financial sector when savers invest their capital in a risky investment or accept the offers of unethical financial institutions expecting a high return (income), while ignoring higher risks. Such cases have occurred as the results of financial crises, when many financial institutions (including the insolvent institutions), fearing losing customers, offered higher interest rates on savings accounts. Many customers, without regard to risk, continued their savings operations, resulting in huge financial losses and losing trust to financial institutions. Insolvent institutions in turn lost their customers, what deepened their inconvenient situation (Yung and Hugh 2013). The rapid and uncontrolled growth of credits can also threaten stability in the financial system, especially when the credibility of borrowers has not been thoroughly analysed and it seems to be questionable. The example of unfavourable impact of expansion of credits on financial stability is subprime loans (subprime mortgage) in the United States, offered lenders with low credit ratings, what were identified as a direct cause of the turmoil in the financial markets and the global financial crisis. The reason for a credit crunch crisis in South Korea in 2002 was 75 million credit cards were issued in order to increase consumption after the crisis of 1997–1998. However, credit cards were not used by the owners in accordance with the government's assumptions, i.e. payments for consumption (with a positive impact on economic development). The issued cards were used to withdraw cash from ATMs and used to settle past liabilities, and the debts were not repaid. As a result of this situation, card-issuing banks have suffered huge losses (He et al. 2005).

Considering the financial inclusion as the supplementing process to monetary policy in achieving the financial stability it is worth stressing that the goals of central banks regarding financial stability and the financial inclusion are not contradictory and they can be mutually reinforcing. Nevertheless, a financial stability, as well as financial inclusion, require adequate regulatory infrastructure, efficient financial markets and well-run, honest and responsible financial institutions. The promotion and supporting the idea of financial inclusion by central banks can contribute simultaneously to improving financial inclusion and strengthening financial stability (Hawkins 2006).

We should also underline the feedback between financial inclusion and financial stability. It means that financial stability or financial instability influence the financial inclusion—see Table 2.

In the analysis of the presented areas of the financial stability impact on the financial inclusion, one should underline the importance of central banks monetary policy for financial inclusion policy by the prism of financial stability. Financial

Table 2 Impact of financial stability/instability on financial inclusion

Kinds of result	Impact of a financial stability on the financial inclusion	Impact of a financial instability on the financial inclusion
Positive	– Consumers trust increase at the financial market – Improvement of financial consumer sentiment – Increase of the interest in financial offers and the scale of their usage	– More careful analysis of threats – More rational policy of financial inclusion – Development of the financial security network, transfer of the centre of gravity from credits to savings
Negative	– Limitation of the financial inclusion as a result of emphasis on maintaining financial stability – Development of an unregulated sector of financial market	– Increasing the risk – Declining the consumer trust at the financial market – Deterioration the sentiment among financial consumers – Declining the level of household savings – The reduction of lending by banks

system supervisors identify, assess and monitor systemic risks arising in the financial system on an on-going basis and take steps to eliminate or reduce these risks. In this way financial supervisors (including central banks) increase or restore the confidence in financial systems, improve the financial consumers sentiment and, consequently, positively influence the scale of the usage of products and services offered by the financial institutions. An important activity of financial supervisors in the pursuit of financial stability is the presentation of the results of analyses of the stability of the financial system, including the assessment of its resistance to possible disturbances.

This increases the knowledge and awareness of financial consumers and the likelihood of positive changes in their financial behaviour without the need for additional actions (interference). Financial instability in turn decreases the resistance to the disorder and increases the susceptible to financial contagion and panic. An increased level of systemic risk is not conducive to effective allocation of funds, which results in lowering the level of savings in banks as well as the disturbances in the widening of bank lending.

Ironically, financial stability also has a negative effect on the financial inclusion. Excessive emphasis on financial stability can undermine the existing level of financial exclusion by preventing financial innovations seen as synonymous of good times in the financial sector. It should be mentioned, that some of the financial innovations on the one hand meet the needs of financially excluded consumers or economically disadvantaged households and at the same time allow for an increase in the range and level of financial offers supplied by banks and other financial institutions. But on the other hand the financial innovations are the source of new risks. For this reason, an attempt to mitigate risk, as the priority of maintaining financial stability in the system, may prevent financial inclusion. A risk elimination or mitigation most frequently takes the form of a regulatory framework for innovative financial services. Too restrict regulations may be the reason for the financial exclusion or the limitation of financial inclusion.

Another example of the negative impact of financial stability on the financial inclusion is the dynamic development of the unregulated (unsupervised) part of financial market—for example financial pyramids (Quisenberry 2017). The prosperity of the financial market is conducive to the development of each financial market segment. The lack of sufficient consumer knowledge and skills can push them towards the unregulated and more risky part of financial market. Moreover, the rapid expansion of entities operating in this unregulated sector may aggravate the financial intermediaries operating in the regulated (supervised) sector and thus reduce the level of the financial inclusion from the perspective of supply side.

Paradoxically, financial instability, which is essentially a negative phenomenon, can have a positive impact on the financial inclusion, as the higher risks associated with it improve the diligence of analyses of appearing threats. This in turn increases the rationality of decisions and behaviour of financially included individuals and households. It also happens that, as a result of the new risk or financial crisis caused by bad debts, the centre of gravity is shifted from credits to long-term savings to improve the resilience of households to the devastating effects of the crisis. In such cases savings become a priority (American Savings Education Council and American Saves 2011).

The conducted analysis confirms the existence of the contradictions in the opinions on the relationships between the financial inclusion and financial stability. But ignoring these relationships can result in costly financial crises and maintaining a resiliently high level of financial exclusion and financial instability. Hence, a financial supervision authorities should take them into account during defining financial stability policy and financial inclusion policy connected with a monetary policy (Čihák et al. 2012).

3 The Meaning of Financial Inclusion for Economic Development

The financial inclusion may support monetary policy also in a pursuit of economic growth. The economic growth is conventionally measured as the nominal value of gross domestic product (GDP), percent rate of increase in real gross domestic product, or real GDP, GDP per capita, but also may be assessed by the level of investment, output, employment, disposable income, consumption, or the size of the capital involved in economy. Each area of financial inclusion may affect the transformation of the economy, but these dependencies are not simple and unambiguous—see Fig. 2. GDP per capita represents achieved economic level by the prism of standard of living.

There is a feedback between the financial inclusion and income represented by GDP per capita, seen as the achieved economic level from the perspective of individuals. In addition each area of financial inclusion represents non-linear relationship and different level and should be considered separately.

It should be underlined that in many countries individuals have an account regardless of the situation in economy. But having an account in financial institutions is

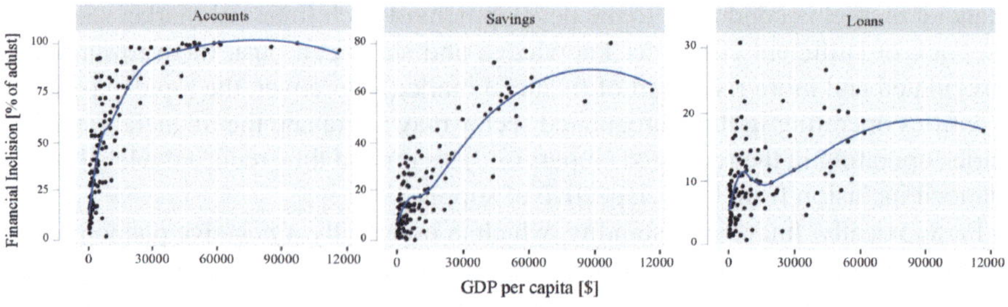

* To determine the shape of dependencies between dependent and independent variables, scatterplots were used and analyzed together with the simple smoothing function applied (LOESS method).

Fig. 2 Relationships between financial inclusion in the area of having account, savings and credits/loans and PKB per capita in the world

very important for economy, because it is starting point to other areas of financial inclusion. Savings as a very important area of financial inclusion play a fundamental role in economy, which is confirmed by a positive correlation between the level of saving and the economic development. Savings of households and businesses are an integral and very important part of the economic system. They are called "private parts" of domestic savings and their level is positively correlated with the level of investment in the economy. Increasing the level of household savings has positive impact on future economic growth. In addition, the level of domestic savings, determining the degree of dependence on foreign capital, affects the financial stability of the country and thus contributes to economic growth and its sustainable development (Sabra and Eltalla 2016).

The positive impact of retail credits/loans on economic development has been proven (documented) by many analyses and studies conducted in different countries. Loans provided by households enable the realization of many actions and investments in many sectors of the economy. An example of the direct im-pact of credit on the economy is the positive impact of mortgage loans on the development of the construction industry (Gostkowska-Drzewiecka and Pestka 2014), car loans on the car industry (KPMG 2017) or other forms of consumer credit including credit cards on financing the purchase of durable goods and supporting producers. These household loans provide an additional consumer demand and promote economic growth. Next very important example of influence the credits and loans on economic growth in longer perspective are educational loans, which may have a very positive impact on the economy due to a better educated society. The level of social education translates into an increase in the number of educated people who constitute the human capital determining economic development.

The economy development also requires a facilitated access to credits and loans by low-income and entrepreneurial individuals. This creates the opportunity to invest in human capital and make the entrepreneurship as a way to permanently reduce poverty. In such cases mitigating the conditions for borrowing money can help improve the quality of credit services and accelerate economic growth. Access to funding facilitates the emergence of new business entities including those run by individuals. Most of the industries in which retail credits drive prosperity play an important role in the economy in both terms of gross value added as well as investment. The investments in these industries, in turn, favour positive changes in many important economic categories characterized by the economy such as production, employment, income from the population, consumption, size of capital and much more. They are also accompanied by positive changes in the standard of living and public safety. In addition, these industries are linked in many ways to other sectors, influencing the effects of their activities.

The role of the financial inclusion in the economic development can be considered in a broader meaning. Increasing the level of financial inclusion associated to launching the new initiatives, affects the competition in business and contributes to the development of entrepreneurship and more evenly distribution of economy development effects (Balakrishnan et al. 2013). In addition, the impact of financial inclusion on economic development can also be considered from the point of view of reducing the inequality of household incomes using financial offers (García-Herrero and Turégano 2015). Households having savings and possibility of borrowing money are more resilient to unexpected shocks and financial crises which usually cause unexpected expenses and income drops. The basic financial sources available under financial inclusion may significantly reduce unfavourable impact of unexpected events.

Despite many arguments for the positive impact of financial inclusion on economic development, there is also evidence of its negative impact on economic processes. Research conducted in 1995–2012 on a sample of 27 European countries confirmed that the corporate loans market positively influences the economic growth, while the market of household loans has a negative impact (Sassi and Gasmi 2014). Another example of negative impact on the financial market and the economies of many countries have had the high risk (subprime) mortgages in the United States, which initiated the global financial and economic crisis in 2007. Results of other research show that Too easy access to credit and loans threatens not only the financial wellbeing of households, but also contributes to the losses of financial institutions lending money. Taking high risks in the process of investing of household surplus can be also dangerous for both financial consumers and financial institutions. It may happen when investment decisions are influenced by psychological, behavioural factors, and financial decisions are irrational and unpredictable. Such decisions and behaviour are source of "noise" in the financial sector and can threaten both financial stability and the whole of the economy.

The financial inclusion influences the economy growth also in an indirect way, for instance by a stabilization and controlling inflation in an economy which is essential for a sustainable economy. But also in the case of inflation—the influence is complex and specific for each area of the financial inclusion, which is a result of various relationships between level of inflation and particular areas of financial inclusion—see Fig. 3.

The impact of financial inclusion on economy growth takes place also Indirectly through the financial stabilisation channel. Financial inclusion as the one of many

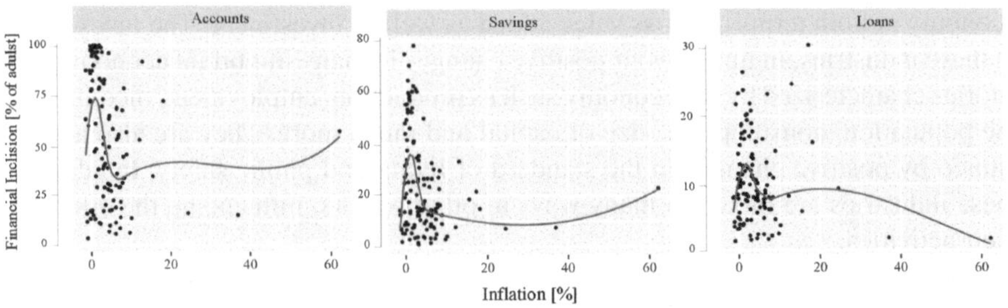

* To determine the shape of dependencies between dependent and independent variables, scatterplots were used and analyzed together with the simple smoothing function applied (LOESS method).

Fig. 3 Relationships between financial inclusion in the area of having account, savings and credits/loans and level of inflation

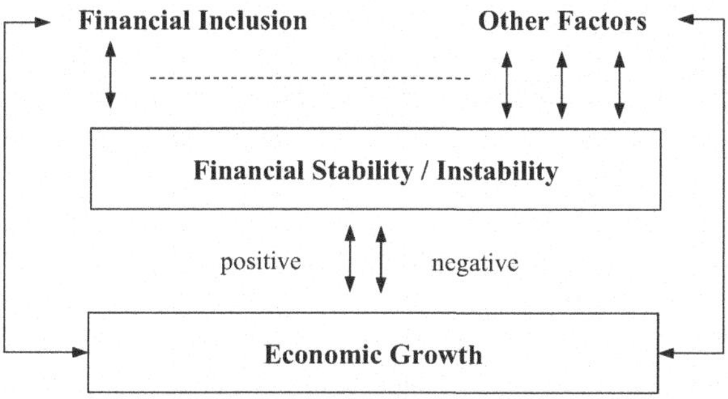

Fig. 4 Financial inclusion as the one of the factors influencing the economic growth

factors influencing the stabilisation in financial system contributes to a situation in economy—see Fig. 4.

For a long time many studies have confirmed the positive impact of well-functioning financial systems (mainly banking) on economic growth, capital accumulation and growth of productivity (King and Levine 1993; Wu and Cheng 2010). The confirmation of the thesis about the positive impact of financial sector stability on economic development is well-functioning financial systems, which overcame the limits of external financing and thus support entrepreneurship and economic expansion (Levine 2004).

The results of research conducted in many countries confirm relationships between many parameters describing the situation in the banking sector (e.g. size of banking sector) and changes in the economic growth and confirm strong correlation between these variables (Vaona 2005). Banking system is one of the most important channels through which the financial system can contribute to the economic growth. The stable economic development is influenced by the improvement of risk diversification and information services of banks and other financial institutions. The dependencies between financial sector development and long-term economic growth are typical for both developing and advanced economies (Burgess and Pande 2005), although many studies indicate that the positive impact of financial sector development on the economic growth is greater and more persistent in developing countries (Mavrotas and Son 2006).

It should be also underlined, that the faster economic growth is not always typical for countries with a better-developed financial sector. In many countries with high economic growth, the degree of financial inclusion is moderate and in many countries with strong and sustainable long-term economic growth there is slow financial market development. Such a situation is typical of many emerging countries (Ekber et al. 2015). And while the situation in these countries in terms of financial inclusion is improving, there are no important changes in increasing the access to more advanced financial services (e.g. more sophisticated investment instruments). This demonstrates that emerging economies move in most degree towards development of banking sector than towards the development of capital market. This does not, however, reduce the importance of the financial inclusion for sustainable economic growth in these countries.

However, there are some views and examples showing that the development of the financial system is conducive to economic growth in varying degrees and depends on the stage of development and the evolution of the financial system. The development of banks' supervisory institutions and the evolution of regulations may result in excessive caution and limiting loans to businesses and households, with further unfavourable consequences for the growth in economy (Haber 2005).

Ambiguous and controversial for economy development is also the influence of foreign banks acting on local markets. On the one hand, foreign banks presence may influence the broadening of financial inclusion, e.g. by increasing the product offering on the local market. In addition, foreign banks as a source of competition improve the quality of the offered products and services and the attractiveness of offers. However, there are results of studies that do not confirm this effect. But on the other hand in many countries foreign banks are a potential source of problems in the credit markets. They often take over the best borrowers, which results in leaving a worse portfolio of borrowers to local banks. In addition, foreign banks are more likely to provide loans in foreign currencies, and the currency risk may adversely affect the financial stability of the country. As an example of negative role of foreign banks at the local markets there is the recent global financial crisis, when many international banks have failed to play a positive role in the local markets (Popov and Udell 2010; Allen et al. 2017).

Conducted discussion on the impact of financial inclusion on financial sector and economy is merely an attempt to identify the different links between these categories. Presented examples confirm that these relationships are varied and it is difficult to assess these interrelations in an unambiguous way and their final effect is the result of many factors.

4 Conclusions

The financial inclusion is strongly connected with many other financial parameters and processes. It influences the financial well-being of households, financial management in enterprises, financial stability and economy as a whole. This impact accompanies the monetary policy of central banks. Financial inclusion enhances the efficiency of usage the different tools and channels of central bank's monetary policy in achieving the most important purposes—financial stability and economic growth. But the complex relationships of many financial categories and processes, including financial inclusion and monetary policy require the develop their coherent policy.

The consideration of the financial inclusion as a supporting process to monetary policy implies further research in two main questions.

The first area of further research should be in-depth research on financial inclusion resulting in increasing its level, especially in the fields of its positive impact on financial stability and economy outcomes. It in turn requires identification of the factors influencing the level of the financial inclusion. Preliminary findings specify demand-side factors and supply-side factors. To the first group belongs income in the macro and micro scale, the level of financial literacy as the result of effective financial education, gender, age and other socio-demographic factors (cultural, religious). In the group of supply-side factors usually are identified mainly terms of access to financial products and services and their quality. Conducted research and preliminary results explore that particular areas of financial inclusion depend on different factors. Having the accounts depends in most degree on automated teller machines (ATMs) per 100,000 adults, level of financial literacy and interest rate spread (lending rate minus deposit rate, %), savings depend on income (GDP per capita) and level of financial literacy and credits/loans depend mainly on number of commercial bank branches (per 100,000 adults) and interest rate spread. Such results show necessity of research conducted on an on-going basis on the financial inclusion impact areas and factors influencing the level of financial inclusion from the perspective of supporting financial markets authorities in pursuit to their main purposes realization.

The second area of further research is the identification and analysis of other processes as supporting the monetary policy in a direct and indirect way.

References

Ahamed, M.M., Mallick, S.: Is financial inclusion good for bank stability? international evidence. J. Econ. Behav. Organ. https://editorialexpress.com/cgi-bin/conference/download.cgi?db_name=RESConf2016&paper_id=120 (2016). Last accessed 20 July 2018

Allen, F., Jackowicz, K., Kowalewski, O., Kozłowski, Ł.: Bank lending, crises, and changing ownership structure in Central and Eastern European countries. J. Corp. Finan. **42**, 494–515. https://doi.org/10.1016/j.jcorpfin.2015.05.001 (2017). Last accessed 27 Nov 2018

American Savings Education Council and American Saves.: In: Fourth Annual Saving Assessment Indicates Many Americans Still Struggling, Washington, DC, https://consumerfed.org/press_release/annual-saving-assessment-indicates-many-americans-still-struggling/ (2011). Last accessed 5 Mar 2019

Andersson, B., Claussen, A.C.: Alternatives to inflation targeting. Sveriges Riks Bank Econ. Rev. **1**, 51–82. http://archive.riksbank.se/Documents/Rapporter/POV/2017/rap_pov_artikel_3_170120_eng.pdf (2017). Last accessed 27 Nov 2018

Aragon, E., Savino, M.: Central Bank preferences and monetary rules under the inflation targeting regime in Brazil. Braz. Rev. Econometrics **29**(1), 79–109. https://pdfs.semanticscholar.org/022f/6b76a39fc0418a98bfde4ab3a624abdeaa12.pdf (2009). Last accessed 27 Nov 2018

Bachas, P., Gertler, P., Higgins, S., Seira, E.: Banking on trust: how debit cards help the poor to save more. NBER Working Paper, no. 23252, National Bureau of Economic Research. http://www.nber.org/papers/w23252.pdf (2016). Last accessed 20 Mar 2018

Balakrishnan, R., Steinberg, C., Syed, M.H.: The Elusive Quest for inclusive growth: growth, poverty, and inequality in Asia. IMF Working Paper, no. 13/152, International Monetary Fund. https://www.imf.org/external/pubs/ft/wp/2013/wp13152.pdf (2013). Last accessed 27 Nov 2013

Burgess, R., Pande, R.: Do rural banks matter? evidence from the Indian social banking experiment. Am. Econ. Rev. **95**(3), 780–795, https://econ.lse.ac.uk/staff/rburgess/wp/aer.pdf (2005). Last accessed 27 Nov 2018

Caruana, J.: Monetary policy for financial stability. In: 52nd SEACEN Governors' Conference Naypyidaw, Myanmar, 26 November, https://www.bis.org/speeches/sp161130a.pdf (2016). Last accessed 15 May 2018

Chaloupek, G.: "Neutrality of money" versus "stability of the price level"—issues of monetary theory within the Austrian school of economics. Paper presented to the 14th ESHET Conference, Amsterdam, March 25–27. http://www.chaloupek.eu/explorer/NeutralityText.pdf (2010). Last accessed 27 Nov 2018

Chauvet, L., Jacolin, L.: Financial inclusion, bank concentration and firm performance. World Dev. **97**, 1–13. http://dx.doi.org/10.2139/ssrn.2903982 (2017). Last accessed 27 Nov 2018

Cottarelli, C., Dell'Ariccia, G., Vladkova-Hollar, I.: Early brids, late risers, and sleeping beauties: bank credit growth to the private sector in Central and Eastern Europe and in the Balkans. J. Bank. Finan. **29**(1), 83–104. https://doi.org/10.1016/j.jbankfin.2004.06.017 (2005). Last accessed 27 Nov 2018

Čihák, M., Muñoz, S., Sharifuddin, S., Tintchev, K.: Financial stability reports: what are they good for? IMF Working Paper, no. 12/1, Washington DC, USA. https://www.imf.org/external/pubs/ft/wp/2012/wp1201.pdf (2012). Last accessed 27 Nov 2018

Debelle, G.: Twenty-five years of inflation targeting in Australia, RBA conference 2018. Speech of Deputy Governor, Reserve Bank of Australia. https://www.rba.gov.au/speeches/2018/pdf/sp-dg-2018–04-12.pdf (2018). Last accessed 20 Aug 2018

Demirgüç-Kunt, A., Huizinga, H.: Bank activity and funding strategies: the impact on risk and returns. J. Finan. Econ. **98**(3), 626–650, https://doi.org/10.1016/j.jfineco.2010.06.004 (2010). Last accessed 27 Nov 2018

Ekberg, J., Chowdhuri, R., Soejachmoen, M.P., Kermanus, B.: Financial deepening in Indonesia. Funding infrastructure development—catalyzing economic growth. Oliver Wyman i Mandiri Institute. https://www.oliverwyman.com/content/dam/oliver-wyman/global/en/2015/sep/Financial_Deepening_In_Indonesia.pdf (2015). Last accessed 27 Nov 2018

Frączek, B.: Edukacja finansowa jako determinanta wzrostu włączenia finansowego. Podejście zintegrowane, Wydawnictwo Uniwersytetu Ekonomicznego w Katowicach (Financial education as a determinant of the increase in financial inclusion. An integrated approach, Publisher of the University of Economics in Katowice) Katowice (2017)

Gadanecz, B., Jayaram, K.: Measures of financial stability—a review. IFC Bull., BIS, Basel, **31**, 365–382, https://www.bis.org/ifc/publ/ifcb31ab.pdf (2009). Last accessed 27 Nov 2018

García-Herrero, A., Turégano, D.M.: Financial inclusion, rather than size, is the key to tackling income inequality. BBVA Working Paper, BBVA Bank, no. 15/05, Madrid, http://bruegel.org/wp-content/uploads/2018/01/WP_Financial-Inclusion-Income-Inequality4.pdf (2015). Last accessed 27 Nov 2018

Gostkowska-Drzewiecka, M., Pestka, E.: Ekonomiczne uwarunkowani rozwoju rynku mieszkaniowego w Polsce – klasyfikacja (Economic conditions for the development of the housing market in Poland—classification). Part I. J. Manag. Finan., Gdańsk University **12**(1), 90–91, http://cejsh.icm.edu.pl/cejsh/element/bwmeta1.element.desklight-bc5bfaf1-617e-477f-96ba-0d3e76a2a673 (2014). Last accessed 27 Nov 2018

Haber, S.H.: Mexico's experiment with bank privatization and liberalization, 1991–2000. J. Bank. Finan. **29**, 2325–2353. https://stephen-haber.com/wp-content/uploads/2014/02/Haber-Mexicos-Experiments-with-Bank-Privatization.pdf (2005). Last accessed 27 Nov 2018

Han, R., Melecky, M.: Financial inclusion for financial stability: access to bank deposits and the growth of deposits in the global financial crisis. World Bank Policy Research Working Paper, no. 6577, https://ssrn.com/abstract=2312982 (2013). Last accessed 15 Apr 2018

Hannig, A., Jansen, S.: Financial inclusion and financial stability: current policy issues. ADBI Working Paper, no. 259, Asian Development Bank Institute, Tokyo. https://www.adb.org/sites/default/files/publication/156114/adbi-wp259.pdf (2010). Last accessed 27 Nov 2018

Hawkins, P.: Financial access and financial stability. In: Central Banks and the Challenge of Development, Bank of International Settlement, BIS, Basel, 65–79, http://citeseerx.ist.psu.edu/viewdoc/download?doi=10.1.1.370.4733&rep=rep1&type=pdf (2006). Last accessed 5 Mar 2019

He, D., Yao, E., Li, K.: The growth of consumer credit in Asia. Hong Kong Monet. Author. Quart. Bull. March, https://www.hkma.gov.hk/media/eng/publication-and-research/quarterly-bulletin/qb200503/fa2.pdf (2005). Last accessed 5 Mar 2019

Issing, O.: Monetary and financial stability: is there a trade-off?. In: Conference on "Monetary Stability, Financial Stability and the Business Cycle", Bank for International Settlements, Basel, 28–29 March 2003, https://www.ecb.europa.eu/press/key/date/2003/html/sp030329.en.html (2003). Last accessed 5 Mar 2019

Khayat, G.: The corridor's width as a monetary policy tool. Working Paper, Aix-Marseille School of Economics—AMSE, https://halshs.archives-ouvertes.fr/halshs-01611650/document (2017). Last accessed 5 Mar 2019

KPMG.: Stan branży motoryzacyjnej w polskiej gospodarce (The condition of the automotive industry in the Polish economy), Raport by KPMG, Warsaw, p. 43. https://pzpm.org.pl/__sk/__sk_files.php?d=1506523216vqrfjrhubkwfumdnyidmcuvqpigjpislykricycdjzjdmnql&u=1113 (2017). Last accessed 5 Mar 2019

King, R.G., Levine, R.: Finance and growth: Schumpeter might be right. Quart. J. Econ. **108**, 717–738, https://www.isid.ac.in/~tridip/Teaching/DevEco/Readings/07Finance/05King&Levine-QJE1993.pdf (1993). Last accessed 5 Mar 2019

Levine, R.: Finance and growth: theory and evidence. NBER Working Paper, no 10766, 865–934, https://www.nber.org/papers/w10766 (2004). Last accessed 5 Mar 2019

Mavrotas, G., Son, S.: Financial sector development and growth: re-examining the nexus. In: Bagella, M., Becchett, I.L., Hasan. I. (eds.) Transparency, Governance and Markets, pp. 217–242, Amsterdam (2006)

Mehrotra A., Yetman, J.: Financial inclusion—issues for central banks. BIS Quart. Rev. March, https://www.bis.org/publ/qtrpdf/r_qt1503h.htm (2015). Last accessed 5 Mar 2019

Mishkin, F.S.: Rethinking monetary policy after the crisis. J. Int. Money Finan. **73** (Part B), 252–274, https://doi.org/10.1016/j.jimonfin.2017.02.007 (2017). Last accessed 5 Mar 2019

Mishra, P., Chauhan, S.: CSR funds in banking sector as an effective means for financial inclusion initiatives in India. Ind. Inst. Forest Manag., http://pioneerjournal.in/files.php?force&file=CSR_Funds_in_Banking_Sector_as_an_Effective_Means_for_Financial_Inclusion_Initiatives_in_India_756999930.pdf (2016). Last accessed 5 Mar 2019

Mukherjee, S., Bhattacharya, R.: Inflation targeting and monetary policy transmission mechanisms in emerging market economies. IMF Working Paper WP/11/229 (2011)

Popov, A., Udell, G.: Cross-border banking and the international transmission of financial distress during the crisis of 2007–2008. European Central Bank Working Paper, no 1203, ECB, Frankfurt, Germany (2010)

Quisenberry, W.L.: Ponzi of all Ponzis: critical analysis of the Bernie Madoff scheme. Int J Economet. Finan. Manag. **5**(1), 1–6 (2017)

Ratnovski, L., Huang, R.: Why are Canadian banks more resilient? Working Paper, WP/09/152, IMF, Washington, DC, http://citeseerx.ist.psu.edu/viewdoc/download?doi=10.1.1.518.6449&rep=rep1&type=pdf (2009). Last accessed 5 Mar 2019

Sabra, M., Eltalla, A.: Foreign aid, domestic savings and economic growth in selected MENA countries. Bus. Econ. Res. **6**(1), 352–362 (2016)

Sassi, S., Gasmi, A.: The effect of enterprise and household credit on economic growth: new evidence from European Union countries. J. Macroecon. **39** (Part A), 226–231 (2014)

Siddik, M.N.A., Kabiraj, S.: Does financial inclusion induce financial stability? Aust. Account. Bus. Finan. J. **12**(1), 32–46, https://doi.org/10.14453/aabfj.v12i1.3 (2018). Last accessed 5 Mar 2019

Song, F., Thakor, A.V.: Relationship banking, fragility, and the asset-liability matching problem. Rev. Finan. Stud. **20**, 2129–2177, https://pdfs.semanticscholar.org/8173/985db2027bcb041b1d787a1fa19dfad5728c.pdf (2007). Last accessed 5 Mar 2019

Svensson, L.E.O.: Monetary policy after the crisis. In: Proceedings, Federal Reserve Bank of San Francisco, issue Nov, 35–49, https://www.frbsf.org/economic-research/files/Svensson2.pdf (2011). Last accessed 5 Mar 2019

Tura-Gawron, K.: The forecasts-based instrument rule and decision making. How closely interlinked? The case of Sweden. Equilibrium **12**(2), 295, https://doi.org/10.24136/eq.v12i2.16 (2017). Last accessed 5 Mar 2019

Vaona, A.: Regional evidence on the finance-growth nexus. Working Paper, no. 30, Department of Economic Sciences, University of Verona, Verona (2005)

World Bank.: Website of World Bank, https://www.worldbank.org/en/topic/financialinclusion/overview (2019). Last accessed 5 Mar 2019

Wu, J.L., Cheng, S.Y.: The dynamic impacts of financial institutions on economic growth: evidence from the European Union. J. Macroecon, **32**(3), 879–891 (2010)

Yung, Ch.P., Hugh, P.: How finance is shaping the economies of China, Japan, and Korea, pp. 269–270, Columbia Business School Publishing, Columbia (2013)

Risk Management in Central Banks in the Context of Monetary Policy Normalization

Aleksandra Nocoń

Abstract In the face of the global financial crisis, central banks have used non-standard and unconventional monetary policy instruments. Firstly, they implemented the interest rate policy, lowering base interest rates to a very low (zero or—in some cases—even negative) level. In the lack of expected results, they also decided on *Quantitative Easing* policy. However, some of them in the following years did not undertake normalizing activities. The main aim of the study is identification of major categories of risk, accompanying the normalization process of modern central banks. Methodology used in the research mainly based on theoretical analysis: selection and discussion of theoretical material and descriptive material, in context, and detailed comparison of risk accompanying individual central banks. The central bank's risk may concern timing of normalizing activities. Too fast phasing out of non-standard instruments can threaten the growing economic growth. While, their too late implementation may pose a risk for long-term macroeconomic and financial stability. An important area of the research, undertaken in the study, is the risk of central bank's balance sheet normalization. This process may take place through active approach—resale of assets, purchased previously by central banks, or passive approach—holding them in the balance sheet until maturity.

Keywords Risk management in central banks · Monetary policy normalization · Risk areas of central banks · Balance sheet normalization

1 Introduction

The global financial crisis has caused significant changes in risk management both in commercial as well as central banks. The risk management system seems to be more significant especially that the largest central banks of the global economy begin activities towards normalization of their monetary policy. Normalization—in general

A. Nocoń (✉)
University of Economics in Katowice, 1 Maja 50, 40-287 Katowice, Poland
e-mail: aleksandra.nocon@ue.katowice.pl

P. Linsley et al. (eds.), *Multiple Perspectives in Risk and Risk Management*, Springer Proceedings in Business and Economics,
https://doi.org/10.1007/978-3-030-16045-6_14

terms—is the process of returning to traditional monetary policy. Most often, it is identified with the restoration of monetary policy to pre-global financial crisis framework (Nocoń 2018). On the other hand, it can mean its transformation towards a new quality, so far unknown to central banks—*new normal*. The lack of previous central banks' experiences in realization of normalizing activities is undoubtedly a factor hindering their implementation. Appropriate definition and implementation of *exit strategies* assumptions is extremely difficult in the absence of theoretical framework (Cecioni et al. 2011). In turn, normalization without clearly defined assumptions, ad hoc implemented, may generate financial risk not only for a banking sector, but for the whole financial system. That is why, so much emphasis is now placed on identifying the main risk areas from monetary authorities' point of view that may accompany the normalization process.

The main aim of the study is identification of major categories of risk, accompanying the normalization process of modern central banks. The experience from the global financial crisis is the basis for determining what the *new normal* in the risk management system should be. Methodology used in the research mainly based on theoretical analysis: selection and discussion of theoretical material and descriptive material, in context, and detailed comparison of risk accompanying individual central banks. Additionally, the following research methods were used: study and critical evaluation of the literature, secondary analysis of empirical data of the major central banks, cause and effect analysis, case studies, observation method, document analysis method as well as synthesis method.

2 Risk Management in Commercial and Central Banks

In recent years, risk management in commercial and central banks has become more and more important. The new regulatory order, implemented after the recent financial crisis, encouraged financial safety net institutions, including regulators, supervisors and monetary authorities, as well as commercial banks themselves to strengthen in many areas the risk management process (Pyka et al. in print). Banks and credit institutions are currently subject to more detailed and restrictive requirements, which mainly relate to:

- tightening capital requirements—in relation to the value and quality (structure) of their capital,
- implementation of liquidity requirements (*Liquidity Coverage Ratio*—LCR and *Net Stable Funding Ratio*—NSFR)—so far not occurring in recommendations of the Basel Committee on Banking Supervision,
- specification of the maximum level of banks' leverage—leverage ratio,

- methods of calculating risk-weighted assets (RWA)[1] for all types of risk within pillar I.[2]

For central banks, involvement in the risk management process is extremely important for their monetary policy. In recent years, monetary authorities have implemented (zero, and in some cases even negative[3]) interest rate policy and significantly increased the size of their balance sheets, which determined essential changes in the risk management framework. Among others, they extended requirements regarding eligible assets for collateral in open market operations, or as a part of the *Quantitative Easing* policy, purchased and now maintain specific securities (also from the non-financial sector) in their assets.

Although, there are many similarities in the methods of risk management of central banks and commercial banks, there are also many differences arising from the public mission and the mandate imposed on monetary authorities. First of all, credit operations and risk mitigation measures are in some ways similar to the lending activity of commercial banks, but in the case of monetary policy of central banks, securities that may be considered as their collateral, as well as an interest rate on the refinancing loan are the same for all borrowers. At the same time, it requires from monetary authorities a risk control framework which aims to achieve risk equivalence across all assets accepted as collateral. Secondly, the overriding objective of central banks is to maintain price stability, while the main aim of commercial banks is to maximize financial income. In addition, monetary authorities in the risk management process primarily take into account macroeconomic conditions, while commercial banks—the microeconomic context, i.e. their individual financial condition and situation on the banking market. Finally, central banks during instability increase their exposure to financial risk by implementing a set of non-standard tools, in order to reduce risks for the financial system. Their goal is to restore financial stability and ultimately maintain price stability. On the other hand, commercial banks in exceptional times limit the amount of risk taken, striving to maintain their own stability, liquidity and solvency. Thus, the risk areas of commercial banks and central banks are in many aspects convergent, but the methods of its reduction and management are significantly different.

---

[1]Reliability and comparability of bank risk estimation models were strongly questioned after the global financial crisis. The Basel Committee, in order to reduce their unjustified volatility and lead to greater comparability, has attempted to normalize them in a new document—Basel IV (The Basel IV assumptions were published on December 7, 2017. They cover the nine-year implementation period, which will start on January 1, 2022 and will last until January 1, 2027). The Basel microprudential instruments are designed to counteract procyclicality and, to a greater extent, protect individual institutions in the conditions of risk materialization, which may lead to a crisis situation.

[2]Pillar I concerns estimation of a sum of the minimum capital requirements for credit, market and operational risk. The minimum capital requirements are based on three basic elements: definition of regulatory capital, risk-weighted assets and the minimum ratio of capital to risk-weighted assets.

[3]The negative interest rate was implemented by the central bank of Denmark, Switzerland, Sweden and Japan. In turn, the central bank of Hungary, Sweden and the European Central Bank decided on implementation of the negative deposit rate.

Central banks in their risk management principles carefully defined, taking into account new areas of risk after the global financial crisis, pay particular attention to protection, consistency, simplicity and transparency (ECB 2015). They imply that, pursuing their mandate, central banks will undertake activities that limit their exposure to financial risk. This concept, which underpins all risk management—also commercial banks—is commonly known in the literature as risk efficiency (Champan and Ward 2004). Central bank's risk management must therefore be an integral part of their decision-making process. In turn, simplicity and transparency are achieved through initiatives, implemented directly in accordance with previously adopted rules, and the highest possible predictability of activities (ECB 2018).

This monetary authorities' commitment to risk efficiency is vital for several reasons. First of all, despite financial independence, the central bank's financial resources are public funds, so any losses suffered by conducting monetary policy are losses for the public purse. Secondly, losses can affect the financial independence of central banks and thus potentially their operational independence. Thirdly, these losses may undermine central bank's credibility and reputation, thereby threaten trust of public opinion in achieving the main objective—maintaining price stability.

3 Main Areas of Risk in Times of Monetary Policy Normalization

The normalization of monetary policy, related to the complete *exit* of non-standard instruments and restoration of the new monetary architecture, requires a revision of the existing or introduction of new rules into the general central banks' risk management framework. Monetary authorities should remain flexible by formulating and implementing *exit strategies*. However, initiatives ending unconventional policy should not undertake higher risk than it is necessary. Therefore, the beginning of the normalization process requires from the monetary authorities identification and then—during its implementation—monitoring risk in the following areas (see Fig. 1):

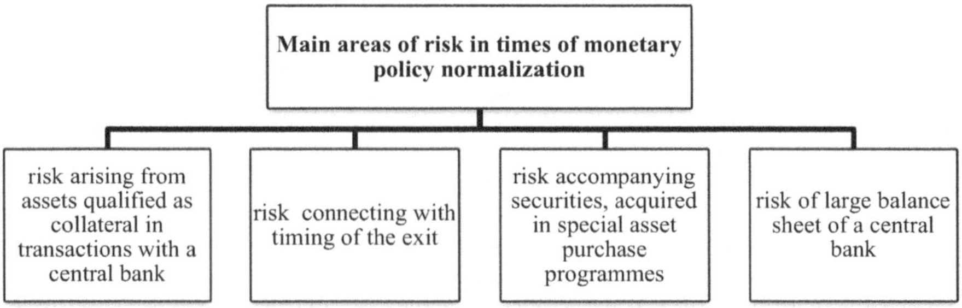

Fig. 1 Main area of risk in times of monetary policy normalization

1. risk arising from assets qualified as collateral in transactions with a central bank,
2. risk connecting with timing of the *exit*,
3. risk accompanying securities, acquired in special asset purchase programmes (APP) implemented during *Quantitative Easing* policy,
4. risk of large balance sheet of a central bank.

Non-standard open market operations, undertaken by the monetary authorities as a response to the recent financial crisis, were characterized by increased frequency, volume of transactions, extension of maturity of refinancing operations, a fixed-rate tender procedure with full allotment, as well as extension of the list of collateral accepted in those operations and counterparties allowed to transactions with a central bank. In conventional open market operations, central banks require specific collateral from commercial banks in order to protect against potential losses of monetary authorities. During the global financial crisis, it was decided to extend the list of eligible collateral in refinancing operations with central banks. This list has been extended by: deposit certificates and negotiable debt instruments in foreign currency (Bogołębska 2012). Moreover, some central banks also accepted private securities as collateral in open market operations (ECB 2010; Nocoń 2016).

Extension of the list of assets accepted as collateral in refinancing transactions was aimed at increasing banking sector's access to liquidity, which at the same time would impact on an increase of commercial banks' lending. So far, central banks have been operating on the concept of a single list, which included a list of assets accepted as collateral in transactions with a central bank, that increased the overall transparency of those operations. However, along with the extension of scale and scope of central banks' activities, this list was also expanded by new types of securities. Therefore, as a part of the monetary policy normalization, its re-revision is necessary in the aspect of minimizing the central bank's risk. Especially that liquidity demand declines. However, it is possible that in the future the list may be extended again, in the view of a need to re-stimulate banking sector.

For many central banks, the risk is also associated with the appropriate time of starting normalizing activities, so when they should stop monetary easing (finish expansionary monetary policy) and start its tightening (begin restrictive monetary policy). Central banks in the world (including Federal Reserve System and Bank of Japan) indicate that this should be the moment when decisions about (Nocoń 2018):

1. the end of an increase of monetary authority's asset portfolio—*tapering purchase*,
2. an increase of main interest rates and start adjusting the asset portfolio to the new steady state,

are made. These are two separate decisions. However, both of them should primarily depend on current economic and financial conditions. Thus, they should not be implemented in a predetermined time. Completion of monetary policy easing should take place when there are justified assumptions that economies will return to a path of growth, towards a higher level of resources use, and inflation will move towards the target, as well as when this path will be maintained despite the withdrawal of non-standard monetary policy instruments. However, it is extremely difficult to

Fig. 2 Too early normalization versus too late normalization

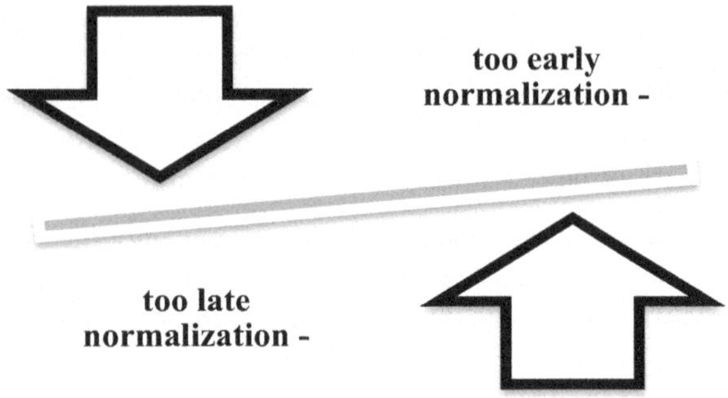

determine when exactly macroeconomic variables will enter the path and be able to keep on it, even when monetary easing and asset purchase programs end. Nevertheless, too fast phasing out of non-standard instruments may threaten the growing economic growth. On the other hand, their too long implementation may pose a risk for long-term macroeconomic and financial stability (see Fig. 2).

Therefore, the question is whether it is more beneficial for monetary authorities to implement normalizing activities early enough, when the first signs of economic recovery appear, or whether it will be better to extend the time of normalization process until the total restoration of financial system stability. Rapid implementation of the normalization process will allow to counteract the excessive expansion of central bank's balance sheet and growing inflation risk. On the other hand, it may cause weakening of the economic growth (or even re-recession), which is a positive effect of non-standard instruments. Previous experience with the withdrawal of unconventional tools points to some irreversible element. This is due to the fact that effectiveness of non-standard policy of central banks depends—to a large extent—on how long implementation of this policy is expected. For example, if only a short-term liquidity support for banking sector is expected, commercial banks are reluctant to increase their lending (González-Páramo 2009).

Moreover, expansion of central banks' assets generates significant costs, which argues quick end of non-standard tools, especially *Quantitative Easing* policy. An increase of size and changes in the structure of central bank's balance sheet may affect its ability for smooth normalization process or social confidence that this process will be implemented in appropriate time without the risk of inflationary pressure. On the other hand, central banks are concerned that the higher value of their balance sheet total and the longer maturity of instruments held in their assets, the greater negative consequences of normalization.

It should also be mentioned that the total effects of extraordinary monetary policy are observed after some period of time, which is due to the existing delays. This indicates that too fast normalizing activities should be avoided (Yellen 2015). On the other hand, deferring a decision to start the normalization process, under full banking sector and financial markets stability, may result in excessive expansion of central bank's balance sheet and growing inflation beyond the target, set in a monetary policy strategy. Normalizing actions taken too late may also increase the risk of loss of central bank's credibility, particularly with regard to the objective to maintain a stable price level. Therefore defining assumptions of the normalization process, it should be taken into account the possible consequences of too aggressive monetary policy tightening, especially in the face of budgetary savings, as well as the risk of too late normalizing actions.

At the same time, delaying the normalization process, risk of financial system instability may increase, by an impact on growth of risky exposures that make *exit* even more difficult. In particular, extended period of low interest rates and liquidity support programs may threaten market mechanisms in effective resource allocation, thus encouraging to rollover loans for unprofitable investments, as well as weakening motivation to improve assets quality in banks' balance sheets. Moreover, too long period of low interest rates may also lead to an inadequate approach to risk by investors and finally threaten stability of financial markets (Yellen 2015). At this stage—a decade after first implementation of the non-standard monetary policy instruments, central banks seem to have chosen the path of late normalization. In the case of the Federal Reserve System, decision on interest rate normalization was made only after total completion of *Quantitative Easing*. Similarly, the European Central Bank declared its readiness to raise a level of key interest rates only when the asset purchase programme will be fully extinguished. Thus, the monetary authorities have recognized that the potential benefits that can be achieved through non-standard and unconventional monetary policy outweigh the possible risks resulting from the prolonged implementation of the *exit strategies*.

Another aspect is how great importance a central bank attaches to the risk of financial stability, when it decides to complete low interest rate policy. Maintaining low (zero or negative) interest rates for too long may foster to undertake excessive credit risk and duration risk by financial institutions, acting as financial intermediaries.

The third area of central banks' risk, resulting directly from the implementation of extraordinary instruments, are threats connecting with asset purchase programmes. Firstly, this risk is a compilation of risk accompanying individual securities, acquired by monetary authorities. In the case of Treasuries (e.g. US Treasury securities purchased by the FED), this risk is negligible. However, along with the modification of the QE policy, central banks purchased more and more new types of assets, including private debt securities (corporate bonds and commercial papers), which were burdened with a higher level of risk. Secondly, central banks bear the risk associated with secondary activities of QE policy—resulting from the reinvestment of funds from maturing securities. It is connected with re-engagement of capital and maintaining high value of balance sheet total. Therefore, some risk control parameters also in this area require recalibration. This is to ensure that—taking into account maturity of some of the securities acquired during the implementation of QE policy, and the reinvestment of funds—the overall risk exposure will not change.

Finally, the fourth risk area of modern central banks results from maintaining large balance sheets, as a consequence of the implementation of a set of non-standard monetary policy instruments—mainly *Quantitative Easing* policy and extended open

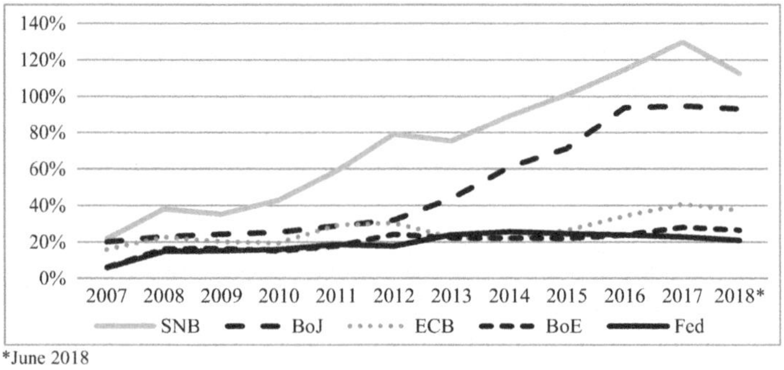

Fig. 3 Balance sheet totals of the largest central banks as a percentage of GDP of their economies

market operations (see Fig. 3).[4] Normalization of the central banks' balance sheet seems particularly problematic and ambiguous. Central banks, in order to normalize their balance sheet, i.e. decrease their balance sheet totals and a change of asset structure, towards reduction of high risk securities, purchased in special asset purchase programs, may (Agostini et al. 2016):

3. hold them until maturity (*passive approach* or *passive unwind*), or
4. resell them (*active approach* or *active unwind*).

In the passive approach, time of normalization may be significantly prolonged, given a long-term maturity of securities, held in monetary authorities' assets. In turn in active approach, balance sheet normalization will not take too long, because a part of purchased assets will be resold. However, both approaches—passive and active—involve some benefits as well as costs, resulting from specific central banks' actions. In the passive approach, it would take several dozen years to make excess reserves—created by the central bank to finance unconventional asset purchases—completely disappeared from the balance sheet. Moreover, the passive approach in the normalization process of central bank's balance sheet may generate financial losses, and thus zero profit distribution to the state budget. A negative financial result may result from natural maturity transformation that occurs in central bank's balance sheet. During *Quantitative Easing* policy, monetary authorities purchased mainly Treasury bonds with a low interest rate. Maintaining them in their balance sheets may cause that interest expenses will exceed current interest income.

The active approach, so their resale, undoubtedly may cause a rapid decrease of the value in the balance sheet. However—as in the passive approach—generating financial losses for a central bank, as a result of low interest rates of purchased assets. The difference—in relation to losses resulting from the passive approach—would only be that they would be resold under conditions of rising interest rates.

[4]According to Reuters, the central banks' total assets in relation to the GDP of their economies is currently at a level of 20.9% for the Federal Reserve System, 26.5% for the Bank of England, and 37.3% for the ECB. A significantly higher value in relation to the Gross Domestic Product represents currently Bank of Japan—93.2% as well as the Swiss National Bank—112.4%.

Against this background, the following potential scenarios of central bank's balance sheet normalization can be identified (Agostini et al. 2016):

1. *Selling Securities outright—active approach*—Central banks can actively sell assets it purchased during different QEs. This will be the most effective in settings of high inflation and future unanchored expectations indicating rise for higher inflation than the central bank's target, or growth overheating than central bank's forecasts.
2. *Maturing assets not re-invested—Passive (Gradual) approach*—Central banks can also take the approach not to re-invest maturing assets back into the central bank's expanded balance sheets. This process will allow a gradual wind down as assets come due.
3. *Reinvesting maturing assets into duration for gradual equally paced long term wind down—Passive (Snail pace) approach*—This approach allows central banks to keep reinvesting maturing assets into new assets, however, with a plan to invest in assets, which when come due, smooth the assets maturity gaps in the long run. This will gradually wind down the balance sheet on a longer horizon in a consistent and orderly manner.
4. *Keeping expanded balance sheet as a "new normal"*—Central banks may accept the new role of having expanded balance sheet forever. Not the best of choices as many central bankers have openly stated that this is not their priority nor role, however, if circumstances of weak global economy consistently exists and inflation constantly undershoots banks target, central banks will look for alternatives and this may become a new normal.

Another issue is the risk arising from the composition of central banks' assets. If, as in the case of the FED, these assets mainly consist of US Treasuries, government agency debt and Mortgage-Backed Securities (MBSs), it seems that the credit risk of this portfolio is relatively low. However, looking at the structure of assets of the Swiss National Bank, approximately 94% of its balance sheet total is located outside of this country. What's more, about 20% of total assets are invested globally in shares, including approximately 88 bln USD in American shares. Thus, the risk of the Swiss National Bank's balance sheet structure is much more higher. However, this problem will be a subject on the further scientific research.

4 Summary

The central bank risk management system must evolve with the passage of time and dynamically changing environment. Experience from the recent financial crisis have to be included in the new normalized financial risk management framework, which will be better adapted to the conventional monetary policy architecture and highly flexible to the changes that are taking place. Central banks should take into account the potential risk areas indicated in the study, as a part of the new risk management framework. This applies both the risk arising from assets qualified as collateral in transactions with a central bank, the risk of too early or too late normalization, risk accompanying securities, acquired in special asset purchase programmes during *Quantitative Easing* policy, as well as the risk of balance sheet normalization. Therefore, modern central banks are now faced many challenges in the area of new monetary policy objectives and tools. It is extremely important to precisely define assumptions of the normalization process of modern monetary policy, in particular setting aims to be achieved. The risk resulting from the normalization process seems to be much higher than that accompanying the *enter strategy* policy, i.e. implementation of unconventional instruments. The lack of previous experience of monetary authorities in realization of normalizing actions is also a kind of barrier, or a fear of smooth implementation of the *exit* assumptions. Central banks can hardly imagine potential consequences of normalization, which additionally slows down their practical actions.

The main aim of the normalization process should not be a desire to return to pre-global financial crisis policy, but to define a *new normal* policy, adapted to current determinants of banking sector functioning and new risk areas that accompany their modern activity. It is possible that these framework will be converged or—to some extent—be similar to those preceding the recent crisis. However, their verification, in terms of appropriateness and relevance in the new paradigm of modern central banking, is crucial (Pyka 2010).

References

Agostini, G., Garcia, J.P., González, Á., Jia, J., Muller, L., Zaidi, A.: Comparative Study of Central Bank Quantitative Easing Programs. School of International and Public Affairs, Columbia University in the City of New York, vol. 155, pp. 36–37 (2016)

Bogołębska, J.: Instrumenty polityki pieniężnej Europejskiego Banku Centralnego w okresie globalnego kryzysu finansowego. In: Mechanizmy funkcjonowania strefy euro. Ed. J. Bilski, E. Feder-Sempach, Acta Universitatis Lodziensis, Folia Oeconomica 264/2012, 58 (2012)

Cecioni, M., Ferrero, G., Secchi, A.: Unconventional monetary policy in theory and in practice. Bank of Italy Occasional Papers 102 (2011)

Champan, Ch., Ward, S.: Why risk efficiency is a key aspect of best practice project. Int. J. Project Manage. **22**(8), 619–632 (2004)

ECB: Central bank risk management in times of monetary policy normalisation. In: Speech by Y. Mersch at the International Risk Management Conference, Paris, 8 June 2018, https://www.ecb.europa.eu/press/key/date/2018/html/ecb.sp180608.en.html. Last accessed 18 July 2018

ECB: The ECB's response to the financial crisis. ECB Monthly Bulletin, pp. 67–69, Oct 2010

ECB: The financial risk management of the Eurosystem's monetary policy operations. July, 23 (2015)

González-Páramo, J.M.: Non-standard monetary policy: five questions about the exit. Speech on the occasion of the Seminar at the European Economics and Financial Centre, London, 6 Nov 2009

Nocoń, A.: Normalization of modern monetary policy. Uni-edition GmbH, Berlin, vol. 7, p. 145 (2018)

Nocoń, A.: System reagowania współczesnych banków centralnych na niestabilność sektora bankowego. Difin, Warsaw, 95 (2016)

Pyka, I., Nocoń, A., Cichorska, J.: Konsekwencje nowego ładu regulacyjnego w sektorze bankowym Unii Europejskiej. CeDeWu.pl, Warsaw (in print)

Pyka, I.: O nowy paradygmat bankowości centralnej. In: Ekonomia i finanse. Współczesne wyzwania i kierunki rozwoju, CBiE, University of Economics in Katowice, Katowice, pp. 485–497 (2010)

Yellen, J.L.: Normalizing monetary policy: prospects and perspectives. In: Remarks at "The New Normal Monetary Policy," a research conference sponsored by the Federal Reserve Bank of San Francisco, San Francisco, 27 Mar 2015

Fund Transfer Pricing and Its Impact on Bank Liquidity Measures

Christian Cech and Ewa Dziwok

Abstract The global financial crisis of 2007–2009 had a huge impact on financial markets and especially on liquidity (understood as the ability of economic agents to exchange existing wealth for goods and services or for other assets). The consequences of the crisis which have been visible till today forced the authorities and supervisory boards to establish new liquidity risk measures as well as to improve existing ones. The aim of the paper is to show bank's approach to FTP (fund transfer pricing) and their impact on main liquidity risk measures. The survey includes an analysis of chosen Austrian and Polish banks.

Keywords Fund transfer pricing · Liquidity risk · Risk measurement

1 Introduction

The latest financial crisis showed that access to liquidity can be limited and is not free of charge. In consequence, the Basel Committee proposed liquidity standards, which oblige banks to measure their level of liquidity risk, which then is monitored by the banking supervision. Some measures use balance-sheet data of banks and can be used to measure liquidity risk at bank level and—by considering all banks in the supervisor's task area level (Federico 2012). Basel III introduced two measures for liquidity risk: the liquidity coverage ratio (LCR) and the net stable funding ratio (NSFR). The LCR is intended to ensure that banks hold a buffer of liquid assets to maintain a short-term liquidity that lets them survive stressed conditions over a 30-days period (BCBS 2013). The NSFR is designed to support stable funding structures and is used to monitor the long-term liquidity.

C. Cech
Fachhochschule des BFI Wien, Wohlmutstraße 22, 1020 Vienna, Austria

E. Dziwok (✉)
University of Economics in Katowice, 1 Maja 50, 40-287 Katowice, Poland
e-mail: ewa.dziwok@ue.katowice.pl

P. Linsley et al. (eds.), *Multiple Perspectives in Risk and Risk Management*, Springer Proceedings in Business and Economics,
https://doi.org/10.1007/978-3-030-16045-6_15

Considering the fact that LCR is defined as a quotient of high quality liquid assets (HQLA) to total net cash outflows over the next 30 calendar days in a predefined stress scenario, its level is strongly influenced by regulatory requirements, market conditions and market participants' behavior. The LCR must be larger than 1, i.e. the number of HQLA must exceed the scenario cash outflows. Hence, in order to fulfill this requirement, banks with an LCR less than one can either increase their HQLA or reduce the scenario cash outflows. The latter can be achieved by e.g. reducing the liquidity and credit facilities or by reducing the level of customer deposit. The requirement to hold sufficient HQLA (numerator of LCR) or an appropriate level of funds (denominator of LCR) enforces banks to find an equilibrium between their balance sheet structures, business priorities and allocation of liquidity costs (Gomes and Wilkins 2013).

Although previous studies (Grant 2011) suggest that liquidity costs need to be transfer-priced similarly to interest payments, the knowledge about the impact of a fund transfer pricing (FTP) system on liquidity measures is still limited. Little is known about the use of FTP in liquidity management processes in Central East European countries like Austria or Poland.

This study analyses the five largest banks in Austria and Poland and examines whether banks are more likely to have a sufficiently high LCR level if they use a FTP system. We point out that having a functioning liquidity management system strongly influences the probability of having a sufficiently high LCR level.

The paper is organized as follows. Section 2 reviews the literature on liquidity risk and liquidity risk measures. Section 3 describes the liquidity management process. Section 4 reports descriptive results from Austrian and Polish banks and Sect. 5 concludes.

2 Liquidity Risk and Liquidity Risk Measures

The global financial crisis of 2007–2009 had a huge impact on financial markets and especially on liquidity understood as the ability of economic agents to exchange existing wealth for goods and services or for other assets (Williamson 2008). The consequences of the crisis which are visible till today forced the authorities and supervisory boards to establish new liquidity risk measures.

Generally literature (Nikolaou 2009) describes three main types of liquidity: central bank liquidity, market liquidity and funding liquidity (see Table 1).

Central bank liquidity relates to the necessary sources provided by the central bank to the financial system through its open market operations. It is monitored via the central bank's balance sheet.

Market liquidity refers to the ability to trade in financial markets and, in the broadest sense, refers to a situation when financial assets can be bought or sold without having an undue impact on prices (ESRB 2016). Hence market liquidity incorporates three elements: volume (any amount of assets), time (can be sold anytime, rapidly) and transaction costs (with minimum loss of value) (Keynes 2003).

Table 1 The role of the different liquidity types

Heading level	Example
Central bank liquidity	Enables to maintain the balance between demand and supply in the whole financial system
Market liquidity	Enables the trading within the market with focus on the value of assets, time of transaction (speed) and costs (price)
Funding liquidity	Enables the institution to settle its obligations with immediacy and without incurring unacceptable losses

Funding liquidity, which this study mainly focuses on, is the ability of a solvent financial institution to make agreed-upon payments in a timely fashion (IMF 2008). Borio (2000), Strahan (2008) and Brunnermeier and Pedersen (2007) define funding liquidity as the ability of banks to fund their positions by raising cash at short notice either via asset sales or new borrowing. Drehmann and Nikolaou (2009) define it as the ability to settle obligations with immediacy. The Basel Committee of Banking Supervision defines the funding liquidity as the ability to fund increases in assets and meet obligations as they come due without incurring unacceptable losses (BCBS 2008).

These three types of liquidity are closely linked to each other and each plays a specific role in the whole financial system. As a consequence, any problem with one type of liquidity causes troubles with another one. The main role of the banking supervision is to properly assess the possible dangers and risks which can influence the liquidity of the whole financial system.

Concerning the liquidity risk, central bank liquidity risk could materialize only in case of hyperinflation or an exchange rate crisis, because a central bank is generally always able to provide money for the financial system.

The market liquidity risk (known also as a trading liquidity risk) is the risk that it is impossible to trade at a fair price with immediacy (Nikolaou 2009). If it materializes it usually has important consequences for the whole financial system. Particularly, it can lead to financial crises which have an influence on the financial stability and in consequence on the real economy. Knowing the significance of market liquidity risk to financial stability, that type of liquidity risk is usually closely monitored by policy makers.

The funding liquidity risk is the risk that over a specific time horizon a bank will become unable to settle its obligations with immediacy (Drehmann and Nikolaou 2012). Funding liquidity risk is measured at the institution level. The most popular measure is gap analysis, where the term structure of expected cash flows and the term structure of expected cumulated cash flows is constructed (Castagna and Fede 2013). Theoretically the most accurate way to measure funding liquidity risk is to model a joint distribution of all underlying risk factors. From a practical point of view however this is difficult to implement as there is often a lack of data needed to calibrate this distribution. There are several studies that try to overcome these problems: Nyborg and Strebulaev (2004) have developed a theory of multiunit auctions, Valimaki (2006) argues that "when the central bank applies a quantity oriented liquidity policy, a positive tender spread may result from money market inefficiencies and banks' risk aversion even if the central bank preferences are symmetric and the markets do not anticipate any changes in the policy rates". Drehmann and Nikolaou (2012) extract an insurance premium from banks' bids in the main refinancing operation auctions conducted by the ECB and propose it as measure of funding liquidity risk.

3 FTP and Liquidity Risk Management

Most of the new liquidity regulations underline the significance of good governance and liquidity management and its influence on asset-liability management (ALM) as well as funds transfer pricing (FTP). The established principles introduced by the Basel Committee emphasize that each bank or institution is responsible for sound management of its liquidity risk to guarantee a sufficient amount of funds to meet stress situations (BCBS 2008). In this procedure the transfer of liquidity made through FTP plays a crucial role. The FTP process allows to assess the costs, benefits and risks of funding liquidity inside a bank.

As a result of regulatory requirements banks and financial institutions are developing their liquidity management frameworks in the fields of (BCBS 2008):

- governance;
- organization and functions;
- basic policies and models;
- metrics, methodologies and limits;
- stress tests and contingency plans;
- reporting and tools.

Following the risk management principles, banks and financial institutions have to implement models that let them integrate the costs of liquidity in management decision processes and monitor the sources of liquidity as well as market indicators.

A key element of effective liquidity risk management is a properly constructed FTP process and its integration into the bank's overall risk strategy. Recommendation 2 of the Committee for European Banking Supervisors to the European Commission on liquidity risk management (CEBS 2008, p. 8, recommendation 2) states that "Institutions should have in place an adequate internal mechanism—supported where appropriate by a transfer pricing mechanism—which provides appropriate incentives regarding the contribution to liquidity risk of the different business activities. This mechanism should incorporate all costs of liquidity (from short to long-term, including contingent risk)".

Concerning governance, new tasks and responsibilities should be established inside the organization and the liquidity risk is added to the decision structure (limits, new products and their impact on liquidity). In every step of the liquidity management process, an implementation of FTP can improve the performance. The process of FTP implementation covers the following areas:

- decision-making (ALCO)
- implementation and management (Treasury)
- control
- internal audit
- reporting.

The Asset Liability Committee (ALCO)—the body responsible (among others) for liquidity strategies—is expected to approve the FTP system and decide on the bank's strategy in terms of regulatory requirements and sufficient liquidity. The treasury department is the creator and director of the FTP system (a bank inside the bank)—it periodically constructs the yield curve and applies the FTP idea across the bank. The division of the FTP process into an ex-ante and an ex-post path as well as the identification and separation of liquidity and interest costs allow to improve the control over the procedure. The main role of the audit is to plan and recommend the FTP system (usually in form of internal procedures and regulations), as well as the evaluation and improvement of the FTP system. Reporting is responsible for the transparency of the FTP to facilitate the decision-making process in terms of speed and accuracy and to meet the regulatory reporting requirements.

The above mentioned procedure of FTP implementation shows that when FTP is used as an integral part of the decision-making process the bank is able to react more effectively. In consequence, it allows the bank to have a competitive advantage.

4 FTP Impact on Liquidity Measures

Lack of precise regulations concerning the allocation of liquidity costs and benefits caused the Basel Committee on Banking Supervision (BCBS 2008) to introduce 17 principles for managing and supervising liquidity risk which were also implemented in the European Union's Capital Requirements Directive IV (CRD IV).

The Committee of European Banking Supervisors, (now the European Banking Authority), also discussed the role of "an effective allocation mechanism for liquidity costs, benefits and risks" (CEBS 2010). It issued regulations in the form of five guidelines which specify the requirements of the Basel Committee concerning the introduction of FTP mechanisms, including liquidity costs, benefits and risks.

Together with the regulatory developments and the linking strategy with regulations, the Financial Services Authority (Financial Stability Institute, FSI 2011) tried to specify what exactly "better practice" means. In its guidelines it outlines proposals for FTP (called there Liquidity Transfer Pricing, LTP) regarding governance and shows how to use FTP to manage on-balance sheet funding, liquidity risk. and contingent liquidity risk. In 2016, the Federal Reserve board of governors (Federal

Table 2 FTP use and the level of LCR of the 5 largest Polish banks

Bank	Assets 2016 (in bln EUR)	Transfer pricing (Y/N)	LCR 2015 (%)	LCR 2016 (%)
PKO BP	64.5	Y (Transfer center)	132	136
Pekao	39.4	Y (Internal transfer pricing)	105	120
BZ WBK	33.9	Y (FTP system)	146	144
mBank	30.2	Y (FTP system)	132	181
ING Bank Śląski	26.5	Y (Risk transfer system)	178	155

Reserve System, FRS 2016) issued its own guidelines which present various methods for pricing liquidity risk using FTP.

In spite of regulators attempting to control whether banks adequately price risk and although several regulatory measures have been introduced over the past years, the internal pricing of liquidity in form of FTP systems is highly complicated and subjective (Elliot and Lindblom 2015). Under the traditional assumptions of the theoretical FTP framework, the cost of liquidity should be added as a marginal cost based on FTP. However, the practical implementations are not as straightforward since the market will not pay for any firm specific risk reductions, banks that are net lenders to the market may find that the market is not willing to pay the liquidity premium. Moreover, the implementation costs, although not accounted for in theory, are highly relevant in practice. As banks have to adapt their existing systems to fulfill the new Basel III regulations the whole process of pricing liquidity costs could importantly influence the way how the LCR and NSFR are calculated.

In case of LCR which requires banks to maintain a liquidity buffer (HQLA) that matches expected cash outflows over the next 30 calendar days, the formula assumes that a stressed scenario would last for only one month, which is unrealistically short. This is why HQLA driven by LCR should be always treated as a minimum volume to maintain. And additionally, because the HQLA value is viewed as a cost, a bank will need to understand the liquidity level of every type of customer's liability to optimize the balance sheet from an LCR perspective. In Basel III regulations one can find the division of liability types into: stable (less risky) and non-stable (with risk of higher assumed outflow). As a consequence banks wish to maximize stable liabilities and minimize non-stable ones, which could be achieved by appropriate fund transfer pricing mechanism (an internal strategy which let them favor different parts of the balance sheet or different customers).

A comparison of the use of FTP systems in Austria and Poland shows that the five largest banks in both countries have implemented FTP systems and have centralized their liquidity management process. All banks fulfill the LCR requirements (Tables 2, 3).

Table 3 FTP use and the level of LCR of the 5 largest Austrian banks

Bank	Assets 2016 (in bln EUR)	Transfer pricing (Y/N)	LCR 2015 (%)	LCR 2016 (%)
Erste Group Bank AG	208.2	Y (FTP system)	122	142
RBI	134.8	Y (FTP system)	142	184
Unicredit Bank Austria AG	105.8	Y (FTP system)	132	134
Raiffeisenlandesbank Oberösterreich AG	39.4	Y (FTP system)	98	117
BAWAG P.S.K. AG	35.5	Y (FTP system)	137	138

An analysis of the five largest Austrian and Polish banks shows that all of them already use FTP to calculate charges for providing liquidity internally. All banks fulfill the regulatory requirements concerning short-term liquidity. The biggest banks which correctly understand the impact of every liability on their net interest income (NII) are able to compensate higher cost of liquidity through a proper asset management mechanism.

5 Conclusions

The liquidity models which are proposed in the literature and used in banks describe the basic mechanisms of liquidity management. Liquidity management helps to explain the fundamental causes of liquidity problems in banks by measuring and assessing the bank's cash flow as well as asset-liability maturity mismatch.

An adequate description, effective measurement and assessment of liquidity using the available tools are associated with several problems. Among others one problem is the models' verification, an excessive simplification (or vice versa—the complication) of the models and finally problems with forecasting the future dynamics of payments and building appropriate liquidity scenarios. As an effect there is a need for further research concerning the process of cash flow estimation, behavior of bank's customers and utility of historical data to forecast future scenarios.

This paper reviews the concept of fund transfer pricing (FTP) and liquidity risk measures. It is visible that large or medium sized commercial banks have the market position enough strong to influence the LCR ratio. They are able (they have educated staff and necessary sources) to recognize how each type of liability (numerator of LCR) influences on bank's balance sheet and revise their strategy to improve it. This means the implementation of funds transfer pricing into the optimization process of the balance sheet to achieve a acceptable level of liquidity ration without losing a competitive position on the market.

References

BCBS Basel Committee on Banking Supervision: Basel III: the liquidity coverage ratio and liquidity risk monitoring tools (2013). http://www.bis.org. Last accessed 14 Aug 2017
BCBS Basel Committee on Banking Supervision: Principles for Sound Liquidity Risk Management and Supervision (2008). http://www.bis.org. Last accessed 14 Aug 2017
Borio, C.: Market Liquidity and Stress: Selected Issues and Policy Implications, pp. 38–51. BIS Quarterly Review November (2000)
Brunnermeier, M.K., Pedersen, L.H.: Market Liquidity and Funding Liquidity, CEPR Discussion Papers 6179, (2007)
Castagna, A., Fede, F.: Measuring and Managing Liquidity Risk. Wiley, Chichester (2013)
CEBS, Committee of European Banking Supervisors: Second part of CEBS's technical advice to the European commission on liquidity risk management, CEBS 2008/147 (2008), http://www.iasplus.com. Last accessed 14 Aug 2017
CEBS: Committee of European Banking Supervisors: Guidelines on Liquidity Cost Benefit Allocation, October (2010). http://www.eba.europa.eu. Last accessed 14 Aug 2017
Drehmann, M., Nikolaou, K.: Funding Liquidity Risk. Definition and Measurement, ECB Working Paper Series No. 1024 (2009)
Drehmann, M., Nikolaou, K.: Funding Liquidity Risk: Definition and Measurement. J. Bank. Financ. **37**(7): 217–382 (2012)
Elliot, V., Lindblom, T.: Funds transfer pricing in banks: Implications of Basel III. In: Elliot, V. (ed.) Essays on performance management systems, regulation and change in Swedish banks. BAS Publisher, Gothenburg (2015)
ESRB: Market liquidity and market-making. European Systemic Risk Board October (2016)
Federal Reserve System: Interagency Guidance on Funds Transfer Pricing Related to Funding and Contingent Liquidity Risks. March (2016). https://www.federalreserve.gov. Last accessed 14 Aug 2017
Federico, P.M.: Developing an Index of Liquidity-Risk Exposure: An Application to Latin American and Caribbean Banking Systems. IDB Technical note No. IDB-TN-426 (2012)
Financial Stability Institute: Liquidity Transfer Pricing: A Guide to Better Practice, December (2011). http://www.bis.org. Last accessed 28 Aug 2017
Gomes, T., Wilkins, C.: The basel III liquidity standards: an update. Bank of Canada Financial System Review, June (2013)
Grant, J.: Liquidity transfer pricing: a guide to better practice. Australian Prudential Regulation Authority Working Paper, Sydney (2011)
https://www.bankaustria.at
https://www.bawaggroup.com
https://www.bzwbk.pl
https://www.erstegroup.com
https://www.ingbank.pl
https://www.mbank.pl
https://www.pekao.com.pl
https://www.pkobp.pl
http://www.rbinternational.com
http://www.rlbooe.at
IMF: Global Financial Stability Report, April (2008)
Keynes, J.M.: Ogólna teoria zatrudnienia procentu i pieniądza. PWN, Warszawa (2003)
Nikolaou, K.: Liquidity (Risk) concepts. Definitions and Interactions. ECB Working Paper Series No 1008 (2009)
Nyborg, K.G., Strebulaev, I.A.: Multiple unit auctions and short squeezes. The Review of Financial Studies **17**(2), 545–580 (2004)
Strahan, P.E.: Liquidity Production in 21st Century Banking. NBER Working Paper No. W13798 (2008)

Valimaki, T.: Why the marginal MRO rate exceeds the ECB policy rate? Bank of Finland, Research Discussion Papers 200/2006 (2006)
Williamson, O.: The New Palgrave Dictionary of Economics. Palgrave Macmillan (2008)

Cyber Risk in Financial Institutions: A Polish Case

Nikoleta Musiał

Abstract The aim of the article is to indicate the most crucial aspects of cyber risk in the financial institutions as well as the problems connected with cyber security system and relationship with a customer. The article reviews the state of the cyber risk as a potentially one of the most dangerous ways of reputation damaging of a firm as well as a financial loss. Every firm must understand the constantly evolving risk and, moreover, the tools and all techniques to protect their systems. There is no difference between small and big companies in terms of risk. Moreover, not only financial services companies may be in danger. The cyber risk management may be seen as a way for a company to distinguish from its competitors which may build a long-lasting relationship between a client and a company. Security in a cyberspace is one of the most important issues for IT departments but not only. Nowadays, it is very popular to organise the large-scale hacker attacks. The reason of organising such attacks is generally the desire of getting the profit and ransom for the recovery of the data or control over the company's computers. The attacks may be organised by both; a hacker or employees. Most of the criminals target financial companies because they strongly believe that it is the most profitable. Online and offline fraud incidents have also raised during the last few years. It resulted in monetary and also reputational losses for all the victims—financial institutions. Improving defenses require implementations of new products or systems and people. If a client is aware of the fact that the financial institution is very committed to prevent a fraud or cyber-attack, a good relationship with a customer may be established, as well as the good reputation of a company.

Keywords Cyber-attacks · Cyber risk · Financial institutions

N. Musiał (✉)
University of Economics in Katowice, 1 Maja 50, 40-287 Katowice, Poland
e-mail: nikoleta.musial@edu.uekat.pl

P. Linsley et al. (eds.), *Multiple Perspectives in Risk and Risk Management*, Springer Proceedings in Business and Economics,
https://doi.org/10.1007/978-3-030-16045-6_16

1 Introduction

All the decisions, which are made in the enterprise, are connected with the determination of condition in the future. It is never possible to determine how all the factors will influence the future based on the decisions made in the past. It may be only predicted but it never may be certain.

The unavoidable progress of science and technology may contribute to the reduction of risk but also may be a tool to introduce new forms of risk. Technological trends may not be the only sources of risk—also the economic reality is worth considering.

The paper aims to indicate the most important and considerable aspects of cyber risk, with a particular focus on financial institutions and also problems which are created in terms of cyber security system. In the conceptual layer, the paper reviews the cyber risk as a way or a chance for criminals to attack a given organisation which may result in losing reputation image of a firm and, moreover, in financial loss as well. Nowadays, a society faces a constant technical development. Thus, each entity should be prepared to fight potential cyber-attacks and defend its customers as efficiently as possible. In case of financial institutions, the safety is crucial by its nature, due to their prominent role in the economy. When a given organisation is considered to be immune to all kinds of cyber-attacks from the outside it may result in having a good reputation among the customers which may cause a good and long-lasting relationship between these two.

The paper is divided into several sections. The second section provides the reader with the definitions of cyber risk and the types of cyber risk. In the third section, the paper discusses an example of one of the most devastating cyber-attack faced by Polish banking system in 2016, with the specification of actions taken against. This example opens a discussion on the challenges of cyber security, which is outlined in section four. Section five offers some considerations on the challenges in managing cyber risk. The sixth section concludes the study.

2 Conceptual Framework—The Understanding of Cyber Risk

2.1 *The Definition and Types of Cyber Risk*

The term risk may be used universally but it is very often attached to the different meanings (Kloman 1990). Defining the risk will depend on the overall context in which the term risk was applied (Charette 1990).

Every unit in the environment, as an enterprise may be called, is exposed to a large number of situations, potentially risky ones or dangerous ones, caused by the economic situation in a given country, permanent changes in the global market, as well as other economic situations affecting the creation of uncertainty. All in all, it may influence both—the company and also its customers (Samuelson and Nordhaus 2004).

The specific definition of risk may vary, it is possible to establish a few main characteristics of risk. The most important is that the potential loss and uncertainty must appear, as well as there must be a choice or a decision to make to deal with the previous two characteristics (Charette 1990).

Nowadays, not all enterprises obtain strategies and decision models which may facilitate the reduction of unpleasant and unexpected activities influencing the creation of risk. As a result, most of the enterprises are forced to react only in a crisis situation. This is caused by lack of external and also internal balance in the functioning of the company (Castells 1997).

All kinds of risk may cause very serious loss of profits which may lead to the bankruptcy of a company or even reputation damage. In economic terms it is said that generally people try to avoid uncertainty about their income and consumption. Aversion to risk may also be distinguished in most of the cases. When the annoyance, which is caused by the option of loss of a given amount of income, is stronger than a pleasure of obtaining the same amount of income, a person may have strong aversion to risk (Samuelson and Nordhaus 2004).

Defining the risk may be rather difficult. The risk is determined on the basis of different sciences and theories, such as behavioral sciences, economics, insurance, legal sciences or psychology. The word *risk* is considered to come from old Italian *risicare* which may be translated as *to dare*. From semantics point of view it is shown as a choice rather than a destiny which cannot be avoided. Defining the risk has been a challenge for many years. According to A. H. Willet, who tried to find a proper definition in 1901, the risk is objective, related to the subjective uncertainty. Unfortunately, the definition introduced by Willet may be seen as a very imprecise due to the ambiguity of the notion of uncertainty. In the USA were published two definitions of insurance risk in 1966. In the first one the risk was defined as certain unsureness about the next action taking into consideration two or more possibilities. In the second one an insured person or object were understood as a risk (Ronka-Chmielowiec 2002).

The understanding of various contexts of the definition of risk is relevant for understanding and defining of cyber risk. Cyber risk emerged with the development of modern technologies. The term *cyber risk* means a loss for the unit connected with the technical infrastructure or the use of technology in a given organization. The loss may appear in many different forms as well as may be caused by different units, for example by the hacker or even by an employee, who has done this accidentally or intentionally (Cheol-Kwon 2013).

The cyber risk exists in a number of forms. Broadly it may be categorised into four types based on the origin of the risk (Cheol-Kwon 2013):

- internal and malicious
- internal and unintentional
- external and malicious
- external and unintentional.

Internal and malicious cyber risk is a purposeful act of the theft or sabotage made by a person inside a company. It is highly possible that it may be caused by a dissatisfied employee who aims to delete or steal data from a central system or to install viruses on a company's computers and machines. Internal and unintentional cyber risk is caused by a person from inside a company, an employee, who is making a mistake; it has to be taken into consideration that even the most qualified, well-intentioned and experienced employee may be accidentally responsible for the disability of a firewall or an internal back-up system. External and malicious cyber risk is related to a deliberate attack made by someone outside the company and this kind of cyber-attack must be taken into consideration the most seriously because this may be infiltration of a data base of a given organisation by a criminal or a hacker. Finally, external and unintentional is an accidental and negative influence on an organisation, for example a software error or natural disasters which may affect the system availability (Cheol-Kwon 2013).

2.2 *Cyber Attacks*

Cyber risks, which come from the cyber-attacks, are limitless. Some of the most dangerous may be distinguished (Hoffman 2014):

- ransomware
- credential-harvesting malware
- social engineering
- personally identifiable information.

Ransomware is a kind of software which is designed to block the access to the device until the certain amount of money is paid to the person responsible for blocking the device. There are a few different types of ransomware which may be distinguished. The first one is called *screen-locker* and it blocks the access to the device by blocking the user's screen until the certain amount of money is paid. It is also possible to solve the problem without paying the money if a user possesses technical knowledge. The second one is called *crypto-ransomware*. It is a very effective kind of ransomware. It is based on blocking the files, also files placed in the Cloud. The attacker may unblock the files after receiving money, generally between $300–$900. Files, which were attacked, are impossible to unblock without paying the ransom. The latest kind of ransomware is called *disk-encryptor*. The task of disk-encryptor is to block whole the disk. Generally, ransomware may look like an invoice, information of a delivery or enclosed CV or an advertisement on the Internet. It is also often placed in an enclosure with e-mails. When a user opens an enclosure, the process begins. After some time, the user may only see the notification on the screen with the instruction on how to pay a ransom (Schofield 2016). Credential-harvesting *malware* is a growing very rapidly threat in the financial sector. It targets all data stored in smartphones. In some cases, the credential-harvesting malware may be used to gain access to the system of network resources and to take control over bank accounts. Both customers and business users must understand that in many cases they are not aware of the attack by, for example, using a cloned website created just to obtain certain information. The newest technique, which is used for credential-harvesting, are digital skimmers, which allow a cyber-criminal to steal data needed to enter online payment forms or login to websites (Torsten 2018). Social engineering appears when a cybercriminal obtains sensitive information from organisations by posing as a representative of legitimate organisations, for example a bank. It is a set of techniques and methods which were created to gain confidential information. Hackers often use the lack of knowledge or naivety and gullibility of their victims. The system is based on the finding the weakest piece in the security system—a human being. Kevin Mitnick helped popularized in the '90s the term social engineering. Social engineering is a very successful way to invade the organisation by criminals. The cyber criminals often pretend to be someone else to gain the data. Careless customers often share their personal data which the criminals which may later be used to hack their bank accounts (Hulme and Goodchild 2017). Personally identifiable information is information about an individual which may be used to distinguish a person's identity or biometric records. Personal identifiable information are divided into two groups called linked and linkable information. Linked information, such as full name, home address, e-mail address, social security number, passport number, driver's license number, credit card number, date of birth, telephone number or log in details may identify a person easily. Linkable information is a kind of information which on its own may not identify a person, but the same information combined with another one could locate, identify or trace a given person. Personally identifiable information are stored in data warehouses by business or government. All the data may be used for fraud and ransom demands and identify theft by cybercriminals (Sweeney and Lubowicka 2018).

3 Financial Institutions Cyber-Attacks in Poland

Poland is one of the countries that has recently expected several serious cyber-attacks, which lead to the discussion on the potential scale and harm of the cyber-attacks. In this section, the example of such attacks are shortly discussed, with a short notion on the actions taken against. The attack took place in 2016 and is considered as one of the biggest cyber-attacks, up to date.

Clients of more than 200 bank branches were attacked by the malware called GozNym. The information was announced by IBM X-force—a team of some of the most-valued IT security analysts in the world. They provide facilities for the IBM X-Force Exchange platform, which is a cloud-based platform for acquiring and intelligently analyzing information about threats. It enables quick exploration of data on the latest threats and aggregation of these data into practically useful analytical results.

GozNym, a malware responsible for breaking into the banks, is a special kind of software because it is a very sophisticated, commonly used in only a few countries.

That means that Poland is now a target for cyber-criminals. The first step in all the action was sending the e-mails to banks with the attachment which after opening the access to the computer is gained by the cyber-criminal. The malware is able to look like and act like a bank which was used by the customers. The website is, obviously, a fake one and it is able to block the access to the real website of a bank. Mostly, the client is not aware that he or she is a victim of the attack.

The expert explains that double transaction authorization methods—SMS messages sent by banks, tokens and one-time codes—may help protect against cybercrimes.

It is expected more and more attacks because the group of criminals may rent existing infrastructure to other cybercriminals. Every teenager will be able to rent infrastructure to attack Polish banks using the bitcoin currency, for example, which is more and more popular in Poland, as well as in other countries.

Attacks on banks have also happened before. In March 2016 mBank became the target of hacker attacks. Cyber criminals using phishing attacks tried to extort account login details and payment card details. It all started with the fact that customers started receiving e-mails with information about temporarily blocking the mBank transaction website. In the e-mail was a link to the fake website which was created by the attackers to gain very sensitive information from the mBank customers (PAP 2016).

Moreover, in 2016 the Internet users investing in the bitcoin virtual currency also had to take into account losses. In August, there was a significant decline in bitcoin value due to the suspension of trading on one of the stock exchanges. 756 bitcoins were stolen which was equivalent to over 64 million dollars. The rate dropped by more than 100 dollars and the virtual currency was paid around 540 dollars (Gawin 2016).

In 2018 the malicious BackSwap Software was responsible for modifying account numbers in Internet transfers and stealing money by attacking clients of 5 Polish banks (mBank, ING Bank Śląski, BZ WBK, PKO BP and Pekao SA). The actions of the malware was for the first time discovered at the beginning of this year. A danger was discovered by Paweł Śmierciak, an analysist of threat. The threat is sent by e-mail with the attachment which looks like an invoice. The BackSwap is installed immediately after opening of the attachment. The BackSwap is able to detect when a user is opening a bank's website. When a person is transferring more than 10,000 PLN the virus unnoticeably changes the account number and money is transferred directly to the cyber criminals (WPA 2018).

In 2017 many incidents of security breaches and data leakage appeared. The information about the theft of data from Equifax, Verizon or Kmart was revealed. The infrastructure of many companies was paralyzed by the attacks of Petya, WannaCry, and BadRabbit. To make massive cyber-attacks, hackers also used IoT (Internet of Things) devices that are becoming more and more popular. Mostly ransomware attacks, malware, phishing, attacks on the network layer, DDoS attacks and botnets, appeared. The most common target of cyber-attacks were companies from the energy, healthcare, retail and production sectors. The financial sector and state institutions were also at risk. Only in the fourth quarter of 2017 Gray Wizard registered

167,324,652 incidents. Daily, the number of incidents was on average 1,394,372. All security incidents and attacks that were targeted at websites protected by Gray Wizard Shield came from France. In second place among the source countries of cyber-attacks, is taken by Great Britain. The countries from which the increased traffic was recorded are also Germany, the United States and Poland. Other countries with a fairly high rate of incidents and involvement of cybercriminals are the Netherlands and Canada (wGospodarce 2018).

4 The Need of Cyber Security

4.1 Cyber Security System

Cyber-attacks are becoming more and more frequent and dangerous. Attackers improve their tactics and techniques relatively faster than modern security systems may be updated. The methods used by attackers are also more sophisticated and creative each year. All financial institutions must face a constantly growing pressure threat from possible cyber-attacks. Fraud is closely linked with all cyber-crimes and the synergies in how financial institutions try to fight cyber-crime and fraud. All financial institutions are forced to invest large amounts of money in the security systems and people to fight cyber-crime. A company is exposed to reputation damage in a case of cyber-attack, apart from the loss of funds. It is necessary to permanently supervise and monitor cyber-crime protection to be sure that measures are improved to face the increasingly sophisticated cyber-attacks each year. New products, new systems and qualified people are required to improve the defenses. All banks must constantly take a view across channels and their clients' behaviours to be prepared to defend in a case of a cyber-attack. Suspicious transactions may be detected by technologies which include machine learning, big data or artificial intelligence. By combining these methods, they are able to get through large amounts of data which may help identify every suspicious action. It is also necessary to remember that the danger may come from a potentially safe channel that has been already checked. Extremely complex nature of all cyber-attacks requires all financial institutions to detect actions, which may be suspicious, more precisely and proactively. In the fight against a cyber-crime, every financial institution should make sure that all clients are constantly informed about the risks. Clients must fully understand why it is so important to implement very strong and complicated authentication systems. The danger that the customers may see the cyber defense as the inconvenience still exists. There is also an opportunity that with the actual and correct information the client will understand and accept the real nature of cyber risk. Moreover, it may encourage all clients to protect themselves stronger than before. It must be admitted that the awareness among corporate clients about the security is raising. One of the most dangerous facts is that a cyber-crime is more lucrative for an attacker than other crimes, so it requires financial institutions to invest a lot of their resources into building a defense. Cyber attackers act like corporates with the development of new products and also offering services which may be integrated with other activities of different criminals, even gangs. In every organization the culture of cyber security should be implemented. All information should be shared and communication should include communication about information-sharing tools. Cyber defenses must consist of modern technology and know-how. All of the clients and staff should be constantly informed about risks, such as social engineering. In the case of all organisations new capabilities are developed and introduced to inform all clients as fast as it is possible about the danger because in the case of cyber-attacks the speed is crucial. Generally, the financial-services industry is seen as being more mature than other industries when it is about planning, preparing and introducing cyber security systems, as well as protecting against appearing cyber-attacks. The are some techniques and methods which help maintain security among financial services (Lepoutre and Mirland 2017):

- ATM black-box style attack
- Artificial intelligence.

ATM black-box-style attack which is used by cyber criminals. Cyber criminals attach hard drive or a laptop to the ATM and at the same time displacing the current ATM software. The result is that the attacked ATM may be remotely controlled and, moreover, the cash may be taken on demand. The way of avoiding the risk of cyber-crime in that case may be making the exterior of the ATM physically harder. That may cause a better protection of the inner components from manipulation (Chin 2018). Artificial intelligence is a try to create a decision mechanism, as much as it is possible, similar to a human brain's decision mechanism. With the constant development of science and technology it was discovered that the human brain is too complicated to be imitated. Decision mechanism is more specific and precise. The researchers have been focused mostly on a specific problem and are still trying to solve the problems, until now. The aim of artificial intelligence is to solve a problem which takes certain amount of time in a very short period of time. Artificial intelligence may be used to detect cyber-crimes. With the help of academic research in the last few years some new products have been improved to successfully detect a cyber-attack (Maloof 2017).

DarkTrace is a global company dealing with artificial intelligence called Technological Pioneer. DarkTrace uses self-learning artificial intelligence to identify and respond to cyber-attacks. By using the technology introduced by DarkTrace a given company may obtain technology, which is based on very complicated self-learning machinery and advanced mathematics, and a tool to detect threats and an effective visualisation platform which enables the analysis of a threat (DarkTrace homepage):

- Big data
- machine learning.

Big data is a term used to name a large and diverse data sets, also the processing and analysis which may be difficult but very valuable, because it may lead to the gaining new knowledge. Big data may allow analysts to clarify and categorise cyber threats very fast. Big data will help visualise cyber-attacks. The Big data sets allow using historical data as well as modern ones. Using the historical ones all abnormalities may be distinguished. The historical data may be also used to create new possibilities to predict models and machine learning. It may give the possibility to predict most of the future events (Gil 2018). Machine learning is a kind of computer science which main task it to enable computers to learn new behaviours taking into consideration empirical data. The target is to allow a computer to learn from the past experience, not from the human interaction. One of the actions of machine learning connected with cyber security is to deal with a spear phishing which the main task is to gather information from a victim by an e-mail sent by the attacker. The traditional detection techniques lack accuracy and the speed. The solution is in the predictive URL classification models. The models are based on the newest machine learning algorithms which are able to identify patterns that may reveal unwanted e-mails prepared by the cyber-criminal. Webshell is a kind of code which is loaded into a website. It allows the attacker to change the web root of the server. This lets the attacker gain access to the data base of a given system. Machine learning models may be prepared to detect the difference between normal behaviour from a malicious one. The algorithms may be used to identify and isolate them from a system before they attack (Kohavi and Foster 1998).

4.2 The Weakest Point of Cyber Security

Some years ago, the cyber security systems or cyber-crimes were only associated with international corporations and organisational. Nowadays, having all personal information, including information about bank accounts, family and health on the smartphones, the security of data is more important for every person than ever before. The tendency to concentrate on modern technologies leads to the reckless behaviour of the users. The most famous hacker in the history—Kevin Mitnick—is sure that most of the cyber-attacks are made with the help of a reckless and trusting customer. Mitnick is considered to be the most talented hacker in the history but not very familiar with modern technology. He was a globally known person in the early '90s when he was searched for by FBI. He proved many times that the social engineering, which means manipulation and gathering valuable information from them, is crucial in gaining the personal data which may guarantee the access to the systems, even in the case of global organisations. Mitnick used his skills connected with social engineering for the first time at the age of 13. The relatively expensive bus tickets forced him to counterfeit the tickets. Later on, Mitnick started using social engineering to break into companies or institutions. He was able to gain such information as the credit card number or social insurance number. It has to be admitted that he has never stolen anything—his aim was to know how the systems work. Mitnick is responsible for hacking the McDonald's company. When the customers wanted to order food in DriveThru all the employees could hear them but Mitnick was the only one who could answer. Mitnick is also responsible for hacking the Motorola company. In that case, Mitnick used his personal skills to convince one of the employees of a company to obtain a special code for one of the systems (Business Insider Polska 2018).

'*Companies spend millions of dollars on firewalls, encryption, and secure access devices and it's money wasted because none of these measures address the weakest link in the security chain: the people who use, administer, operate and account for computer systems that contain protected information*' (Business Insider Polska 2018). It is said that most of the attacks connected with a cyber-crime in the public institutions are organised with the help of its employees. Simple measures, for example encouraging all employees to log out while having a lunch break and to choose reliable and complicated passwords, may dramatically enhance the security without the money needed. The passwords should be made of at least six characters, including a mixture of numbers, punctuation marks, as well as letters. A given user should remember to have a different password for each system and the password should never be revealed to anyone. The technology security may not be enough to defend successfully against cyber-attacks. The users must understand and keep the set of security policies. Human Firewall Council is a group to promote this approach. The group is sure that a user has a very important role in maintaining security. The best solution to protect against cyber-attacks is to combine the proper knowledge of a user with anti-viruses software and relevant configuration of firewalls (The Economist... 2002).

5 The Challenges of Managing Cyber Risk

To manage the cyber risk, all organization should assess the probability and possible impact on of an event and to create the most appropriate way of dealing with a risk, which is consistent with a widely adopted framework of risk management. The assessment leading is one of the most important parts of risk management. The process starts with defining the goals of a given organisation, as well as internal and external factors which may possibly influence the success. Risk assessment under ISO 31000 consists of three steps: risk identification, risk analysis, risk evaluation. The first one is connected with the application of a systematic process which helps understand the consequences of actions taken before. Risk analysis is connected with understanding of risk likelihood and its conseqeunces. The last step is connected with the effect of the actions (Purdy 2010).

Cyber risk, as any other type of risk, cannot be totally eliminated and any institution has an unlimited budget or personnel to fight all risks. The risk management is helping manage the negative effects of uncertainty in a way which helps use the company's resources the most effectively and efficiently. In a good system of risk management the most important is clear communication and awareness among all units in a given institution about the possible risks. It makes the risk decisions more precise, well considered and efficient. The risk management tries to identify all risks very early and implement relevant mitigations to avert unwanted incidents or negative impact.

While Planning a cyber risk management program certain, the following elements should be taken into consideration (Tobar 2018):

- The culture of cyber security and risk management in an organization. The necessary is to structure a communication process and establish appropriate leadership in a company. Also, the training is important to maintain the expertise to help deal with new kinds of risk.
- Information sharing process should consist of criteria for communicating in a case of escalating risks.
- Priorities in an organisation because of a limited budget. It is important to efficiently prioritise risks and responses, such as trends, impact and time horizon.
- Flexibility in an institution is highly required because it is not possible to be immune to all risks.
- Speed has a crucial meaning when a given organisation is exposed to the risk. The speed of actions may minimize the negative impact of a danger on a company. Response to an event and recovery depend on preparation and planning. The plans should be accomplished regularly.
- Threat environment which is often omitted while organising cyber-security. Insiders, malicious or accidental, are mostly the cause security problems.
- Cyber hygiene practices is a basic point of cyber risk management. It focuses mostly on activities to secure all organisation, prevent and reduce risk.

The cyber risks rapidly continue to grow making the cyber risk management really important. It is very important to implement an efficient risk management program to protect the data from attacks (Tobar 2018).

Undoubtedly, banks, regulators, financial institutions and legislators are keenly aware of the problem of cyber threats. The threat continues to grow rapidly. Hackers and cyber criminals are more and more clever and sophisticated in the creation of ways to break into even the most protected and intelligent security system. It has to remembered that the easiest way to break into a company is through its employees. Organisations must monitor not only their employees, but also customers' behaviour to be able to fight against cyber criminals. The insurance market is trying to develop new products which may respond to new needs and treats. Cyber risk insurance may be offered by many insurers. Not only payment of compensation is offered but also more and more popular crisis management services as a part of the insurance coverage. Required is to introduce the cyber risk management at a highly advanced level to be ready to constantly defend a company against changing methods and ideas of cyber criminals (Camillo 2016).

6 Conclusions

Nowadays every company may be the victim of a cyber-attack. The development of new technologies is unavoidable. It may help every organisation protects its customers, but it also may be a source of new problems appearing almost each day.

Cyber risk nowadays is one of the most dangerous problems which every company must face. The cyber-attacks may influence a company is a various of ways. One of the most dangerous risks is losing a good imagine and reputation of a company which may result in losing the customers' trust and also losing money which may, in result, lead to the bankruptcy of a given organisation.

It has to be admitted that not only financial institutions may be in danger but, in fact, they are in the danger from the very beginning. It is simply because it is believed by the criminals that it is the most profitable and effective to attack a financial institution because there is money.

The protection against criminals and cyber-criminals is crucial. Security must be implemented from the very beginning in every company. The good way to keep a company safe is introducing an effective risk management, especially cyber-risk management which may definitely make easier for the company to deal with cyber-security problems and challenges.

It must be remembered that the attacks may be organised not only by the criminals or cyber-criminals. It most of the cases it is done by an employee who wants to get the profit and control over a company. The hygiene of work as well must be implemented and conducted. It is also very important to teach the stuff members to work safe. Attacks may be done also by getting by the cyber-criminal very sensitive information from the employee of a given company.

Every given organisation should remember that in fast changing reality the company is more and more in danger caused by the development of new technologies and the creation of new methods of attacks by cyber-criminals. If a firm is able to maintain the safe in their institutions it may result in having a long-lasting, very profitable and efficient relationship with its customers.

References

Castells, M.: The Power of Identity. Blackwell Publishers, Massachusetts (1997)

Camillo, M.: Cybersecurity: Risks and Management of Risks for Global Banks and Financial Institutions. Henry Steward Publications, United Kingdom (2016)

Chin, L.: Financial services: emerging cybersecurity threats and regulations. https://www.securityroundtable.org/financial-services-emerging-cybersecurity-threats-regulations/ (2018). Last accessed 1 Dec 2018

Charette, R.: Applications Strategies for Risk Analysis. McGraw-Hill, USA (1990)

Cheol-Kwon, L.: Introduction of a cyber security risk analysis and assessment system for digital I&C systems in nuclear power plants. IFAC Proc. Volumes **46**(9), 2140–2144 (2013). https://doi.org/10.3182/20130619-3-ru-3018.00311

DarkTrade Homepage: https://www.darktrace.com/. Last accessed 1 Dec 2018

Gawin, M: Największe ataki hakerskie w 2016 roku. Te firmy padły ofiarą cyberprzestępców. https://www.bankier.pl/wiadomosc/Najwieksze-ataki-hakerskie-w-2016-r-Te-firmy-padly-ofiara-cyberprzestepcow-7489739,2.html (2016). Last accessed 1 Dec 2018

Gil, P.: What Exactly is 'Big Data'?. https://www.lifewire.com/what-exactly-is-big-data-4051020 (2018). Last accessed 1 Dec 2018

Hoffman, J.: Cyber Security: Managing Your Risk, Protecting Your Assets. https://www.psafinancial.com/2014/07/cyber-security-managing-risk-protecting-assets/ (2014). Last accessed 1 Dec 2018
Hulme, G.V., Goodchild, J.: What is Social Engineering? How Criminals Take Advantage of Human Behaviour. https://www.csoonline.com/article/2124681/social-engineering/what-is-social-engineering.html (2017). Last accessed 1 Dec 2018
Kohavi, R., Foster, P.: Glossary of Terms: Machine Learning. Kluver Academic Publishers, Netherlanads (1998)
Kloman, H.F.: Risk management agonists. Risk Anal. **10**(2), 201–205 (1990). https://doi.org/10.1111/j.1539-6924.1990.tb01039.x
Lepoutre, P., Mirland, P.: Cyber security: trends and implications in financial services. https://www.securities-services.societegenerale.com/en/insights/technology/cyber-security-trends-and-implications-financial-services/ (2017). Last accessed 1 Dec 2018
Maloof, M.: Artificial intelligence: an introduction. http://people.cs.georgetown.edu/~maloof/cosc270.f17/cosc270-intro-handout.pdf (2017). Last accessed 1 Dec 2018
PAP: Potężny atak hakerów. Na liście ponad 200 banków w Polsce. https://tvn24bis.pl/tech,80/potezny-atak-hakerow-zaatakowano-ponad-200-polskich-bankow,638642.html (2016). Last accessed 1 Dec 2018
Purdy, G.: ISO 31000:2009—setting a new standard for risk management. Perspect. Risk Anal. **30**(6), 881–886 (2010). https://doi.org/10.1111/j.1539-6924.2010.01442.x
Ronka-Chmielowiec, W.: Ubezpieczenia—rynek i ryzyko. Polskie Wydawnictwo Ekonomiczne, Warszawa (2002)
Samuelson, P., Nordhaus, W.: Ekonomia. PWN, Warszawa (2004)
Schofield, J.: How can I remove a ransomware infection? https://www.theguardian.com/technology/askjack/2016/jul/28/how-can-i-remove-ransomware-infection (2016). Last accessed 1 Dec 2018
Sweeney, M., Lubowicka, K.: What is PII, non-PII, and Personal Data? https://piwik.pro/blog/what-is-pii-personal-data/ (2018). Last accessed 1 Dec 2018
Business Insider Polska, Słynny Haker Radzi, Jak Chronić Dane Przed Atakami Wykorzystującymi 'Inżynierię Społeczną'. https://businessinsider.com.pl/technologie/nowe-technologie/socjotechnika-w-atakach-hakerskich-kevin-mitnick/wn98szh. Last accessed 1 Dec 2018
The Economist, The Weakest Link, if only computer security did not have to involve people. https://www.economist.com/special-report/2002/10/24/the-weakest-link (2002). Last accessed 1 Dec 2018
Tobar, D.: 7 Considerations for Cyber Risk Management. https://insights.sei.cmu.edu/insider-threat/2018/02/7-considerations-for-cyber-risk-management.html (2018). Last accessed 1 Dec 2018
Torsten, G.: The Foundation of Cyber-Attacks: Credential Harvesting. https://www.securityweek.com/foundation-cyber-attacks-credential-harvesting (2018). Last accessed 1 Dec 2018
WPA: Atak na polskie banki. https://www.computerworld.pl/news/Atak-na-polskie-banki,410295.html (2018). Last accessed 1 Dec 2018
wGospodarce, Cyberataki w 2017: Nikt nie był bezpieczny. http://wgospodarce.pl/informacje/46727-cyberataki-w-2017-nikt-nie-byl-bezpieczny (2018). Last accessed 1 Dec 2018

The manufacturer's authorised representative in the EU is Springer Nature Customer Service Centre GmbH, Europaplatz 3, 69115 Heidelberg, Germany. If you have any concerns regarding our products, please contact ProductSafety@springernature.com

Printed and bound by CPI Group (UK) Ltd, Croydon, CR0 4YY
05/10/2026
02228130-0008